TUDOR SECRETARY

Sir William Petre at
Court and Home

To

MARC FITCH

1. SIR WILLIAM PETRE, 1567
Aged 61

TUDOR SECRETARY

Sir William Petre at Court and Home

F. G. EMMISON
County Archivist of Essex

LONGMANS

LONGMANS, GREEN AND CO LTD
48 GROSVENOR STREET, LONDON W1

RAILWAY CRESCENT, CROYDON, VICTORIA, AUSTRALIA
443 LOCKHART ROAD, HONG KONG
PRIVATE MAIL BAG 1036, IKEJA (LAGOS)
44 JALAN AMPANG, KUALA LUMPUR
ACCRA, AUCKLAND, IBADAN, KINGSTON (JAMAICA)
NAIROBI, SALISBURY (RHODESIA)

LONGMANS SOUTHERN AFRICA (PTY) LTD
THIBAULT HOUSE, THIBAULT SQUARE, CAPE TOWN

LONGMANS, GREEN AND CO INC
119 WEST 40TH STREET, NEW YORK 18

LONGMANS, GREEN AND CO
137 BOND STREET, TORONTO 2

ORIENT LONGMANS PRIVATE LTD
CALCUTTA, BOMBAY, MADRAS
DELHI, HYDERABAD, DACCA

PRINTED IN GREAT BRITAIN BY
RICHARD CLAY AND COMPANY LTD.
BUNGAY, SUFFOLK

Contents

CONTENTS

APPENDICES

ABBREVIATIONS

A.P.C.	*Acts of the Privy Council*, ed. J. R. Dasent
B.M.	British Museum
Cal. Pat. Rolls	*Calendar of Patent Rolls*
D/DP	Petre archives in Essex Record Office
Dom. Cal.	*Calendar of State Papers, Domestic*, Vol. I, 1547–1580
E.R.O.	Essex Record Office, County Hall, Chelmsford
For. Cal.	*Calendar of State Papers, Foreign*
H.M.C.	Historical Manuscripts Commission
L. & P.	*Letters and Papers, Foreign and Domestic, of the Reign of Henry VIII*, ed. J. Gairdner and R. H. Brodie. (Refs. after vol. nos. are to the numbered docs., not to pages.)
P.R.O.	Public Record Office
S.P.	P.R.O., State Papers (originals)
Span. Cal.	*Calendar of State Papers, Spanish*
Ven. Cal.	*Calendar of State Papers, Venetian*

Plates

1 SIR WILLIAM PETRE, 1567, aged 61 *Frontispiece*

Artist unknown (formerly attributed to Holbein). 'The painter was probably a Fleming by birth; the style is much in the manner of Steven van der Meulen, a migrant Court painter who was working in England in the fifteen-sixties.' (*Petre Family Portraits: A Catalogue*, by David Piper, Assistant Keeper, National Portrait Gallery: E.R.O. Publications no. 26, 1956.)

Wearing a black gown trimmed with brown fur and a black cap with ear-flaps, and holding a white wand of office. Petre was the first Chancellor of the Order of the Garter to be given a special badge—the red and white Tudor rose within the garter, inscribed HONI SOIT QVI MAL Y PENSE, hung on a ribbon. Coat of arms with two renovated lines below. That he was Secretary to Elizabeth, as stated in the later inscription, repeats Holinshed (1st edition, 1577) and subsequent writers; after his resignation in 1557 he seems to have been titular Secretary.

Another version (probably that which belonged to Lord Lumley in 1590) is in the National Portrait Gallery and bears the same age inscription, and a seated variant is at Exeter College, Oxford.

(On view in the Long Gallery, Ingatestone Hall.)

2 SIR WILLIAM PETRE, aged 40 *Facing page 16*

Artist unknown. It is conceived in a Netherlandish tradition and has certain affinities with a group of portraits painted in the 'forties and 'fifties associated but not convincingly with the name of 'The Regent Master'.

The ring on the forefinger was occasionally used for official papers (see p. 302); that on the fourth finger is evidently his Secretary's signet seal with the Tudor rose, otherwise unknown except for one little known variation of the usual Holbein pattern of Thomas Cromwell's portrait.

(In Lord Petre's private apartments, Ingatestone Hall.)

Illustrations in the text

Plates 2, 4, 5, 6, 8–13, 15–18 and illustration on p. 85 are reproduced from photographs by the Essex County Council's Visual Aids Service; Plate 3 from a photograph by Vincent Bibbings. Text illustrations on pp. 85, 91 and 264 are Crown Copyright; reproduced by permission of the Controller, H.M. Stationery Office.

Preface

I HAVE gradually been convinced that the story of Sir William Petre's life and the supporting evidence both present unique features. His record of continuous service is unmatched in mid-Tudor politics. The double survival of abundant archives not only of his public career but also of his domestic affairs appears to have no parallel in his generation and rank. Like many of the 'New Men', he acquired a large estate, built a fair mansion and founded a county family; in his case, exceptionally, all three have been perpetuated to this day. His house still belongs to the family and is the home of his direct descendant, the seventeenth Baron Petre.

No other Secretary served three successive sovereigns; and apart from Petre, only two of the twenty Privy Councillors in 1544, when he joined them, were retained by Henry VIII's children. They were Paulet Lord St. John, later Marquis of Winchester, whom Mary put under house arrest before overcoming her suspicions and reinstating him; and Cheyney, who died a month after Elizabeth's accession. Petre's unbroken service on the Council until 1567, the date of his retirement, was without equal in that he alone escaped all hazards of its membership: execution, imprisonment, confinement, exile, disgrace, fine, dismissal, enforced resignation, or merely rejection by a new monarch. By middle life he had acquired the label of indispensability. The state papers reveal him as an almost ubiquitous figure, and the chronicle of his career runs as a continuous thread through political history. Long before the appearance of Permanent Secretaries, Petre, like Cecil, virtually became a permanent Secretary. Petre is the chief link between the two great Tudor Secretaries: he received his administrative training largely from Cromwell, Cecil largely from Petre, though being as reticent as Petre it is unlikely that the full extent of Cecil's debt will ever be discovered.

For Petre's court life, his steward's account-books are a valuable new source supplementing the state papers. Fortunately, there are also separate account-books and other important documents dealing with his country life, which afford a good picture of his family, wards and guests, their food and drink, the servants, the building and gardens, and the management of the household. On some of these aspects of home life, Petre's own detailed accounts, enhanced by their precise nature, are immeasurably more valuable than generalizations based on secondary sources. When the present Lord Petre entrusted his extremely rich archives to the Essex Record Office in 1939, it became clear that the domestic scene at Ingatestone Hall could be reconstructed, more fully perhaps than for any other mid-Tudor house of medium size. In 1953 Lord Petre leased to the Essex County Council a large part of his home for an educational experiment which so far has no counterpart. Since then, exhibitions of Essex archives lasting the whole summer, with a different theme each year, have been held there in an ideal setting. As an aid to the teaching of history and local topography to thousands of children, the success of the scheme has already given it a permanent place in Essex education. The thousands of adults who come do not have education in mind. They come to see an interesting display in an historic house, but all the same they learn much about the county.

As county archivist, I became custodian of these premises and these records. The perennial interest of visitors and others in the building and its builder made it seem very desirable to produce a book about Ingatestone Hall and social life there in Petre's time. My colleague, Arthur Edwards, the county history adviser, tried to dissuade me from confining it to domestic affairs, as Petre happened to be a national figure lacking an adequate biography. Although I was willing to give a good deal of personal leisure to examining the archives in my charge, it was obvious that even a brief study of Petre's political life would involve much time in the national repositories. A Leverhulme research award in 1954 enabled me to take three months' special leave of absence. My sponsors for the application were Sir John Neale and Professor S. T. Bindoff. They emphasized that Petre offered a rare opportunity for telling the story of a Tudor minister of middle social position from two angles, public and private; and of course I capitulated—to a six-year instead of a three-year task.

The book thus covers both aspects of his life. It is written not only for the general reader, but for all those who wish to know more about Sir William Petre and about the pleasant home which he planned for the enjoyment of his relatively little rest away from the rigours of the Court.

I wish to thank three writers of recent biographies of Secretaries of State who shared the office with Petre: Dr. Mary Dewar, author of a Life of Sir Thomas Smith compiled for a London Ph.D. thesis (1956), for her friendly advice; Dr. S. R. Gammon, now American Vice-Consul at Milan, for his great kindness in lending me for some months his Princeton Ph.D. thesis (1953) on Sir William Paget, later Lord Paget; and the late

Professor Conyers Read, distinguished American historian, for allowing me to draw freely from his *Mr. Secretary Cecil and Queen Elizabeth* (1955).

My book also owes much to the two main authorities on the secretarial office—Dr. G. R. Elton and Dr. Florence Higham (*née* Evans), whose *Tudor Revolution in Government: Administrative Changes in the Reign of Henry VIII* (1953) and *Principal Secretary of State: a Survey of the Office from 1558 to 1680* (1923) left the intermediate period coinciding with Petre's term to be investigated. This I have not attempted to undertake. It is a subject for a specialist in constitutional history; and in any case it was impossible for me to make long searches in uncalendared classes of material in London.

Some may well feel that the head of a very active local record office should confine himself to archival duties. My temerity in writing a Life of Sir William Petre, despite lack of qualifications for the task, arose from the unusual events and circumstances already related. 'It has therefore seemed to me an excusable ambition, if not a paramount duty', to quote Sir John Neale on his infinitely bigger work on Tudor parliamentary history. Had another writer appeared, no one would have been more pleased than I to put both archives and local knowledge at his disposal. Some years before part of Ingatestone Hall came under my care, an old friend, the late E. A. B. Barnard, author of *A Seventeenth Century Country Gentleman* (1944), had been tempted by my long-term deposit of the Petre account-books for his study in the Cambridge University Library to begin research, but he soon gave up on realizing the extent of the material. A little later, Professor H. R. Trevor-Roper suggested a thorough examination of one aspect of the Petre archives to Mr. W. Emerson, a Rhodes scholar from Yale. For his Oxford D. Phil. thesis (1951), 'The Economic Development of the Estates of the Petre Family in Essex, 1540–1640', I transferred hundreds of the Petre estate documents to the Bodleian Library. His conclusion that Sir William was just, even generous, to his tenants seems to be fully borne out by my own research, but I have recalculated, with some modification, Dr. Emerson's figures of the cost of building up the Essex and West Country estates.

For some years I had felt that county archivists should proclaim how much of their material is of national as well as local interest. The story of Sir William Petre bears this out. Pioneer work in this direction was done by Arthur Edwards, formerly senior history master at Maldon Grammar School, and Arthur Brown, when they compiled *English History from Essex Sources* for 1550–1750 and 1750–1900, both books issued by the Essex Record Office in 1951. In the previous year Dr. A. L. Rowse, in his

England of Elizabeth, had declared: 'There are immense riches in local archives. . . . I believe that the marriage of local with national history has more to offer us than many more sought and over-cultivated fields.' My good friends, Dr. W. G. Hoskins, who founded the Leicester University Department of English Local History, and his successor Dr. H. E. P. Finberg, insist that their academic subject is important enough to stand on its own feet, as indeed local record offices do, without 'support' from national resources. These stimulating opinions are not necessarily contradictory.

Historical research has the happy result of widening the writer's circle, all the more so in the case of a book dealing with both political and social aspects. Those to whom I am indebted make a long list of old and new friends.

I am grateful to the following for help on specific sections: Dr. W. G. Hoskins, Dom J. Stéphan, Dr. J. Scarisbrick and Miss Joan Sinar, County Archivist of Devon (ancestry and early years); Professor M. D. Knowles, Dr. Joyce Youings and Dr. G. W. O. Woodward (religious houses); Mr. J. Harvey and Mr. M. Girouard (architecture); Professor F. J. Fisher, Dr. Joan Thirsk and Mr. G. E. Fussell (food and agriculture); Sir James Mann, Master of the Tower Armouries, and Mr. W. Tucker (armour); Dr. W. L. Woodfill, Mr. Thurston Dart and Mr. L. G. Langwill (music); Mr. J. C. T. Oates, Cambridge University Library (books); Mr. Wentworth Day (sports); Mr. V. A. J. Swain, Dr. F. N. L. Poynter, Librarian, The Wellcome Historical Medical Library, Mr. L. M. Payne, Assistant Librarian, Royal College of Physicians, Miss A. Lothian, Librarian, The Pharmaceutical Society of Great Britain (surgery and medicine); the Rector of Exeter College, the Keeper of the College Archives and Mr. R. W. Southern, Fellow of Balliol (Exeter College); Professor J. Hurstfield (wards); and Mr. W. H. Challen (Kyme genealogy).

My other academic obligations of a more general character are very heavy. I owe a great deal to Professors Neale, Bindoff and Hurstfield for their kindness in inviting me to join their post-graduate Tudor seminars, despite my infrequent attendance, and to Dr. P. Collinson, Miss N. Fuidge and other past and present members; to Sir Goronwy Edwards, formerly Director, Mr. A. Taylor Milne, Secretary, Mr. E. L. C. Mullins, and to other friends at the University of London Institute of Historical Research; to Dr. G. R. Elton, Dr. A. L. Rowse and Professor H. R. Trevor-Roper; and to Professor W. K. Jordan, who invited me to lecture at Harvard in 1959 when I needed a break and for his generous hospitality there and at his country home in Vermont.

I am grateful to the Librarians of the Society of Antiquaries, the Royal

Historical Society and the Inner Temple; to two old friends G. E. Glazier, County Librarian of Bedfordshire, and J. G. O'Leary, Borough Librarian of Dagenham, and to many other public librarians for their long-term loans; especially to my Essex colleagues, K. J. Lace, County Librarian of Essex, and Miss I. Woodhams, Reference Librarian, for invaluable help and special facilities in connection with rare and out-of-print books.

It is very pleasant to acknowledge ready help from many members of my own profession, especially Francis Steer and Felix Hull, former colleagues and now County Archivists of West Sussex and Kent, Miss J. Godber, Miss I. Darlington, Mr. P. I. King, Miss E. D. Mercer, Mr. M. P. Statham and Mr. E. H. Sargeant, County Archivists of Bedfordshire, London, Middlesex, Northamptonshire, West Suffolk and Worcestershire, and Mr. M. F. Bond and Dr. A. J. Hollaender, Archivists at the House of Lords and the London Guildhall. I am most grateful to the Assistant Keepers of the Public Record Office who have been so helpful, especially Dr. N. J. Williams, Mr. E. K. Timings and Mr. A. W. Mabbs, to the staff of the Manuscripts Department of the British Museum, and to Mr. Roger Ellis, Secretary of the Historical Manuscripts Commission, and Miss D. Coates, Registrar of the National Register of Archives. I wish to thank the Marquis of Salisbury and Mrs. Woodfill (*née* Iselin) and Miss C. Talbot, his archivists at Hatfield House, for permission to consult and for help from the manuscripts there.

My colleagues at the Essex Record Office, who are thankful that I have at last buried Sir William Petre, have given me immense help, especially Hilda Grieve, John Holmes, Kenneth Newton and Nancy Briggs; by far my heaviest debt is to Arthur Edwards, whose aid and criticism I sought and received in such generous measure as to lead me to rewrite several chapters.

My appreciation is due to the members of the Records Committee of the County Council for their encouragement in agreeing to recommend its inclusion in the *Essex Record Office Publications* if not accepted by a London publisher, and to Mr. Christian Berridge, Clerk of the County Council, for his untiring efforts in bringing the Ingatestone Hall scheme into being.

I acknowledge with pleasure help also given me by Mr. A. Fellows, Mr. M. Craze, the Rev. R. R. Lewis, Mr. D. T. Piper, Mr. W. A. Foyle, Mrs. E. D'Esterre (*née* Middleton), Miss A. C. Shrubsole, Miss E. Burton and Mrs. M. Clutton (*née* Petre), who wrote about 1930 a Life of Sir William Petre, based chiefly on the printed calendars of the public records, and most generously lent me her unpublished manuscript. This Life, too, would not have been published had it not been for the public-spirited action of Lord Petre in placing his archives in the Essex Record Office; and I am indebted to his lordship for many kindnesses and for giving me permission to reproduce portraits and other subjects at Ingatestone Hall.

Only those who have spent six (or more) years of their leisure, on top of a busy professional life, can realize what my wife's constant encouragement (more important than her frequent help) has meant and how many joint social pleasures my family has sacrificed to prevent the six years stretching out indefinitely.

For the generous award which enabled me to take the initial three months special leave I have to thank the Trustees of the Leverhulme Research Fellowships. I wish to record grants of £100 each towards the publishers' costs made by the Trustees of the Marc Fitch Fund and by the Friends of Historic Essex, whose chairman during the major period of writing the book was my friend Marc Fitch. To him many historians, archaeologists and antiquaries already owe much and a far greater number will be indebted to him in the future.

Essex Record Office and Ingatestone Hall.

CHAPTER I

Early Life

WILLIAM PETRE came of old South Devon stock on both sides. His father's and mother's families belonged to Tor Brian and Woodland, adjacent parishes near Totnes and Ashburton and about twenty miles south-west of Exeter. He was the son of John Peter and his mother was Alice the daughter of John Colling. A pedigree owned or compiled before 1630 by Thomas Westcote, a Devon antiquary, traces William's ancestors to his great-great-grandfather, William, who was born not long after 1400. They all lived at Tor Newton, in the parish of Tor Brian. The Peters were numerous in Devon before the sixteenth century, and the name is spelt indifferently Peter, Petyr, Petur; William himself always signed Petre. A present-day authority on Devon reasserts that 'the Peters, among others, were members of franklin families with pedigrees and lands going back two or three hundred years'.[1]

In the national subsidy lists of 1523 John Peter of Tor Brian was assessed on goods to the value of £40, as was a relative, Otis Peter, in the neighbouring village of Ipplepen. There were fewer than 500 taxpayers at this level in the whole of Devon.[2] Wood, the first historian of Oxford graduates, described John as 'a rich tanner'.[3] This is a detail that could hardly have been invented, and it fits well with the known activities of the big Devon farmers of John's generation. He was almost certainly a prosperous cattle farmer, with tanning as a lucrative sideline. In the same way as a 'butcher' in the early sixteenth century could be a substantial farmer with a great number of cattle, a 'tanner' might also be a well-to-do person. Prince, the Devon historian, writing about 1700, was indignant with Wood's description; William, he declared, was 'not of mean or mechanic parentage, as some' (he quotes Wood only) 'either ignorantly or maliciously suggest, but of gentle and worshipful progenitors: for this was a name of note in these parts long before this gentleman brought so much lustre and eminence to it'. Citing Westcote's pedigree, Prince shows that John was an esquire and his father a gentleman.[4] William, however, was to be the first armigerous member. The rank of esquire may be regarded as a fiction of Westcote, restated by Prince because of his own ignorance of what a tanner's position could be in Tudor times. The place of William Petre's father in the social scale, as a rich farmer and freeholder of the manor, probably lay between that of yeoman and gentleman. His mother's immediate forebears, the Collings or Cullyngs of Woodland, like his father's, would have been called 'franklins' in the fifteenth century.

The manors of Tor Brian and Tor Newton were both acquired about 1528 by Thomas (later Sir Thomas) Kytson, a London merchant who was then building Hengrave Hall in Suffolk. John Peter, or Petyr, William's father, was a tenant around 1500 of land within the manor of Tor Brian.[5] The manor of Tor Newton was apparently sold by Kytson to John;[6] but the date has not been ascertained.*

Tor Brian, a tiny village not far from Dartmoor, lies quietly remote from the main thoroughfare beyond Exeter to South Devon. The lane approaching the village is narrow and winds steeply up and down to a group of old houses and cottages close to the church, with its ancient rood screen and fragments of stained glass (plate 3). Tor Newton stands above Tor Brian on a hill affording a fine view. A considerable portion of the fourteenth-century manor-house of Tor Newton is incorporated in the present building.

William Petre was born in 1505 or 1506. His contemporary portraits bear the inscription 'Ætatis suæ 61, Anno Domini 1567'.[7] An ancient book of hours used, like later family bibles, by the Petres for entering births and deaths, states that he died on 13 January 1571–2 in his sixty-sixth year.† Although he was termed the eldest son in the herald's visitation of Devon in 1564 and subsequently in the College of Arms archives as well as by Prince, an old family tradition accorded seniority to John, 'a theory so far confirmed by his (John's) being styled "of Tor Brian"'.[8] This John was either the purchaser of the manor of Tor

* In November 1535, Kytson, lord of Tor Brian, granted to 'John Peter of Tor Newton' a certificate of his free condition as a tenant of Tor Brian manor (E.R.O., D/DP F44); this somewhat rare type of document was based on the evidence given by other tenants at a court held two years previously to the effect that John, his parents, ancestors and kinsfolk of the surname of Peter always held by free, not servile, tenure; the tenants' testimony of 1533 may mark the date of John's acquisition of the manor. It is not clear whether this John was William's brother or father; the late Mr. Tapley-Soper showed that the latter has been wrongly identified, in place of his nephew, as a mayor of Exeter (H. Tapley-Soper, 'A Chapter in the History of the Peter or Petre Family of Devon', *Trans. Devon. Assoc.* (1918), i, 417–30). A few lords of manors about this time were trying to revive claims to serfdom on their manors. John the brother was accorded the status of gentleman on his death at Tor Brian in 1568 (West Suffolk R.O., E3/15). 'How little [contemporary] relevance the distinction of bond and free had to social or economic status' is discussed by A. R. Wagner, *Eng. Genealogy* (1960), 124–5. The Devon probate records and the valuable genealogical notes (including those on the early Peters) made by Mr. Tapley-Soper were lost in the heavy air-raid on Exeter in 1942.

† This fifteenth-century illuminated manuscript was sold last century (the only family archive to leave the Petres' possession) and was recently bought by Mr. W. A. Foyle of Beeleigh Abbey, Essex. All the births and deaths are printed in the work referred to in reference 8 (p. 323); see also pp. 124 n., 125 n.

Newton from Kytson, or his son who inherited it. A younger son was also christened John, who became custom-house officer of Exeter. Another William was apparently the fourth son, but little is known of him.* Richard, the fifth son, became Archdeacon of Buckingham. The youngest, Robert, rose to be an Auditor of the Exchequer and died a wealthy man. The three daughters were Wilmot, Alice and Thomasine (plate 4).

'Where William had his school learning, whether at Exeter or in the country, 'tis not very material to determine, if we could.'[9] To this unhelpful remark nothing can be added. But the next stage is clear. In 1520, about the usual age of fourteen, he went up as a commoner to Exeter College, Oxford, which had been founded in 1314 by Walter de Stapledon, Bishop of Exeter, for scholars from Devon and Cornwall. Small landowners, aware of the increasing number of lucrative posts in Church and State open to men of ability and education, were ambitious to send one of their sons to a university. It was a period of vigorous intellectual life. The first public Greek lectures had been given before the close of the previous century by the great pioneer of Greek scholarship in England, William Grocyn, at Exeter College; at Oxford, as at Cambridge, its study had met with strenuous opposition. Petre became an accomplished Latin scholar, but there is nothing to show whether he studied Greek. Times were changing. The law was no longer the exclusive preserve of ecclesiastics; lay lawyers were being promoted to high office. Moreover, the influential group of Oxford scholars was about to be succeeded by a younger generation of Cambridge men, many of whom Petre was to meet in later life—Cranmer, Ridley, Bacon, Cheke, Ascham, Smith and Cecil.

In 1523, when he was seventeen or eighteen, he was elected a fellow of All Souls College, and graduated bachelor of civil and canon law on 2 July 1526.[10] Among his immediate predecessors who had achieved the distinction of becoming a civilian as well as a canonist was Edmund Bonner, later Bishop of London; and Stephen Gardiner, the future Bishop of Winchester, did likewise at Cambridge. Having thus at a relatively early age made himself proficient both in Roman law, that of the

---

* The younger John is known as 'John the customer' to distinguish him from his cousin John, mayor of Exeter, who is called in the city records 'John the merchant' and married Wilmot, sister of 'the customer'. A 'Mr. William Petre' was a visitor to Ingatestone Hall in 1548 (E.R.O., D/DP A3); he may be the same 'William Petre of London gent.' who was appointed jointly with Sir William as Chief Steward of the Savoy lands in 1549. It was not unusual for the same name to be given to two living children: for a contemporary instance of a Devon man with four sons named John, see D. E. Gardner and F. Smith, *Genealogical Research* (Salt Lake City, 1959), ii, 134.

administrator, and in ecclesiastical law, he was elected about 1527 Principal of Vine Hall, or, as it was sometimes called, Peckwater Inn; they were in fact two almost contiguous buildings. Every Oxford scholar had to live in one of the numerous halls, each under a responsible warden elected by them. That under Petre's care was the centre of the study of the civil law and was shortly afterwards absorbed by Henry VIII in Christ Church, where the name Peckwater Quad survives. Petre now looked for further advancement.

Almost the only evidence of the beginning of his public career is Lloyd's *State Worthies*, a curious book written nearly a century after Petre's death and of only 'slight biographical value';[10] but behind Lloyd's fulsome phrases there are clearly sources of reliable information no longer available. He states that Petre owed his preferment to the Boleyn family, having become tutor and then companion to George, son of the Earl of Wiltshire.* The date of the tutorial appointment is not known; it may be as early as 1526 or as late as the spring of 1529. In June of the latter year Petre was selected as one of the additional 'proctors' [proxies] in the 'King's Affair', when a declaration of the invalidity of Henry's marriage was being sought in the legatine court presided over by Cardinal Campeggio and Wolsey.† Later in the year George Boleyn was sent to France as an ambassador, and Petre may well have accompanied him after the annulment case had been revoked to Rome that summer. He was free to do so, as he was no longer needed as King's proctor; moreover, in that same summer, an unknown doctor of divinity, Thomas Cranmer, had suggested that the most sensible way to solve Henry's problem would be to consult the universities of Europe on the validity of the marriage. The idea appealed to the King, who commended Cranmer to the care of Wiltshire. Early in 1530 Henry dispatched Wiltshire, attended by

* Sir Thomas Boleyn, father of George and Anne, the future queen, was created Viscount Rochford in 1525 and Earl of Wiltshire in 1529. 'Tutor' had two senses—service in a big household or in foreign travel. Lloyd used both and probably employed 'companion' in the latter sense and 'earl' anachronistically.

† 'The proctors on the king's part were Doctor Peter which was after made the king's chief secretary and Doctor Tregonell' (G. Cavendish, *Life of Wolsey*, ed. R. S. Sylvester (Early Eng. Text Soc., 1959), 79). Cavendish wrote in Mary's reign and is regarded as factually reliable (G. R. Elton, *The Tudor Revolution in Government* (1953), 75). Tregonwell had been principal of Vine Hall before Petre. The two leading advocates had been authorized to appoint substitutes (Lord Herbert, *Life and Reign of Henry VIII* (1672), 261, quoted by G. Burnet, *Hist. of the . . . Church of Eng.* (1679-1715)). Dr. Sylvester identifies 'Doctor Peter' with Dr. Peter Vannes because by contemporary custom secretaries were referred to by their christian names (e.g. 'Doctor Stephens', *ibid.*, 79, certainly denotes Stephen Gardiner). Vannes became the King's Latin secretary but could not have been mistermed the King's chief secretary by Cavendish, and the editor admits that Vannes was in Rome at this time (*ibid.*, 225-6). On the other hand, the fact that Petre did not get his D.C.L. till 1533 is an understandable slip on Cavendish's part.

Cranmer, to Bologna to meet the Emperor Charles V and the Pope in order to urge his cause, and he also sent a number of learned lawyers to Italy, France and Germany to seek the opinions of divines and canonists in the universities. Even if Petre did not accompany George Boleyn, he certainly went abroad. Lloyd wrote:

> The Earl of Wiltshire first pitched upon Petre for his son's tutor, and then for his own companion. Cromwell's quick eye one day at my Lord's [Wiltshire's house] spyeth his personage, and observes his carriage. Nothing would satisfy him, but that the young gentleman should come to Court, and go to travel. King Henry loved any All Souls man, but was enamoured with him, in whom concurred the three perquisites [requisites] of that society.
>
> 1. A gentile extraction.
> 2. A graceful behaviour.
> 3. Competent learning.
>
> The young man designed for business, was to travel for education, and the scholar for experience.
>
> 1. His pension is allowed him, £125 a year.
> 2. His tutor is assigned, who had been there before, and could instruct him what he should see, where he should go, what acquaintance to entertain, what exercise or discipline to undergo.
> 3. His instructions were drawn up; as,
>
> That he should keep a diary of what the chiefest places and the eminent persons, either apart or in conventions, yielded worthy of remarque and observation.
>
> To have before him a map or card [chart] of every place he goeth to.
>
> Not to stay long in any one place.
>
> To converse with no Englishman but agents, ambassadors, or such grave persons as his Majesty should direct him to.
>
> To endeavour after recommendations from persons of quality in one place to those in another; keeping still his correspondence with the most public and eminent persons of every respective place.
>
> Within five years he returned a complete gentleman, correcting the vices of one country with the virtues of another; and being one happy composition of every region. Two things improved his travel:
>
> 1. An artificial and careless freedom, that opened others.
> 2. A natural gravity, that shut him up, and was more capable of observing their virtues and escaping their vices.

Whatever may be Lloyd's merits as a historian, these last sentences carry conviction. Again and again in the future, Petre owed his success as a public servant to his ability to 'shut up' himself and to 'open' others.*

He returned to Oxford on 17 February 1533, to be admitted doctor of civil law. It was then, or even later, that he probably came to Cromwell's notice. Nothing more is known of his five years abroad and little of the months that followed. He became a clerk in Chancery, where, says Lloyd, 'his first employment was the charts, the Latin letters and the foreign negotiations'.† Of his subject Lloyd does give, however, an effusive

* It is impossible to deduce from Lloyd whether Petre was first introduced to the Court by the Boleyns or Thomas Cromwell. Wolsey was much occupied in the late 1520s with his Oxford foundation of Cardinal College (afterwards Christ Church), and Cromwell, going there in his train, may possibly have brought Petre to Wolsey's notice. Cromwell was Wolsey's secretary and drew up the foundation deeds, but had little personal influence before his master's fall at the end of 1530, and there is not the slightest trace of any Wolsey–Petre association. If Petre did not come to notice at Oxford, his being in the Boleyn household made it unnecessary for Cromwell to discover him, and that meeting is probably apocryphal. Pollard (*D.N.B.*, s.v. Petre) says that 'Anne Boleyn also sent Petre presents, and promised him any pleasure it was in her power to give' (I have been unable to trace the source of this statement), and surmised that it was through Anne's influence that Petre was chosen for government service, but her father was also powerful at Court, even earlier, when he was one of the leaders of the anti-Wolsey faction. George's confession in 1530 (*Letters and Papers of Henry VIII*, iv, pt. iii, no. 6539) about his weak knowledge of Latin and Italian points to his need of a 'companion'. Petre's assignation for a period of study-travel abroad was in no way remarkable. Almost every Tudor diplomat and secretary of state began his government career similarly, e.g. John Mason received a royal exhibition for study in Paris in 1530, and soon after 1532 was sent through France, Spain and Italy with instructions to forward information about foreign relations and places visited (W. G. Zeeveld, *Foundations of Tudor Policy* (1948), 747); and the youthful Roger Ascham's ambition was to become tutor to a nobleman's son, with foreign travel in the suite of an English ambassador (*D.N.B.*). Petre's allowance of £125 a year seems generous, but Cranmer's 6s. 8d. a day was about the same. Whether Petre was with Boleyn abroad has not been substantiated; perhaps it may be surmised that they were together in France on at least one of the embassies with which George was charged, though the *D.N.B.*'s statement that Petre's residence on the continent was chiefly in France appears to rest only on a secondary authority citing no source (C. W. Boase, *Register of . . . Exeter College, Oxford* (1894), lxxxi).

† For his doctorate, see Foster's *Alumni Oxonienses* (1891), iii, 1151. The Oxford Register of Congregations in which the entry occurs (f. 282 v.) states that Petre and three others were incepted in a 'solemn act', i.e. an official ceremony; that they were so *realiter* seems to make it certain that Petre attended in person. I am indebted to my friend Mr. I. G. Philip, Secretary of the Bodleian Library, for his opinion on the original entry. The authority for 24 January 1533 (Wood's *Fasti Oxonienses* (1815), i, 93) cannot be found. Evidently confusing this with his double baccalaureate, Lloyd credited Petre with a doctorate also in canon law. The statement has been repeated more than once, but seems to have no factual foundation. The royal agents' correspondence about the negotiations in the courts and universities of Western Europe does not yield any conclusive evidence of his absence abroad. Apart from his solitary appearance in 1533, there is however no definite proof of his being in England during 1530–5 (several references to him in the printed calendars for these years have been misdated), and Lloyd's assigning him to foreign travel for nearly five years cannot therefore be challenged. 'Charts' appears to mean charters or grants, a sense now obsolete but in use in Lloyd's time and not inappropriate for Petre's work as a clerk in Chancery; it does not denote maps, for which Lloyd employed 'card', a contemporary but equally obsolete term.

vignette which, despite his balanced antithetical style, runs in no way contrary to the known character of Petre in later life.

His capacity was contemplative, and his genius active; observing, rather than reading; with his eye more on men than books; studying behaviour, rather than notion; to be accomplished, rather than knowing; and not to err in the main, rather than to be excellent in circumstance. His body set off his parts with a grave dignity of presence, rather than a soft beauty of aspect. His favour was more taking than his colour, and his motion more than favour; and all such, as made his early vices blush, and his riper virtues shine.

CHAPTER II

Visitor of Monasteries

BY 1535 the Reformation in England had already gone a long way. Henry had broken away from Rome. In January he first exercised the royal supremacy in ecclesiastical matters, recently bestowed on him by Parliament, when he made Thomas Cromwell, his Secretary, his Vicar-general. This appointment was soon to mean much to William Petre, but his career might have been very different had other prospects of promotion materialized. In the following November, Cranmer, now Archbishop of Canterbury, wrote to the Secretary: 'I thank you for your favour to Dr. Petre. I had intended to make him Dean of the Arches, and shall do so if you think fit. There is no man so meet for it.'[1] Dean was the customary name for the judge of the Court of the Arches, the Archbishop's all-powerful, unpopular court of appeal. As it turned out, Petre was not advanced. Instead, a new appointment was conferred on him. Twelve months after the Vicar-general had received the royal authority, Petre was commissioned by the King to act as Cromwell's deputy in ecclesiastical matters.[2]

By a singular mark of confidence, Petre was thus given exalted rank in the Church of England, a rank for which there was no precedent. It soon brought him into unexpected prominence. In June 1536 a crucial Convocation for the province of Canterbury met in St. Paul's: a notable gathering of bishops, abbots and priors. The second session opened on the 16th. There entered a layman, one Dr. William Petre, who claimed the right of sitting in the Archbishop's place and of presiding over the assembly. He argued thus: the King was Supreme Head of the Church of England and therefore should occupy the highest seat in Convocation; in his absence, the Vicegerent in spirituals should preside; in Cromwell's absence, the first place should be assigned to him as Cromwell's 'proctor', or deputy.[3] The Church, it is true, had acknowledged the King's supremacy, but few of its dignitaries could have anticipated ever having to sit under a lawyer scarcely thirty years old. Yet they had to recognize the logic; and Petre gained his point. Cromwell himself presided at the next session a few days later, when Cranmer's annulment of Anne's marriage was obediently confirmed; in the meantime Henry had secretly married Jane Seymour. Petre's first election to Parliament may have occurred in the same month. This cannot be proved, but if he did serve as a member of the Parliament of June–July 1536, it was as Cromwell's nominee and his seat was Downton in Wiltshire.* Petre's close association with Cromwell is also illustrated by a letter in the King's name sent three months earlier directing the University of Oxford that none be given a medical degree without the vote of the Professor of Medicine, and signed 'Thomas Crumwell, Gulielmus Petreus'.[4]

Early in 1535 Henry had commissioned Cromwell to undertake a general visitation of churches, monasteries and the clergy. So it was, without knowing how complete the destruction would ultimately be, that the nation-wide inquisition into the internal condition and finances of the religious houses was organized. While one chronicler named Cromwell's deputies in the first visitation of 1535-6 as 'Richard Layton, Thomas Legh, William Petre, Doctors of the Law, and Dr. John London, with others',[5] Petre's name has been left out by all modern historians, who have relied on the evidence of the incomplete records abstracted in the printed calendars. But a Barking Abbey account kept by William Pownsett, the receiver-general of the abbey, makes it clear that Legh and Petre were there, probably at the end of September: 'Paid to Dr. Legh for his visitation 22s. 6d., to 5 of his servants 10s.; paid to 4 of Dr. Petre's servants 10s. 4d.' Legh is otherwise known to have visited London houses in that month, and Petre may therefore also have shared the task.[6] Petre's name also occurs in an account-roll of Dunmow, the Essex house linked with the famous custom of the flitch. The prior's expenses for January 1536 included: 'reward to Dr. Petre and his clerk, 15s.; my costs to London and back, 41s. 1d.' A similar item has been found in an uncalendared account of St. Osyth's Priory near Colchester.[7] An unnamed commissioner had been in the Dunmow district two months earlier, as a result of which the prior had had to spend 48s. 10d. on apparel for the novices sent away by the visitor. Whether Petre had descended on these and other houses in Essex or remained in London cannot be deduced. The royal agents had power to punish those convicted of serious crime and to investigate the charters of each house. About half the number visited that autumn and winter were given incriminating reports; of the remainder the commissioners spoke indifferently or even well. Early in 1536 Parliament was persuaded, after some opposition, to pass a bill for the suppression of those with incomes of less than £200 a

---

* For this reference I am indebted to Mr. R. Virgoe (History of Parliament Trust), who discovered in 1958 an undated note, seemingly in Cromwell's hand, of what he concludes to be his nominees for Bishop Gardiner's three boroughs in the 1536 Parliament, Gardiner then being abroad (B.M., Cott. MS., Otho C. x). Cromwell's parliamentary career began with Taunton, another possession of the see of Winchester (cf. G. R. Elton, *The Tudor Revolution in Government* (1953), 78-9).

year.* It was then generally believed that the larger and more orderly houses, stirred to self-reform, would continue to flourish.

The surviving records of the dissolution of the lesser houses are also incomplete. Though Petre is not found to have taken any part, in the autumn of 1536 he was certainly engaged in the work of a second visitation, which included the more important abbeys and priories. On two days in September he was at St. Augustine's Abbey, Canterbury: 'Dr. Petre, being sent of the Lord Cromwell to visit all the clergy throughout all Kent, did visit this abbey, making enquiry of the observing of the injunctions which we in the first visitation received by Dr. Layton.'[8] From this venerable abbey Cromwell received his subordinate's diffident report: 'Albeit I have deferred to write because I would not trouble you unto such time I might myself wait upon your lordship, yet forasmuch as these two days I have examined two matters in Canterbury of more importance, I thought it my bounden duty to signify my proceedings, which I have sent by this bearer, to whom also I have showed in what places I shall be during the visitation in Kent, to the intent (if your lordship will command me any further service concerning these matters) he may the more easily send the same unto me.'[9] It is the earliest of Petre's surviving letters. A visit to Christ Church Cathedral Priory would be expected of him and may be the second 'matter of importance'. A Canterbury monk and a Thanet priest were accused in 'Dr. Petre's circuit in the visitation',[10] and he appointed arbitrators in a dispute about a legacy to Wye church.[11] No more of his Kentish itinerary can be traced except for visits to Rochester and Dartford a week before Christmas: 'I have taken the compromise [delegated authority] for the election of the prioress of Dartford [one had just died], which I now send, sealed with their convent seal. I have also taken an inventory. This day I ride to Rochester and from thence to certify your lordship of my proceedings with all speed.' On the following day, in fact, he was back in the capital, examining witnesses on Cromwell's orders about an attack by London ruffians on some Frenchmen.

Although Parliament had expressly excluded the larger monasteries from confiscation, Henry and Cromwell coveted their immense wealth. Agents were therefore sent in 1537 through the counties to enquire into their conduct. The general aim was to obtain possession, ostensibly by voluntary surrender, but by bribery where necessary; and pensions were

* A list of all houses in thirty-three English counties and in Wales, distinguishing those worth 'above 300 marks' annually, is in the possession of Mr. W. A. Foyle of Beeleigh Abbey, Essex. The hand is easily recognizable as that of Petre, who may have drawn it up in his capacity as deputy Vicar-general.

offered at rates much above those given to the inmates of the smaller houses. The Dissolution gave the commissioners a great deal of other work, such as making inventories of stock and surveys of land, stripping the buildings of lead, jewels and plate, and putting in temporary bailiffs to safeguard the interests of the royal exchequer.

In the spring, Hyde Abbey near Winchester was expecting to receive Dr. Petre, and his being granted in May a munificent annuity of £40 by Fountains Abbey in Yorkshire may perhaps be the result of a favourable report after a visit by him, but it is to be noted that this substantial grant, much larger than his other monastic annuities, was made on the King's recommendation. Petre is not definitely known to have been active again until the summer. Then, glad no doubt to leave London which was scourged by plague, he was solely responsible for the mitred Abbey of Chertsey in Surrey, the first of the large houses to fall in the south. In November he suppressed the priory of Lewes in Sussex, with its rights over the cell of Castle Acre in Norfolk, and with Layton he visited Bedforshire, dissolving Warden Abbey and taking the first steps at Woburn Abbey. A note of Cromwell's in November about sending Petre to Coventry and Combe may refer to preliminary visits to two neighbouring Warwickshire houses, eventually dissolved by another commissioner.

In February 1538 the great Abbey of Abingdon in Berkshire, renowned for its ancient origins, surrendered to Petre. A Suffolk priory was the next objective, and Petre reported in March: 'We have this day received the surrender of Butley, to which the convent has assented very quietly. It is the best leaded house I have ever seen. The lead is worth £1,000, but there is no other riches but cattle.' A fortnight later, Petre and Tregonwell rode westwards to dissolve the important Abbey of Evesham, where they exposed an ancient blood 'miracle', and also Llanthony Priory in Monmouthshire. From the latter Petre wrote to Cromwell: 'I have been at Evesham and there received the resignation of the abbot, which he was contented to make immediately upon sight of your lordship's letters, saving that he desired me very instantly that I would not open the same during the time of my being here because (as he said) it would be noted that he was compelled to resign for fear of deprivation'; his cellarer had betrayed him, so he wisely accepted the terms which Petre had previously negotiated.[12] After a hard ride back to London to report progress to Cromwell in person, Petre journeyed into the New Forest, where Layton and he dealt with Beaulieu and Southwick Abbeys. The former had special rights of sanctuary. As the privilege could be for an indefinite period, the fugitives were expected to work. Cromwell was told how they found thirty-two men, many aged, some very sick; all craved to stay there for life. The debtors were allowed to remain, the murderers and felons bidden to depart.

In April Petre suppressed Kenilworth Abbey in Warwickshire. A few weeks afterwards he was again at Woburn, which had been given up to Legh a day or two earlier. There both were involved in taking depositions from the disloyal monks which led to the devout abbot being charged with treason; but Petre was not one of the judges who tried and hanged him in the abbey grounds in June. In that month he dissolved Welbeck Abbey in Nottinghamshire, the chief house of the Premonstratensian Order (White Canons), and three days later Roche Abbey in Yorkshire. He seems to have been busy in the north during July, but there are only meagre details of his movements, which included the suppression of Matersey in Nottinghamshire[13] and apparently a journey back to the Court to report to Cromwell. Early next month, he posted into Norfolk and took the surrender of Walsingham Priory (the shrine of Our Lady there had once been visited by Henry and his first queen), and West Dereham and Wymondham Abbeys.[14] Twelve days later he wrote to Cromwell from the Gilbertine Priory of Malton that he had nominated a conformable prior of Newburgh and received the resignation of the abbot of Whitby (dissolved in 1539 by others); he had ridden to York and was proceeding to Beverley; thence he was making for the Gilbertine Priory of Clatercote in Oxfordshire. The last he dissolved on 22 August. Sempringham Priory in Lincolnshire, the first and chief Gilbertine foundation, was suppressed by Petre in September. Before mid-October he received in rapid succession the submission of eight subordinate Gilbertine priories, all in or near the same county, except for Matersey. There was no opposition because Robert Holgate, the accommodating Master of the Order and 'a creature of Cromwell',[15] rode round with the royal agent—and was rewarded in 1540 with a princely pension.

Returning to London, Petre dissolved the hospital of St. Thomas of Acon in the Cheap and the nunnery of St. Helen in Bishopsgate; also, with Layton, that of Malling in Kent, whose prioress had begged Cromwell that her house should be visited by Petre, a mark of esteem. It was in the last month of 1538 at the mitred Abbey of St. Albans that Petre and Legh first met with determined opposition. 'I would rather choose', the abbot declared, 'to beg my bread all the days of my life than consent to any surrender.' So they were obliged to ask Cromwell to dispatch Layton, whose sterner methods prevailed. The magnificent shrine of St. Alban was utterly destroyed, probably by the use of gunpowder, and its jewels and ornaments were sent to the King.

There are no records to show to what extent Petre had kept in touch with his relations in the West Country since he went up to Oxford as a youth. But early in 1539 he returned there with royal authority, visiting monasteries in his native county, as well as in Wiltshire, Somerset and Dorset.[16] Pursuing his course, he went to Exeter, where his cousin John Petre, later to become mayor, had married his sister Wilmot. In successive days he dissolved St. John's Hospital in Exeter and Polslow Priory near by. Perhaps he stayed at Tor Newton, his birthplace, a few days later, on his way to suppress Torre and Buckfast Abbeys. His companion was Tregonwell, both chosen no doubt because they were Westcountrymen. John Smyth and Sir Hugh Pollard, with two or three others, were added later. Their work in some places went easily, at Buckland, for example, where Petre took possession from an intruded pro-Cromwell abbot. In contrast, the Carthusian priory of Hinton put up a struggle, and did not surrender until two months later. Among the monks who then got pensions was one who expressly denied the royal supremacy. 'We have not yet done anything touching this man,' Petre and Tregonwell informed Cromwell to their credit, 'but (not putting him in any fear) have let him remain until your lordship's pleasure be known herein.' He wandered about the local taverns, a pathetic figure, upholding the Pope's supremacy. So fell England's last Charterhouse. When they saw the impending confiscation, the heads of many houses resorted to a form of self-protection by granting leases of their lands, but Cromwell was insistent on the unmasking of this quasi-deception. At Lacock, for instance, Petre disclosed a case of nepotism involving the abbess and her relations, members of a wealthy Wiltshire family, to whom she had recently leased various manors. The question is dealt with in several reports, for example, that from Tregonwell and Petre, in February: 'We have with as good expedition as we might taken surrender of the houses of St. John's in Bridgwater, Athelney, Buckland Monalium, Taunton, Donkeswell, Canonlegh, and Polslow, and in all these houses have found as much conformity as might be desired. Saving that in many of them we have found great waste and many leases of late passed which nevertheless we have stayed and called in again as near we might.' Their strength having just been augmented, they intended to control these abuses more effectively by splitting into two pairs, 'so that two of us being at one house, the other two may in the same time dispatch another'. By this means they hoped to complete the visitation before 25 March, thus ensuring that the half-yearly rents due at Lady Day went into the royal coffers. Under this plan Pollard joined Petre. Bearing down on the Prior of Montacute, they found the Abbot of Bruton closeted with him. They accused the abbot of having had 'privy conference' with the prior, making him as obstinate as the former, and having raced to lease all the Montacute demesnes on the eve of their arrival. It was Petre who took both their surrenders some weeks later, but their resistance was apparently overcome only by the offer of munificent pensions. One courageous lady withstood the combined assault of Tregonwell, Petre and Smyth. 'Albeit we have used as many ways with her as our poor wits would attain', they had to admit, 'yet in the end we could not by any persuasions bring her to any conformity.' The prioress was not tempted by material gain. 'If the King command me to leave this house', she retorted, 'I will gladly go, though I beg my bread; and as for pension I care for none. Trouble me no further, for I have declared my full mind.' She was deposed, but her stout defence won a further nine months' life for the house.

The trouble arose because the reformed religion had scarcely taken root in these parts, where the monasteries retained a good deal of popular support. The task of securing their possessions for the King was primarily that of Tregonwell and Petre, sometimes separately, sometimes working together, as Legh and Layton had done in the north. The table has been reconstructed from the dated deeds of surrender and their dispatches to Cromwell.

ITINERARY OF THE WEST-COUNTRY HOUSES, 1539

Surrendered on	*Dissolved by*
JANUARY	
16 Pulton Priory, Wilts.	Petre
16 Marlborough Priory, Wilts.	Tregonwell & Petre
16 Bradenstock Priory, Wilts.	Tregonwell
(16) Malmesbury Abbey, Wilts. (Tregonwell and Petre 'did nothing because the abbot was in London'.)	
20 Lacock Abbey, Wilts.	Tregonwell & Petre
23 Keynsham Abbey, Som.	Tregonwell & Petre
26 Hinton Priory, Som.	Tregonwell & Petre
27 Bath Cathedral Priory, Som.	Tregonwell & Petre
FEBRUARY	
3 St. John's Hospital, Wells, Som.	Tregonwell
7 St. John's Hospital, Bridgwater, Som.	Tregonwell
8 Athelney Abbey, Som.	Tregonwell & Petre
10 Minchin Buckland (Monalium) Priory or Hospital, Som.	Tregonwell & Petre
12 Taunton Priory, Som.	Tregonwell
14 Donkeswell Abbey, Devon	Tregonwell

Surrendered on	Dissolved by

FEBRUARY

16	Legh (or Canonlegh) Abbey, Devon	Tregonwell
19	Polslow Priory, Devon	Petre
20	St. John's Hospital, Exeter, Devon	Petre
22	Hartland Abbey, Devon	Tregonwell
23	Torre Abbey, Devon	Petre
24	Launceston Priory, Corn.	Tregonwell
25	Buckfast Abbey, Devon	Petre
27	Buckland Monachorum, Devon	Petre
27	Bodmin Priory, Corn.	Tregonwell

MARCH

1	Plympton Priory, Devon	Petre
2	St. German's Priory, Corn.	Tregonwell
3	Tavistock Abbey, Devon	Tregonwell
8	Forde Abbey, Devon	Petre
8	Newham Priory, Devon	Tregonwell
(?9)	Montacute and Bruton, Som. (Petre met with opposition.)	
11	Middleton (or Milton) Abbey, Dors.	Tregonwell
12	Abbotsbury Abbey, Dors.	Petre
13	Tarent Abbey, Dors.	Smyth
14	Bindon Abbey, Dors.	Tregonwell
15	Cerne Abbey, Dors.	Tregonwell
15	Witham Priory, Som.	Petre
18	Sherborne Abbey, Dors.	Petre
20	Montacute Priory, Som.	Petre
23	Shaftesbury Abbey, Dors.	Tregonwell
25	Wilton Abbey, Wilts.	Tregonwell
(30)	Amesbury Priory, Wilts. (Tregonwell, Petre and Smyth met with opposition: surrendered to others, 7 December.)	
31	Edington Priory, Wilts.	Petre
31	Hinton Priory, Som.	Tregonwell

APRIL

1*	Bruton Abbey, Som.	Petre

The winter itinerary can be extended from the general list of monastic plate—and in slightly more detail from Petre's own indenture of the receipt for the treasures brought from the West to London;[17] the latter,

* Petre left London again on 16 April and dissolved Hyde Abbey, Hampshire, a fortnight later; that marked the end of his work in the West.

dated 2 May, arranges the places by counties. The houses surrendered tally exactly, except that the list and receipt add to the itinerary the small priories or cells of Colwick, Marsh, Dunster and St. Anthony, in Devon, Somerset and Cornwall. Of more importance, they name the churches from which the commissioners removed 'superfluous plate', which were: Salisbury Cathedral, Wells Cathedral, Exeter Cathedral, Glastonbury Abbey and Malmesbury Abbey.

Little would otherwise have been known of the legalized plunder of these renowned churches, apart from Wells. There, the chapter's letter of 6 March to Cromwell stated that Tregonwell and Petre had been 'lately' to take so much of their jewels and plate as they deemed expedient for the King's use: no complaint was breathed, merely a plea against further spoliation. Their days had been so fully occupied that the descent on Wells (and probably Glastonbury) must have occurred between 3 and 7 February when they were active in Somerset. Although Petre had told Cromwell that they 'did nothing' at Malmesbury on 16 January because the abbot was in London, the indenture shows that they looked after the needs of the royal treasury in his absence.

The schedule of jewels and plate is a composite one. The visitors required only a discharge for the total treasure, weighed and assayed. It was indeed a haul fit for a king. Henry received, for instance, 'a small cross of gold with one image garnished with 15 emeralds, 6 garnets and certain small pearls weighing together with the stones and pearls $12\frac{3}{4}$ oz.', and 'seven chalices of gold with seven patens of gold', as well as 'a super-altar [consecrated portable stone slab] garnished with silver and gilt and part gold called the great Sapphire of Glastonbury'. The agents brought in, surprisingly enough, 'a crown of gold plated with silver called King Henry the Sixth's crown'; where this was found is not disclosed. Not all the loot was up to this standard: some of the stones were 'counterfeit'. There was also a rare object: 'a great piece of an unicorn horn, as it is supposed', which it would be wrong to dismiss merely as a curiosity. The sceptical comment is that of one ahead of his time, for the existence of the one-horned animal was still generally believed. Whether horn of the sea narwhal or of the Syrian antelope, it was valuable. Not many of the objects were specified. The great mass was lumped together in the final entry, '45,000 oz. of gilt, parcel gilt, and white plate, broken and whole'. A train of pack-horses, strongly guarded, must have been needed to transport the one and a quarter tons of treasure to the Tower.

Soon after the end of the parliamentary session, visitation was resumed. Petre apparently did not renew his own inquisitions until the late summer, when he secured Dartford Priory, which he had first visited in 1536. He

Sᵗ Wᵐ Petre;   Ætatis,
                                                                  Suae:XL.

2. SIR WILLIAM PETRE
Aged 40

3. TOR BRIAN, DEVON
Petre's birthplace

spent a busy time in London during October. The prioress of Holywell gave up her house to Legh and Petre. Alone, Petre received the surrenders of the celebrated Priory and Hospital of St. Bartholomew, Smithfield, and of the important Priory of St. Mary Overy, Southwark.* He was also one of the commissioners who dissolved the Priory of St. Mary Spital without Bishopsgate, London.

Petre then rode to Bury in Suffolk. There, on 4 November, the vast Abbey of St. Edmund fell, a monastic stronghold of remote antiquity with a colossal income. Although the deed of surrender was taken only by Petre, the pension list shows that his colleagues were Sir Richard Rich, Sir Anthony Wingfield, Richard Southwell and John ap Rice. The last had been at St. Edmundsbury a year earlier and had reported sardonically on the relics found there; these included some of the coals that roasted St. Lawrence, the parings of St. Edmund's toes, with as many pieces of the cross of Our Saviour as would make a large whole cross. The new report, sent direct to the King three days after the surrender, dealt with money, not miracles. As the abbot was very conformable and aged and the yearly revenues were 4,500 marks (£3,000), they suggested that he should have a pension of 500 marks and a house. They had removed the plate and the ornaments and sold the other goods. The lead and bells would be worth 4,500 marks. They asked if they were to deface the church. In the meantime they would survey the lands. Their letter to Henry is signed by all five, together with Thomas Mildmay, an auditor of the Exchequer. The abbot was awarded his annual pension (equivalent to £10,000 at present), but died before getting his first payment.

On 14 November the oldest English nunnery and one of the largest yielded to Petre: Barking Abbey in Essex, a few miles east of London, said to have been founded in 666. Two dealings which he had had with the abbess and convent in 1538 were to settle where his future country home would be.† A week later he helped to secure Syon in Middlesex.

In the New Year he took a leading part in the closing scenes of the long act of Suppression. Westminster Abbey surrendered to Petre on 16 January; pensions were settled a few days later by Rich, Petre, Sir Thomas Pope and Mildmay. Two days before the submission of Westminster, Petre had obtained that of St. Thomas's Hospital. While in Kent, he and two subordinates had also dissolved Leeds Priory. But Canterbury was the main objective. 'The mother monastery of England, Christchurch',

---

* The former was soon to be re-founded by the King in connection with the Corporation of London as the hospital known to generations as 'Barts'; the latter is now Southwark Cathedral.

† See Chapter III.

an Anglican historian wrote, 'though marked to have fallen among the first, had struck the awe of caution into the breast of the spoiler. It had been visited again and again.'[18] The final commission to receive possession of Christ Church Cathedral Priory and Rochester Priory, signed by Cromwell and dated 20 March, was given to Cranmer, Rich, Petre, Nicholas Bacon, Solicitor of the Court of Augmentations, Ap Rice, and four others, 'or any two of them'. The most experienced member, deputy Vicar-general Petre, was one of the quorum. On 15 April he was reimbursed £26 paid by him to the Rochester servants when their establishment was given up.[19]

The indefatigable Petre completed the Dissolution of the Monasteries by taking the surrender of Waltham Abbey in Essex. This he did on 23 March, and was accompanied, appropriately enough, by Edward North, Treasurer of the Court of Augmentations, who thus visited the last house that yielded its wealth to the royal coffers.* Of the magnificent structure, the present parish church is but a part. Yet the great Norman abbey church might have survived intact, had the scheme for additional dioceses been carried out. A list, in Henry's handwriting, of 'places for the new intended bishops' seats' begins with Essex, the see to be at Waltham. In like fashion, St. Albans and Bury St. Edmunds were to become cathedrals of new dioceses of Hertford and Suffolk. But Henry's plan, despite his vast confiscation, remained for the most part a dead letter, and Essex was not to be a separate diocese until three and a quarter centuries later, when Waltham Abbey was one of the churches again proposed in vain as a new cathedral.†

All Cromwell's agents were lawyers. On three of them, Layton, Legh and London, many abusive terms have been heaped by their contemporaries and by historians. A fellow visitor, for instance, found Legh's 'insolent and pompalique behaviour' intolerable, and Cromwell reprimanded him for his 'sumptuous usage and gay apparel' on visitation journeys when he was always attended by fourteen men in livery. Recent writers have shown that the most sinister charges may be forgotten.[20] If their blackness has now assumed a dark shade of grey, Petre's conduct takes on a paler hue. Certain it is that Layton, Legh and London, but never Petre, were branded with such vices as cruelty, bribery, rapacity,

---

* Waltham Abbey suffered a musical as well as material loss. Thomas Tallis, the organist, was dismissed but was soon able to find a place in the Chapel Royal, in which Henry, a friend to music, maintained a high standard. Tallis kept his appointment there through the three reigns which followed, and worked with an even greater composer, William Byrd, whose Essex patron was William Petre's son.

† The real work of the Dissolution ended at Waltham Abbey, but it may be added that St. Nicholas' Hospital, Portsmouth, surrendered to Petre in June.

cupidity and adultery. The worst the Church historian, Dixon, could say about 'the omnivorous Petre' was that he 'must be named the next in prowess (if better he exceeded not them both) to the experienced Legh and Layton'.[21] Petre would not have resented this imputation of hard work in the King's service. Though diligent, he was neither rapacious nor a rogue; and that, perhaps, is why his share in the Dissolution has attracted little comment. The original sources, indeed, yield a few encomiums.

One of these comes from Abingdon Abbey. There Petre and Tregonwell were assisted by Wellysburn, who told Cromwell that they had handled the inmates so as to leave them with no grudge. He also wrote to Thomas Wriothesley, Cromwell's chief administrative officer: 'I never was in company with more discreet and honest men'; and a little later: 'My trust is such in Mr. Petre's honesty that all the lewd priests in England cannot cause him to go beside honesty. Methinketh him a man of such honesty and so I leave the matter in an honest man's hands.'[22] Of the two meanings of 'honesty' then current, probity in its wide sense is that probably implied in this unsolicited testimonial. Wriothesley, who had secured grants of Beaulieu and Titchfield Abbeys on opposite sides of Southampton Water, received this from his bailiff, writing at Southwick:

> I am thankful for goodness shown me by Drs. Petre, Layton, and Freeman in the sale of all such things as I have bought of them. I was much more bound to Mr. Freeman and Mr. Petre than to Mr. Layton. Where they gave me some things he afterwards took them from me, yea, some such things as I had before bought of them. One thing they gave me for my house was 20 bacon hogs hanging in the roof, of which he took from me 12 of the best. He also took three great coffers, trussed the bacon in two of them, and in the third had all the church books. He likewise used you at Bewley, for your bacon, as your steward can tell you. I do not declare this for any displeasure, but his associates would wish to be accompanied by some other honest man, for by his such usage they take some shame. They wish you should know of him, but not by them.[23]

Petre's diplomacy is shown in this shrewdly managed message. Although possibly nauseated by Layton's methods, he was glad not to be the direct complainant, but to use the outpourings of the resentful bailiff to get the information through to Cromwell.

Whether Petre had found the long Dissolution task unsavoury in any way is not known. In all the correspondence of the time the keynote is entire compliance with the King's will. Most of the abbots and priors, in anticipation of handsome pensions, were subservient. The blackest chapters, the executions of the abbots of Reading, Glastonbury and

Colchester, who stoutly refused to give up their houses, are devoid of the barest reference to Petre's name.

Petre had done a great amount of travelling, from the visitation of Kent in 1536 until the dissolution of the last great abbeys in 1540. North as far as Whitby, south, east, and west down to the borders of Wales and Cornwall, his commissions had taken him, riding with servants and packhorses. And the journeys he actually made were certainly more numerous than the extant records disclose. The agents' arrival for putting into effect the formal take-over is known to have been preceded in some cases by more than one preliminary call, during the general inquisitions of 1535–8 or in preparation for the final arrangements for dispossession. The knowledge of England Petre thus acquired was to stand him in good stead in the coming years. But it had been a long and fatiguing assignment. Cromwell tolerated no slackness. He knew pretty accurately how much work was involved. Had he not himself visited the small priories of Thoby, Blackmore, Stansgate and Tiptree, all in Essex, in 1525; surveyed, inventoried and valued them, and reported to his master, Wolsey, intent on suppressing them to furnish funds for the building of Cardinal College at Oxford? Petre certainly wasted no time on his own work and travel in the vast business scheme controlled by Cromwell as general manager.

Petre's sole grant from the Crown for his share in the labours of the Dissolution was one small monastery, and even that was not acquired without securing influential support, nor was it an outright gift. In May 1538, when sending a report to Wriothesley, Petre went on to say: 'Would to God, if my lord [Cromwell] go to the King at any time before our return, it would please his lordship to remember our suit, wherein I pray you to remember your goodness. This I write because I think these times most meet for that purpose in which I am occupied in his business'; remarking somewhat naïvely in a later letter, 'I think the more secret the thing is kept the better, for fear of other suitors.'[25] In August he wrote from Yorkshire direct to Cromwell begging him to remember his suit; and proceeded towards Clatercote. In December Petre was rewarded with this house and the priory manor, its neighbouring manor of Fenny Compton in Warwickshire and other small properties.[26] The grant, almost certainly the object of his suit, was made 'in consideration of good and acceptable service to us performed', a phrase that may be taken literally. No purchase-price was stated. Its annual value was reckoned (on a conservative basis) at £34 13s. 4d. Petre's second account-book shows a payment in 1544 of £99 13s. 6¼d. to the King 'for the purchase of the late priory of Clatercote with the advowson of Westwell', which may represent the annulling of the rentcharge. It is possible to estimate the capital value of the Clatercote estate a little more accurately. In 1546 Petre re-granted it to the Crown in part exchange for the manor of Brent.* He then certified that it was worth £70 clear a year, which, calculated on the usual basis of twenty years' purchase, meant a value of about £1,400 on the land market.

Although Clatercote was the only Crown favour earned by all his Dissolution exertions, annuities were granted to him by nineteen chapters in the hope of postponing their fall or improving their pensions; some of the royal agents did better in annuity business. By 1540 this source gave him just over £100 a year, the £40 from Fountains being by far the largest and apparently the first.† In addition, £80 in annual rents was received from leases of six impropriate rectories, chiefly in Kent, made to him by Rochester and Winchester Cathedral Priories, which he visited in 1536-7; Petre had sub-let these rectories. Today most if not all of the annuities would be considered bribes; but the Tudors gave small salaries to their officials, knowing that there were many perquisites to be had for the asking.

* See p. 268.
† The houses in addition to Fountains were: Barking, Sempringham, Kenilworth, Wells, Wilton, Taunton, Edington, Battle, Merton (Surrey), Southwick, St. Mary Spital-without-Aldersgate, Evesham, St. Albans, Godstow, Montacute, Malton, Clatercote and Robertsbridge.

Ingatestone Hall

1 Purchase from the Crown

ESSEX became the adopted county of Dr. William Petre, whose ancestral origins lay deep in Devon, as a result of three influences—marriage, land and London. He did not marry until he was approaching thirty, and then chose for his wife Gertrude Tyrell, the youngest daughter of Sir John Tyrell of Little Warley Hall, a cadet of an ancient and prolific south Essex family. Their main seat was Heron Hall in the neighbouring parish of East Horndon, only twenty miles from the capital. How the rising official met his future wife, when and where they were married, and what her dowry was, cannot be ascertained, but it may be surmised that the wedding took place in 1533.[1]

The only glimpse of William and Gertrude reveals them in August 1537 at Wriothesley's Hampshire home. A servant of the host, writing to his master, shows Petre enjoying the pleasures of the chase: 'Mrs. Petre and the rest at [Meon] Stoke be in good health. Dr. Petre sends commendations. On Sunday I dined at Stoke with my mistress and him. That afternoon he rode to [Bishops] Waltham and killed a buck and pressed me to ride with him to Southwick' (near Titchfield).[2]

The Petres' first-born, John, died in infancy.[3] Dorothy, the next child, is recorded as being born in 1535 and her godmothers were Lady Norwich and Dame Dorothy Barlee, the aristocratic abbess of Barking. The second daughter, Elizabeth, had as her godmothers Lady Cooke of Gidea Hall, Romford (the Cookes were neighbours of the Tyrells), and Wriothesley's wife. Their births took place in London.[4] Though William acquired a number of relations of knightly and gentlemanly rank in Essex through his marriage, there is no evidence of any closer association with the county until 1537, when he obtained possession of two manors in south Essex probably with the intention of making one of them his country home. In October he secured a lease for £30 a year of the manor of Great Burstead Grange, near East Horndon, from the abbey of Stratford Langthorne in West Ham.[5] Next month, as 'William Petre of London, gentleman', he purchased from one William Kyrkeby of Tonbridge an estate and reputed manor of some five hundred acres called Bayhouse, which lay in the Thames-side parish of West Thurrock. It cost him £504 and produced a net annual revenue of about £25.[6] From Bayhouse a short ride inland would bring the Petres to the Tyrell country, and the water route to

22

London was conveniently short for a government official. Events, however, provided him with another Essex estate, and it was there, in preference to Great Burstead or Bayhouse, that he decided to make his seat. The former lease was soon disposed of, but he retained Bayhouse.

He had been assigned to make the customary enquiries at the renowned nunnery of Our Lady and St. Ethelberga of Barking. Whether the family friendship with the abbess arose because Gertrude's sister was a nun there or because of an earlier visit is not known. The convent was one of the wealthiest of English nunneries, gave good education to daughters from manor-houses in the Eastern counties, and could well afford to be accommodating to an experienced Crown nominee whose beneficent influence might ease the threatened revolution. On 1 February 1538, 'for good considerations them thereunto moving', the chapter granted the visitor, Dr. Petre, an annuity of £10 charged on their estates. That was not all. Exactly three months later, they gave him a forty-year lease, to begin at the following Michaelmas, of their most important country property —the manor of 'Gyng Abbess called Abbess Hall lying in Gyng Abbess'.[7] Throughout medieval times it had other names such as 'Ging ad Petram': in English, 'Yenge atte Stone', whence Ing-at-stone. Petre, still described as of London, was to pay an annual rent of £15 and the convent was to bear the cost of repairs, taxes and other outgoings. The tenants, Thomas Breynwood and his wife Margaret, were compensated. Petre secured his lease just in time, for an Act of 1539 annulled all such leases made within a year of dissolution. It included the 'mansion place', but not the windmill or the warren, nor the rights to present to the church (the advowson) and to hold the manor court. The new tenant had to provide 'honest lodging, sufficient man meat and horse meat and litter' for the abbey steward, receiver and servants for two days and nights each year when they came down to hold courts. The immediate uses to which Petre put his property must remain conjectural, as its history during the next year and a half is a blank.

Some great houses, owing to their good reputation or to the successful intervention of a royal agent, had been allowed an extended term, but inexorably the Crown pursued its aims. The days of their community numbered, the abbess and thirty nuns of Barking assembled for the last time in their chapter-house on 14 November 1539 to execute and hand to Dr. Petre the deed of surrender, ostensibly a spontaneous act. Among those who signed away their abbey, church and all their corporate possessions were ladies of such well-established Essex families as Fitzlewes, Mordaunt, Tyrell, Wentworth, Drury, Sulyard and Kempe. Twelve days later Petre settled the annuities. Abbess Barley's pension of

£133 13s. 4d. was one of the two largest awarded to the head of a nunnery.

On 15 December the manor of 'Gynge Abbess', with the house and the advowson (plate 5), was granted by the Crown to Petre.[8] That his letters patent bear this date is clear proof of his having put his intimate knowledge of the Court of Augmentations and its officers to speedy use, for it was on the previous day that Cromwell and Rich, its Chancellor, were authorized to sell Crown lands at twenty years' purchase, that is, at a capital price of twenty times their full, official current valuation, which was then the usual basis of assessment. It follows, therefore, and it must be emphasized in view of earlier mis-statements, that the grant was neither a gift nor even a very cheap bargain. The sum payable to Henry VIII was its normal market price, which worked out at £849 12s. 6d.; and the property was charged with an annual rent of £4 13s. 6d. to the Crown, from which it was to be held by service of a twentieth of a knight's fee (tenure by knight service and rent of one-tenth of the value were recent statutory provisions).[9] In accordance with contemporary Augmentations practice, the purchaser did not have to pay outright. Petre was allowed to spread the purchase-money over four years, as the little file of receipts for the instalments bear witness (£400 paid on 16 December; £100 in November of 1540, 1541 and 1542; balance of £149 12s. 6d. on 31 October 1543).[10] By a play on words, reminiscent of Christ's 'Thou art Peter, and on this rock [Wyclif reads 'stone'] I will build my Church', Petre promptly modified the alternative name 'Ginge ad Petram' to 'Ginge Petre'.* (Plate 6.)

Study and law at Oxford, study and travel abroad, the law courts in London, work and more travel in England—such had been his life for nearly twenty years. Petre had now acquired a small estate, and risen to an 'esquire' (he was first so termed in May 1539, before becoming lord of the manor of Ginge Abbess [11]). He had achieved the ambition of most men of affairs, a country retreat where from time to time he could take his ease.

In February 1540, only two months after acquiring the manor of Ingatestone, Petre bought for £133 6s. 8d. from the Crown, through a third party, a neighbouring grange called Handley, which he then let; this also had been a possession of Barking Abbey. In the previous October

* St. Matthew xvi, 18 (cf. 'To Symount he put name Petre', St. Mark iii, 16.—Wyclif). Two of the last documents which he signed, one being his will, still maintained the double name; the will gives 'Ingatstone alias Ging Petre', the other, 'Ging Petre alias Ingatstone'; sometimes one alternative was used, e.g. 'the manor place of Ging Petre', 1571 (E.R.O., D/DP A86), but 'Ingatstone' was generally adopted for the parish. The modern spelling Ingatestone obscures the fact that a sarsen stone (still surviving), not a gate, gave the village its suffix, Essex being virtually stoneless.

he had secured from the Court of Augmentations a twenty-one year lease of the demesnes of the Priory manor of Montacute in Somerset for an annual rent of £98 10s.;[12] and a year later, by another indirect purchase from the Crown for £131 15s., the manor of Westwell in west Oxfordshire, which had belonged to Edington Priory; each house, incidentally, had granted him an annuity before its demise.[13] By the end of 1540, therefore, his expenditure or commitments for Bayhouse, Ingatestone and these three properties had reached a total of £1,619, with nearly £100 a year for Montacute, and his available resources for investment must have been extended to the limit. But in a short time Petre had emerged from the Dissolution as a not inconsiderable landowner.

Setting aside Petre's earliest purchase, that of Bayhouse, which was his only estate formerly in lay hands, it is clear that his purchases and leases were of properties of which he had first-hand information as a Visitor, and he was therefore able himself to estimate their immediate income and potential value. In this connection he may have secured the Cotswold and Somerset estates for profitable sheep-farming. His duties, which included searching questions about the management of the monastic estates and buildings, had also given him much practical knowledge and experience that was to stand him in good stead as a rising landowner.

A 'declaration' of his properties and annuities, which agrees fully with the evidence of the state papers and his earliest personal account-book,[14] reveals that in 1540 he had a total income, from rents and monastic annuities, from Ingatestone manorial dues, and from sales of timber, cattle, wool and other produce of the demesnes, of over £500. Of this, at least £380 was assured, but the accounts are not in a form that allows a clear distinction between fixed income and casualties. He was farming the whole of his Ingatestone demesne, employing a bailiff. The Oxfordshire and Somerset estates were also kept in his hands and were looked after by Edward Napper of Holywell, Oxford, who remained his West Country agent for many years. His official income as a master in Chancery was the annual fee of £6 14s. (A full list of his accounts is in Appendix A.)

The same account-book, which extends to 1544, shows that Clatercote and Montacute sales of cattle and sheep at Coventry and Cold fairs yielded nearly £100 each year, and about the same sum was realized by sales from the Ingatestone demesnes to butchers of Ingatestone or London, the latter mostly at Uxbridge fair. The small November fair attached to Ingatestone manor brought him an average of 22s. a year. The accounts give no details of the actual profits of sheep-farming because some entries combine rent and wool sold. Income from the Cotswold wool is exemplified by £14 15s. 10d. 'for 3 packs of wool lacking 10 lb.' sold to a Worcestershire man at 5d. a lb. (December 1542) and £4 10s. from Ingatestone for 270 lb. at 4d. (October 1544). The wolds produced the better wool, the lowland pastures the fatter sheep. Petre evidently kept his wool-clip for a few months before selling it, this being a common practice among larger farmers who could afford to wait for the seasonal rise in price.[15] Only a negligible quantity of corn was sold, from which it is clear that the remainder was consumed by the household at Ingatestone.

Gertrude died on 28 May 1541 leaving the two infant girls.* Petre also found his second wife Anne Tyrell in Essex. They were married by March 1542,[16] and she, too, gave birth to two girls, though one may have died by 1544. Born in 1509,[17] she was the daughter of William Browne, a London merchant who had died during his term as Lord Mayor of London in 1514. She had been first married to John Tyrell, son of Sir Thomas Tyrell of Heron Hall, in the parish of East Horndon, who was a distant cousin of Petre's first father-in-law. They were mere children when their fathers signed an agreement in 1513 for the marriage to take place before 1521.[18] Anne's marriage portion had been 400 marks; she was sole heiress of her father; and her husband died without male heir in 1540.† From Anne came a substantial accession to Petre's wealth: the lease of a farm at Dunton just beyond East Horndon, the contiguous manors of Shepreth and Meldreth in Cambridgeshire, and the manors of Avon Tyrell and Milton in Hampshire. Rents from these estates and other income of his wife's produced £280 in 1542, his total receipts from all sources then being £889. The big increase over the figure for 1540 is due, apart from his profitable re-marriage, chiefly to sales of cattle and wool (£201) and to rents from additional small properties.

The account-book gives Petre's expenditure for one year only (1543). It amounted to £815. In the main only a summary statement, it is useful as a basis for comparison with later years. (See Appendix B.) Petre was not yet a man of substance, but he had already made a material advance.

---

* Practically nothing is known of their married life. Gertrude is commemorated by a slab within the altar rails in Ingatestone church, bearing the date of her death. For Petre's children, see Chapters VII and XIV.

† An interesting little Tyrell account-book for Heron Hall and Dunton, 1539–40, is preserved (E.R.O., D/DP A16). 'Watching my husband' during his last sickness is followed by a bailiff's account for a few months to 'my mistress'. Anne's brother 'Mr. John Browne of London' is mentioned. From her came the book of hours, which was given to her by the 4th Lord Mountjoy, who was both her step-father and uncle. He inscribed verses on their relationship in the book. (J. J. Howard and F. H. Burke, *Geneaolgical Collections . . . Roman Catholic Families*—Part i (1887), Petre, 49.)

2 The Country House

When Dr. Petre bought the manor of Gynge Abbess from the Crown in December 1539, he evidently intended to establish his position by building a country house with relatively easy access to the capital. He found 'the commodity [convenience] of the ground to be such as he could well like'; in other words, a pleasant site and good land.[19] But the existing dwelling, known as Abbess Hall, was 'an old house scant meet for a farmer to dwell upon'; so he 'forthwith' pulled down all the ancient buildings, and then began to erect 'new houses, very fair, large and stately, made of brick and embattled'. By his time, brick was the recognized building material for most homes of consequence in this stoneless county.*

He also followed the fashion of designing the main dwelling on a courtyard plan, with an outer court containing most of the home-farm buildings. There was no longer need, except in areas remote from Henry's strong government, to build manor-houses inside moats or even in semi-fortified plan, with windowless outer walls. Ingatestone Hall, it is true, was partly crenellated, but the parapet battlements were so harmonized with the crow-stepped gables and the bases of the chimney stacks as to please the eye, and were probably for decoration rather than defence. In 1551 Petre received the Crown 'licence to embattle', with pardon for having already done so, by that date almost a double formality.[20]

The new building on or very near the old site was probably started in 1540, and the main quadrangle was completed about four years afterwards. Only for 1543 is there a brief record of his expenditure, which included 'buildings and reparations, £153 11s. 9d.', with no further details. William and Anne were evidently living in the house from the end of 1542 if not before, and he may be assumed from evidence which is related later to have superintended the building operations whenever he was free from his duties in London. Their daughter Thomasine was born at Ingatestone in April 1543. He probably used his position to obtain the services of a first-class ex-monastic architect, but the possibility of his being his own architect should not be dismissed, having regard to his recent visitation experience and to known facts about the building of

* Recent research has shown that brick was used in post-Roman Essex as far back as Norman times, but it is doubtful if it was used extensively by wealthy landowners before the late fourteenth century. There is fairly early fifteenth-century brickwork in Faulkbourne Hall, and it is known that about 1414 Lewis John rebuilt Old Thorndon Hall of brick. All the surviving Tudor courtyard houses in Essex, except one, were built of brick. Probably the bricks for Ingatestone Hall were made on the estate; this was the usual practice, and was certainly adopted a generation later by Petre's son in rebuilding Thorndon Hall.

some other contemporary houses. It is regrettable that his detailed accounts, which begin in 1549, are too late for the main building period. In that year they merely disclose finishing touches, such as flooring and ceiling several of the smaller rooms, making extra doors, and gilder's work; and those of later date reveal that Petre's building operations were directed solely towards providing extra carthouses and the like. By good fortune, however, a great deal of information about the house has been preserved in three documents, each remarkable in its own way.[21] In 1566 Petre commissioned Thomas Larke to prepare a full survey of the manor, demesne and park; the description of the house, which is illustrated by a crude, diagrammatic plan (plate 9), is enlivened by Larke's narration of how Petre tackled drainage problems before laying the foundations. The other records were prepared for Petre's son and heir. One is a long inventory, compiled in 1600, of the whole mansion except certain rooms and of the outbuildings. The other is a map of the manor (plate 7), made in 1605 by John Walker and his son, the astonishing accuracy of whose 'perspective' drawings has recently been proved beyond all doubt; indeed, their representations of larger houses are almost equivalent to scale drawings in miniature (plate 8). The relatively few building entries in the account-books of Petre's son are a reasonable guarantee that no major changes were made by him, so that most of what can be learned about the structure from the two later documents would also be true in William's day. The house that he built has survived. Though much altered since his time, the records in brick and tile are even better than those on parchment and paper.

Petre's house was approached by a lane which turned out of the London to Chelmsford highway at 'London gate', just before reaching Ingatestone. Half a mile along, the lane widened into a 'cawsey' leading to the porter's lodge—the present drive leading to the archway—which was in the centre of the west side of the outer court, or base court. The causeway approached it obliquely. The house, therefore, did not come into view until the gatehouse arch was reached (plate 10). The 'outermost gate' was a simple two-storey, gabled building without turrets, far removed in conception from the multi-floored brick gatehouse of Layer Marney Towers (Lord Marney's extravaganza) or even Rich's ornamented gatehouse at Leighs Priory, both in Essex. There were also gables at each end of the gatehouse range. The square base court was lined on three sides with continuous two-storey ranges, substantially built, and occupied by the outside servants; the lower storey was of brick, the upper being plastered. Then came the smaller middle court, without any buildings except walls, beyond which was the inner court, or mansion proper. It was stately, pleasing to the eye, but unpretentious; showing many a stepped gable and massive chimney-stack with clustered chimneys, but not displaying any ostentatious, purposeless ornament. No stone was used in the exterior, not even for dressings or in the doorways; nor was there any stone in the windows which were constructed with mullions and transoms of brick. The entrance front of the main quadrangle was symmetrical; of its seven bays, the three alternate inner bays were gabled. The single doorway was in the middle. This façade is a fairly early example of the practice, through Renaissance influence, of imposing an outward, superficial uniformity upon a building, the essential internal arrangement of which was still largely medieval and asymmetrical in conception. It is difficult to say whether the façade was broken by a porch or other projections in the builder's time, as it certainly was by 1600. But the front was very modern, with plenty of windows. Behind the gable above the entrance door was a chimney, and there were chimneys at each end. With the aid of the three records of 1566–1605 and after examination of the existing structure, conjectural plans have been prepared showing the positions of the rooms on both floors (pp. 30, 31).

The 'great door' of the house not only had a strong stock-lock and bolt but also within one leaf of the door a small wicket—either at ground level like that surviving at Leighs Priory or higher up to serve as look-out. Inside the entrance, there was doubtless the usual passage known as 'the screens'; on one side, the buttery hatch, on the other, the screen separating the hall from the passage. Generally called the great hall, this was the common living and dining room and meeting-place for the servants and the ordinary guests. Medieval halls had been open to the roof, and the smoke from the central open hearth escaped as best it could through the louvre above. With the use of brick in place of timber came chimney-stacks and the division of the hall into two storeys, and Ingatestone must have been one of the first major houses to have a low-ceilinged hall; the 'hall chimney' is mentioned in 1552. It was about forty feet long and twenty feet wide, and was 'wainscotted', or panelled. Besides an oak table with draw-leaves, there was a huge elm plank standing on four fixed dormers, and as the hall had to seat up to a hundred folk on occasion the walls were lined with benches. Beyond the buttery and beer cellar lay the kitchen, larder and scullery. By 1550 the lord no longer dined with the company in a country establishment, but the hall, presided over by his steward, was still its life-centre. Petre followed the prevailing fashion in placing his private panelled 'dining parlour' next to the hall, on the opposite side to the kitchen. Behind the parlour and for personal use were another pantry and beer cellar, as well as his wine cellar (in Tudor

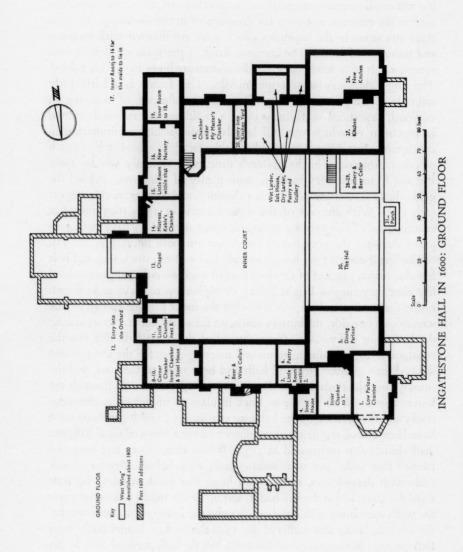

INGATESTONE HALL IN 1600: GROUND FLOOR

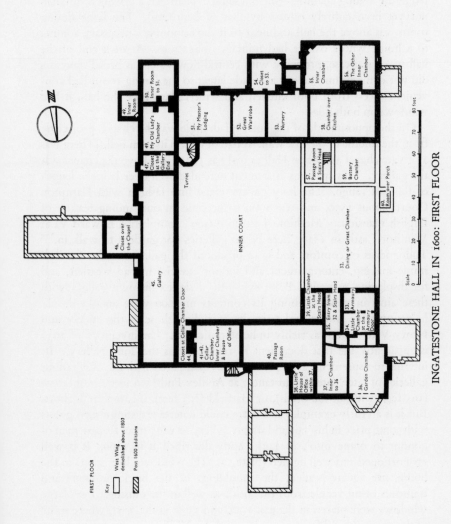

FIRST FLOOR

Key

☐ West Wing demolished about 1800

▨ Post 1600 additions

N

49. Inner Room

50. Inner Room to 51.

54. Closet to 53.

55. Inner Chamber

56. The Other Inner Chamber

48. My Old Lady's Chamber

51. My Master's Lodging

52. Great Wardrobe

53. Nursery

58. Chamber over Kitchen

47. Closet at the Gallery End

Turret

57. Passage Room & Stairs Head

59. Buttery Chamber

46. Closet over the Chapel

INNER COURT

60. Room over Porch

45. Gallery

32. Dining or Great Chamber

Scale

0   10   20   30   40   50   60   70   80 feet

44. Closet at Cellar Chamber Door

39. Little Chamber at the Stairs Head

41-43. Cellar Chamber, Inner Chamber & House of Office

35. Entry from 32 & Stairs Head

33. Armoury

34. Little Chamber at the Armoury Door

40. Passage Room

38. Little House of Office within 37.

37. Inner Chamber to 36

36. Garden Chamber

INGATESTONE HALL IN 1600: FIRST FLOOR

31

times the word denoted a storeroom rather than an underground room).*
The parlour was small, and when Petre entertained important guests they
fed in the 'dining chamber' (the old sense of chamber, a private room, had
not yet been entirely ousted by that of bedroom). The large dining
room was above the hall and next to it the armoury, a necessary adjunct
to a house whose owner had military obligations. At each end of the
hall was a staircase, probably with central-newel steps as broad staircases
did not come in until about a decade later; so the dining room had convenient access from both kitchen and wine cellar. Like the hall, it had
windows on both sides.

On the opposite side of the inner quadrangle was the chapel, projecting
from the middle of the east wall. It had of course its own bell. (There was
a private chapel at Abbess Hall as early as 1225.[22]) Above the chapel was
the gallery. This spacious apartment extended well over half the length
of the east range. The long gallery came into fashion with Hampton
Court, about 1530, and was soon to become an outstanding feature of
English mansions. 'Methinks I am in prison', complained Edward VI at
Windsor Castle in 1549, 'here be no galleries nor gardens to walk in.'[23]
Tudor ideas of comfort and taste produced the gallery for the family's
music-making, entertainment and indoor exercise in bad weather, and
for displaying portraits. Petre evidently designed his own gallery with
these aims in view. Among its contents in 1600 were an old shove-
ha'penny table and several portraits, including those of the builder and
Henry VIII, as well as richly upholstered chairs. The inventory of 1639
is apparently the first document to refer to it as the 'long gallery'. Its
internal measurements are 94 by 18 feet. Compared with the ostentatious
galleries of later date, for instance, at Audley End (226 feet), Montacute
(165 feet, without the oriels), or Hatfield (163 feet), Ingatestone is short.
But it is an early example, and Petre could entertain distinguished guests
with some pride in his 'fair and stately gallery or walk meet for any man of
honour to come into', as Larke aptly described it in 1566. It is well
proportioned and well lighted (plate 12). The windows, like others in the
house, are square-headed, the mouldings of the brick mullions and
transoms being visible from the inside as well as the outside. Two large
windows were placed in the east wall, and three in the west, where some
of the original heraldic stained glass with Sir William's arms still remains.

* Although it was unusual to have any cellars on the far side of the parlour from the hall,
there is a plan by John Thorpe, c. 1600 (in the Soane Museum), of an unnamed house, showing
an exactly parallel arrangement to that of Ingatestone (information kindly given by Mr.
M. Girouard). Perhaps Petre wished to have his wine and better quality beer more readily
accessible to his dining parlour or did not entrust the key to his butler. The absence of
substantial underground cellars may have been due to the springs mentioned later.

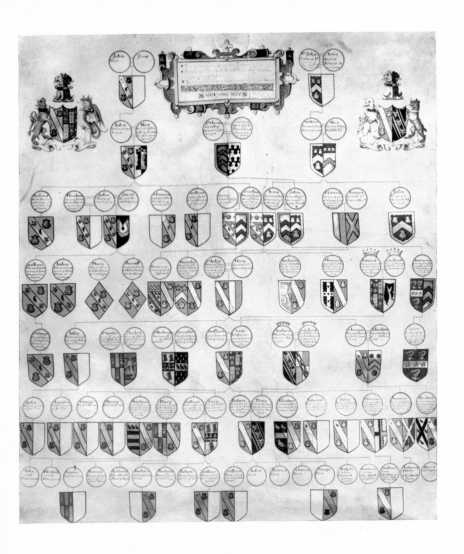

4. ARMORIAL PEDIGREE ROLL, 1634

William's two marriages and those of his second wife appear in the first full line

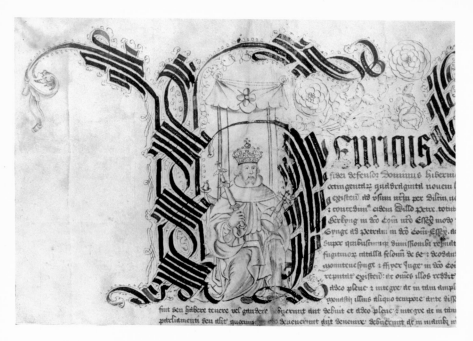

5. CROWN GRANT TO DR. WILLIAM PETRE OF THE MANOR AND ESTATE OF 'GYNGE ABBES *alias* INGERSTONE *alias* GYNGE AD PETRAM', 1539

6. PART OF THE STONE OF ING-AT-STONE BY THE SOUTH DOOR OF THE CHURCH

One quarry bears the arms of Petre impaling Tyrell (for Gertrude, William's first wife), another has Petre impaling Browne (for Anne his second wife), the third has Browne only. An adjacent pane with his motto, 'Sans Dieu Rien', may also be contemporary with the building. (See Appendix C and plate 13.)

The gallery was wainscotted and open to the roof. An unusual feature of Petre's structural plan was his provision of a closet behind the middle of the east wall, next to the fireplace and chimney-stack. This was built to enable the family attending mass to look down into the chapel without sitting with the servants. 'In the middest of the gallery a door, which door leadeth into the chapel chamber over the chapel, where the priest in his ministration from beneath may very well be heard.' The surveyor, writing in 1566, could not refer to the mass, which was probably heard there in secret by Lady Petre, hence his cautiously ambiguous phrase. Yet, although uncommon in its siting, the arrangement was similar to that recommended by Andrew Boorde a few years earlier: 'Let the privy chamber be annexed to the great chamber of estate . . . so that it may have a prospect into the chapel.'[24]

In the north-west corner of the main quadrangle, next to the dining parlour on the ground floor, were the 'low parlour chamber' and another room. Beyond the pantry, wine and beer cellars were three rooms, probably bedrooms, the largest being the 'corner chamber'. Above the low parlour chamber was the 'garden chamber' with its flattened four-centre arch, a room about twenty-four feet on each side, which overlooked the garden (plate 15). Between it and the gallery were bedrooms, the largest being the 'passage room'.

In the opposite range, an unnamed room forty feet long near the kitchen and larders may have been Lady Petre's day-room. In 1550 she bought 'stuff from a pedlar in her hall', perhaps this room. On the other side, in the south-east corner, lay the 'new nursery' (John had just been born at Ingatestone) and 'Mistress Keble's [Petre's mother-in-law] chamber'; both are mentioned in 1550 and the names remained in 1600. Above the long room was 'my master's chamber', or main bedroom, next to which was the usual 'wardrobe' room. On either side were more chambers, including the 'nursery' (for the older children). Garrets ran along the top of this range (but nowhere else in the house); there no doubt the maidservants slept. Diametrically opposite the stairs in the north-west corner were more newel-stairs, built inside an octagonal turret, which led up to the first floor and the attics.

The main court was designed as a self-contained habitation for the family and their personal servants and guests. Under its roof were sixty rooms; this number includes various closets but not the garrets. But it was far from being the whole of Ingatestone Hall. The outdoor servants worked and slept in various ancillary buildings, which were roughly equal in overall accommodation to those of the inner court.* The west range of the incomplete base court (or outer quadrangle) included the gatehouse chamber and its inner room, and the porter's lodge and chamber. In the south range were evidently the falconer's, gardener's and brewer's chambers, hawks' mews, west and east cheese store-rooms, carters' hall, chamber and buttery, bakehouse, boltinghouse, outer and inner milk houses, brew-house and fire-house. The bailiff's chamber and the 'two bed chamber' were perhaps in the short north wing, that is, on the left-hand side after emerging through the gatehouse. Close to the south range were the great stable with a garret, and the slaughter-house, wash-house and fish-house with a chamber above them for making candles. The wood-barn and wood-yard lay outside to the south of the causeway. To its north, as now, were the main barns and yard of the home farm and 'the mill house'. The granary, apparently built in 1559, was a substantial brick structure of two storeys, with crow-stepped gables at its north and south ends. It was set almost at right angles to the causeway and formed the shortest side of a nearly complete pentagonal enclosure to the north-west of the outer court. Also flanking the causeway were the wheat-barn and oat-barn to the north and the carthouse and 'strangers' stables' to the south. The mill house was evidently between the granary and the barns. It was a horse-mill, working a pair of stones, with stable below and granary above. Every outhouse served a useful purpose in making the house as independent as possible of external needs. Thus, in the boltinghouse meal and bran were sifted; in the still house fragrant herbs were distilled in retorts; and the verjuice house, above the horse-mill, contained a press for making from crab-apples a sour liquor used in cooking, to be virtually superseded in later years by vinegar.

A brick house could be safely supplied with plentiful chimneys. Nine of the private rooms, as well as the hall and the kitchen, had fireplaces in the 1600 inventory, which omits one-fifth of the house. Fireplaces were also installed in the rooms of the more important outside servants living in the base court, the plan of which shows five chimneys to serve these rooms, the brewhouse and other offices. The interiors of several rooms, besides the gallery and the hall, were panelled. The house itself had glass windows throughout. The hall and the 'low parlour chamber', and perhaps some other rooms, each had a 'great window'. Even the dovecote

---

* The location of the rooms, etc., in the outbuildings is based on the same three main sources, but their relative position is hypothetical in a few cases.

could boast of glazing in 1549, though the mill house had only wooden 'latticed windows', as in medieval days. With its abundant fireplaces, wainscotting and fine glass windows, Ingatestone Hall ranked as a modern, comfortable home. It was both a knightly residence and a substantial farmhouse.

To the north-west of the house was the private garden—nearly square, divided into six rectangular beds by wide 'walks or alleys'. It was laid out in the formal fashion of the time and was enclosed by a brick wall except at the two corners on the south against the half-side of the base court and against the parlour, the outer door of which led into the garden.

The house was surrounded except for its west front by a large walled orchard. Projecting from the north-west corner and the adjacent sides of the wall were six little structures at regular intervals. Two of them covered spring-heads; the rest sheltered 'fowls that be bred and brought up in the orchard' and the gardener's tools. Larke was evidently impressed with the fowl-coop.

> For the better cherishing of those fowls there is devised by the east side of the orchard from the north-east corner unto the broad gate leading into the hop yard a frame made of thin plank, lattice-like with partitions to keep them in, and is placed from the wall at the least 16 foot and so continueth his breadth. In this frame both partridges, pheasants, guinea hens, turkey hens, and such like do yearly breed and are severally fed and brought up, so as they become tame as other chickens.

The orchard was 'well planted with young trees upon every bank and border of the best fruit that can be and set in good order and proportion, one distant from another equally, and round about the orchard be divers large walks well kept and maintained'. The bowling alley, first mentioned in 1555, was in the orchard.

In the south-west corner of the orchard was 'the banqueting house well and fair builded'. This high-sounding name denoted in Tudor days a summer-house or small pavilion in which the banquet (the final sweet or fruit course) could be served to the guests when the weather was kind. In 1600, if not before, the upper floor of the banqueting house included 'a little study', probably for the young heir, and 'the schoolhouse chamber' may also have been under the same roof. On the side opposite to the garden was another walled enclosure. It lay between the orchard, the south range of the outer court and the stables, and included 'the cook's garden', a 'brick dovehouse very well replenished with doves', and the brewhouse pond. The last was only one of many stews well stocked with fish always ready for the table. 'Within some of these ponds,' moreover, 'the swans do use to breed and have many cygnets which be spent in the house'. Larke's words convey a vivid picture of orderly, pleasant grounds.

Although in a different category to the gallery, the drainage and water-supply scheme formed a double feature of unusual interest, and it drew forth even more of Larke's admiration of Petre's ingenuity. The surveyor revealed the lawyer as a man of resource who solved a drainage problem arising out of the site, for the nuns' old manor-house stood 'under the side of a hill, full of springs, and the ground very subtle to build upon'.

Sir William, foreseeing well the great danger and inconvenience that might have ensued, devised with himself (before he took in hand to build any part of his house) for the sure avoiding and ready conveyance of all such waters, to make divers vaults and gutters of brick, very large, under the ground, round about the whole situation of the house, conveying the waters from every office, the surplusage of any ponds about the house, the rain water or otherwise, from the one to the other unto the lowest part of the river southwards.

The river is the now tiny stream, a few yards beyond the south wall of the orchard; a little below it runs into the not much larger river Wid. Petre had instructed Larke that all these vaults and gutters, by 1566 already 'unknown to any but to himself, nor by any means to be seen without opening', should be 'made manifest to those which shall be hereafter inheritors and owners of his house'; so Larke set out in his survey 'the whole secret thereof' and drew a coloured 'plat', or plan, under Sir William's supervision (plate 9), with a key to it.

The key is a little more specific than the survey about Petre's installation of a water supply for the house and the farm buildings, which was conveyed in leaden pipes from two brick-covered wells near the east wall of the orchard. Thus, although Larke's chief eulogy is of the underground drainage system, Petre's piped supply of 'very clear and sweet' water running 'into every office of the house none excepted' was an equally able achievement.★

The drainage vaults and gutters are readily recognizable on Larke's plan. Three vaults ran from underneath the parlour and the corner chamber and from the door of the adjacent cellar, all on the north side of the house, and they were united inside the courtyard, whence the drain

★ When a drain was blocked in 1952, Lord Petre asked the Essex Record Office to produce the 1566 plan, which at once helped him to locate the trouble. That Ingatestone Hall lies 'under the side of a hill', albeit a low one, was forcibly demonstrated in 1958, when a farmyard wall collapsed under the weight of water after an exceptionally severe thunderstorm and the torrent swept through the north range of the base court and the north wing of the house.

ran below the south range into the brewhouse pond. A long drain extended parallel and close to the north, east and south sides of the mansion; it started in the garden and ran into the first drain near the pond. From the beer cellar below the buttery near the hall door a vault ran under the kitchen, then beneath the banqueting house, and fell into the river. Another long drain was constructed from 'the lowest alley' of the garden, under the wall, where a vault from below the parlour window came in, thence diagonally 'overthwart' or beneath the base court, beyond which it joined a subterranean drain coming from the farmyard pond under the causeway just outside the gatehouse; into the latter a short vault from beneath the garner also drained.

The most elaborate 'ground works' were underneath four rooms of the north range, where the earth was excessively moist. To make a really sound job, Petre had dug trenches over two feet deep, in the beds of which charcoal cinders were laid, and above them crosswise long timber joists, the interspaces being filled with more cinders up to ground level. This had been so efficacious in absorbing the water as to lead Larke to declare that no trouble had since occurred. But to make doubly sure, Petre had also constructed brick gutters along each side of the four rooms, as well as from the middle of each side into a sump-hole in the centre of every room, 'much like unto a washing bowl', from which the water ran away along deeper gutters into the vaults meeting in the middle of the inner court. Larke's delineation of this complicated system is commendably clear.

The vaults were mostly for taking away surface-water entering them through 'vents', all of which were covered by iron gratings. The triple-branch vault from under the north range also served to get rid of the inner courtyard water, which entered it through a vent on the opposite side. There were twelve such vent-holes, the exact positions of which are given by Larke, and ten of them served to drain all three courtyards, farmyard, causeway and garden. Rainwater 'from the leads above' the house fell from or down two spouts into a vent where the drain under the parlour window began. The vault starting in the common beercellar also received the kitchen waste-water through a 'great vent'. Above the main drain which circuited the house, about ten yards away from the middle of the chapel wall, was 'a great vent covered with a great board wherein appeareth the leads conveying the water from the conduits into the house'. This was apparently a combined inspection and flushing vent-hole at the point where the leaden pipes crossed over the drain.

The water pipes ran a considerable distance from the 'conduits', or covered wells, which were a stone's throw beyond the chapel. Three brass cocks are mentioned, but there must also have been one in the kitchen. At the far south-west corner of the base court was 'a small cock of brass', presumably a standpipe, 'whereat any man may have water from the conduits at their pleasure to use'; the other cocks were in the wash-house and fish-house. An interesting problem arises as to whether the water-supply intended for drinking, cooking, brewing, washing and laundering was also for sanitary use. The medieval castle or manor-house had its draughty garderobe, often in a turret with a hole in the floor above a groundpit. In contrast Petre's house had 'houses of office' or 'stool houses'; no fewer than five are mentioned in the incomplete inventory of 1600. Each had a close-stool, its seat covered with leather, velvet or cloth, and a pewter pan; also one or two chamber-pots from the adjacent bedroom. The stools in the privies belonging to the 'low parlour chamber' and the 'corner chamber', both in the north range, probably stood above two of the drainage gutters, which may have been flushed from a tap in the pipes that served 'every office', not meaning merely 'house of office'. There is no hint whether the pipes supplied the first floor nor any mention of a servants' latrine, with or without water; a solitary item in the accounts refers to 2s. spent in 'making clean the jakes about the house'. 'Jakes' is the one good English word, apparently of Tudor origin, which avoids the numerous euphemisms for privy. On balance, the evidence suggests that the sanitary arrangements at Ingatestone Hall were roughly midway between the garderobe and the water-closet invented by Sir John Harrington before 1600 but not in general use until much later.

Larke's laudatory account of Petre's draining and plumbing schemes prompts the question, Did they represent domestic improvements in advance of contemporary ideas, or did Petre copy a plan which he had seen elsewhere? If the question is applied to domestic buildings of medium size, there is perhaps justification for claiming that he was something of a sanitary engineer, but printed material about mid-Tudor houses of the size of Ingatestone Hall is scanty. A piped water-supply and flush-drains had been installed in some of the largest monasteries and royal palaces four centuries before Petre's time. A plan of the water-supply at Christ Church, Canterbury, belongs to the twelfth century; Bury St. Edmund's and St. Alban's Abbeys and the London Charterhouse also had such a system. Petre was present at the fall of the first three houses.

Ingatestone Hall still stands—and is the home of his direct descendant. The survival of the house is in fact partly due to its having been built as Sir William's home: big enough for his own needs and tastes, but, judged by the new architectural fashions of his last years, too plain and unadorned. Retirement from the Court and advancing years saved Petre from the ambitious challenge which drove younger colleagues like Cecil to erect private palaces in which they could worthily entertain their Queen. Petre's widow was to continue at Ingatestone Hall, but the heir acquired a larger house (Thorndon Hall) a few miles away, which he rebuilt in splendid style. He handed over most of Ingatestone Hall in 1600 to his own son and daughter-in-law so that they might gain experience in household 'government'. This heir in turn treated his son in the same way in 1623. And for many years to come Ingatestone Hall served as the house for the widow or the heir-presumptive and was sometimes, especially at Christmas, the alternative residence of the head of the family. Thorndon Hall was superseded by a grand Palladian building, completed in 1770 on a fresh site a mile away, Old Thorndon Hall being razed to the ground to provide building materials.* A century later, New Thorndon Hall was too badly damaged by fire to be rebuilt. After the 1914–18 War, changed social conditions led the family to return to their ancient ancestral home. Then, skilfully restored where it was necessary to remove sash-windows and later doors, it once again became the family seat.

How much of the house built by Sir William Petre survives? Briefly the answer is: the inner court, except for the middle half of the west range which contained the hall; two of the three sides of the base court including the gatehouse, the south range having gone; and the brick granary with some of the barns (plate 11). The west range was 166 feet in length. Its central section of nearly 70 feet, containing the great hall with the dining chamber above, was demolished at some time between 1798 and 1810. There is now therefore no imposing front and porch, but instead, as a compensation, the delightful view of the gatehouse especially from the long gallery across the opened courtyard. The foundations of the great hall were recently found just below ground level. The once gabled bay of this range, to the north of the hall, containing the dining parlour with the armoury above (figs. 1 and 2, nos. 5, 33–35, 39), was not demolished, though it was to some extent rebuilt with the old bricks. Being partially offset from the line of the north range, it now forms a wing slightly projecting to the south. The miniature drawing on the Walkers' map of 1605 (plate 8) clearly shows this projecting bay.

The three crow-stepped small gables above the low parlour chamber and the next rooms (fig. 1, nos. 1–4) are all original, though a good deal

* The site of Old Thorndon Hall was excavated between 1957 and 1959, under the direction of Mr. K. Marshall; evidence was found of two periods of building in the fifteenth century, of John Petre's remodelling between 1575 and 1595 and of the chapel completed to Leoni's design before 1739.

of the brickwork has been renewed at various times. Some of the windows of Sir William's time have been blocked up or altered, but most of the long gallery windows are original. Nearly all the chimney-stacks have been preserved, some with crow-stepped bases, others with octagonal or hexagonal shafts; but the tops of a number have been rebuilt.

Interiors of houses undergo more drastic changes than exteriors. The most important room to the present-day visitor—Sir William's gallery—has on the whole preserved its chief features, though its original roof with wind-braced purlins is no longer visible because of the modern ceiling, the panelling has gone and the fireplace was blocked up in recent years. Nor is it possible to look down into the chapel from the closet, part of which has been merged into the gallery to form an alcove in which hang works by Romney and Raeburn, artistically the most valuable of the family portraits. Sir William's portrait (frontispiece) hangs on the wall of the gallery proper, as it did in the days of its builder, and it is now in the company of those of many of his descendants.

Ingatestone Hall Park had a short history. Petre received a Crown licence to impark three hundred acres of enclosed land as a deer-park. This lay mainly between the Hall and the London–Chelmsford road. But he seems to have relied chiefly on Crondon Park, two miles north-east of the Hall, for supplies of venison; and Ingatestone Park had been disparked by 1605.[25]

CHAPTER IV

Secretary to Henry VIII

1 Master in Chancery and King's Councillor

IN 1536, after serving for several years as one of the six clerks in Chancery, Petre had risen to be a master. The Lord Chancellor was assisted by twelve masters in Chancery, the chief of whom was the Master of the Rolls. The masters' ranks were frequently filled from the advocates practising in the Court of Arches. Petre is found as an active master until 1541. His name also appears among an undated list of 'counsellors appointed to sit together daily in the King's Court of Requests'.* A few of his more unusual tasks as a government lawyer may be related.

A clause of the Royal Supremacy Act strictly enjoined all who possessed papal bulls, licences and dispensations to give them up. William Petre, Thomas Bedell and John Tregonwell, all masters in Chancery, had been appointed in November 1536 at Cromwell's instance to receive and examine all such faculties and to burn them.[1] Before surrendering the bulls, and hoping that Henry might be reconciled with Rome, the abbot of Woburn had copies made to help in proving the ancient privileges; and he got into considerable trouble with Petre for so doing.†

The leaders of the two rebellions in 1536—that in Lincolnshire and the more serious rising in Yorkshire known as the Pilgrimage of Grace—were examined by three masters in Chancery, Layton, Legh and Petre. The

---

* Select Cases in the Court of Requests, 1497–1569 (Selden Soc., xii (1898), 52), citing B.M. Lansdowne MS. 12, f.125. The heading of this list, '20 Hen. VIII' (1528–9), is misleading; several spaces in the original (in a hand of c. 1570) indicate additions of later date than 1529. Petre's name follows such a space. A similar list, also c. 1570, is in Add. MS. 25,248, f.9. A brief examination of some of the papers of the Court did not yield anything of interest bearing on his work as a Master of Requests. Petre's law-books, still extant in the family archives (E.R.O., D/DP L27–35), were probably acquired by him for reference at this period; they include contemporary copies of the Year Books for 1–4 Edw. III and of the Statutes of 1 Edw. III–6 Hen. VI and other MS. precedent books.

† Petre put the bulls he received to utilitarian use, and about a dozen were found in the family archives serving as covers to court rolls of the manor of Ingatestone and to his steward's account-books (E.R.O., D/DP Q1/1–10, A4, 5). The majority were published, with transcripts (despite mutilations) by Professor C. R. Cheney as 'Some Papal Privileges for Gilbertine Houses' (Bulletin Inst. of Hist. Research, xxi (1948), 39–58); these relate to Alvingham, Lincs., which Petre dissolved, and to Watton and Malton. Another bull, c. 1150, originates from his descent on Southwick Priory. Petre's steward also used more than one service book, apparently of Barking Abbey, for similar purposes; they are of late medieval date and only slightly illuminated. A few fifteenth-century monastic title-deeds, e.g. of Holywell Priory, also stayed in Dr. Petre's (and his present representative's) custody; more surprisingly, the original deed of surrender of Titchfield Abbey, 1537 (E.R.O., D/DP 248, 249, 256, 284, etc.).

41

latter revolt had been organized by Robert Aske, whose interrogation was taken at the Tower early in 1537 by Legh, Petre and the Lieutenant.[2]

Cromwell appointed Petre an administrator of the will of the ex-Queen Catherine. Her death was soon followed by the executions of Anne Boleyn and her brother. Their father, the Earl of Wiltshire, surrendered his office of Lord Privy Seal in favour of Cromwell. Thus, the members of the all-powerful family to which Petre had owed much in the early days of his public career were suddenly removed. After Catherine's marriage had been nullified, her daughter Mary was adjudged illegitimate and deprived of the title of princess. This forbidden address was used in 1536 by the wife of Lord Hussey, then Mary's guardian at Hatfield, and Petre was assigned with Wriothesley to examine Lady Hussey about her offence.[3]

A complicated dispute in the Court of Admiralty, in which Petre took a leading part, reveals him in another sphere. 'Rochepot's affair', as it was called, was a grand case for the lawyers if the welter of records is a fair criterion. In 1537, after the truce between the Emperor and the King of France, a Hamburg merchant's ship was captured off the coast of Flanders by a French captain, whose brigantine belonged to Monsieur de la Rochepot. Following a counter-attack, the prize was brought safely into Whitby. The evidence is confusing; the law still more so, involving a statute of Edward III as well as the privileges of the Hanse. The ownership of the prize was settled by a decree made at Whitehall by Drs. Petre, Tregonwell, Bonner and Carne. This was on Candlemas Eve, 1538. But Rochepot was Governor of Picardy and brother of the Constable of France, and the 'doctors' opinion' in favour of the Germans did not suit the French. So it became a top-level dispute, involving Henry VIII and Francis I in personal correspondence. From the evidence of these and other records there emerges a faint picture of Petre's judicial activities.[4]

In April 1539 the King and Cromwell summoned three learned canonists, 'the eminent Doctors Layton, Petre and Tregonwell', to help in preparing a penal statute which would embody the 'Six Articles'[5] and enforce transubstantiation, private masses, confession and clerical celibacy. Appointed to draft alternative bills were two committees, each comprising an archbishop, two bishops and a lawyer, Petre being on one and Tregonwell on the other. The King approved that of the second committee. Soon the 'Act for abolishing of diversity of opinions', the notorious Heresy Statute, became law. This is the session for which there is the first mention of Petre's parliamentary duties—as a master in Chancery;[6] but, as in 1536, there is no means of knowing whether he had been elected a member.

In September the office of Master of the Faculties, the principal judge of the Archbishop of Canterbury's court for the granting of licences and dispensations under the Peter's Pence Act of 1538, was shortly to become vacant by the nomination of Dr. Nicholas Wotton to an archdeaconry. Cromwell told Cranmer that he would like to see Petre as Wotton's successor. But, Cranmer replied, glad as he would be of Petre's advancement 'for such good qualities as I know of him of old', he had promised the office to another, so Petre continued to serve the State rather than the Church, and remained attached to Cromwell's household.[7] As one of the assistants to the bureaucrat behind all the administrative reforms of the 1530s and the modernization of the central government, Petre was gaining invaluable knowledge and experience.*

In 1537 Queen Jane (Seymour) had borne a male heir—the future Edward VI—but she died shortly afterwards. Early in 1539 Henry listened favourably to Cromwell's proposal that he should marry Anne of Cleves, a German Protestant princess, as the alliance would give England important political advantages. Cromwell looked around for the right man to conduct the delicate negotiations and his choice fell on Petre. To seek a woman's hand for a thrice-married king would demand a different technique from that of a monastic visitor. Very detailed 'Instructions for Dr. Petre', signed by Cromwell, were drawn up, probably in June or July. He was to join with Dr. Wotton, then ambassador at the Court of Cleves, and to use all his 'wisdom and dexterity'. The rumour that Anne, the elder unmarried daughter, had been betrothed when a child was a matter on which the widowed Duchess must be persuaded to 'open the bottom of her stomach'. If Anne was already under contract but her younger sister was free, Petre and Wotton, feigning spontaneity, were to 'say merrily' that Henry would be equally pleased. Desiring to see both ladies, in order to advise him on their attractions, the diplomats were also to secure the sisters' portraits and to send their opinion on them as likenesses. It was of course Holbein who painted the flattering picture of Anne which was to lead to trouble. 'A memorial for Dr. Petre when he should have been sent to Cleves', endorsed on the instructions, tells laconically of his having escaped, by luck or plan, from the ill-fated embassy.[8] He had been destined for another matrimonial mission a few weeks earlier, when a marriage was contemplated between Henry and the Duchess of Milan, the lady who was reported to have said that had she two heads she would wed him;[9] but the German project superseded the Italian. Anne of Cleves became Henry's fourth wife. On New Year's Day 1540 the King rode

* See G. R. Elton, *The Tudor Revolution in Government* (1953), for a full assessment of Cromwell's reforms.

out from Greenwich Palace to meet his bride. At the head of her cavalcade were 'the counsellors learned, with other his counsel at large, as Dr.
Petre', and others.[10]

Cromwell soon knew that the Lutheran union was a disastrous failure.
There ensued a struggle in the Privy Council between his party and that of
Stephen Gardiner, Bishop of Winchester, who with the Duke of Norfolk
led the strong conservative reaction. In April 1540 the anti-Cromwellian
faction was stunned when Cromwell was created Earl of Essex (the earldom was an ancient and honourable one); it was indeed a spectacular elevation for the King's Secretary. The new earl, in a last desperate gamble to
retain royal support, secured urgently needed money supplies from Parliament. But his days were numbered. Each of the two violently contesting
parties in the Council was sending its own victims to the Tower. Among
them was a principal ally of Gardiner, Bishop Sampson of Chichester,
whose arrest pointed to Cromwell's temporary ascendancy. It seemed
likely that Sampson would be followed by five more papistical bishops,
including Cuthbert Tunstall of Durham, an able politician. Accused of
treason, Sampson pleaded he had acted under Tunstall's influence. At this
crucial stage Cromwell again chose Petre as prison interrogator.[11] In June
the Court was astonished when the King, momentarily free from financial
worries, allowed Cromwell to fall. In full Council Norfolk, Cromwell's
bitterest enemy, declared without warning, 'My Lord of Essex, I arrest
you of high treason'. Cromwell was dispatched to the Tower. It is
possible that Petre carried the bill of attainder from the Lords to the
Commons, as the day of the arrest was one when he was so engaged. On
the same day the French ambassador wrote that Cromwell had been 'admonished of late by some of his servants that he was acting contrary to his
master's wishes and to the statutes of the realm'.[12] Had Petre a share in
this eleventh-hour warning? There is a hint that Wriothesley and Petre
were assigned to examine him.[13] Of all the men whom he had advanced
or with whom he had worked, only Cranmer raised his voice to inter-
cede. So far from helping Cromwell, who had made his fortune,
Wriothesley was ready 'to throw his benefactor to the wolves at a nod
from the King'.[14] Another hostile witness was Rich, Chancellor of the
Court of Augmentations, who had gained an evil notoriety for his part in
More's trial and was now one of the most powerful and obnoxious of the
King's ministers. On 28 July, four days after Parliament was dissolved,
Cromwell went to the block. Petre thus ceased to be deputy to Henry's
only Vicar-general.

The farcical alliance with Queen Anne had already been severed.
Wriothesley and Petre were given warrants to search Cromwell's house

for vital evidence as to whether she had contracted to marry during her minority, 'wherein Dr. Petre could tell much'[15]—even if he had not been to Cleves. With undue haste Convocation met and appointed eight churchmen to deal with her case. Next day, four lawyers including Petre and Tregonwell were added to the commission, but Petre took no prominent part in the proceedings.[16] The marriage was declared null on grounds of pre-contract and non-consummation; and the record of the judgment was witnessed by the same four laymen. In the meantime, Gardiner had become omnipotent among the councillors, who charged Wriothesley with embezzlement, from which he was not exonerated for some weeks.

Whatever suspense Petre may have suffered on his master's fall was eased after a meeting of the Privy Council at the royal palace of Moor Park, Rickmansworth, on 5 October 1540, when 'Dr. William Petre, doctor of the law, was sworn to be one of the King's Council, and appointed to the place in the White Hall which Dr. Thirlby, elect Bishop of Westminster, had before he was bishop'.[17] The distinction between the Privy Council and the King's Council is material, because the former, in contrast with the medieval privy council, had emerged only a short time before 1540 as an inner ring with greater powers than the rest who were known as 'ordinary counsellors' or 'counsellors at large'. Vaguely classed with them were 'counsellors learned [in the law]', as in Anne of Cleves' procession. The most recent view on the Tudor privy council's origin dates it between 1534 and 1536, rather than in 1540 when that body started a register of its proceedings and appointed a clerk.[18] The Privy Council was differentiated from the unorganized body, who were concerned with routine or judicial business, in the Courts of Requests and Star Chamber, for example, thus relieving their seniors. In October 1540, the Privy Council decided to rid itself of the burden of hearing some suits, which were to go to the King's 'Ordinary Council' appointed for such purposes; and Heath, Bishop of Rochester, was appointed one of the King's Council and joined with Thirlby 'to hear causes determinable in the White Hall'. Petre was promoted two days afterwards to fill Thirlby's place on the Ordinary Council.* The peripheral position provided Petre with

---

* Later in the same month the King wrote to his ambassador with the Emperor about his wish 'to fish out the bottom of the matter touching the marriage of the French King's daughter' and his hope that the Emperor would 'disclose his heart frankly' (phrases reminiscent of 'open the bottom of her stomach' in Petre's instructions for going to the court of Cleves). Henry ordered him to inform the Emperor that he (the ambassador) had obtained advice from 'his great friend (in whom he had special trust and affiance), being one of our Council (though not of our Privy Council), but a man of gravity and learning, and one that hath great intelligence with our near councillors and such as be about Us'. The attributes fit Petre's legal cap closely. (State Papers (1849), viii, 456.)

opportunities for widening his experience and increasing his reputation in readiness for further promotion.

Only a week after he had joined the outer ranks of the Council Petre was summoned into the inner circle as a defendant. Appearing before them at Moor Park, he heard John Barkley of Canterbury charge him 'with concealment of a book of treasons put to him against the prior of Christchurch at his visitation' several years earlier. He denied the accusation, and Barkley was remanded to bring proofs. In the meantime he was commissioned with the Sheriff of Surrey and Sir Robert Southwell another former Visitor, now also an ordinary councillor, to examine certain cases of riot and arson. At the next meeting Petre attended in a double role. Southwell and he duly reported; and Barkley brought his proofs, but 'the matter appearing false and malicious, Dr. Petre was discharged'. Apparently it was the result of idle gossip with an ex-monk, who was given a short term of imprisonment.[19] The Privy Council register is not uninformative about Petre's work during the next three years; even so, the recorded assignments may represent only part of it. But none of the eight disputes or charges which were referred to him with one or two colleagues is of special interest.[20]

A month after the marriage with Anne of Cleves was dissolved, Henry wedded his fifth wife, Catherine Howard. Within a year she was found guilty of misconduct. In December 1541 the aged Duchess of Norfolk was examined by Wriothesley, and Petre was appointed to go to her house at Horsham to collect evidence about the Queen's pre-nuptial behaviour, in which Lady Rochford, the widow of his former patron George Boleyn, was implicated as an abettor. But 'Dr. Petre was out of town and the King's Solicitor went to Horsham in his place';[21] so, once again, he avoided being embroiled in his sovereign's matrimonial affairs. Were all three escapes fortuitous or the result of shrewdly timed evasive action? Parliament attainted Catherine and her go-between, and they were beheaded.

This Parliament, which assembled on 16 January 1542, is the first of which Petre can be definitely traced as a member. He had been elected as one of the knights of the shire for Essex. The other county member and the Essex borough members are unknown; it is fortunate that the incomplete returns for 1542 preserve Petre's name.[22] There are no extant returns for the Parliaments of 1536 and 1539, to both of which, as already explained, he may have been elected.

In 1542 Petre was again employed as a Dissolution agent. About seventeen small religious colleges, each having a few inmates and an endowment now coveted by the King, had survived. Most of them surrendered spontaneously during 1541-2. For the few requiring persuasion Petre was the principal commissioner, and he visited Mettingham College, Suffolk, Higham Ferrers College, Northamptonshire, and Vaux College, near Salisbury.[23] 'My expenses to Sarum, 50s.' in August 1542, in his personal accounts,[24] tallies with 'the charges of the two commissioners to take the surrender [of Vaux College], 100s.' entered in the official record. But his little account-book, unlike those of later date, yields nothing more about his public activities.

2 Principal Secretary, Privy Councillor and Knight

January 1544 was a memorable month in Petre's life. What was going on in the highest spheres is not easy to trace. On New Year's Day Sir Thomas Wriothesley, who had been rapidly rising to a position of great influence, was created Baron Wriothesley of Titchfield. On Cromwell's own elevation to an earldom four years earlier, his office of Secretary had been conferred jointly on Wriothesley and Ralph Sadler, another of Cromwell's chief assistants, who were both knighted on appointment. The former now resigned his secretaryship, but was given an annuity of £100 (he and Sadler were the first to be given that sum each as salary) until being 'advanced to any office the yearly fee of which amounts to £100': Lord Audley the Chancellor was dying, and Wriothesley succeeded three months later. One of the two offices of King's Principal Secretary was vacant. It was filled by Petre. His appointment is dated the day before Wriothesley's resignation, 21 January, when 'William Petre, knight, King's councillor', was granted the salary of £100, the first payment to be received on the following Lady Day 1544.[25] He had made his way into high politics.

The official with whom Petre shared the secretaryship was William Paget, an able man whose political career was to be more conspicuous though more chequered than Petre's.* Of about the same age, Paget had been born of humble parentage. Educated at Cambridge, he became a member of Gardiner's household. The bishop sent him to study at Paris. Later he was employed in several diplomatic missions to France and Germany. In 1540 Gardiner's influence secured his appointment as clerk of the Privy Council, but he soon went as ambassador to the French court. On his return in April 1543 he became joint Secretary in place of Sadler who was sent as envoy to the court at Edinburgh. John Mason, who had been

* The most detailed account of Paget is an unpublished thesis, 'The Master of Practises: A Life of William, Lord Paget of Beaudesert, 1506-63', by Dr. S. R. Gammon (Princeton Univ. 1953).

acting during Paget's absence, secured the clerkship of the Council. Petre's knighthood evidently coincided in date with that of his new appointment, and Paget seems to have attained similar rank at the same time. The presumption is that Henry conferred the knightood on Petre when he received the signet seal from the King's hand.*

It is not known to whose influence Petre owed his advancement. It has been said that Petre's reforming sympathies earned him a place at the Court: Wriothesley 'had been reckoned a mainstay of the conservative party; but any effect on his promotion was minimized by the accession to his office of Secretary of Petre, who was reckoned of the other side'.[26] There is, however, no evidence of Petre's religious leanings, and it is more likely that his ability as well as early legal training and foreign travel and his more recent experience earned the advancement.

No formal record of his appointment exists (his successor was to be the first Secretary to obtain the office by patent). In climbing the stairs of State service, Petre had skipped one step, recent holders of the secretarial appointment having first graduated as a clerk of the Council or of the Signet; and he did not have to wait, like Paget, nearly a year for his knighthood.

The office which Petre had secured was of ancient origin.† For several centuries the King's secretary had been a minor minister in his household. As writer of the King's letters he had held a position of trust and as one of the royal mouthpieces his personal influence counted occasionally. He was also custodian of the signet, the most personal of the King's seals, the great seal and the privy seal having each in turn become used for purely official documents. Gardiner gave a better status to the office, but it was Cromwell who raised it to heights of great importance by using the secretaryship as the medium through which he wielded abnormal influence. It has recently been argued that the division of the secretaryship in 1540 was not a cautious ruse on Henry's part to prevent the rise of another powerful bureaucrat, but a step taken for administrative convenience. 'The intention seems to have been to have one secretary permanently in attendance

---

* Several mis-statements must be rectified. *D.N.B.* is in error in dating Petre's appointment as 'early in 1543'; and the standard lists of Secretaries (e.g. Royal Hist. Soc., *Handbook of British Chronology*) give March 1544, apparently following the editorial note 'March?' in *L. & P.*, xix, pt. ii, 701, derived from pt. i. 278(4). Shaw's *Knights of England* gives Petre's name among those who were knighted some time in 1543, and assigns Paget to '[?1543–4]'; *D.N.B.* is inaccurate in knighting Paget on 18 Oct. 1537: he was still unknighted on 26 Dec. 1543 (*L. & P.*, xviii, pt. ii, 526), but is referred to as Sir William on 17 Jan. 1544 (*ibid.*, pt. i, 80(27)). *L. & P.*, xix, pt. i, 1036, is also incorrect in terming him a knight in May 1543 (the original gives 'armigerum', E.315/236, f.38).

† The chief authorities for the office are G. R. Elton, *The Tudor Revolution in Government* (1953), and F. M. G. Evans (Mrs. Higham), *The Principal Secretary of State* (1923), which in the main deal respectively with the periods immediately before and after Petre's term.

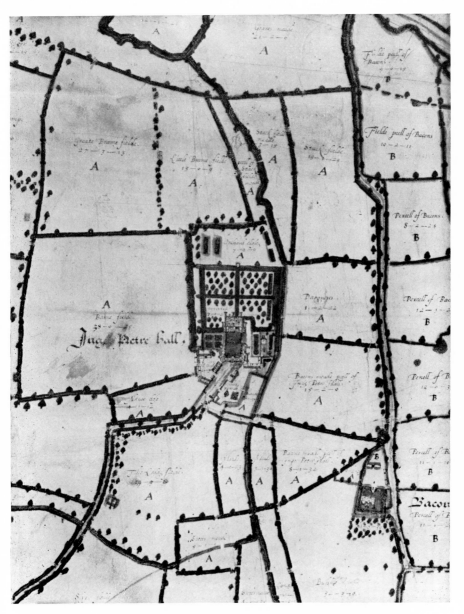

7. MAP OF INGATESTONE HALL AND THE DEMESNE, 1605
By John Walker, Senior and Junior

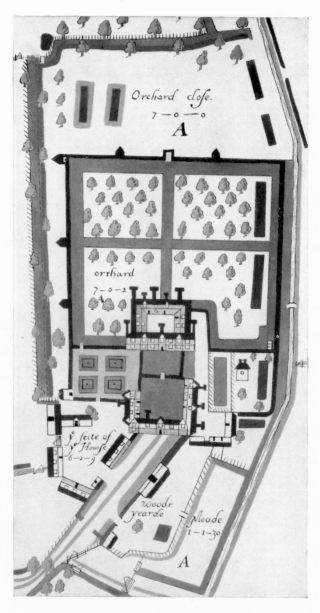

8. INGATESTONE HALL

Enlarged re-drawing from the Walkers' map of 1605

on the King, and the other permanently in attendance on the Lord Privy Seal' (i.e. Cromwell).[27] After the latter's fall, the existence of two Secretaries proved useful in a similar way. When the sovereign was on progress or otherwise away from the capital, state business demanded that some members of the Privy Council, generally including one of the Secretaries, should remain at Westminster. One of them also was occasionally sent abroad on short-term, special diplomatic missions for which early training had equipped Petre. The two officers were equal in status and privy to each other's affairs, though as explained either could act if the other was absent.

The title of Principal Secretary distinguished him from the subordinate French and Latin secretaries. His duties fell mainly into three categories, two of which concerned his relations with the King and with the Privy Council. The pre-Cromwellian Secretaries' correspondence had largely been confined to foreign affairs. That alone embraced many letters to foreign monarchs and the English ambassadors at their courts. The latter involved giving the envoys instructions and guidance for pursuing intricate negotiations. There was also close contact with this country's trade representatives in Western Europe. But Cromwell's 'great addition to the office was government at home: he made the Secretary supreme in the internal administration of the state'.[28] The sphere of domestic affairs included some supervision of the vastly increased number of royal grants of land following the Dissolution as well as the appointment to numerous national and local offices in the gift of the Crown, all of which, with many licences and other documents, had to pass under the signet. Since the Secretary had almost daily access to the King, his own chamber was in effect one of the chief ante-rooms to the Privy Chamber.

As Secretary, he was automatically promoted a member of the Privy Council, and his second main responsibility was as a councillor and as liaison between King and Council, because the sovereign rarely attended meetings. He drafted the agenda, or added any confidential items to the draft submitted by the clerk of the Council, who was excluded when matters of secrecy were discussed (which explains why many matters were not recorded in the Council's register). The Secretary's attendance, generally more regular than that of other members, gave him an added influence in debate, and as the growth of conciliar business led to more frequent delegation of important matters to commissions and committees, one of the Secretaries was usually put on them.

The Secretary also had an important role in Parliament. By a statute of 1539, it was enacted that he should sit in the Upper House on one of the Woolsacks. The warrant of 1540 providing for two Secretaries varied this. Instead of sitting solely in the Lords, they were normally to appear singly in each House in alternate weeks, because of 'the good service' they could do the King in the Lower House; but this impracticable plan may never have been put into force.[29] Future Secretaries, too, were usually members of Parliament in virtue of their office. Each received a writ of assistance, which meant that he sat in the Lords at the opening and ending of Parliament and was theoretically on call for the work of that House, but doubtless spent most of his time in the Commons.[30]

Cromwell had extended the Secretary's power and patronage to the farthest limits, chiefly because of his own personality. After it became a dual appointment, the Secretary's chances of attaining outstanding influence were accordingly reduced. Apart from that, no second Cromwell appeared. But there remained ample opportunities, involving speculative and dangerous risks for those who wished to take them.

The secretariat comprised the Principal Secretaries' private clerks with the four signet clerks.* The French and Latin secretaries, although they had their own specific duties, probably gave help when required, and the three clerks of the Council worked under the Principal Secretaries' direction. The amount of paper work which devolved on this group of officials was immense. The Secretaries' status was specified in the warrant of 1540. They took precedence after all peers spiritual and temporal and the four executive officers of the royal household—Treasurer, Comptroller, Master of the Horse and Vice-chamberlain.

The personal income accruing to the Secretary was fourfold. In addition to the salary of £100, he was entitled as a member of the royal household to free board and lodging in whichever palace the Court might be. These were important emoluments, but it is not easy to assess their exact monetary value. The Secretaries were entitled to two messes (or diet allowances for each meal), sufficient to provide also inferior diets for their servants as well as for the French and Latin secretaries. The figures given in the household ordinances made by Henry at Eltham in 1526, as revised about the time of Petre's appointment, are somewhat confusing. These apparently value the two messes together at £813 a year;[31] in addition, each Secretary had his 'bouche of court' (or rations of bread, wine, fuel and lights) worth £34 a year, together with stabling for eight horses and three (probably double) beds for servants. These sources were thus fixed; the other income was unpredictable. One source was the yield of the signet office. After deducting expenses, the profits were

* One of the signet clerks was John Cliff, a relation of Lady Petre by marriage. An agreement, 1557, between the four clerks, including Cliff, regarding fees is printed in full by F. M. G. Evans, op. cit., 353-4.

allocated according to recognized fractions between the Secretaries and the clerks, the ministers' share being equally divided, irrespective of the number of documents passing under each Secretary's signet. For example, of the 6s. 8d. fee for a private warrant each took one-tenth, and for perpetual land grants each received 20s. The Secretary's net income from his fees varied considerably from year to year, but averaged about £150, exclusive of the fixed annual salary of £100 to each.*

The other source was the receipt, with other ministers of the Crown, of gifts in money or kind which a host of suitors for appointments, grants, pardons, introductions or information were expected by ancient usage to make. The Secretary was well placed for bringing suppliants' requests to the magnates among the councillors and to the sovereign himself, and those seeking favours would recognize the wisdom of securing the Secretary's support.

A few weeks after Petre assumed office, Henry's 'not so perfect health' led him to authorize two magnates to use a royal signature stamp for certain Crown documents; the notification was addressed to six officers including 'William Paget and William Petre, knights, the two Principal Secretaries'.[32] In the national repositories, at Hatfield House, and in some other family archives can be seen large numbers of letters signed by Henry's privy councillors. Of these, hundreds beginning in 1544 bear Petre's signature, usually the last as befitting the Secretary. In the state papers are his own drafts of many letters. Occasionally he added a postscript in his own handwriting to a Council letter written by Paget, who at first corrected some of Petre's drafts.[33] The minutes of the Council for his year of office are missing, so it is not known how regular his attendance was or whether any special directions were given to him. His personal accounts for this year help to fill the gap in some ways. The second of the extant books gives his daily expenses from 17 January 1544, four days before his preferment, until 1 December.[34] On the first page he wrote, 'The account of John Keyme of money by him paid for me.' 'John Keme his servant' is first mentioned at the time of dissolution of Rochester Priory. By now he was clearly Petre's steward.† An almost day-to-day record, it confirms that Sir William had taken up his secretarial duties by

---

* See Appendix J and S.P. 10/18/30. The figures quoted by F. M. G. Evans, op. cit., 207, 354–5 for 1540–2 show an even wider variation. On becoming Secretary, Petre lost his fee as a master in Chancery.

† The accounts are those of Petre's expenses at London and the Court, and are more detailed than his brief disbursements for 1542–3. Apart from the initial heading, the book is in Kyme's writing; every page is signed at the foot 'W. Petre', who ran his quill through it to signify personal audit. Keyme (or Kyme, as he usually signed himself) was a son of John Cayme of Lewes. Like his father in 1512 he was in 1544 a trustee of Lewes Grammar School. John Cayme, probably the father but possibly himself, was M.P. for Lewes in 1543.

February. He had lost no time in having a black damask gown and a velvet coat trimmed with silk made for him, which cost as much as £9. He was already the tenant of a small house in Aldersgate Street, which was soon to be the nucleus of a much bigger one; this he used as a convenient pied-à-terre when he was not in attendance at the Court (pp. 82–5). 'Boathire from the Court to the Blackfriars 6d.; in reward to Mr. Paget's cook 4d. and to Mr. Paget's servant 5s.', on the 9th, possibly indicates Petre's first appearance at the Council Board, followed by a celebration dinner given by his fellow Secretary, whose house was in the Blackfriars. There are hundreds of entries in these and later accounts for 'boathire to the Court'—often the only record of his being in or near London and sometimes the sole evidence of his taking part in important events. Kyme accompanied his master almost everywhere, and paid all expenses out of the privy purse, for ready money was rarely carried about by the nobility and gentry. Lady Petre was attended by her own servants, whose travelling expenses were also paid by Kyme. By mid-February Sir William had taken possession of his official chamber at Westminster and his wife had appeared at the Court. The usual river journey thither, with a groat to a royal porter, occurs on 5 March, the date of his earliest Council signature (no Council letters for his first seven weeks survive). Thus the accounts reveal a little about Petre's activities before his officially recorded presence at the Council.

On the 6th, the day's business included a visit to Cranmer at the archbishop's palace: 'My master's boathire to Lambeth and from thence to the Court, 4d.; ditto. from the Court to Paul's wharf [the nearest landing-stage to Petre's house in Aldersgate Street], 3d.; my lady's boathire to Lambeth and home again, 8d.' On the following Sunday Petre returned Paget's hospitality at Aldersgate. Their personal friendship was developing, for Paget's cook twice got further 'rewards' later in the month. The first recorded gift—a gelding—from an influential man came from Robert Holgate, the former Master of Sempringham who was now President of the Council in the North and was soon to become Archbishop of York.

At the end of May 1544 his accounts suddenly strike a sterner note, with 10s. 4d. paid to an armourer for dressing Petre's 'harness' [body-armour], 'a great basket' for it, and making two dozen bows. In that month Edward Seymour, Earl of Hertford, with a force of 10,000, was conveyed to the Forth in a fleet commanded by John Dudley, Viscount Lisle. Desultory warfare against the Scots had been going on for two years. Francis I of France had supported the anti-English party in Scotland, and for that and other reasons Henry and the Emperor Charles V had made a pact to invade France in June, when Henry's expeditionary force was to be reinforced by transporting to France Hertford's troops who had recently ravaged parts of Scotland. In the muster book Petre was set down to send a score of footmen—the smallest contribution among the councillors; but he was only beginning to establish his position as a landowner with tenants liable for military service.[35] The sale of Crown lands to provide funds was entrusted to Cranmer, Hertford (just returned to Court), Thirlby and Petre.* The significance of this commission can be gauged from their realizing over £73,000; Petre himself bought lands costing £250.[36]

'Boathire to the Lord of Hertford's and from thence to the Court' is the prelude to a fresh appointment. Two days later, on 7 July, a week before Henry crossed over to take command, his sixth wife, Catherine Parr, was made Regent. To advise her he chose five special commissioners—Archbishop Cranmer, Chancellor Wriothesley, Hertford, Thirlby and Petre, who was also among the few ministers authorized to use Henry's signature stamp in his absence. Wriothesley or Hertford was to be resident at Court; if neither could be there, then Cranmer and Petre were to remain with the Queen, but 'when convenient all five shall attend her'.[37] For most of the time it was a Regency Council of four, as Hertford joined Henry next month.

During the spring and early summer Petre's presence at the Court had taken him no farther than the palace at Greenwich, most of his work having been done at Westminster or St. James's. It was customary for the Court to leave London in the summer because of the risk of plague. Soon after the King's departure, Petre therefore journeyed with the Queen, with all the attendant inconvenience of combining work and travel. The peripatetic Secretary's movements may be traced in his steward's accounts and his official letters.[38] The Queen removed first to Hampton Court, then on to Woking. There Petre was present at various meetings of the Regency Council between 1 and 24 September; on the 22nd he drafted their letter offering the King congratulations on his successful siege of Boulogne. With four servants he made a hurried journey via Kingston back to London, thence to Hampton Court and on to Nonsuch Palace, Henry's architectual extravaganza near Cheam, and by way of Croydon to rejoin the Queen at Eltham. The King came home on 30 September, the Court having proceeded to Leeds Castle in Kent to meet him there. After stopping at Otford, Henry stayed in the archbishop's palace at Foots Cray. The Court then went on to Greenwich and was back at Westminster by the middle of October. On the following Sunday Petre paid a call at Lambeth to see Cranmer, who had lent him a packhorse for his

* From this time onwards Secretary Petre was placed on scores of commissions; only the more important will be mentioned.

baggage (Thirlby had also sent him an Irish hobby just before the progress).

The campaign in France gave Petre his first real opportunity to prove his ability as Secretary.[39] No sooner had Henry reached the French shore than Petre prepared a circular letter demanding loans for the prosecution of the war. 'For my master's part of the benevolence, £10' (Petre's accounts, 21 June) is evidence that some money had been raised by this means before the King's departure.[40] Petre was responsible for drafting nearly all the letters from the 'Council with the Queen'—to Holgate, to the Earl of Shrewsbury, Lieutenant-general in the North, to Wotton, now ambassador at the Emperor's court in Flanders, to Thomas Chamberlain, the King's representative in the Low Countries, to Stephen Vaughan, financial agent at Antwerp, to Lord Wharton, in charge of the Scottish border; most of them addressed some of their official letters to him personally. He drew up a few of the Queen's own letters for her signature.*

But his chief business, of course, was the constant correspondence with the King's Council overseas. Paget had been sent across beforehand to plan the campaign. A week before the premature death of Dr. Layton, who had become Dean of York and was on diplomatic service abroad, Paget sought Petre's influence at home to secure some of Layton's preferments for Wotton; he obtained the deanery a month later. Except for a few weeks when Paget was temporarily back in England Petre was left in sole charge of the secretarial office and was kept unusually busy with the Council's preparations on this side of the Channel, as well as with the mass of routine business.

After Henry's return, the tone of some of Petre's drafts is more severe. The Secretary already knew his master's mind, and worded the letters to the Council left behind at Boulogne in no uncertain terms. For instance, Rich, the treasurer of the expeditionary force, was rebuked for submitting an account for £55,348—only part of the cost of the campaign. 'The Kings marvels that, whereas they write that their number is but 8,000, their expenses for these fourteen days have been more than the ordinary wages of the whole army.' Petre added, 'You must send over with diligence a more plain declaration'. Rich replied with a whine, 'The poor soldiers may ill forbear their money'. The Dukes of Norfolk and Suffolk, too, were informed of Henry's annoyance, and Petre drew up the missive: the King had been 'advertized that, notwithstanding his pleasure signified sundry times for your abode there, you daily send his soldiers homewards, as if indirectly to enforce your own retirement'. Some of Petre's drafts

* Queen Catherine rewarded him a few months afterwards by standing as godmother to his daughter—Catherine (her other godmother was Princess Mary).

were amended in Henry's own hand; he appears, for instance, to have gone minutely through the important instructions to the Boulogne Council, written at the end of October.[41] A late Elizabethan story quoted Henry as telling Petre not to brood at his drafts being corrected by the King, 'for it is I, said he, that made both Cromwell, Wriothesley, and Paget good secretaries, and so must I do to thee. The princes themselves know best their own meaning and there must be time and experience to acquaint them with their humours before a man can do any acceptable service.'[42] This anecdotal pearl may be accepted as genuine.

On appointment as Admiral of the Fleet against the French, Sir Thomas Seymour, Hertford's younger brother, was handed a 'memorial' of instructions for 'the assembling the whole navy from London, Harwich and Dover', which bears Petre's corrections. He got further injunctions in November, all compiled by Petre, also a strong letter from the Council complaining of waste: 'Have henceforth a more wary eye to your victuals, considering with what difficulty and charge they are brought to you.' The orders to the naval commander off Scotland came from the same pen.

Petre had now been tested as Secretary to the King and to the Queen Regent, and in effect as Secretary for home and foreign affairs, for war and for the navy. The evidence is clear. Without being able to share the responsibility with Paget, who did not return till mid-November, Petre was involved soon after his appointment in nearly all the state correspondence at home; for three months he was not even able to consult the absent King. He was dealing, for the most part, with the nobility and the highest officers: men senior in every sense to the newly promoted official, magnates who would guess who had prepared the Council letters from London and might resent their language. It must have been a singularly anxious time for him, but there is not the slightest hint of rebuke from the King downwards.

The year 1545 began with the French attempt to recapture Boulogne, which was foiled by Hertford's able counter-attack. In the meantime there was trouble with the Emperor over his orders to seize English merchants' ships in retaliation for our capturing a fleet of Flemish vessels. Wotton having failed to secure restitution, the task was given to Paget, who left England again on 24 February. For the second time within his first year Petre carried on alone. Suddenly remembering a vital point at 5 a.m. when about to sail from Dover, Paget's clerk was told to add a postscript to the overnight letter to Petre: 'You will find Fontaney's cipher among the other ciphers written upon, with Greek letters, Bertheuilles cipher.' And some hours later Paget scribbled at Calais: 'Arrived here about 3 p.m. I was so sick that I would have given 1000 li. (if I had been a rich man) to have been on land.' His letters to Petre already betoken warm friendship and mutual trust. Receiving grave news from another source about Lady Paget, he wrote: 'Ah, Mr. Petre, if she be dead, I am the most unhappy man in the world and desire no longer to live. Be good to my children' (there were nine of them). His grief was premature, and his wife, like Petre's, was to outlive him. The strained commercial relations with the Low Countries were eased by Paget's diplomacy within a few weeks, and it was agreed that the complaints should be referred to representatives of both sovereigns, with executive powers of arbitration on outstanding claims. Accordingly, on 28 April, Henry appointed Thirlby, Petre, Tregonwell, Carne, the English ambassador in Flanders, Vaughan and Chamberlain. The Emperor's chief representative was Chapuys, his late ambassador at London and a man of no mean ability.

It was now Petre's turn to keep the Secretary left at home informed, and a brisk interchange of letters followed. On 9 May the envoys arrived at Calais, 'having (as they said) as fair a passage as might be desired, but for my part', wrote Petre, 'was never in all my life so sick, and was the very worst of all the company'. Senior commissioner after Thirlby, Petre knew that he was being tried again. 'I will employ myself to the best I may to your good advices, and I shall most heartily pray you to continue this your gentleness; so, having no language and as little experience I know how unmeet I am to serve in this thing, but the goodness of my most gracious master comforteth me.' The prevalent plague worried him: 'I thought myself ever a tall [courageous] man, and not to fear over much the plague till this morning. I was not more afraid of the like in all my life; the thing cometh so suddenly and so dangerously.' He concluded anxiously: 'If I have not done well to address this letter to the Council let me have your advice; I will amend the next. Because this matter be long and tedious I thought it not wise to address the same to the King's Majesty.' Henry's irascible nature must have given Petre constant concern at this early stage of his secretarial career; the King, however, must needs have precise reports, and would suffer no delay. Brief but insufficient, or full but wearisome? Official or personal address? These two problems for the administrator were the same as now.

By mid-June Petre's reports reveal growing self-confidence. He was able to tell Paget that lately they had not had 'so hot schools [debates]; in many of our conferences a man might learn to brawl mannerly'; and they 'always end with good and merry words'. But it was important to profess to have taken great pains. 'I pray God we may serve to the contentation of the King's Majesty, and that our good medicine shall take away all the sourness of this diet', he added punningly, the negotiations being known as the Diet of Bourbourg, from their place of meeting near Calais. Paget quickly reassured him that the King 'liked his proceedings', and offered him a valuable lesson in contemporary diplomacy. 'Chapuys', Paget wrote, 'is a great practiser [intriguer], by which term we cover lying, dissembling and flattering. This matter must be handled sleytly [subtly], and, as you have learned to scold, so you must, if you will deal with him, learn to lie.' And he concluded with further verbal ammunition backed by the promise of forces: 'We have prepared three great armies against the enemy's landing. My Lord Suffolk may fortune to pass the seas with 25,000 Englishmen and 3,000 light horses. And this brag you may, as it were soberly, throw out to the commissioners. Marry; you may make the number greater if you list.' Whether Petre produced facts or lies is not disclosed; but Chapuys gave him full credit: when confronted with an awkward suggestion, 'Petre changed the conversation', feigning the excuse that he must not forget to relate something about which Paget had written. Petre had equal respect for oral fencing: 'We are matched with two old foxes, and yet with reason (as God help me) I think we have answered them; marry, in words they overcome us, and yet we begin to learn to talk prettily, and shall learn daily more, for we have a good school, and none ill schoolmasters for that purpose.' He drew an animated pen-portrait of the English commissioners' opponent in another letter, of which two lines will suffice: 'There is nothing in Chapuys but poison, malice, and a lewd liberty of speech; sometimes he setteth a countenance to tell a fair tale devised before.' Of the letters signed by the envoys, some are addressed to the King himself, a few in Petre's own hand. The list of grievances on both sides, with supporting documents, is immense and would fill a book.

Their endeavours met with little success. Petre was still anxious to know whether the King was satisfied. His secondary concern was to ride into Essex: 'Let me have a word by you whether I may not in my way to the Court steal one day or two to see my house; it is very little out of my way, and yet I will not go thither except you shall so advise me': wise man, to seek leave of absence. There is no record of royal or conciliar approval of his efforts as ambassador to Charles V.

On the day (18 July) when Petre returned, invasion was attempted by French ships. The King was at Portsmouth, reviewing his navy, on which he had spent much of the royal and monastic wealth, when two hundred enemy sail were reported off the Isle of Wight. Next day they harried Henry's becalmed fleet and severely damaged the *Great Harry*, famous in

English naval annals. Suddenly the wind arose; his frigates came out swiftly; and disaster was averted. Sir William got his desired leave to go to Ingatestone. He joined the Court at Titchfield, Wriothesley's home, on the last day of July.* After the meeting, he seems to have enquired into the state of the navy, following the recent encounter, so that he would know how to hold his own with Admiral Seymour, a haughty and impulsive man, with whom the cautious Secretary probably had little sympathy. His draft of a Council letter early in September shows clearly that he was well aware of the danger of further attempts at invasion. Except for two weeks in mid-August when Petre apparently went home again, both Secretaries were in constant attendance as the Court journeyed towards Windsor, staying at noble houses and royal palaces, by way of Cowdray, Petworth, Woking, Oatlands and Cobham. One day the councillors momentarily turned from public affairs because three Essex men had 'wrongfully slandered' Secretary Petre. Penitently confessing that the offence had 'proceeded of lightness without any ground', the men were released from prison.[43]

The Court removed to Westminster in readiness for the opening of Parliament on 23 November. Petre was again a member. Of its close, on Christmas Eve, he unwittingly turned chronicler. 'A letter from Secretary Petre, written on the last day of the session puts its history in a truer and very different light: "the book (i.e. bill) of the colleges", he writes, "escaped narrowly and was driven over to the last hour, and yet then passed only by divisions of the house. . . . The bill of books, albeit it was at the beginning earnestly set forward, is finally dashed in the common house, as are divers others." '[44] The recipient was Paget, who had been sent with Tunstall and Tregonwell to Calais to treat with French commissioners.

The rest of Petre's letter is of outstanding interest, as it contains a description of Henry's renowned address, similar to that in Hall's *Chronicle* (the only other source).[45] All the more fortunate indeed that Petre was not confined to his sickbed, for Vaughan, who was back in London, had written two days before to Paget: 'Sir William Petre, Secretary, yesternight at Court fell suddenly diseased [ill], but is well again', adding a gratuitous comment, 'the man is of a weak nature, and cannot bear such great pains as such secretaries as ye two be are wont to be charged and laden with'.[46] Tregonwell, rather than Tunstall, is probably the other envoy referred to, but in the event Vaughan himself was

* This is his first recorded attendance in the Privy Council registers, for the volume from July 1543 to early May 1545 is lost, a new book having been begun on the day after he landed at Calais; for the next twenty-two years the registers are of course a primary source.

PRINCIPAL SECRETARY, COUNCILLOR AND KNIGHT

to die within four years and Petre despite his 'weak nature' was to outlive
Tregonwell by seven. Perhaps convalescent, he dictated the letter for
Paget to John Mason,[47] French secretary and a clerk of the Privy Council,
whose offices involved acting as a senior assistant to the Principal Secretary.* To the nation's assembled representatives Henry had stressed the
need for religious unity. 'Supreme Head of a national church which was
independent alike of Rome and Continental Reform, he had consistently
refused to countenance any tampering with Catholic dogma or discipline.
[But] Henry's measures certainly did not put an end to religious discord.
The King admitted as much in the famous speech.'[48] It was a moving oration in which he earnestly begged them to show more charity to each
other. According to Hall, he gave 'his subjects there present such comfort, that the like joy could not be unto them in this world'. Petre's own
comment is couched in like phrases. The speech, he told Paget, was 'such
a joy and marvellous comfort as I reckon this day one of the happiest of
my life'. His letter tells graphically how, contrary to custom at the close
of a session, Henry instead of his Chancellor replied to the Speaker. This
'he did with such a gravity, so sententiously, so kingly or rather fatherly,
as peradventure to you that hath been used to his daily talks, should have
been no great wonder (and yet saw I some, that hear him often enough,
water their plants)'. This curious picture of weeping members is re-
drawn later in the report. Thanking them for their financial aid in agreeing to a subsidy and to confiscation of the chantries, the old King broke
down with emotion. 'I hear, quoth he, and alas, the while; that the special
foundation of our religion being charity between man and man is so
refrigerate (for this was his term) as there was never more dissension
and lack of love between men and men.' For exposition of the
Scriptures, men should resort to the learned, not to 'every tavern or
alehouse'. (Hall has it that the King deplored how the Bible was 'disputed, rhymed, sung and jangled in every ale-house and tavern'.) Learning that Petre had been 'very sick', Paget was glad his colleague was
'amended'. 'Reading your recital', Paget thanked his informant especially
'for the repetition therein of the most godly, wise and kingly oration'.[49]

The genuineness of the devotional attitude to the monarchy has been
doubted. 'When Henry's secretaries bartered encomiums on their master,
the interceptor is not bound to take such coinage at its face value: and if
Hall is a less official, he is hardly a less obliged, panegyrist.'[50] Mason may
possibly have had a share in Petre's letter beyond writing from his senior's
dictation. One or two phrases, even allowing for the occasion, may sound

* The signature is erased, but the editor of the L. & P. rightly attributed the letter to Petre
and it was he, not Mason, who received thanks from Paget three days later.

59

too fulsome for Petre, though 'watering their plants' is not a more vivid metaphor than his 'fishing for men in the tempestuous seas of this world', a later and well known allusion to official corruption. A modern writer declared that caution in accepting Henry's speeches as genuine 'need not apply to those borrowed from chronicler Hall'.[51] Referring to Henry's address, he added: 'It is probable that Hall, whose chronicle was published within three years of the delivery of the speech, used one of the various copies which were made at the time. Petre sent to Paget a long summary of the speech on the day on which it was delivered.' How much Hall's version was dependent on Petre's may never be known, but there is little doubt that the Secretary's language was inspired by the remarkable tone of the address.

On 5 April 1546 Petre and Wotton were appointed to treat with Skepperus and Van der Delft, Charles V's representatives in London, over mercantile matters.[52] A week later Petre was again left in charge, Paget being dispatched with Hertford, Lisle and Wotton to Calais to treat for peace.[53] After a month's stiff negotiations a settlement about Boulogne seemed assured. The French plenipotentiaries agreed to pay two million crowns over eight years, after which England would cede Boulogne. Paget urged Henry to accept. The procrastinating terms led him to regale Petre with an anecdote about one condemned to die by Louis XI. To save his life the man undertook to make the King's favourite ass speak within a twelve-month. 'What?' said a friend, 'it is impossible.' 'Hold thy peace', he answered; 'for either the King will die, or the ass will die, or the ass will speak, or I shall die.' So, before the time of payment came, the optimistic Paget thought that the English might make some new bargain to keep Boulogne, the French might forfeit it by non-payment, the French King might die and his son not care so much about it, or some other pretext for not returning it might arise. Henry would not agree until a new boundary line was surveyed, which delayed matters.

Petre received from Viscount Lisle several personal letters which were cordial in tone. The Admiral told him, for instance, about a 'shameful and unhappy wretch who ran a shallop, the *Phoenix*, aground and forsook her like a knave'; but 'she ended as honestly as ever a ship could do'. John Dudley the sailor was tired of his shore job and diplomatic delays. 'For God's sake', he urged Petre, 'help to an answer, for it is time.' He could brook it no longer, and dashed out to sea to fight some French galleys that had fired on the camp. In his absence the French commissioners refused to go on with the parleys, which led Paget to send him a hasty recall in sharp terms to accomplish his mission on land. 'In last letters you asked my advice and I sent it: but I see that great men sometimes ask advice only for manners' sake.' Smarting under his colleague's censure, he forwarded the letter to Petre explaining that he had not sallied forth without the King's command and Paget's consent. Shortly afterwards Lisle sent Petre a report on money matters, on which he was out of his depth and so took Petre into his confidence: 'You are wise enough to take the sense and not the letter. Wrap up my follies together and keep them to yourself.' It was a high compliment from the Admiral to the Secretary. He joined in Henry's sycophantic chorus, declaring to Petre his readiness to spill his heart's blood for the monarch. Paget also had to stomach a rebuke—from the King, who 'misliked', so Petre had to explain, his frequent advocacy of peace. Paget replied at night, desperately fearing that he would be dubbed a pacifist. 'My body trembleth and mine eyes water. Wherefor? For myself? No, no, Mr. Petre!' On his knees he begged his Majesty believe him, and what he wrote to his 'dear companion' might be shown to the King if Petre thought fit. Paget dragged in a reference to his 'long and penciful care and labour of mind'. Paget and Wotton of course did the real work, the noble ambassadors keeping on good terms in a different sphere. While the first official was inspecting boundaries with his French counterpart and the second was busy 'with the President to see the penning of the treaties', the English and the French admirals went hunting. So Lisle informed Petre; perhaps a Dudley had humbled himself too much, and it might serve to remind him that there were two social strata among ambassadors, as among councillors.

Paget used his influence with Hertford to try to secure an unnamed appointment on behalf of the Secretary at home. But Hertford regretted that he could not help. 'I cannot gratify Mr. Petre's desire', he wrote from his camp to Paget a short distance away at Guisnes, because he had already importuned the King to grant the office to a friend, although he was 'ready to do Mr. Petre pleasure as any friend he has'. Hertford added: 'At my coming forth the attorney of the Court was departed, which room if it please the King's Majesty to bestow upon my said friend, Mr. Petre might then have the other.' It is impossible to know what 'the other' preferment was. At last, on 7 June, the Treaty of Camp (as it was termed) was signed, and peace was restored.

While Petre alone had been responsible for the King's correspondence, the Court had been at Greenwich, except for the second week in May when the Secretary was in personal attendance on Henry at Westminster, the Council remaining at Greenwich with Gardiner as their letter-writer. Council and Secretary were in daily touch, and among those whose names figure in the lengthy corresondence is Hugh Latimer, who was destined to achieve an undying fame. Opposed to the Act of Six Articles, he had resigned his bishopric of Worcester in 1539. In May 1546, he became involved with Edward Crome, a protestant divine, who had preached against the mass. Dragged from his seven years' retirement, Latimer, with Crome, was summoned before the Council at Greenwich, and was promptly committed to the Tower. Petre acted as intermediary between the Council and the King in the matter of the two offending clerics and sent back Crome's depositions with a strong hint that before submitting them to Henry the document should be 'written in a fairer hand and better order'![54]

In the meantime elaborate preparations had been ordered for the reception of the French ambassador, the Admiral of France, who arrived at the end of July bringing the treaty for ratification. Petre was among the courtiers appointed to attend on him and was told to provide two of his own servants for the magnificent banquet given in the great hall at Hampton Court.

The treaty had left over for arbitration England's claim of arrears of pensions of 512,000 crowns due under an obligation given by France in 1529. This dispute was now referred to two commissioners from either side. Petre was selected as the senior, with William May, doctor of civil laws and Dean of St. Paul's. Their instructions were specific.[55] Setting forth the equity and justice of the debt, they were to use all dexterity to induce the French to pay. Failing that, they were to inform the King of the motives for disagreement, and await further orders. If the French were adamant, they were, with good words, to bid their opponents farewell, declaring that the royal masters would doubtless go further into the matter. The envoys arrived at Calais on 2 September, tarrying in vain for the French commissioners, 'the time appointed by the treaty expiring within two or three days', as Petre anxiously reported on the 5th. It expired, and the four did not meet until several days afterwards. Their terms of reference were therefore technically invalid. One matter had to be referred to the King; the state of Petre's nerves is indicated by his endorsing a letter to Paget: 'Hora ix diei; wind at east. Haste! Haste!' At last, on the 23rd, the real business began, Petre and May giving three good reasons why the money should be paid. But the French gave them 'more sophistications than reason and they mind nothing less than to come to the point', the exasperated Petre told Paget: the packet of letters had just arrived at 2 a.m., and he was writing without delay to catch the forward post to Calais at 3 a.m. 'Whereunto', the diplomats reported to Henry personally, 'we having debated all the points by two whole afternoons, and agreeing upon no point material', the French asked them to subscribe a document to that effect. They refused, 'for the treaty would have had us meet and end this matter before the 7th instant, and it was the 8th before we heard of their coming, and we never heard of commissioners who met without doing anything, making any writing'! The King was also told of their very cordial parting, the French leader having taken Petre apart and asked him to advocate a settlement by the princes themselves. He told Paget that they intended to ride next day from Guisnes, where they had wrangled, to Boulogne, which they had not seen since its conquest, and thence to see 'the King's pieces' (forts, not cannon), 'more for their comfort and strengthening against the seas than for any skill to judge of such things'. Petre would then hasten towards Court as fast as his 'ill back' would allow; it had so troubled him in the past week that it would be 'painful to ride'. Were he not, he confessed, one of the worst sailors (Paget was equally bad), he would rather voyage by 'long seas' than make this journey. It is patent that Petre expected no thanks from the King as a result of the *impasse*, but was anxious to convince his colleague at home that they had done their best. Their rivals had remarked on appointment that they marvelled about the matter having been referred to an even number of commissioners, quoting a text from civil law that arbiters should be chosen in *numero impari*. Was Petre, himself a civilian, tactless for once, in reiterating this weak point in the terms of the recent treaty, which had left Paget to bask in his master's sun, but in Petre's opinion was predestined to send himself home to a cool reception?

Among the multifarious matters with which the Secretary had to be conversant was public finance. From the middle of 1545 it is possible to trace the part which Petre played in negotiating foreign loans—from the renowned Fuggers, the German bankers, from Bartholomew Compagni, a rich Italian merchant in London, and others; and his earliest association with Thomas Gresham, who was to become England's most sagacious financial adviser, also dates from this period.[55] The royal pleasure with Petre's successful efforts to borrow money abroad, details of which are incomplete, had at any rate been signified by the Council in August when he was absent. The vast cost of the French war resulted in further forced sales of the former monastic estates. Early in the year both Secretaries had been added to another commission charged with this work. In conjunction with Wriothesley, Paulet Lord St. John, Gardiner and Sir Anthony Browne, they were also given the big task of examining the state of the revenue courts, and were granted wide powers to collect all they could by the most stringent means and with the utmost speed.[57]

It was at Windsor on 5 October that he rejoined the Court, which soon removed to the palace of Oatlands, where Henry was attended by four of his ministers, including the Earl of Arundel and Petre.[58] The main body was now governed by Hertford and Lisle and was meeting mostly at the latter's house, Ely Place in Holborn; Paget was also with them. Among the councillors a struggle was going on between the Catholics and the Protestants, who were bent on undermining Gardiner's influence.* The bishop must have realized that his position was weakened from Henry's somewhat scathing letter to him early in December, apparently drafted by Petre.[59] The King returned to London just before Christmas. Now very infirm, he kept himself, or was kept, in great seclusion, seeing few beyond his ministers, and engrossed with charges of high treason against Norfolk and his son the Earl of Surrey. The Howards had planned to secure the government (and young Edward), Henry being too old to govern, by murdering the whole Council. And Surrey, committing a grave heraldic error, had assumed a quartering which belonged only to the heir apparent to the throne. The offending escutcheon had been displayed at Kenninghall, his father's Norfolk mansion. At his trial, Surrey voiced his opinion of the 'low' officials who were ousting the old aristocracy. 'Thou, Catchpole', he called out to Paget, 'thou hadst better hold thy tongue, for the kingdom has never been well since the King put mean creatures like thee in the government.'[60] In this category Surrey also included Hertford, an opponent of old, and Wriothesley, who helped to prosecute him. Surrey's remark was to be echoed, in varying tones, throughout the next three reigns, until the 'New Men' of the Reformation and the Dissolution had established themselves too securely to pay attention to impoverished scions of the ancient nobility. The Howards were sent to the Tower. Petre had a share in the examination of the witnesses.[61] Surrey was beheaded. Norfolk's life was saved by a few hours, because of Henry's death on 28 January. The heir was the nine-year-old Edward.

* In the following January Gardiner granted Petre on the ground of 'friendship' an annuity of £100 from the income of his bishopric. There is no means of telling whether this substantial sum was a bribe to gain Petre's support or a reward for past services. Whether or not made 'without fraud or covin', as the confirming Crown patent of 1552 declared (*Cal. Pat., Edw. VI*, iv, 179; E.R.O., D/DP T303), it was a powerful politician's acknowledgment of Petre's influence. See also p. 66.

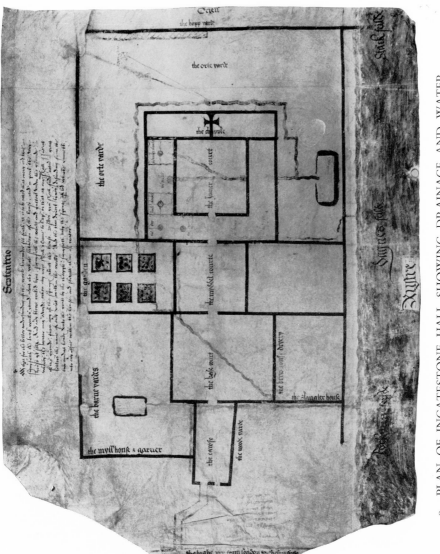

9. PLAN OF INGATESTONE HALL SHOWING DRAINAGE AND WATER
    SUPPLY, 1566

By Thomas Larke

10. INGATESTONE HALL: THE GATEHOUSE

11. INGATESTONE HALL

CHAPTER V

Secretary under Somerset

1 Petre, Smith and Cecil

AT the meeting of Edward's Privy Council held on 13 February 1547, Paget and Petre, 'Chief Secretaries to the King's Majesty', were ordered to surrender their signets, whereupon Edward restored them by his own hand.[1] The language implies that there was no effective break in their tenure. But for two reasons Petre's (as opposed to Paget's) hope of appointment to secretarial or conciliar office cannot have been bright, despite his having been chosen as the Council's mouthpiece in conveying their 'grief' to Van der Delft, three days after Henry's death. Under the Succession Act of 1544, Henry's will, made in December 1546, nominated his young heir's council of sixteen, who were to govern by virtue of their status as executors. Henry also named, it is true, twelve assistant executors, but their services were only to be called upon if required; Petre, in company with Arundel, Thirlby and Rich, was among the supplementary dozen. Henry's intentions with regard to religion were made manifest by his balanced choice of conservatives and reformers. There were several significant exclusions, in particular, Gardiner, whose antagonism to the Protestants was well known. The reformers included Cranmer, Hertford, Russell and Lisle; the Catholics, Wriothesley, Tunstall and Browne. St. John, Paget and North were an intermediate Council group, whose latitudinarian views would have a steadying influence when religious feeling ran too high.

The will gave Petre a second jolt. Henry's legacies to the executors were generous. Some got £500, the others £300; and £200 was left to every assistant executor—with the single exception of Petre, who was accorded nothing. Apart from failing to receive this last mark of royal favour, his being left out of the Council is almost as puzzling, for he seems to have exhibited no religious bias. Henry had appointed Petre a member of the Regency Council in 1544; since then the evidence is that he had discharged his onerous duties ably, acting as sole Secretary for three periods, besides taking senior responsibility in two embassies abroad. No clue has been found to suggest why he was passed over, and a clerical slip for as large a sum as £200 is improbable.* The councillors were

---

* In checking the printed versions (L. & P., xxi, pt. ii, 634; cf. Rymer, Foedera) I examined the original will and the draft list of legacies (P.R.O., E.23/4) in case either MS. had suffered a mutilation which could have contained Petre's name; that is not so.

slow in paying the legacies, because the treasury was nearly empty. Paget, for instance, did not get his until 1549. But on 6 October 1547, early in the series of warrants, the Council register notes, '£200 for the bequest to Sir William Petre, one of the Principal Secretaries, made to him by the King's Majesty deceased'![2] This unexpected entry raises questions of authority and motive. Henry, on his deathbed, was alleged to have empowered his executors to implement any of his unfulfilled promises of favour. That the Council felt the need to reward the Secretary whom the old King had treated shabbily seems the most likely solution of the little mystery.

Four weeks after his resumption of the secretaryship, all the assistant executors were added by royal commission to the Privy Council. The personnel was then much the same as under Henry, except for Gardiner and Thirlby. Not until this meeting was Petre formally re-instated as a councillor.*

In the meantime, some strange, strategical movements had taken place. Hertford had been scheming to increase his influence. His initial struggle for power had been eased shortly before Henry's death. Of his former rivals, Norfolk and Surrey, one was in the Tower, the other in the grave; and Gardiner was out of office. Hertford proceeded to fortify his position by a still closer alliance with the resourceful Paget, who had helped him to control the Council in Henry's last weeks. His death was kept secret for three days and then announced to Parliament by Wriothesley; Paget read the will, suppressing part of it. On the same day the executors chose Hertford, uncle of the boy King, as Protector of the realm and governor of his person. Edward VI gave his assent. The *coup d'état* had succeeded. A few days later Paget read another document—to the Council. It declared Henry's intention to bestow honours and the Howards' attainted estates on his executors. The Lord Chancellor was authorized to prepare the patents, by reason of which Edward Seymour, Earl of Hertford, became Duke of Somerset; William Parr, Earl of Essex, became Marquis of Northampton; John Dudley, Viscount Lisle, Earl of Warwick; Thomas Wriothesley, Earl of Southampton; and Richard Rich, Baron Rich. But other dignities, including Paget's, were to be deferred. Among those not promoted was Petre; nor did he get any of the Howard lands. He was, however, 'to have the £100 fee of my Lord of Winchester'.[3] The receipt of this 'fee for the office of high steward of all the possessions of the Bishop of Winton' in his accounts for Michaelmas 1547 confirms how his own

* Petre's memorandum for reorganizing the Council's business, mis-dated as 15 Feb. 1547 in *Dom. Cal.*, 1547–80, 2 (cf. A. F. Pollard, *England under Protector Somerset* (1900), 80, 88–9), has been assigned by me to early 1553 (see p. 102).

finances benefited by Gardiner's downfall. Gardiner's annuity to Petre and the fee for this office must be identical. Another powerful minister was soon removed, unexpectedly. Shortly after his elevation to an earldom, Wriothesley committed a serious error in procedure as Chancellor and was adjudged to have forfeited office. He was placed under house arrest and obliged to give a bond for £4,000 for payment of a fine to be fixed by the Council. Rich became Lord Chancellor. All immediate rivals had thus disappeared from the Protector's path.

On 18 August the seal *ad causas ecclesiasticas* was 'by special order of the Lord Protector's Grace' committed to Petre's custody. He thus took over, in succession to Paget, the symbol of royal control over the Church. The power of restoring to the bishops and others their pre-Reformation jurisdiction was now to be exercised only by licence under his seal.[4] A general visitation of the Church was begun, following the King's letters issued to the archbishops in May, Petre being one of the signatories.[5] It was under these injunctions that so many stained-glass windows were smashed and wall-paintings whitewashed. The new translation of Erasmus's *Paraphrase of the New Testament* had to be provided in every parish church, and Petre's accounts show that he paid 5s. 'towards buying' a copy in November 1548, probably his contribution to that for St. Botolph-without-Aldersgate, where his town house lay. After the visitation, the keeper of the ecclesiastical seal was given specific authority to seal all bishops' commissions.[6] This offended them because of the irksome burden of sending their legal instruments to Petre.*

Paget had been appointed in June as Comptroller of the Household and sole Chancellor of the Duchy of Lancaster, both sinecures but influential posts. Petre then became sole Secretary. He occupied the office alone for nearly a year, but was overshadowed by Paget in matters of policy.†

* A memorandum drawn up at Edward's death about their grievance stated that the seal 'was some profit unto him' (P.R.O., S.P. 10/18/30), but entries in his own accounts credit him with an average of only £12 a year (see Appendix J).

† The standard lists of Principal Secretaries (*P.R.O. Lists and Indexes*, XLIII; F. M. G. Evans, *The Principal Secretary of State* (1923), 349; and *Handbook of British Chronology* (Roy. Hist. Soc., 1939), 89), which have overlooked this point, are therefore deceptive in not stating that Paget ceased to hold this office in June. In March the Council Register had termed Paget 'our Chief Secretary' and Petre 'one of our two Principal Secretaries'. By August Petre was 'the King's Majesty's Principal Secretary' or 'Chief Secretary' (*A.P.C.*, ii, 114,116,148,153); the French ambassador in London referred to 'le premier secretaire d'Etat Petre' (*Correspondance Politique de Odet de Selve* (1888), 186); and Van der Delft alludes to two letters from the Emperor being passed by the Protector to 'the First Secretary, Dr. Petre' (*Span. Cal.*, ix, 194, 227). The evidence suggests that Petre no longer shared office with Paget, and the sharp decline in the number of ambassadors' letters Paget received in contrast with those addressed to Petre confirms this view (*Foreign Cal.*, *Edw. VI*). Further, when Paget took over his higher office the Council paid his fee as Secretary up to Midsummer Day, that is for only three-fourths of the year (*A.P.C.*, ii, 101).

In the late summer of 1547 Somerset, as Lieutenant and Captain-General, conducted the English army to Scotland. During his absence, Cranmer, Russell, Paget, Browne and Petre were the most active deputies.[7] On 30 August Paget informed Somerset that they had 'divided themselves into two bands, one to wait continually one week and the other band the other week, and upon Sundays to be always together at the Court'; he added, 'Mr. Secretary was somewhat diseased',[8] but Petre's illness must have been only a short one. The campaign resulted in the massacre of the Scots at Pinkie near Musselburgh. In November, while Somerset's reputation remained high after the victory, Edward's first Parliament was summoned. It seems to have been freely elected, and few of the former members re-appeared. Several of the Protector's strongest supporters on the Council were equally zealous in the Lower House, the leaders of which were apparently Paget and Petre,[9] who was again returned for the county, with Thomas Darcy, a prominent Essex landowner. The period of uneasy calm which followed the consolidation of Somerset's position continued during 1548. Very little of Petre's secretarial correspondence for 1547–48 has been preserved. His official work would in fact be obscure were it not for some drafts about foreign affairs and his letters from the English ambassadors, Wotton in France, Carne in Flanders and Thirlby in Germany, and the Spanish ambassador's dispatches to the Imperial Court. One of the last, for November 1547, dealing with the perennial trade negotiations, reveals St. John, Paget and Petre as guests at Van der Delft's house. 'After dinner', he reported, 'they announced that the Protector had commanded them to communicate with me respecting my complaints about the customs. Great disputes ensued, some growing quite heated in their arguments.' Van der Delft and Petre were still arguing two days after Christmas about a proposed renewal of the commercial treaty for ten years, and the same four were wrangling over the same matter thirteen months later.[10] These are meagre records of a busy Secretary. His own account-books add a little. In December 1547, when the private day-to-day record of the Secretary's expenses is resumed, Lady Petre was with him at Court. Parliament sat until the 23rd. On the 20th he paid to Lord Mountjoy's executors the substantial sum of £6 13s. 4d. for a silver-studded horse harness. On 'Christ's Day' Petre gave 8d. to a priest to say mass, and again on St. John's Day (the 27th), when he crossed over to Lambeth, presumably to visit Cranmer. That evening he dined again with Van der Delft. Petre moved with the Court from White Hall to Hampton just before New Year's Day, 1548. His steward's first list of 'rewards' to the bringers of New Year gifts names some of Petre's fellow office-holders and subordinates.

Rewards given for bringing of New Year gifts, 1548

Mr. Vannes' servant for bringing of 10 yards of black satin, 5s.

Mr. Hunning's man for bringing of a looking glass and a case of knives, 6s. 8d.

Mr. Baker's servant, bringing of 2 sovereigns 40s., 5s.

Mr. Vaughan's servant bringing a salt with a cover gilt having my master's arms, 6s. 8d.

Sir Thomas Pope's servant bringing 2 sovereigns 40s., 5s.

Mr. Godsalve's servant bringing 2 new pieces of gold and 4 pieces of silver, 5s.

Mr. Taverner's servant bringing 3 yards black satin, 5s.

The Bishop of Durham's servant bringing 6 li. 13s. 4d. in gold, 10s.

Mr. Armell's servant bringing a pair of mittens lined with velvet and an hour glass, 5s.

John Godsalve was a clerk of the Signet, Armigell Waad (also termed 'Mr Armil' and 'Mr Armigell') and William Hunning (or Honnyng) were clerks of the Council, and Dr. Vannes was Latin secretary. Others whose work often brought them into touch with Petre were Sir John Baker, Chancellor of the Exchequer, Sir Thomas Pope and Stephen Vaughan, now Under-treasurer of the Mint. It is curious that Pope was to be the most constant donor of New Year presents to Petre, but, except for their early association at the surrender of St. Alban's and Westminster Abbeys, never appears in Petre's public life again. Tunstall, Bishop of Durham, is the only councillor, and this great politician, who was evidently on very friendly terms with Petre, sent a similar sum more than once in later years. What New Year gifts cost Mr. Secretary in 1548 is not known, apart from £9 5s. to discharge the customary offerings to the Royal Household from the gentlemen ushers to the scullions; ten years earlier he had given twenty rials (coins worth 11s. 3d. each) to Cromwell, who got scores of similar 'gifts'.

Other presents arrived in the following weeks. Browne, the Master of the Horse, sent his compliments, first with half a hind, then twice with two whole ones, the last on Maundy Thursday—an acceptable gift against the end of the Lenten fast. A natural sequel was the reward of 4s. 4d. to the royal household servants 'for baking half a red deer in the [royal] pastry'. Petre also received a dozen marten skins from Sir Anthony St. Leger, the Lord Deputy of Ireland, who was probably soliciting aid in his suit (in September he was superseded and returned to England). More gratifying was a goshawk from the Lord Chamberlain (Arundel), which called for 20s. to the bringer. Arundel was the only aristocratic member or the Council and a leading one.

On 17 April 1548 a second Principal Secretary, Thomas Smith, took his seat at the Council table at Greenwich.[11] He was born at Saffron Walden in 1513; his father, a man of substance, had been Sheriff of Essex. In 1540 he graduated at Padua as doctor of civil laws. Returning to Cambridge he became LL.D. there. A man of pronounced Protestant views, he entered the Protector's service early in 1547, having held a Council clerkship for a short time before his promotion. The 20d. 'reward to my Lord Chancellor's cook' on the day of Smith's appearance perhaps marks Petre's presence at a complimentary dinner in London given to the new official by Rich, whose country home lay midway between Saffron Walden and Ingatestone. The Council had apparently recognized an all-round growth in the administrative burden of the secretariat, though it is impossible to say whether Smith's appointment was intended to relieve Petre; a reduction in his Signet fees certainly coincided with Smith's advent.

On 27 May Petre bade farewell to Smith, who departed for Flanders to negotiate for the levy of mercenaries and to seek the Emperor's support, as a French invasion of Boulogne seemed inevitable. The state of England is reflected in Petre's spending £6 on his own armour and £18 for 'setting forth of two demi-lances and two light horsemen'. He supped at the Lord Chancellor Rich's table, with Baker, and with William Garrard, a rich city haberdasher and perhaps his closest friend outside the conciliar circle. When the Court removed to Oatlands in August, Petre found some leisure for the pleasures of the chase; and in the same month royal warrants brought him three bucks, from Byfleet, Kimpton and Woking parks, as well as a sorrel colt from the King a few weeks later. Arundel sent the Petres an invitation to supper and his own barge to fetch them. Two hats were bought for the occasion, his of taffeta costing 8s. and hers of velvet costing 24s.! It was the third token of esteem from the earl within a year. On Christmas Day Sir William dined with the Venetian ambassador, but there is no hint of his participating in the Court festivities. He rode into Essex on Twelfth Eve, without his wife. Although he had been frequently at Ingatestone in 1548,* he saw little of it in 1549, which was to prove a time of abnormal stress, of great changes in political, social, religious and parliamentary affairs, with grave events crowding one upon another. They obliged the Secretary, month after month, to abandon hope of rural peace on his Essex manor, forcing him indeed on one occasion to concentrate on avoiding the Tower. He was back in London by the middle of January, when Parliament approved, after some modification, the draft of the great work which was largely Cranmer's—the first English Prayer Book.

While the Archbishop had been busy with doctrinal plans, the Admiral

* See Chapter VII.

was engaged in sinister plots. Somerset's brother, Lord Thomas Seymour of Sudeley, had for some time been under grave suspicion of piracy and of scheming to subvert the government and to marry Princess Elizabeth. He was now deeply involved in a fraud affecting the Bristol mint. The Council sent him to the Tower. Next day detailed instructions, prepared by Petre, were issued for searching his house in Wiltshire.[12] To take action against one who had had some dalliance with the girl who might succeed to the throne, one who was of the Protector's own blood, was an assignment which Petre cannot have relished. The Protector, on the Council's advice, appointed Russell, Southampton and Petre to examine scores of hostile witnesses. At Hatfield, that treasure house of political archives, is preserved much of Petre's scribbled handwriting bearing on the case, including his 'minute of the interrogatories' to be administered touching Seymour's treasonable attempt also to bring about a marriage between the King and Lady Jane Grey, daughter of Henry Grey, Marquis of Dorset.[13] Questioned by Petre, Dorset deposed that the Admiral declared, 'By God's precious soul, I will make this the blackest Parliament that ever was', and disclosed how he had sent pocket-money to young Edward because 'his uncle of Somerset kept him very strait'. Petre made abstracts of Dorset's 'confession', which, 'perhaps with the design of screening this nobleman from being implicated in the treason of the Admiral, are so drawn up as to give a very imperfect account of what passed between them'.[14] On 12 February, in this period of stress, Petre dined with the duke. Next day, the Secretary was at the Comptroller's house, where Paget and he were perhaps compiling their report. A month went by before the evidence was complete. To give Seymour the chance of purging himself, the Council visited the Tower in force but in vain; and they cautiously left the final verdict to Parliament, which attainted him. His treason did more than anything else to weaken the Protector's position. Somerset received a call from Petre two days after the bill was passed. Petre's is among the signatures to the execution warrant; Somerset's is first, as it had to be. A tip to 'the late Lord Admiral's cook' and boathire from the Tower to the Court, entered on the second day after the traitor went to the block, are laconic references to the event.*

* Soon afterwards Petre was granted the eighty-year lease which Seymour had obtained in the previous year of fourteen manors of the Dean and Chapter of Westminster in Gloucestershire and Worcestershire, the rents of which brought in over £200 (*Cal. Pat. Rolls, Edw. VI*, ii, 182–3), but apparently he soon disposed of the lease. The groat to the porter at Sir Edward North's on the eve of the admiral's execution perhaps indicates a dinner to arrange the terms of the lease, for North was Chancellor of the Court of Augmentations in succession to Rich.

The monasteries and the churches having been 'reformed', it was now the turn of the universities. They were already suffering from the troublous times, and the number of scholars had been rapidly diminishing. In May 1549 both universities had to submit to the King's visitors. Because the treasury was empty, the previous Parliament had entrusted to the government the college and chantry endowments which were made over to Henry for life. Exempted from the Act were Oxford and Cambridge. Among the commissioners for Oxford were Warwick, Paget and Petre. The visitors imposed new statutes on the university, and they ordered a great burning of books and manuscripts. Petre did not descend on his *alma mater*. His steward provides him with undeniable alibis in frequent boathire between Greenwich and London in the first half of May and 'my master's dinners and suppers at the Court from 14 to 28 May'. In contrast to the holocaust, 'binding certain books of my master's that came from Master Wotton' is set down—by no means the only accession to Petre's library from his diplomatist friend at Paris.

Somerset had been grappling with formidable tasks. The risk of insurrection at home and the hostility of France, the Empire and the Papacy were major causes of concern, and these were aggravated by the economic instability. During the last years of the preceding reign, England's coinage had been progressively debased. Each act of debasement resulted in a sharp rise in prices. The labouring man was the chief victim, because wages lagged behind prices, mainly owing to the increase in unemployment; and the spread of vagabondage became a growing menace. Several councillors, antagonized by the liberal-minded Protector's attack on these social and economic abuses, remonstrated with him. The depopulating of some villages by enclosures for sheep-farming had led him to issue commissions in June 1548 for redressing the grievance; and some dispossessed tenants were already pulling down hedges and park-pales. Somerset refused to condemn them. 'Maugre the devil', he declared, 'private profit, self-love, money, and such-like devil's instruments, it shall go forward.' But he was forced by May 1549 to issue a proclamation through the Council against breakers of enclosures, and Petre drafted it.[15] The government was virtually bankrupt, and had to borrow from Flemish Jews at rates as high as 14 per cent. Part of the interest was shamelessly paid in lead and bell-metal recently confiscated from churches and chantries, following the making of inventories on conciliar instructions to county commissioners, also drafted by Petre.[16] Somerset, however, must be given credit for reducing the royal household expenditure by one-fourth, and Petre had been helping him in a parallel task by his work for a small commission set up in the autumn of 1547 to investigate the Crown revenues.[17] Nothing has been found to suggest that Petre was in any way a policy-maker at this time, nor are his views about Somerset's reforms on record.

It was in Devon and Cornwall that revolt first broke out. The insurrection started on Whitsunday, 1549, when the new Prayer Book was to come into use, though economic discontent was an equally strong underlying cause. Lord Russell, who had received the rich estates of Tavistock Abbey in Devon, was deputed to suppress it; separate orders were given to the brothers Sir Peter and Sir Gawen Carew, who arrived first, and their violence aggravated the rebellion. 'We will not receive the new service, because it is but like a Christmas game', the insurgents had proclaimed, and they demanded the restoration of half the monastic lands. Petre must have anxiously awaited news from his native county, in which he now owned the manors of Brent and Churchstow, former possessions of Buckfast Abbey. In Exeter, the fighting was fierce. A Catholic with more zeal than marksmanship let off with his cross-bow at a presumed heretic, and instead hit Petre's younger brother John, the Customs officer, and his best friend, a good Papist, as the records say; but with no serious results. Progress in suppressing the revolt was slow, and fresh instructions were sent to Russell. To the draft, which he had much corrected, Petre added these vigorous words: 'Because sundry ill and seditious persons for the better achievement of their devilish purposes have spread abroad such lewd and untrue rumours as they imagine may best set forth their naughty purposes, the said Lord Russell shall search out the authors, causing them to be punished according to their deservings.'[18] Sir William Herbert, a privy councillor whose parks had been invaded, was sent with reinforcements to Exeter, now besieged; and the Devon justices of the peace received a missive from the Council written by Petre[19] at Syon House on 26 June, with directions to induce the rebels to retire peaceably.*

In the summer there were other disturbances, notably the Norfolk revolt led by Ket. During July Petre was constantly journeying between London, Westminster and Richmond. Many crossings-over to Lambeth in August may indicate that Cranmer and Petre were bearing an extra burden in the absence of colleagues on military service. The Norfolk rising obliged the Council to order the gentry of Essex to equip as many

---

* The revolt scarcely figures in *A.P.C.* or *Dom. Cal.*; but copies of as many as fifteen dispatches from the Council to Herbert between 29 June and 12 Sept. are in the Inner Temple (Petyt MSS., 538/46, ff. 432-65); only that of 27 Aug. does not include the signature of Petre, who probably drafted most of them.

demi-lances, or light horsemen, as they could, and to muster at Saffron Walden. Petre's steward noted:

A 'pertizan',* 6s. 8d.; 12 bows at 2s. 2d. apiece, 26s.; 14 pikes at 20d., 23s. 4d.; 3 handguns with their apparel, 31s. 6d.; 6 lb. powder, 4s.; a 'carre' to carry it, 6d.; feathering 4 sheaves of arrows with 7 new shafts and 4 girdles, 5s. 8d.; for mending my master's crossbow, string and 4 crossbow bolts, 2s. Kerseys for coats for the wars—4 pieces of Northern kerseys 16 yards apiece at 20d. the yard, with 12d. over, in the whole £5 7s. 8d.; for the dyeing yellow of the same kerseys at 3s. apiece 12s. and for the dressing 4s.

The 'great horses' in the Ingatestone stables were got ready again. Petre's own mount was equipped with a new saddle of black velvet and Spanish skins, a double harness of black leather, white girths and a double surcingle. On the last day of June his steward had paid various bills grouped together as 'provision for the wars'—either the South-Western rebellion or a further but unsuccessful campaign against the Scots at the end of 1548, which had led Petre earlier to lay out £2 in equipping a 'light horseman and two great horses against the war'. He apparently slipped away from the Court for a flying visit to see for himself whether mid-Essex 'remained in a quavering quiet', as Arundel had recently informed him was the state in Surrey. Parts of Suffolk, Essex and Kent were in fact involved, but not seriously, in Ket's rebellion.[20]

The revolt accounts for Petre's first recorded association with William Cecil, whose appointment as Somerset's personal secretary must however have brought them in touch earlier. Born in 1520, Cecil had studied at Cambridge, where he came under the influence of the great Greek scholar, John Cheke, whose sister Mary he married shortly after going up to London. She died within three years, having given him a son, Thomas, one day to become Earl of Exeter. His second wife was Mildred, eldest daughter of Sir Anthony Cooke of Gidea Hall, Romford, neighbour and friend of Petre; she, like her father, was noted for academic learning.† Cooke was governor, or preceptor, to Edward, and Cheke was also one of his tutors. After Cecil had read law at Gray's Inn, the Protector made him master of his court of requests. On 13 August 1549, the Privy Council charged a committee of three with the duty of exercising a censorship of all printed books:

An order was taken that from henceforth no printer should print or put to vent [sale] any English book but such as should be examined by Mr. Secretary Peter, Mr. Secretary Smith, or Mr. Cicill, or the one of them, and allowed by the same.[21]

* See Appendix H.   † Lady Cooke was one of Elizabeth Petre's godmothers.

Here, in company, are three of the Fathers of the Civil Service, all biblio- philes. Their task, however, was no literary one, but the suppression of seditious books and pamphlets. Within two months the trio was broken up and Petre was the sole censor for the rest of the reign. Unfortunately nothing is known of this sphere of activity. Later, under Mary's heresy commission, 'heretical and seditious books' were included in its wide powers of search. Falling naturally within the Secretary's scope, licensing and censorship of books were duties firmly linked with the office in the ensuing century.

2 Somerset's First Fall

The prelude to the crisis which was rapidly approaching is one of the most obscure periods in Tudor history. The revolts had further weakened the Protector's position. The Catholic element in the Council was ready to overthrow him in the hope of securing a reversal of his religious policy. The initiative, however, was taken by Warwick, 'the subtlest intriguer in English history', in the words of Somerset's best biographer.[22]

Soon after 18 September Somerset and Edward moved to Hampton Court. It was apparently not until 5 October that the Protector suddenly sensed dangerous opposition from Warwick's party. On that day he issued an appeal to the people to muster at Hampton, and dispatched couriers to summon to his side the victorious army of Russell and Herbert, already on their way back from crushing the Western insurgents. With Somerset were Cranmer, St. John, Paget and Petre, all of whom had signed a Council letter to Lord Cobham, the Deputy, or Governor, of Calais, dated from Hampton the day before; Smith and Cecil were probably also there. But the statement by Somerset's biographer that Cranmer and the two Secretaries had been engaged on routine Council business at Hampton Court for some time before that date cannot be maintained.* Cranmer and Smith, at any rate, were adjudicating in the trial of Bishop Bonner at Lambeth on 23 September and 1 October (p. 113), and Smith was absent from the Court until about the 4th or 5th. Petre was enjoying a brief rest at Ingatestone when Bonner was sentenced on 1 October, but he was back in London next evening, when he visited Lambeth, and again the following day.

On the morning of Sunday 6 October, Somerset's opponents met at

---

* 'The documents discharged in the paper war in which Somerset fell', Dixon wrote (op. cit., iii, 154), are nearly all preserved in the state papers (Dom. Cal., 1547–80). 'Some of them have been printed by Foxe, Burnet, and Tytler: one or two by Strype, and by Mr. Froude.' Dixon gives an annotated list for the period 5–11 October. Those in the Petyt MSS. (Inner Temple) were printed by Pocock, Troubles connected with the Prayer Book of 1549 (Camden Soc., 1884).

Warwick's house, Ely Place in Holborn.* Besides Warwick, their number included Arundel and Southampton; also St. John (apparently presiding), who had cast his lot with Warwick and may have stolen away from the Court the day before.[23] The councillors had reviewed the grave condition of the country and the neglect of their oft-proffered advice by the Protector, 'minding to follow his own fantasies'. They determined, however, with feigned loyalty, to make another friendly remonstrance to him and to repair at once to Hampton Court. But as they were about to depart, Petre rode up to the gates, demanding in the Protector's name to know the reason for their session and warning them that if they descended belligerently upon Hampton Court they would be arrested as traitors. How much of Petre's message followed the terms of his instructions, how much represented his own views, it is impossible to say. 'He was sent', Edward wrote in his Journal, 'to know for what cause the lords had gathered their powers together, and if they meant to talk with the Protector, they should come in a peaceable manner.' The Protector, in a letter written the following day, said that he had 'sent Mr. Petre with such a message, as whereby might have ensured the surety of his Majesty's person, the preservation of his realm and subjects'.[24]

As Petre had made his way towards London, he knew that he was facing a turning-point in his life. Either way might quickly lead to Tower Hill. He may well have questioned the unfortunate choice of himself, instead of Smith, Paget or Cecil.

Whether Petre was 'soon satisfied that the Protector was wrong and the Lords were right',[25] or whether he was swayed by threats or self-interest, the fact is that he remained with the London councillors. In vain Somerset waited till dusk for his return. Alarmed by the silence, he decided that Windsor would provide a safer defence against an attack from London. Taking the King, he rode with Cranmer, Paget and Smith through the night to the castle, to await reinforcements from the West. Next day (the 7th), each side weighed its chances of victory, and important messages were sent in both directions. Somerset's letter (in Smith's hand) to those in the capital reveals a spirit already wavering:

> His Majesty and we of his Council here do not a little marvel that you stay [detain] still with you Mr. Secretary Petre, and have not vouchsafed to send answer to his Majesty, neither by him nor yet any other. Ye shall find us agreeable to any reasonable conditions that you will require. Praying you to send us your determinate answer by Mr. Secretary Petre, or, *if you will not let him go*, by this bearer.[26]

* For the whole of the following week, a vivid record has been preserved in a fresh register of the 'London' Privy Council (*A.P.C.*, ii, 330–44), the previous book finishing with the business at Hampton Court on the 4th.

The letter from Ely House to Windsor declared that the message brought by Secretary Petre had grieved them because their fidelity was doubted. Reassuring Edward on that account, they did not hesitate to blame Somerset, who had always refused to hear reason. It is preserved in the form of the draft as well as the original with the signatures including Petre's and the copy in the Council register.[27] The draft is partly in Petre's writing, partly in Southampton's.[28] Petre began carefully at first, making more than one amendment as he went on. The councillors were making a direct approach to the King. Could they be sure that Edward had no great respect or affection for his uncle? Could they destroy what confidence he had in the Protector? In the heat and confusion of the moment, it was perhaps the most difficult letter which Secretary Petre had ever had to write. He was addressing a king scarcely twelve years of age, a precocious boy already aware of his future responsibilities. How much did the writer, a man in his forties, really know of the mind of his sovereign? On their knees they most humbly beseeched him, Petre wrote, 'not to give from henceforth any such credit to the Duke of Somerset your uncle nor to any other as may bring as your Highness' true subjects'. Not 'the Protector', it is to be noted; but the phrase was dangerous, and its bad construction reveals a distracted mind. Petre scored out the whole reference to Somerset. He was uncertain about the legal status of the body for whom he was acting while drawing up the letter. To a man of his training, the affair had an unconstitutional flavour. So he wrote 'do at this present assembly', only to put his pen through it and substitute 'have at this present time consulted together'. 'Assembly' had a treasonable sound (but the Lords decided later to use the word). His writing then deteriorated into a hurried scrawl. It had been a fateful day for him, and it was imperative that Edward should be acquainted with what had taken place, and that without delay. But Petre was determined to clear his own character from any accusation of disloyalty, and he explained his failure to return. 'Almost all your Council being here, we have for the better service of his Majesty *caused your Secretary to remain here with us*': those words might save his head from the block, might even keep him out of the Tower, should the London group's plan go awry. And having written thus far, he handed the quill to Southampton, who continued without so much as starting a fresh line.*

Events of the preceding hours had doubtless tended to embolden

* The editor of the *Calendar of State Papers* detected the change; and close examination of this and other documents in Petre's and Wriothesley's hands leaves no doubt about the point at which the latter snatched up the pen.

Somerset's opponents. Lord Chancellor Rich, who may also have been at Hampton Court, had deserted the Protector and joined Warwick, bringing the Great Seal with him, and evidently presided at their meeting on the 7th. Their number had been further strengthened by Sadler, Baker and several others. Now a majority of the Council, they were no longer the Ely Place faction; and they communicated with the King, not with the Protector. Even if the two italicized passages do not connote forcible detention, it is debatable whether Petre's behaviour amounted to defection, a term applied by more than one historian. If not physically intimidated, logic convinced him of the futility of attempting to return to a tottering Protector.

On the same 7 October Warwick and his allies also addressed a warning to Cranmer and Paget; it was drawn up by Petre.[29] Aimed at alienating their support of 'the Duke of Somerset', the letter declared their resolution to deprive him of the status of Protector, urged Cranmer and Paget to persuade him to submit to justice and reason, and concluded with even more ominous hints about the 'inconveniences' which might ensue if their advice were not heeded. Petre was probably also given the task of preparing the proclamation, dated the 8th, condemning Somerset's 'evil government', a sure sign that the London party was already optimistic about his surrender.[30]

On the 8th, no less than three letters were written at Windsor and delivered post-haste at Ely Place by Sir Philip Hoby (Thirlby's successor at the Emperor's court, from which he had recently returned). The King, no doubt at his uncle's dictation, appealed to the councillors in London not to use extreme measures against Somerset; Cranmer, Paget and Smith hinted that he was willing to resign if his life were spared; Smith addressed a personal note to Petre deprecating violence. The last letter, between the separated Secretaries, is refreshing in its contrast to the plotting and counter-plotting. Confirming that the Protector was 'content to refuse no reasonable condition', Smith craved Petre's influential aid.

Having by reason of vicinity and office with you most acquaintance, I am boldest to write unto you. Now is the time when you may show yourself to be of that nature whereof I have heard you, that is, no seeker of extremity nor blood, *but of moderation in all things*. To require with blood that which may be had with persuasion and honour, I cannot think it should be in any of my Lords there, and as little in you. I pray you join with us on that side, that things may be brought to moderation; and rest not to labour herein. You shall do the best deed, I think, that ever any gentleman did, tho' you be but an earnest motioner herein. . . . For my part, I am in a most miserable case. I cannot leave the King's Majesty, and him who was my master, of whom I have had all; and I cannot deny but I have misliked also some things that you and the rest of my Lords there did mislike—as you know, no man better, yourself. But now let Christian charity work with you, Sir, for God's love, the King's and the realm's; refuse not the offer which is so good, so godly and so honourable unto you, that this realm be not made in one year a double tragedy.

The last phrase was an allusion to the recent execution of Somerset's brother. Full of misgivings, Smith added another desperate plea in a post-script: 'And, if you may, I pray you write to me, though it be but two words of comfort.'[31] Whether one concludes that Smith was honest, or like Petre was 'stayed', there is no doubt about the estimation in which Petre was held; a man of moderation might be counted upon to temper the attitude of the more unruly confederates.

He would have been foolhardy, in his uncertain position, to risk any written answer to Smith. But a further, little-known letter reveals that Petre had responded to his friend's appeal by arranging to send Smith's brother George, a city merchant, to Windsor Castle with first-hand news.[32] It was a generous-minded act. Smith wrote:

I thank most heartily my Lords of Warwick, Arundel and you that my brother George had leave to come and visit me. Which was both mine and his great comfort. For the love of God, Sir, help to bring this tumult to some moderate thing. . . . I am sorry it is come so far and to so much extremity. I am not able to judge of your doings but I would have wished that proclamation which I hear say is abroad had been stayed a while. If ye can, I pray you let me have knowledge by my brother in what state I stand in myself. I trust my tarrying here can not be prejudicial unto me when I can not go away. And I cannot tell what might be said though I might go away, if I should now leave the King's Majesty. And I repose much in your friendship to answer for me if anything be objected, and shew now such a part for me as you would wish I should for you in the like case, and I shall not forget it whiles I live.[33]

All other feelings had evidently given place to fears for his career, if not his life. It was now his turn to be insistent that he was held fast. This second letter is undated, but mention of the proclamation of the 8th and his silence about Hoby's return to Windsor on the 10th assigns it to the intermediate day. On that day, too, Russell and Herbert dashed the hopes of those at the castle by refusing to give aid.

Meantime, in collusion with the London councillors, Hoby started back to Windsor; then, according to Smith, pretending that he had lost their letter, he told his servant that he must return for another one, and sent him on with the false assurance that 'all would be well'.[34] The Warwick–Southampton group dispatched Hoby to Windsor once more, on the morning of the 10th.[35] He carried two sets of messages, both drafted by

Petre, open and secret. He declared his open one to the King, the Duke, the Archbishop, Paget and Smith; Cecil also being 'present', it is to be noted. Nothing could be more reassuring to Somerset. They intended 'no manner of hurt to him, but only to give order for the protectorship'. This also is quoted from Smith's own report. The reaction was that those at Windsor 'wept for joy, and thanked God, and prayed for the Lords. Mr. Comptroller [Paget] fell down on his knees, and clasped the Duke about the knees, and weeping said, "Oh, my Lord, ye see now what my Lords be." ' [36] The scene at this end is the most villainous of the whole drama. His suspicions allayed, Somerset allowed his guards to be removed. But Paget had evidently established a private agreement with Warwick and Southampton, and on the previous day he had sent his servant to the London Council with secret advice how they might best take Somerset. Accordingly, Wingfield was sent to Windsor with orders (written by Petre [37]) to present himself to Cranmer and Paget, and not only to secure the Protector but also to confine Smith and Cecil[38] to their chambers until the victors' arrival on the 12th, when they 'presented themselves to the young King most humbly on their knees', and Edward accepted their explanation. The final scenes are brief. Smith was dismissed from the office of Principal Secretary and removed on the 13th to the Tower, to be joined next day by Somerset. Cecil was also dispatched thither—although 'his part in the whole business was an obscure one'.[39] Petre drew up a stiff order to the Lieutenant to keep the prisoners under close guard; he had already supervised the composing of a lengthy report on the recent events as well as a circular letter to the lord lieutenants of several counties;[40] but the proclamation dated the 10th, and probably drafted a day or so earlier, was compiled by Southampton.[41] Warwick's *coup d'état*, like Somerset's less than three years earlier, had been achieved without fighting.

The story of Somerset's fall, of the loyalties and disloyalties of those who figured in it, has often been told; but the mass of conflicting evidence confused the older historians' verdict. One open mind registered both alternatives—'treachery or benevolence' in the case of those who were at Windsor and 'perfidy or prudence' on Petre's part.[42] The earlier indictments of Paget and Cranmer for betraying Somerset are no longer repeated with vehemence. Smith's petition to Petre that the Duke's life should be spared was granted. And in Paget's defence his recent biographer speaks: 'Evidence of Paget's understanding with the leaders of the opposition is shadowy. It rests on only three points. His continued and unavailing forecasts of doom during the last eighteen months had been fulfilled to the last degree. Most of the calamities could have been averted if only his advice had been followed. Secondly, the reward which he received from the victorious rebels would not have gone to a last-minute convert to their cause. To fill the gap between these points there exists a remarkable letter from Smith to Paget, written from prison after the fall of the Duke'.[43] This is a fresh document. It implies that Paget and Petre, who had been paired so often before, were both to go as emissaries to London.

> I first commend me unto you as humbly and heartily as I possibly may. And whereas I had thought that ye had taken that already I had opened all my heart unto you, I perceive by a word cast out to my wife that ye do not even fully take it so. First, that I ever conspired your death or heard of any such thing in my presence, I do fully deny it and renounce God if ever I did, who now at this time hath most need to help me. I do not deny that on the Sunday in the morning, I trow it was, or Saturday late at night, when my lord's grace first opened this broil unto me (for ye knew before I was away) I told him if it were so, that you did know what it was, no doubt. Then he told me that he had sent you and Mr. Petre away. To that I said 'Alas, Sir, then have you done evil. For there is no man so able to help it in the world as he is, and could better do it, and if you had had more of the Council about you, it had been better. For the love of God, stay him about you, and I would wish Mr. Petre too. And herein use their advice; all that remaineth here else hath no experience, and ye shall be sure they will less attempt violence against you having them here.' 'No,' saith he, 'I think he be as evil as the best of them.' 'Though he be, Sir,' quod I, 'yet I am sure he will invent something for you.' 'Well,' sayeth my lord, 'go your ways, and help Cecil to make some more of those letters which he is amaking, and if he be not gone already, I will have him tarry here.'[44]

The date is lacking, but immaterial. What is of interest is the new light it throws on the early days of the crisis. 'If he be not gone already' apparently refers to Paget, not to Cecil; and, if so, the Protector must have cancelled Paget's orders shortly before he was about to leave for Holborn.

In the welter of double dealing, it is impossible to trace a single councillor working for the country's interests. The problem of Petre's motives remains unsolved, though on balance the theory that he hoped Somerset's fall would bring a return to more orthodox religion seems weak in contrast to the view that his action was influenced by the strength of Warwick's party and the ineptitude of Somerset's policy. There is no indication that Somerset and Petre were ever on intimate terms; and Petre's personal accounts reveal their having dined together only once.

On Sunday 13 October the Privy Council was a united body again, in name though not in spirit. Its minutes give an attendance at Windsor of twenty-four members, headed by Cranmer, Rich and Warwick, and including Paget and Petre. The King went back to Hampton Court.

There, on the 15th, the Council appointed Wotton, Petre's old diplomatic friend and Dean of Canterbury and York, as Secretary in succession to Smith. A conservative replaced a reformer, while Petre remained in office. Next day he resumed routine work where he had left off on the 4th, with a secretarial letter to Cobham at Calais ending with the news of the latest arrivals in the Tower and of Wotton having been 'joined with him in office': a cautious, factual letter suppressing personal comment. The government removed to Westminster on the 18th. The period of chaos had ended, and those with consciences at last had a little time for thought. The £20 paid 'for my Lady Smith' on the 28th was perhaps the outcome of Petre's own heart-searching into the devious ways, leading away from the Tower, which he had followed. Petre seems to have been honest, even generous, in handing Smith his share of the secretarial fees on his release six months later: 'To Sir Thomas Smith in full payment of £114 1s. paid unto him by my master's commandment for the signet, £44 1s.'

The epilogue is delivered by Petre's accountant, though very faintly. The cost of 'my master's supper at London' on 2 October included that of his servants. The state of unrest in the city, especially after Somerset's proclamation for a muster, is confirmed by the expenses for the 6th, the day when Petre was 'stayed' (torch, alms and tip to the Newgate porter). Payments for servants' meals show that twelve of them, including Cliff his Signet clerk and Ingatestone tenant-farmer, remained ready with horses for any emergency. On the 11th he dispatched one of his men into Essex, perhaps to give his pregnant wife the good news of his own safety, and on the following day his men accompanied him to Windsor. The end of the crisis is marked by his sending home several Essex retainers who had ridden up to give military service, by a reward to the Aldersgate porter, and by substantial bonuses to Edward his horsekeeper and Mistress Wells his London housekeeper for extra work. On Petre's return to Hampton Court, he settled a Kingston innkeeper's bill for fodder 'left unpaid' when he and his escort had ridden to London, not to return at once; and some weeks later a baker there got 8s. 6d. 'for horsebread spent at the time of the Duke of Somerset's apprehension'.

3 The Town House

When the sovereign was living near the capital—at Greenwich or Hampton Court—Petre was not completely freed from his judicial duties in the law-courts, especially the Star Chamber, and at certain periods during term-time he was obliged to travel frequently by river between

Westminster and the Court. The irksome necessity of attending in both places, among other reasons, had led him therefore to find a town house for himself and his wife. Immediately after becoming Secretary early in 1544 his choice fell on a property on the west side of Aldersgate Street, just outside the city gate. It was a small house, and he rented it.

Later in the year he bought it and three adjoining dwellings for £36. In the same week he also acquired for £13 6s. 8d. a row of four small houses in the same parish of St. Botolph-without-Aldersgate, formerly belonging to St. Bartholomew's Priory. From contemporary and later evidence it appears that the eight dwellings were contiguous. It is possible that Petre intended either to convert or rebuild them in keeping with his improved circumstances. In the event neither project was put in hand, for by 1549, if not before, he secured the tenancy of a much larger adjacent house from the Drapers' Company, who were to sell it to him in 1552 for £80.* It lay between the streets now known as Long Lane and Little Britain.[45] An extension took place two years later, when 'two tenements lately appertaining to the Swan' were referred to as 'now annexed to my master's house', and probably were 'the new house' referred to in later years in contrast to 'the old building'. Aldersgate Street had already gained a reputation for its fine houses.

Some idea of the substantial size of Petre's town house may be gauged from the rooms given in the inventory of 1562,[46] most of which are also mentioned in his accounts. There were the hall, dining chamber, outer and inner great chambers, great and little parlours, chapel and parlour chambers, 'the chamber wherein my master lieth', the chamber over the parlour, the cook's and Kyme's chambers, the wardrobe chamber, the servants' lodgings (which had partitions), garrets, and of course more than one house of office. Of more interest perhaps was the gallery; 'towards the flooring of my master's gallery next the street with plaster of paris' a plasterer was given an initial payment of £2. 'My master's study at the end of the gallery' and the making of 'heavy clothes racks' in it prove that it was not an external gallery. Other rooms were the nursery, the chamber in which 'the gentlewomen lieth', the schoolhouse, Mr. John's chamber, the winter chamber, porter's lodge, servants' chambers, horsekeepers' chamber, and at least six smaller rooms. Besides kitchen and stable there were numerous other offices—buttery, wet and dry larders, cellar (under Kyme's chamber), bakehouse, boulting-house, fish-house, workhouse, washing-house and woodyard. Petre's own bedchamber was well

* Part of the premises acquired in 1544 apparently continued in his occupation, the remainder being leased to various persons. In 1571 his brother Robert Petre, an Exchequer official, had the tenancy of three of the houses.

furnished. The walnut bed had a tester of cloth tissue, chequered with cloth of silver, fringed with red and white silk, and curtained with red and white taffeta. The walls were tapestried with rich arras worked with a typical pastoral design of sheep and red flowers.

The width of the house against Aldersgate Street was 48 feet, and it was on the north side of Petre's earlier acquisition. The plot of land was an irregular one, between 121 and 136 feet in length, the west or far end adjoining the brick-wall boundary of Lord Rich's mansion, which had been the residence of the Prior of St. Bartholomew, and the tenement of 'Mr Burgon' (Thomas Burgoyne).[47] Rich had 'collected around him, in houses in Bartholomew Close, many of the officials of the Court of Augmentations, which was no doubt a convenient arrangement.'[48] Among them were Sir Edward North and Sir John Williams, successively treasurer and keeper of the monastic jewels, and Thomas Burgoyne and Walter Mildmay, successively auditors of the Augmentations. Petre also had probably felt it desirable to live in or near this coterie, and it will be remembered that it was he who had dissolved the priory and hospital. His well-stocked garden and stables adjoined Mildmay's house, and part of his garden wall abutted on the land owned by Rich, who allowed Petre because of their 'friendship' to lay a half-inch lead pipe under the wall to convey water from his main supply-pipe to Petre's house.[49] A good deal of other incidental information can be gathered from the accounts about the mansion and outbuildings.*

The Petres did a certain amount of entertaining at Aldersgate. His accounts give the impression that he was more often a guest than a host, but this is due to the fact that visits to his friends' or councillors' houses led to 'boathire' entries, whereas the cost of his own hospitality was entered in the housekeeper's books, which are not extant.

Apart from short embassies abroad and royal progresses, Secretary Petre spent his time mostly between the palaces in or near London, his town house and Ingatestone Hall. In broadest outline, his life was divided fairly equally between the three, but the proportions varied greatly from year to year. Petre's periods of residence at Aldersgate Street ranged from single nights to fairly long stretches. Sometimes only his wife and children were living at Aldersgate Street for a few weeks. But, unlike Ingatestone Hall, the town house was never really regarded as a home, and now and again, especially when he accompanied the sovereign on progress, it is clear that it was left in the sole charge of the housekeeper (p.153).

---

* Petre's son apparently rebuilt it. In later years it became known as Petre House and still later as London House, and was not pulled down until the end of the last century. (E. A. Webb, *The Records of St. Bartholomew's, Smithfield* (1921), and Guildhall MSS., L.37/9512-3.)

From the steward's accounts can be gained an insight into 'my master's chamber at the Court', as he called the room assigned to Secretary Petre and his wife in each of the favourite palaces. The few items of movable furniture consisted of his two chests and her trunk, bedstead, candlesticks and snuffers, coal-basket, trenchers and table linen; and there were occasional purchases of mats and rushes and of course 'an urinal'. Board was free (the 'bouche of court'), and the only extra expense is illustrated by a month's 'charges in the kitchen at the Court—to my master's cook for so much by him provided for dressing my master's meat, 5s. 3d.'

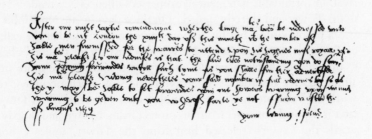

SOME OF PROTECTOR SOMERSET'S PRIVY COUNCILLORS, 1549

A brief letter from the Council at the time of Ket's rebellion. Signed by Edward Seymour, Duke of Somerset; Thomas Cranmer, Archbishop of Canterbury; Richard Rich, Lord Rich, Lord Chancellor; William Paulet, Lord St. John, Great Master of the Household; Thomas Wriothesley, Earl of Southampton; William Paget, Lord Paget, Comptroller; Sir William Petre and Sir Thomas Smith, Principal Secretaries; William Parr, Marquis of Northampton; and Sir John Baker, Speaker.

CHAPTER VI

Secretary under Northumberland

1 Somerset and Warwick

SOMERSET'S protectorate had ended; power was now in the hands of Warwick. Utterly selfish and unscrupulous, he lacked Somerset's religious convictions and ideals, despite his being in the van of the extreme Protestant party. The victor lost no time in trying to crush his former rival. A formidable statement of Somerset's offences was tendered to him in the Tower and abjectly signed. On three days in late November Petre was a prison visitor, but his accounts give no hint whether the calls were on Somerset, Smith or Cecil. He was also busy on the Council's behalf in examining the public accounts and trying to remedy the more pressing administrative disorders. As Secretary he was much occupied, too, in work for Parliament, which assembled on 4 November.[1] A few weeks later it deposed Somerset from his protectorship by Act, and shortly afterwards the Council released him from the Tower, under a bond of £10,000 to stay at Sheen or Syon, both on the Thames. Other Acts aimed at suppressing all anti-enclosure agitation, thus reversing Somerset's policy, and ordered the wholesale burning of the prohibited Latin missals and service-books. The Council's injunction to the bishops for their destruction followed hard on the heels of the statute. Petre did not sign the order, dated Christmas Day, nor did North, now Chancellor of the Court of Augmentations, with whom he supped that evening; but that cannot be construed as lack of sympathy with the reformers.

The New Year 1550 brought Petre 'a gilt bowl with a cover' from the King; the messenger's gratuity, which was customarily about one-tenth of the value of the gift, suggests that the royal plate received was worth about £10. The domination of Warwick's party was emphasized by the issue of a New Year's honours list. Warwick himself had recently become Lord High Admiral. Russell and St. John were raised to the dignities of Earls of Bedford and Wiltshire and were appointed Lord Privy Seal and Lord Treasurer. The Comptroller was elevated to the peerage as Baron Paget of Beaudesert, his Staffordshire seat; and Wingfield became Comptroller in his place. Petre's name did not appear, for he had already gained preferment. The treasurership of the Court of First Fruits had conveniently become vacant through death. It was granted on 20 October 1549 to Petre and entitled him to £120 a year for life, but the inclusive salary had to provide also for 'the diets of him and his clerks, for chests, boxes, bags, parchment, paper, ink, green wax, cloth, boat and carriage hire, with other necessaries'.* As Treasurer, he received frequent Council warrants to make payments for various purposes out of the Court's income. Petre's was a mediocre reward in comparison with others: fitting, no doubt, for a man of moderation whose tongue had been more than usually slow in offering an opinion in the time of crisis; but ample recompense for being 'stayed' from returning to the King. Having been required to remain with the London group, he probably expected little more than to be allowed to retain office, which was not conceded to two prominent supporters, of whose influence Warwick was jealous. Arundel, the Lord Chamberlain, was dismissed on a charge of peculation, amerced in the fantastic sum of £12,000, and confined to his house, though his liberty was soon restored and two-thirds of his fine remitted. Southampton was compulsorily retired from the Council. He was allowed to leave London in the following June, but restricted under penalty of 5,000 marks to Hampshire, his home county, where he died next month, possibly by poison self-administered. Under his will made shortly beforehand he named Petre as overseer and bequeathed him a basin and a silver ewer. Of the same age, his rise to power had been more spectacular than Petre's but he had suffered two sudden falls. So far from helping Somerset, both Arundel and Southampton had given Warwick powerful aid in the previous October; yet they were betrayed. Warwick had revealed himself in his true colours. Cecil and Smith were soon liberated on parole under bonds of £1,000 and £3,000 respectively.

Warwick's first act of foreign policy was to negotiate peace with France, which had taken advantage of the revolts in the previous summer to attack the fortresses around Boulogne. Bedford, Paget, Petre and Mason were chosen to treat for the surrender of the town.

Before going abroad, Petre slipped away from Court to see his wife and baby son, John, born five days before Christmas. Without returning to London, he joined his colleagues at Gravesend, the place from which the overland journey to Dover usually began. His train of fourteen horses and seven servants had made the short ride through Horndon-on-the-Hill to Tilbury ferry on 22 January, 'what time they brought my master to the waterside, going towards Calais'. A storm in mid-Channel drove the envoys' ship back to Dover, and the start of the conference was further delayed by arguments over the place for the meetings. The emissaries' instructions embraced other matters in dispute. As their task was difficult

* His personal accounts give quarterly sums of £30. By the same patent Petre was also assigned a task: to receive to the King's use the income from the recent clerical subsidy (*Cal. Pat.*, *Edw. VI*, iii, 24). The patent is in the family archives (E.R.O., D/DP O49).

they were given wide discretionary powers, and Petre had already been occupied in working out their *modus operandi*.[2] To retain the Boulonnais had become impracticable. The cession of Boulogne, if it could be agreed upon without loss of honour, would bring in a large sum of money and put an end to the heavy cost of maintenance. Paget, advocate of peace, was insistent that England should give way on any reasonable basis and drop all claim to the twenty-year-old debt of half a million crowns. The French commissioners, who included the redoubtable Gaspar de Coligny, Duke of Châtillon, knew their own strength. Negotiations were concluded with remarkable speed by 24 March. The price demanded by Warwick and finally agreed for handing over the town and fortresses intact was 200,000 crowns on delivery of Boulogne and another 200,000 crowns soon afterwards. The peace terms secured were favourable to England. Much of the credit goes to the silent, formidable Petre, to whom Lloyd's oft-quoted remark by Châtillon refers. ' "Ah, we had gained the other 200,000 crowns", the French commissioner declared, *"but for the man who said nothing"* ':[3] a rare testimonial for an able diplomat to use of another, and a substantial figure saved for the treasury. It is a memorable remark because Secretary Petre left behind so much more evidence of his work than of his personality. He made the last stage of the return journey to London on 29 March: 'To the Lord Paget's servants being watermen in reward for bringing my master from Gravesend, 3s. 4d.'

The term 'Mr. Secretaries Peter and Wotton' re-appeared in the Council attendances next day, but not for long. On 23 April Petre sailed again, in company with Paget, Cobham and Mason (the French secretary), as the plans for the surrender of Boulogne were to be made at the French court. Mason had just been made a councillor, and Cobham, the Deputy of Calais, had occasionally had friendly dealings with Petre; for example, at the previous Christmas, when he arranged to send over to Petre a hogshead of French wine—perhaps free of duty. If any reports were sent home they have not been preserved. After Mass at Amiens Cathedral, there was a great ceremony when, according to Edward's journal, the envoys were cordially received by the nobles.[4] A gratuity of a sovereign to 'one of the King's wardrobe for bringing certain of the King's apparel for my master' before his leaving England suggests that Petre was arrayed in costly satin and rich gown. Mason remained as ambassador. The Deputy and Petre, Van der Delft informed the Emperor on 11 May, 'are leaving tomorrow for England; the King has presented them with silver-gilt plate'—Petre in fact got six pieces.[5] Before returning home, he also invested in silver plate, eight candlesticks, four bowls, four salts and a dozen trenchers being bought from William Abeel of Calais for an unknown sum, of which

£41 6s. 8d. was the second and final instalment. For £10 he bought four pieces of cloth containing a hundred ells in all through Sir William Dansell, the King's agent in Flanders and Governor of the Merchant Adventurers. Edward's diary refers to his emissaries having brought back the treaty and a 'testimonial of the oath which confessed that I was supreme head of the church of England and Ireland, and also King of Ireland'. He was clearly gratified with the work of his Secretary, who had discharged his second mission to France in 1550 with satisfactory results. Such embassies often proved costly to the envoys, who habitually complained about their personal losses. On 27 May 22s. was given by Petre's steward to the messenger who brought him £266 13s. 4d. 'by the Council's warrant', which had been authorized a few days before his departure: 'Warrant for 400 marks in reward to Mr. Secretary Petre towards his furniture [equipment] at his voyage into France, and for 4 li. diets by the day, whereof two months beforehand at his journey into France.'[6] This scale of remuneration seems reasonable, if not generous.

Petre was then involved in the final negotiations for ceding Boulogne and for receiving the 400,000 crowns, which his taciturnity had wrung out of the French, instead of half that sum. Their ambassadors, including Châtillon, with four Marshals of France, were to come over to London to obtain the King's ratification of the treaty. The first half of the money was safely transported. So the Frenchmen must be received with every mark of respect. Petre visited Paget and supped with Sir Anthony Aucher, the Master of the Jewel House, to discuss the ceremonies. Aucher was to lend plate for feasts and to release more for gifts. That was not enough. On the day of Petre's return to the Council Chamber (23 May) a further gift of £1,500 in cash was authorized: no wonder that Petre sent his steward at once to Sir John Godsalve of the Mint. Durham Place was set aside for the ambassadors' residence. Paget and Petre attended them there and at their reception by the King; they also introduced the ambassadors one day at the Council Board.

Petre had reported about the mission on his rejoining the Council, which was augmented by two—a new member, Lord Clinton, and an old one, the Duke of Somerset. But the Secretary was not surprised by the presence of the ex-Protector, for on the previous day he had called on Paget, who doubtless explained how the 'whole Council' recently decided on reinstatement. He was absent from meetings throughout August, when the Court went on progress in Surrey owing to the outbreak of plague in London, but he was with the councillors again at Oatlands on 5 September.* Their number was further increased by two—the

* The steward's accounts ended 10 July; those for the next 3½ years are not preserved.

Earl of Huntingdon, an adherent of Warwick, and William Cecil, Somerset's former secretary and from that day Principal Secretary in place of Dr. Wotton, who had resigned that office but remained a councillor. What Cecil's status had been since his release from the Tower at the beginning of the year is very obscure.[7] Of Wotton's eleventh-month partnership with Petre, practically nothing is known. Wotton must have taken away or destroyed all his correspondence on resignation.

Petre's attendance was almost continuous during the autumn and winter of 1550–1. By that time the plight of England was even worse than at Henry's death. Foreign loans had still to be sought, at exorbitant rates. The cloth trade was suffering from acute depression. Poverty was increasing. A bad harvest aggravated the prevailing distress. Injunctions, drawn up by Petre, were issued in an attempt to keep down the high price of corn, and councillors met under the threat of further insurrection. Warwick's party in the Council was determined not to allow the former Protector to become omnipotent again. Sir John Allen, the Lord Chancellor of Ireland, received a letter from Petre, who added to the Council's formal dispatch his own words of encouragement—language of the sort one associates with the writer, always anxious to help a colleague looking after the good of 'the common wealth' in distant parts but getting little official recognition.[8] The country had every need for the advice of such sober men as Petre and Cecil, for a period of bitterness and intrigue almost unparalleled in the annals of the Council was ahead. What advice was tendered by the Secretaries, how much of it was accepted, it is impossible to say. The tone of the minutes becomes increasingly sinister; and behind the matter-of-fact entries can be heard angry words and violent strife. For these months there are preserved a few of Petre's letters to Cecil— doubly welcome in the absence of his personal accounts—which tell of the kindlier relations existing between the less exalted councillors. The first was sent from Ingatestone on 4 March 1551.

I thank you for your gentle letters which I received by this bearer, the sight of whom at the first made me a little sorry for that I suspected I had been sent for, and had appointed certain things of my own to be done tomorrow; but your news made me sorry indeed, being all of such sorrowful sorts as are too heavy for my weak stomach to digest, but God will amend all this if we amend ourselves among the rest. I am glad of the likelihood of my Lord Paget's placing in the room of my Lord Chamberlain, for so shall he that can well serve have good occasion to tarry at the court. For the rest I defer till our next meeting which I intend God so willing shall be upon Sunday next. I thank you for your book. My little ones, when they shall be able, shall send you some taste of their profit in

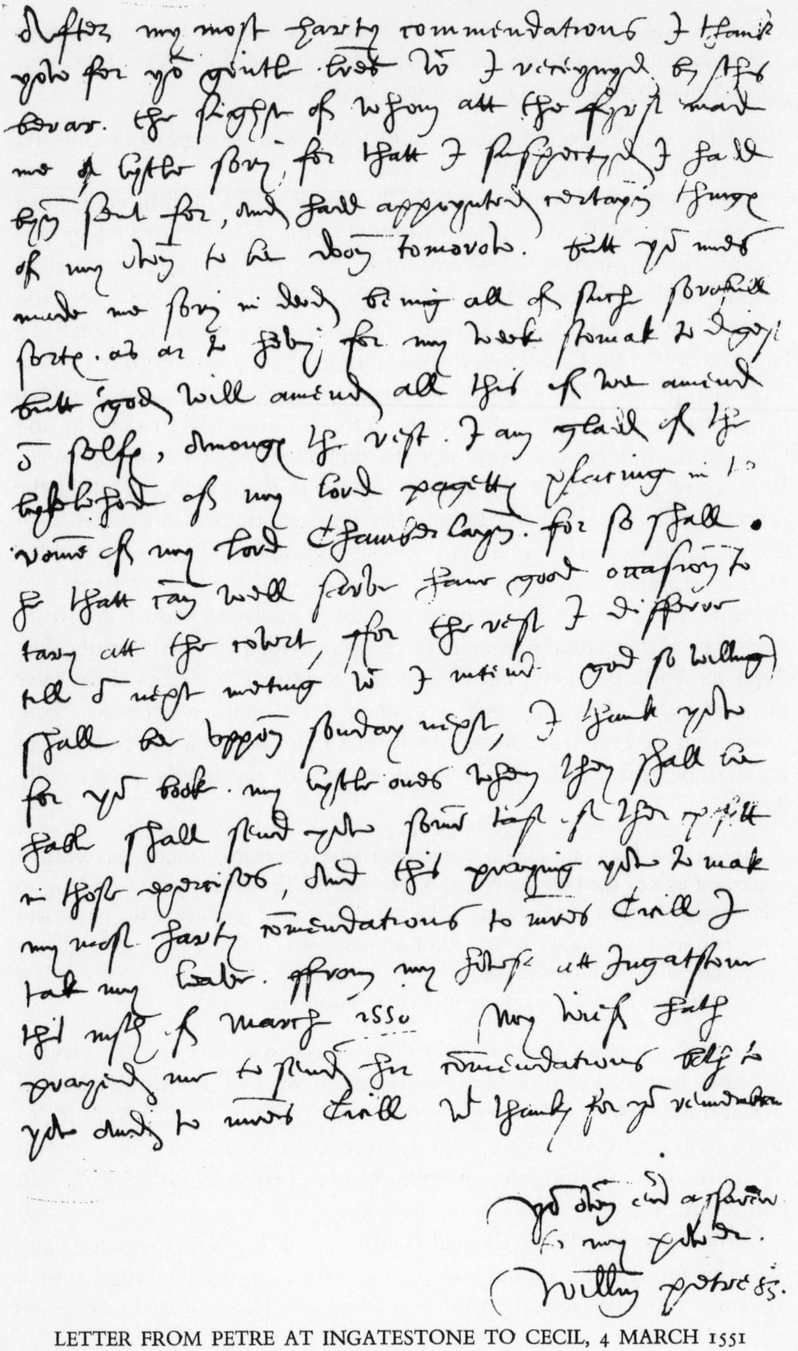

LETTER FROM PETRE AT INGATESTONE TO CECIL, 4 MARCH 1551

those exercises. And thus praying you to make my most hearty commendations to Mistress Cecil I take my leave. My wife hath prayed me to send her commendations both to you and to Mistress Cecil.[9]

The 'little ones' were Thomasine and Catherine, now nearly eight and six years old; John was well over a year.

Paget's hopes of becoming Lord Chancellor a few months earlier had not been realized;[10] nor was he promoted to the office of Lord Chamberlain on the death of Lord Wentworth, who had replaced the Earl of Arundel and was succeeded by Lord Darcy. The rift between Paget and Warwick widened. Aware that his influence was weakening, Paget had begun to avoid the Council in the summer of 1550, and after May 1551 he seldom appeared. His single surviving account-book, for 1550-2, which names his guests, has one reference to Petre.[11] On 12 March 1551, he and Cecil were 'bidden and came not' to dinner at Paget's London house. Both Secretaries were at all Council sessions in these weeks. During the preceding half year, Cecil's biographer laments, there is no evidence of the younger Secretary having any special assignment; 'Petre was used for high level, diplomatic purposes'.[12] Throughout the eclipse of Paget and Arundel, Petre and Wiltshire must have been in charge of such constructive work as they could persuade the faction-divided Council to authorize. After 12 April, however, Petre's seat was to remain unoccupied for over three months. The long gap is explained by another letter to Cecil, written on 14 May from Petre's manor of East Horndon (six miles from Ingatestone and a little nearer London), where the family occasionally stayed.

> I thank you for your sundry letters and advertisements, among the which I account one of the best the recovery of your health which I pray God long to continue. As for mine, whether it be this ill favoured weather as the physicians say it is, or my naughty body full of humours that is the cause, my fit still remaineth with me howbeit not so sore as it was in the beginning. So gentle is it that it giveth me leave to write these few words unto you.[13]

Cecil's sickness was a brief one, but Petre's gave some anxiety to his friend Wotton, who had resumed ambassadorial duties with the Imperial court at Augsburg. He was genuinely relieved, he told Cecil on 10 August, 'to hear of Mr. Petre's recovery, whose presence at the Court will give you the more leisure to enjoy the sweetness of your private life at home, which you so much desire'.[14]

In the meantime Warwick had been using all his craft to secure sway over the young King's mind and arranged for him to attend the Council meetings in person, secretly primed in advance. 'He instigated Edward to dispense with counter-signatures upon his documents. In this way he gradually freed Edward from the restrictions of his minority and at the same time bound him closer to himself.'[15] The relations of the King's Secretaries with Warwick were becoming increasingly difficult.

Further stages in the downward path of the government were reached in the summer of 1551. By two proclamations in June and August the coinage was successively lowered, first the tester (1s.) to 9d. and the groat (4d.) to 3d., then, after a shamefully short interval, to 6d. and 2d.[16] The undated draft of the latter is in Petre's hand.[17] The city companies at once raised prices, especially those of victuals, despite the Council's remonstrances. Within a week of his rejoining the councillors and a week in advance of the second depreciation, Petre asked them for a special receipt for £7,000 delivered by him as Treasurer of the First Fruits to the Mint 'before the [first] proclamation and of the decaying of money'.[18] His wisdom in covering himself in these days of crumbling currency is significant. An echo of his actions during the time of the councillors' suicidal juggling with coinage, when inside knowledge gave them abnormal scope for dishonest practices, was heard in March 1553. It told how his attempts to deliver cash into the royal coffers, well before the double debasement, had been frustrated by another's obstinacy. At the time of the first on 9 July 1551, Treasurer Petre had £10,134 in his hands, which thereon fell in value to £7,601, and on 17 August he had £3,930, which was 'abated' that day to £2,620, a total loss of £3,843. Before the earlier proclamation he had 'made often declaration and tender' of the treasure remaining in his office to the late Cofferer, who refused to receive any of it. Baker, Chancellor of the First Fruits, was given a warrant to allow Petre the full sum.[19]

The drastic debasement was all the more disgraceful because the Crown had recently made yet another great haul, by appropriating most of the endowments of the religious colleges and chantries on the ground that they existed for superstitious uses. The task of surveying and suppressing these foundations, unlike the dissolution of the monasteries, had been decentralized by the appointment of county commissioners. Choral and other elementary schools were to be abolished with the chantries, but grammar schools attached to chantries were to be preserved if recommended by two special commissioners for the whole country. These were Sir Walter Mildmay, General Surveyor of the Court of Augmentations, and Robert Kelway, Surveyor of the Court of Wards and Liveries, who had been joined with St. John and Petre in the previous year to look into the Crown revenues. Mildmay and Kelway were now given discretionary power to assign suitable endowments for continuing such grammar schools, which were then deemed in accordance with official sycophancy to have been founded by Edward. Among the medieval schools thus saved from extinction was one at Chelmsford, maintained from the income of a chantry in the parish church. By its continuation warrant, dated February 1551, it was to have a corporation of four governors. The nominees were Sir William Petre, Sir Walter Mildmay, Sir Henry Tyrell and Thomas Mildmay, for term of their lives. It was they, with the inhabitants of Chelmsford and district, who petitioned the Crown to establish the school, and it was only natural that it should be under their control. Thomas Mildmay of Chelmsford, a monastic visitor, had secured in 1540 the manor of Moulsham in Chelmsford and built Moulsham Hall, a fine mansion. Walter was his fourth son. Tyrell, of ancient Essex family and Sheriff this year, was Thomas's brother-in-law, and closely connected with Lady Petre. So it was that the 'Chelmsford Free Grammar School of King Edward VI' was resurrected, after the Crown had confiscated the income of the two parochial chantries and re-endowed it with almost twice the sum from three other Essex chantries and gilds. The letters patent, dated 24 March 1551, authorized the governors to appoint a master and usher; also, with the advice of the Bishop of London, to make statutes. The 'foundation' of the school was thus due to a family group of mid-Essex gentry, most of whom were also officials of the central government.* 'That there are so few Edward VI Grammar Schools' (the number in the whole country is less than twenty) 'we owe to the rapacity of the boy-king's ministers of state';[20] but the Principal Secretaries may be exonerated. It is an interesting commentary on the privy councillors' local influence that, of the nineteen schools in Essex reported on by the chantry commissioners, only one other school was continued; that was at Saffron Walden, where Sir Thomas Smith had been educated.

The Council had left London because of the mortal sweating sickness for Hampton Court, where Petre was at work on 2 August. Three weeks

* Although its contents were known from the official enrolment, the 'original' school charter was long believed lost. It was in fact entrusted to the senior governor, was carefully preserved by his descendants, and, with other school archives, was rediscovered when the present Lord Petre in turn entrusted all his family muniments to the Essex Record Office in 1939 (D/DP O28-42). Only a few weeks later, I was also fortunate in acquiring for the County the Mildmay archives from Thomas Mildmay's descendants, among them the finest early map of an Essex estate (D/DM P1); it shows a detailed drawing in elevation of the 'wholesome and gentlemanlike house', converted into the school, which had been the refectory of the suppressed Grey Friars' house in Moulsham on the south bank of the river; the building was rented from Thomas Mildmay. This stimulated a faithful master of the Grammar School, J. H. Johnson, M.A., to write a history of it in good time to arouse interest in its quatercentenary (*Essex Review*, liv-lv (1945-6); re-issued as a book in 1946). For other Essex grammar schools, see A. L. Rowse, *The England of Elizabeth* (1950), 498-9; for Felsted School, see below, p. 257.

later (p. 121), he was commissioned to visit the Lady Mary at one of her Essex mansions. Riding thither and then on to Windsor to report, so soon after his getting back into the official saddle, brought on a recurrence of leg trouble. Petre left the Castle, a sick man again, filled with gloomy forebodings. His prophecies were to be fulfilled before he returned in October. This second interval is bridged by three more letters to Cecil, the first two from London. On 9 September Petre wrote:

> I doubt not but that Cliff my man hath declared unto you the state I have been in sithens your departing and even so I do continue but with good hope of short amendment. This day lying in my bed I heard of your return towards the court, whereof like as I was glad so was I further requested to pray you to be good unto this bearer in his suit which he will open unto you. He sayeth he is chosen to be one of the Savoy according to the order of their foundation. I have been desired to help this man, wherein because I could do nothing being absent, I have thought it good to pray you to be their good master with your advice and further as you shall see occasion. If he shall be found otherwise meet, in my poor opinion he shall be so much the more worthy to enjoy the thing for that he is chosen (as they say) according to their statutes.
>
> Touching myself I can write yet nothing certain of my return for that I am outstaying when the flux of humours in my leg shall be so stayed as I may be able to endure labour and standing. The physicians do think this to come of the dregs of my long sickness, for that the humour falleth into a weak place hurt not long sithens.[21]

The next letter shows that the invalid had been reflecting much on good and evil, especially the endless angling for places. The Council had recently ordered the clergy to preach against greed. Perhaps Petre remembered the trenchant words of Thomas Lever's sermon at Paul's Cross: 'Covetous officers', he declared, 'have so used this matter that those goods which did serve to the relief of the poor be now turned to maintain worldly, wicked, covetous ambition.'[22] A government appointment was vacant. The Savoy, rebuilt by Henry VII as a hospital, had been granted a charter by his son. As chief steward of the Savoy lands, Petre had some influence in filling the office of master, especially having lent the master and brethren £240 on mortgage for five years.[23] His mind dwelt on the prize and the many anglers, some of whom would have no qualms about diverting the stream of charitable funds into baser channels. So Cecil found that his correspondent had 'waxen a preacher' himself. Petre's own text was also 'Thou shalt not covet'. Not constrained to sober, official language, he broke into vivid metaphor. To him the prevalent sin was 'fishing in the tempestuous seas of the world for gain and wicked mammon', instead of 'fishing for men'. Despite what he had recently done for Chelmsford Grammar School his conscience disturbed him and he voiced his misgivings to the younger man. Dated 14 September 1551, this is perhaps the most self-revealing of Petre's letters.* The seemingly casual remark at the end refers apparently to William, his fourth son (p. 125) and illustrates his generation's acceptance of a very high infant mortality rate.

I thank you for your letters and also for your pains for the Savoy. I doubt not but there be (as you write) good or rather great plenty of anglers for it; if they do angle for the good continuance of the poor men and of the house I like their angling well. And whosoever has most desire to do so I would he might take the fish; marry, I would all things were done in order, and every man called to such place specially rather of other men's vocation than of their own labour. At the beginning the apostles left their fishing of fishes and became fishers of men, and now we who talk much of Christ and His Holy Word have, I fear me, used a much contrary way; for we leave fishing for men and fish again in the tempestuous seas of this world for gain and wicked mammon. Thus you see lying here alone I am waxen a preacher.

I do send you herewith a notice of a commission for the visitation of the Savoy. W. Say was not in London and therefore I did it myself, you may put on as you think good. I have put a clause that the commissioners may reform things; which I did for that when they shall know my Lord's pleasure they may do the same after their advertisement without any new commission.

My leg, I thank God, beginneth well to amend. Tomorrow I intend to ride towards my house in a litter. I go there rather to comfort my weak wife, who is somewhat troubled with the death of her young son.[24]

Next month the councillors chose a lawyer and one of their own number, Sir Robert Bowes, as master of the Savoy. The third letter, written on 30 September, came from Ingatestone.

I was in good hope at the receipt of your letters that I should within few days have been able to travel towards the court, for my leg was in good towardness of amendment, and about four days past I rode four miles thinking to essay what I was able to endure. The same night the humours had again such a flux into my leg that the next day my leg brake out again and ran more and was in worse case than it was yet at any time. Sythen that I have again kept my bed and so do still, which rest I perceive is the only remedy for this flux, which (I assure you) hath and doth much trouble me for fear of the continuance thereof; I will from henceforth learn to be more wise.[25]

---

* In December 1549 he had obtained the stewardship of the lands jointly with his brother 'William Petre of London gent.' at an annual fee of £4 (E.R.O., D/DP Z13/3). In 1555 Petre's accounts show his receipt of £14 for 3½ years' fee. Some leaden pipes from the Savoy were carried in 1554 to his town house.

The fact of Petre's being still tied to his couch is important in the light of events about to take place; without this knowledge, there might have been reason for thinking that he, like other leading councillors, was suspected by Warwick; had he been under suspicion, he would have been dispatched to the Tower.

Hinting darkly about a reaction in favour of Somerset, Warwick had been aiming at complete mastery through deep-laid schemes which probably matured in September, when Somerset was kept away from the Council by sickness in his household.[26] On the day Petre wrote from Essex, they had summoned Somerset to attend again. Warwick's next step was a further distribution of honours among his party. He himself was created Duke of Northumberland, and Dorset (Lady Jane Grey's father) became Duke of Suffolk. Paulet, Earl of Wiltshire was made Marquis of Winchester, and Herbert, Earl of Pembroke. Knighthoods were bestowed on Warwick's cousin Henry Dudley and on Cecil, 'who had deserted Somerset for Warwick'.[27] Northumberland, now equal in rank with Somerset and temporarily *persona grata* with his recently elevated supporters, felt strong enough to crush rivals. The Council resolved to investigate Somerset's debts owing to the Crown. He was sent to the Tower, where he was soon joined by Paget, whose influence in the government had made him too formidable for Northumberland's peace of mind. On Paget's movements shortly beforehand, fresh light comes from his West Drayton steward's account-book.[28] After the meeting when the new honours were announced, he evidently withdrew again to his Middlesex home, whence he posted back to London on the morning following Somerset's confinement. Whether this was at the Council's summons or whether like Somerset he felt it wise to show his face is not known, but he had been placed at once under house arrest.[29] At last the able Paget was struck down. The excuse which Northumberland gave himself for action was an alleged plot of Somerset's to invite him, with Northampton and Pembroke, to a meal at Paget's house and there assassinate them. The list of guests at Drayton disclose how Lord and Lady Paget had entertained 'the Duke of Somerset and his train' to supper on 21 September. But the intended victims in this incredible story did not sit at Paget's table (his steward's daily lists bear the stamp of completeness). It is of some interest, however, that on the day of Paget's commital to the Tower the Earl of Huntingdon and his brother Sir Edward Hastings supped at Drayton.[30] Were they merely trying to console Lady Paget? In the wake of Somerset and Paget followed many others, including Arundel (his second fall in two years) and Wingfield.

Petre did not return to the Council until 28 October. He was not among those recently summoned to London. Convalescence had absolved him from implication in either party's machinations. Though not in complete sympathy with Somerset and Paget, he knew that the charges leading to their incarceration were flimsy enough; but the vacant seats betokened extra need for keeping his wonted silence. The proceedings in Somerset's one-day trial before his peers on 1 December were grossly partial. Moreover, the fact that the assassination plot was not mentioned, nor was Paget brought to trial, made it fairly conclusive that it was a fabrication.[31] The Duke of Somerset, the King's uncle and former Protector, was beheaded on Tower Hill three weeks later. His execution was 'the crowning-point of Northumberland's infamy'.[32] Petre was absent from the Council for three weeks—two before and one after the trial.

Petre did not remain at Court for its Twelfth Night festivities. On 4 January 1552 he rode towards Ingatestone, though himself in no festive mood. True, he had again avoided loss of liberty and office, but it was a time of insecurity and anxiety. A week before Christmas his old acquaintance, Lord Rich, had suddenly surrendered the Great Seal in somewhat mysterious circumstances. Petre was among the 'eligible persons' to be Keeper during the Chancellor's actual or alleged sickness.[33] Edward gave the Seal to Goodrich, Bishop of Ely. Rich retired to his Essex mansion at Leighs; yet another victim of Northumberland's hostility, he had narrowly escaped a term in the Tower.[34] Petre reached his own country house, glad to leave the bleakness of government affairs for the warmth of the family circle and to enjoy a fortnight's leisure; but still free to return to Court. He did so shortly before the fourth session of Parliament. Its lasting memorial is 'The Second Prayer Book of Edward', properly the personal memorial to Cranmer. There is nothing to show Petre's reaction to it.

A bill concerning 'clothiers in towns' was committed* to Petre, whose knowledge of the woollen industry extended to manufactures in the West Country as well as Essex and East Anglia, for his name is prominently connected with the Glastonbury scheme of 1551, when a colony of Flemish weavers had been settled by the Duke of Somerset in the abbey buildings.[35] On the Protector's fall a commission was appointed to investigate the Glastonbury plan. Petre compiled the administrative documents. The winter and spring of 1551–2 was a period of continuous toil on parliamentary and conciliar affairs. In April Paget was ignominiously stripped of both Garter and George. He was also dismissed from the

* 'Mr. Secretary Petre' is written against the entry of the bill in the Commons' Journals. 'Usually such a note indicates a committal'; in the early journals, however, not 'a formal committal for the purpose of amendment' but rather that the house entrusted the bill to the member named for perusal. (J. E. Neale, 'The Elizabethan Acts of Supremacy and Uniformity', Trans. Roy. Hist. Soc., lxv (1950), 311.) Cf. pp. 105, 165.

chancellorship of the Duchy of Lancaster for alleged corruption.[36] The Court of Star Chamber fined him £8,000 in June, on his humble submission. He was released from the Tower that month, but confined to West Drayton. Later he managed to discharge the fine, mitigated to £4,000; but lay low, awaiting the time for his revenge on Northumberland.

On arrival at Greenwich on 14 June, Petre found that the duke had left for the north a day or two earlier; he was in fact to be away ten weeks. The Secretaries had immediate consultation on outstanding business; then Cecil quitted the Court for five weeks. Although the King's health had begun to cause concern during the past winter, he recovered sufficiently to travel south-westwards on a summer progress. When he left Westminster for Oatlands on 7 July Edward recorded: 'My Lord Chamberlain, my Lord Privy Seal, Mr. Vice-Chamberlain [Darcy, Bedford and Gates], and Mr. Secretary Petre went with me this progress.' It was a slightly incomplete list, but his note that 'my Council was dispersed' was true enough. Cecil re-appeared at Guildford on the 20th. It was then Petre's turn for leave. On the day of their changing places a report addressed to them both came from Wotton and Thirlby. 'As for the Latin' (they were referring to some long allegations), 'if you will take the pains to read it over, if you have none other time to spare, while you ride a-hunting, you shall well perceive that there hath been much labour taken.'[37] It conjures up a curious scene of the never-idle Secretaries having to pore over Latin memoranda in odd moments snatched between the chamber and the chase. They also received from Wotton a personal note, in his jocular style, revealing a warm, friendly personality.

If your answer be as well taken as we have well taken labour for the searching of it, I would trust it might be worth to me a warrant not for £1,000 out of the Exchequer (for my Lord Treasurer would think that too much) but of a buck out of Eltham Park to make merry withal among my neighbours at Canterbury, where I trust to be shortly, not being appointed to follow the Court this progress. But if my answer seem not worth so much (as *Veritas* is not ever to all ears most pleasant), then shall my neighbours, instead of a buck, be content with a fat goose or a duck. When my Lords of the Council's letters came last day to us, my Lord of Norwich [Thirlby] said, That letter indeed was the Lords of the Council's but the deviser and the causer of it was a good fellow called Mr. Secretary Petre, who thought long to come away from the Court and was afraid lest he might be stayed there awhile for this answer, and therefore made haste to have it; but I, you know well enough, could not believe that.[38]

The subject of the report which Wotton had striven to prepare, so that Petre might depart for home, was the Anglo-Flemish commercial treaty and all that lay behind it. For the past four or five months Petre had been engaged in interviews with Scheyfve, Van der Delft's successor in London. Firstly, Scheyfve, about the refusal by English customs officers to allow certain exports to Flanders. Northumberland, the spokesman, called for Petre's opinion. The Imperial ambassador disagreed with Petre, who rejoined that the treaties reserved the laws that either might make for the public weal. Next, it was the English who protested, Petre descending upon the ambassador with a fine sense of grievance. A Flemish ship had fired on an English vessel to make her lower sail; she refused and turned a boarding attack into a capture of her assailant which was discovered to be a pirate ship. Then there was trouble over harbour-dues that Flemish merchants had to pay. Petre referred to his earlier negotiations with Van der Delft and refused to budge. Three months later, when trade relations with France became embittered, Petre was deputed to settle the argument.[39] There is little doubt about his reputation in this sphere.

He was with the King again at Basing, Winchester's house, on 9 September, the Court having progressed as far as Southampton where it turned homewards. Northumberland resumed attendance at Wilton, Pembroke's house, a week earlier; the duke had been accompanied by Pembroke in his northern expedition, because (as rumour had it) he did not trust the earl.[40] Hampton Court was reached at the end of September.* Edward had been on progress for nearly three months. Petre then rode off to Ingatestone for a few days' sojourn. Thereafter, for some months, he put in an almost uninterrupted spell of duty.

2 Edward and Petre reorganize the Council's Work

It is not easy to gather what was going on in the leaders' minds in the winter of 1552–3. How far Edward's own ability led him to withstand Northumberland's baneful influence and to think independently is a further problem. It was apparently about the beginning of 1552 that Edward first began to have official dealings with Secretary Petre, who was

---

* On the return journey, Northumberland, Darcy, Cobham, the Secretaries and Sir John Cheke held a visitation of Eton College, where they settled differences between 'the master and the fellows' and amended certain college statutes deemed to be 'superstitious' (*Edward's Journal*). C. Read, *op. cit.*, 91, 'Petre took a month off and left him (Cecil) to carry the whole administrative load', is not correct (cf. *A.P.C.*, iv, 140, 144–5, and the *Journal*, 29 Sept., which shows that Petre was soon back in London, in company with Wotton and Smith, to meet two French envoys about another trade dispute).

acting more as liaison between the King and the Council than as writer of the royal letters. This association has scarcely been noticed, partly because of the serious misdating of certain documents a century ago. If the fresh evidence on the reorganization of the work borne by the Council has been correctly interpreted, it seems clear that, whilst Northumberland preferred secretarial contact with Cecil, Edward chose to consult Petre.* Cecil was still inferior in status, which was natural enough at this stage as Petre was his senior in office and age, but 'it is surprising to discover', writes his biographer, 'that not one of the surviving drafts of letters which went from the King or the Council to English agents overseas bears traces of his [Cecil's] composition, though many of them are in Petre's hand'. There is a further comment. 'Petre seems to have outranked him and to have handled the official contacts with foreign diplomats. . . . Cecil's responsibilities were confined to the details of administration. He remained a competent servant, he never became, as he was to become under Elizabeth, a great minister. For that matter no one did under Northumberland.' Petre indeed was standing in relation to Cecil much as Paget had stood to Petre when they shared office. 'Some significance may attach to the fact that Cecil was selected (in 1551) as the spokesman of the Council, to set forth the official version of Somerset's plotting to the Imperial ambassador, though Petre, who was present, would normally have handled such matters.'[41] At that time Edward refers to Cecil merely as 'another Secretary' and hardly mentions him by name, in contrast to Petre who frequently figures in his journal, though it discloses little about the boy's opinions of his ministers.

The Council had already become overburdened with work in 1551. About the same time the emptiness of the treasury forced the government to prosecute every means of replenishing it. These factors resulted in the appointment of several 'commissions', in effect, committees of the Council, to whom were added a few non-members. On 30 December, Edward recorded in his journal: 'Commission was made out to the Bishop of Ely [Goodrich], the Lord Privy Seal [Bedford], Sir John Gates, Sir William Petre, Sir Robert Bowes, and Sir Walter Mildmay, for calling in my debts.'[42]

Two months later reorganization of the work by committees was initiated. Edward's diary, on 3 March 1552, adding a little to the language of the patent roll,[43] emphasized the need for quicker dispatch of affairs. Neither Secretary was troubled with nomination to the commission given

* For a more detailed examination of the material, see F. G. Emmison, 'A plan of Edward VI and Secretary Petre for reorganizing the Privy Council's work, 1552–53' (*Bulletin of the Inst. of Hist. Research* (Univ. of London), xxxi (1958), 203–10).

executive powers to deal with 'the great number of suits and requests which he daily exhibited unto us and the importune calling of the suitors of all sorts'. Nine commissioners were appointed to examine the machinery of the revenue courts in order to raise the maximum income. It appears from their report that only six met; 'nothing is known about the reasons for which Petre', Treasurer of the First Fruits, who is named in the patent but not in the journal, 'stood down'.[44] Edward also listed twenty councillors including both Secretaries 'to attend the matters of the state'; and added: 'I will sit with them once a week to hear the debating of things of most importance.'

Once established, the committee were not allowed to rest even during the summer recess. New and enlarged commissions were issued in July for further sales of Crown lands and for collecting the debts. Petre served on the latter body; their powers were strengthened this time to secure the personal attendance of debtors, who could be imprisoned or fined at discretion. These commissioners were appointed, it has been stated, because of 'the King's necessity and the jealousy [distrust] of the integrity of the officers that handled and received his revenues'.[45] As Treasurer of the First Fruits, Petre was called upon to produce his own account: it has been preserved in the public records, a book with upwards of a thousand entries.[46] But the Treasurer of the Augmentations, Sir John Williams, got two months' imprisonment.[47]

Early in 1553, if not before, a second reorganization of the Council's business was being considered. Knowledge of this rested mainly on a long, undated note by Edward in his journal and entitled 'Certain articles devised and delivered by the king's majesty for quicker, better and more orderly dispatch of causes by his majesty's privy council'. The plan was designed to relieve the Council of extraneous matters, to regulate procedure by standing orders, to settle how much progress could be achieved when attendances fell below the prescribed figure, and to provide for transaction of urgent affairs. It also laid down that on Friday afternoon the Council would prepare a statement of business completed and outstanding, which the Secretary would show to Edward next morning, and that on Sunday the Secretary would present him with the next week's agenda, which Edward would thereupon allocate to 'Monday afternoon, Tuesday, Wednesday, Thursday, or Friday morning': a vivid outline of Petre's seven-day week. It has not been previously noticed that Edward's 'articles' are similar in content to an undated memorandum in Petre's hand, probably because it was assigned to the beginning of the reign, the six-year error in dating having been followed by later writers. Petre's notes, instead of belonging to February 1547, are of later date than

Edward's, if only by a few days. It is surprising, too, that Edward's insistence, in the articles, on his being personally consulted by the Secretary, which makes nonsense in the case of a boy of only nine years, should not have puzzled historians. The main emphasis is in fact on the measure of control of Council's activities which Edward envisaged, an important point which clearly emerges from collation of his and Petre's versions. The Secretary's is a rationalized form, about half the length of Edward's, although none of his articles is omitted. All Edward's amendments were adopted by Petre, who also incorporated Edward's marginal addition, 'Provided that on Sundays they [the councillors] be present at common-prayer'.*

Edward was now just fifteen. His journal reveals a degree of intelligence above the average, but historians and educationalists do not agree in their rating of it.[48] In November 1552 the Imperial ambassador confirmed an earlier note in Edward's journal by reporting that the King 'had begun to be present at the Council and to attend to certain affairs himself; he is allowed a good deal of freedom; but this fact only serves to enhance suspicions':[49] a ruse of Northumberland to deceive Edward into thinking that he now held the reins seems to be implied. Futile as it is to assess the extent to which the new scheme for ordering the Council's programme was a product of the young King's brain or the result only of discussion with Petre, it may perhaps be suggested that he showed his scheme to Petre, who went through it with him, when they decided on three additional articles; these Edward wrote hurriedly in much less tidy script, whilst he remembered them. Petre afterwards drew up his official version, ignoring juvenile phrases, condensing it into the essentials and recasting the articles (now nineteen in all) into their logical groups—next week's programme, the quorum and questions of debate. Each of the supplementary articles fell into one of the three groups. There remained two final standing orders governing matters that were 'busy' (in the now obsolete sense of involving much work) or required urgent attention (Petre used his own favourite 'depech', dispatch).

* Edward's memorandum is on f. 81 of his journal (B.M., Cott. MS. Nero C. x, printed by Burnet, op. cit., v, 121–4). For Petre's, see P.R.O., S.P. 10/1/15 (Dom. Cal., 1547–80 (1857), 2), where it is assigned to 15 Feb. 1547. A. F. Pollard, England under Protector Somerset (1900), 80, 88–9, accorded some prominence to Petre's version. S.P. 10/1/15 merely has a modern pencil endorsement, 'Feb. 1546/7'; 10/1/16, described in the Calendar as a copy of 10/1/15, is a much later copy and has a MS. note at the head, 'probably temp. late Hen. VIII or Edw., prob. in the hand of Dr. Petre', and is endorsed in pencil, perhaps by the editor, 'circa Feb. 15, beginning of E. VI', i.e. the day of Paget's honours declaration. Dixon (Hist. Church of England, iii, 446) and Froude (Hist. Eng., v, 102) mention Edward's articles, but wrongly assigns them to 1552. Both documents have recently been printed side by side, with notes, by F. G. Emmison, op. cit.

Any 'busy' question was to be referred to a committee appointed to 'rough hew' it.*

Whatever influence Northumberland may have had in earlier (or later) months, it is clear that he took no part in the Edward–Petre organization and methods team of 1552–3, as the duke's return to the Court after a long absence did not occur until a fortnight after the day (15 January) when the articles were to be submitted to the Council. It was a day on which the Council met; that neither Petre nor the scheme is mentioned in the register does not preclude its having been discussed. Graver problems and conciliar strife, however, must have led to its remaining in abeyance. The reason is not difficult to find.

3 Northumberland's Conspiracy and Jane

The King's health was rapidly worsening, and over Christmas his weakness began to cause general alarm. The early promise of a responsible mind, of a sovereign who would go far to rescue the country from its miseries, made the tragedy all the worse to anticipate. Northumberland realized that his own power would cease on the King's death, for Edward would be succeeded, in accordance with his father's will and the statute of 1544, by his half-sister Mary, who would restore popery and punish the statesman who had so violently widened the breach with Rome. Nemesis was now shadowing Northumberland continually. About this time, too, he had pains abdominal as well as mental. 'I fear to be sick', both Secretaries were told in language betraying over-anxiety, 'for that I burn as hot as fire.'[50] On 23 November they were advised in a jointly addressed letter that, as 'his Highness hath nominated personages for managing this weighty and secret affair', no time should be lost; but its nature is not disclosed.[51] These and other letters from the beginning of December were sent from Northumberland's Chelsea house, where he was lurking as well as ailing. When he entered the Council chamber on 29 January it was the first time for over three months, a period for which little is known about English politics—or about Petre's activities. And the next three are equally obscure except for Parliament, which Northumberland had been driven to call for 1 March, after making desperate but inadequate efforts to

* The curious term 'rough hew' was reminiscent of that applied in October 1551 to the commission of thirty-two men for the reform of the canon laws, Petre being one of the eight members assigned first 'to rough hew' or draft it; he was in fact the leader of the civilians, the remaining twenty-four being bishops, divines and common lawyers. The commission was renewed in 1552, Petre again being one of its chief members. (*A.P.C.*, iii, 382, 410, 471; *Edward's Journal*, 10 Feb. 1552; Dixon, *op. cit.*, iii, 351–2, 439–40; Strype's *Cranmer*.) Before they completed their task, the religious tide was to change.

raise funds by a final appropriation of church treasures. His corrupt influence secured the election of many nominated members, but he got little more than a subsidy from an obstructive assembly, which he dissolved after a month. Parliament had committed to Petre, who shared the representation of Essex with Sir John Gates, the Vice-chamberlain, a bill about 'wearing apparel'.[52]

In the spring of 1553 Northumberland made a desperate and ingenious effort to ensure his personal and political survival. Of 'Northumberland's Conspiracy', a recent historian has written:

> We do not know how early he conceived the scheme which, instead of the intractable Mary, should give Edward a successor as docile as himself, but before the end of 1552 it was common talk that he was tampering with the succession. The scheme itself was worthy of the clever, crooked mind which had begotten it. Northumberland had one unmarried son, Lord Guildford Dudley. This youth was to marry one of the four granddaughters of Mary, younger sister of Henry VIII, and the dying King was then to make the bride a wedding-present of his crown. Of the four potential queens Northumberland eventually chose Jane, eldest daughter of Henry Grey, Duke of Suffolk, and the marriage took place on Whitsunday, 21 May 1553.[53]

It was probably a few days before the wedding that Edward had been persuaded to approve Northumberland's draft of the 'Device for the Succession' and to copy it out in his own hand. Edward thereby drastically altered Henry's settlement in order to exclude both his sisters and to prevent Mary from leading England back to Rome. Should he have no heir male, the crown was to pass to 'the Lady Jane's heirs male'.

The two Secretaries regarded the future with acute anxiety. Cecil was walking in Greenwich Park one day in mid-April 1553 when he imparted secret news to Alford, his confidential servant. Knowing that his support would soon be solicited by Northumberland, Cecil declared he was 'a misliker of that device, and Sir William Petre too' (every lawyer abhorred it). Fearing assassination, Cecil 'went about armed, contrary to his usual practice', and from 22 April stayed away from the Council until 11 June. Petre had been absent for the two middle weeks of April, returning a day before Cecil's disappearance. Fear of violent death was not confined to Cecil. Scheyfve the ambassador wrote in cipher to the Emperor that all the councillors were buying up armour and weapons. The Cecil–Alford conversation has to be taken with caution as it was first written down twenty years later when Alford recalled these events for Cecil's benefit.[54] The chronology may be somewhat unreliable, and it seems more likely that Cecil's bodily peril coincided with the date of his belated return to Court. His truancy may indeed have been protracted towards the end of

May because Petre sent him news too grave to put on record, but the first four of the five letters from Petre (all written at Greenwich and cited below) as far as mid-May express concern only for Cecil's restoration to health. His modern biographer minimizes the imputation of wilful absence and feels that it was due solely to sickness, of the genuineness of which Northumberland was not sure.[55]

On 30 April Petre saw no reason why Cecil should not finish dealing with his private affairs before returning to Court. 'And I must confess to you of my self', he added, thinking of Ingatestone as well as of Cecil's pleasant country house at Wimbledon where he was convalescing, 'that my old affection homewards is not less than it was wont.' A week later Petre wrote: 'Albeit I had presently no other matter but to signify unto you my earnest desire to understand of your recovery, yet could I not, hearing of a messenger ready to go towards you, but write these few lines.' On 12 May he sent another message, warmly intimate and still revealing no political anxiety. Both Edward and Northumberland wished to learn if Cecil felt fit enough 'to be at the Court at Whitsuntide, when the Ceremony of the Feast of the Order shall be kept'. (Cecil had been appointed Chancellor of the Garter in the previous month.) 'And that his Majesty would be glad to understand somewhat from you therein. And thus well praying to God to send you perfect strength, I wish you as well as your heart desireth.' Three days later: 'I am glad with all my heart to understand your beginning to amend, which I trust with your good order will daily more and more increase. I have delivered your letter to my Lord's Grace of Northumberland, and have done as much as I might to get you a quick answer; but it could not be. In the end it was said that, when Garter shall come to the Court, they will resolve upon the fashion of your robes, etc. They would all be very sorry you should by any means hazard your health by over soon coming abroad. We have no news. God deliver you from the physicians, and yet I fear me (as ill as I love it) I must shortly come to them.'[56] Then finally there is Petre's letter of 18 May, telling Cecil that the Garter feast had been postponed as the ceremony would overtax the frail King and that Northumberland was ill at ease.[57] Not until Cecil got this note did he necessarily scent new trouble.

The secretariat was shaken a few weeks later. On 2 June Sir John Cheke, Cecil's brother-in-law, was sworn by the Council as 'one of the King's Principal Secretaries', or third Secretary. Cheke lost no time in taking up his duties.[58] Nor did Cecil in resuming his, after the news reached him. It may be surmised that Petre, too, realized that his own political career was in jeopardy. On 11 June the councillors included all three Secretaries. That day the ambassador reported: 'The Duke has formed some mighty plot against the Princess Mary and Cheke, the King's schoolmaster and a great heretic, has been made Secretary in place of Dr. Petre, who is said to have demanded permission to retire.'[59] Having known Petre for three years, Scheyfve is unlikely to have confused him with Cecil. If the ambassador's information was accurate, it was Petre who had had enough of it. For many weeks he had been attending the Council regularly enough to sense the quickening pulse of imminent violence. A recent opinion that, after all, Cheke's appointment was directed more against Petre than Cecil, because Petre's 'enthusiasm for the new religion was much more questionable than Cecil's',[60] may be right, as there is little doubt about his distrust of any form of religious extremism. The appointment of a third Secretary, not resorted to by any other Tudor sovereign, did not however necessarily imply the impending resignation or dismissal of Petre or Cecil; and, in the event, neither left his post. Resignation from high office was not a simple act in the sixteenth century; it savoured of treason, and a seat in the Council chamber, despite the over-heated atmosphere, was more comfortable than a draughty bench in the Tower. Petre succumbed and compromised. The learned Cheke's conciliar career was to be short, is meagrely documented, and his shadowy part as Secretary calls for no further comment.

Edward had not long to live. He had become a victim of what was probably acute pulmonary tuberculosis. A document recently discovered in the National Archives at Brussels furnishes definite evidence of the date when this grave deterioration was confirmed by Edward's doctors.[61] It was 28 May. The King would not survive the autumn. Jane Grey could not produce a son in time. So it must have been very shortly after Northumberland learned the verdict that a further act of conspiracy took place. He and Edward met in secret conclave. As a result the dying boy was persuaded again to alter the succession. The amendment, which is apparently in the King's hand though this is still a controversial matter, converted 'Lady Jane's heirs male' into 'Lady Jane and her heirs male'.[62] Only by violent threats did Northumberland clear the remaining hurdles.

A transcript of the juvenile script, which scorings and interlinings had made too significantly untidy, was then made.* Edward certified it, for delivery to the judges. On 11 June, Chief Justice Montague received a letter signed by the Council, which had capitulated, requiring the attendance next day of five judges. 'Secretary Petre sent for Montague, and informed him that the affair required speedy dispatch.'[63] A few

---

* That 'this was done by Secretary Petre', as stated by Nichols, seems to be due to his confusing it with the engagement referred to shortly: no wonder, with so many parallel manuscripts.

days later, the judges declared that they would be traitors if they set aside Henry's will. Northumberland, trembling with rage, challenged them to personal combat. They fled, only to be summoned again next day to the Council. Montague afterwards declared that his treatment was extremely cool, 'as though they did not know him'. One 'bade him hurry': that was Petre. He was Principal Secretary to King Edward, whose implicit orders must be executed, to his shame as a doctor of laws and an assistant executor of Henry's will. Pleading for indemnity from their utterly unconstitutional act, Montague, the highest guardian of the law, in the end complied. Under Northumberland's relentless pressure they drew up in this second week of June the deed or will in the form of letters patent by which Edward settled the Crown on Lady Jane Grey and her heirs male.

Legal scruples having been disposed of, the duke proceeded to inculpate the councillors (including those in disgrace), peers, judges, ecclesiastics and leading citizens of London, over one hundred in all, by extracting their signatures to the settlement, which bears the date 21 June. If Petre showed any hesitation about his own signature, there is no record of delay. Cecil, after doubts, had agreed to sign, but only 'as a witness'—a meaningless distinction. In the last scene of the documentary plot the Secretaries were at any rate not involved, for they were excluded from the company of the noble Lords of the Council.[64]

The Council's final surrender was all the more abject, because they signed yet another document, undated but coincident or nearly so with the settlement. The King or the duke (it matters little) directed the preparing of a further engagement, which is wholly in Petre's hand. The councillors thereby pledged themselves, under their mutually imposed threat of 'most sharp punishment', to maintain the succession as limited by Edward and never to 'vary or swerve' from it.[65] The satellites had to revolve around Northumberland or fall.

There is a second document written by Petre which must belong to the short period before the 'Device' was amended. Bearing Edward's signature at the top, it set out minutes, or notes, of the less important items to be incorporated in his will.[66] One historian has suggested that they were taken down from his own words, another that 'they were probably transcribed by him [Petre] for the King's autograph, as was done with the Device'.[67] Anticipating that his heir would be an infant, Edward enjoined his executors not to lead the country into any war nor to alter the existing religion, to pursue his recent efforts to pay off his debts, and to keep down the royal household expenses.

The last Council agenda for Edward's reign are also in Petre's writing:

that of 3 June wholly, that of 11 June also except for two items added by Cecil, who reappeared in the government that day.[68] In the ante-rooms and galleries the councillors hung around, whispering, planning and plotting. Some were thinking about their monastery lands. Would Mary, if she established her rightful claim, restore them to the Church? Those who, like Petre, had had experience of her determination, did not put it beyond her.

All, Northumberland especially, awaited the King's death. During a month of suspense, the duke took what military and naval precautions lay in his power. The event for which the nation's ears were strained took place on 6 July, when the fell scheme was put into effect. But it was too late, for Arundel contrived to send a message to Mary, who had already escaped from Hunsdon, her home on the Hertfordshire–Essex border.[69] Riding post-haste by Cambridge, she reached Framlingham Castle in Suffolk, once the property of the Duke of Norfolk. In the meantime Northumberland moved quickly. Mistrustful of many of the councillors, he carried them all off to the Tower. His mistrust was well founded.

Lady Jane Grey, eldest daughter of Suffolk and daughter-in-law of Northumberland, a girl of sixteen, succeeded a boy of fifteen. Arriving at Northumberland's mansion, Syon House, on 9 July, she was received by him, Pembroke, Northampton, Huntingdon and Arundel. Petre, with the rest of the Council, took the oath of allegiance to her. Mary challenged them to proclaim her as rightful sovereign, appealing to 'the rolls and records', which the Council knew were irrefutable. The three Secretaries were among the signatories to an insolent reply. The court went without delay to the Tower, and the heralds proclaimed Jane the Queen to a silent and bemused crowd.

In the Council, each one for himself was the undeclared order of the day. All was uncertainty and intrigue. In this maze of plotting and counter-plotting, it is not easy to follow the tortuous path which Petre, as confused as the others, was pursuing. On the day when Jane had been proclaimed, the Council had deputed 'two Secretaries, Petre and Cecil', to repair to the Imperial ambassadors and to express the hope that 'the ancient friendship between the two countries would be preserved'. If the ambassadors' facts were correct, Petre and Cecil had already crossed the dangerous interregnal gulf: they were Acting Secretaries in the interim period before formal appointments could be made; and Cheke also got over. Northumberland then sent Cobham and Mason to browbeat the ambassadors. There were four at this time, among them Renard; his dexterity baffled the emissaries, who returned, not to the duke but to Bedford, Arundel, Shrewsbury, Pembroke and Petre, all known friends of

Mary. These seven on the 13th invited the ambassadors to a conference at Baynard's Castle, Pembroke's riverside house. Petre had evidently thrown in his lot with Northumberland's opponents.[70]

By the 12th, several Catholic nobles and their retainers had reached Mary; Sussex was on his way, as well as 'innumerable companies of the common people'; and strong forces led by Huntingdon's brother, Hastings, were mustering on her behalf at Paget's house at Drayton and elsewhere.[71] The most pressing problem which confronted the duke was the choice of a commander to meet Mary's forces. Among his few friends, none of those capable and available could be firmly relied upon. If he took command himself, he would have to entrust the Tower and the disaffected city to Suffolk, the inefficient leader of his crumbling party. On the 14th he took the latter alternative, and left London, which immediately revolted. Both military and naval forces mutinied against Northumberland; and the people of East Anglia, contrary to his expectations, rallied in force around Mary.

The ordinary folk, going about their work, knew little beyond two facts which could spell disaster: the King was dead; there were rival Queens. Current bewilderment is exemplified in the dating of a deed of 15 July by a cautious Essex attorney as 'in the seventh year of Edward the sixth *late* of England . . . King'.[72] Trustworthy contemporary evidence of the anti-Northumberland revolution is scanty. One is obliged to rely partly on Cecil's written 'submission' presented to Mary a little later (a 'miserable apology' for his dissembling actions during the crisis) and on the narrative of his actions in Alford's statement made in 1573.[73] They reveal his careful avoidance of every act which might implicate him. Petre was equally involved with Cecil and cannot be excluded from the general condemnation. Cecil's dislike of the 'device' for upsetting the succession has already been referred to; 'of my purpose to stand against the matter, be also witnesses Mr. Petre and Mr. Cheke', his apology of a few weeks later adds. After further confessing to various acts of dissimulation, Cecil comes to the days after Northumberland's departure from the Tower. 'I practised', he was to write shortly, 'with the Lord Treasurer [Winchester] to win the Lord Privy Seal [Bedford]', in order to secure Windsor Castle for Mary; 'I did open myself to the Earl of Arundel . . . and to the Lord Darcy', both of whom were well disposed to his suggestions, 'whereof I did immediately tell Mr. Petre for both our comfort [encouragement]. I did also determine to flee from them if the consultation had not taken effect, as Mr. Petre can tell, who meant the like.' But Secretary Cheke dissuaded his brother-in-law from flight overseas, urging him to study his Plato's *Dialogues*, 'where Socrates, being in prison, was offered to escape and flee, and yet would not'.[74] The classics had given the Cambridge men some stability.

The Council heard from Rich, Lord Lieutenant of Essex, that Mary's forces had been augmented by those of his north Essex neighbour, the Earl of Oxford, from Hedingham Castle. At their morning meeting on the 19th they replied to Rich, who was arming, with a stern warning to remain loyal to Queen Jane; any councillor who flinched from subscribing stood in peril of Suffolk's assassin. A later historian added, significantly, that this letter 'was penned by Cheke; for Secretary Cecil was absent, and Petre, though present, did it not, though he signed it'. Paget's signature shows that he was once again in the body of councillors.* But immediately after the session, their warder, Suffolk, was evidently too alarmed to restrain them further; all knew that Northumberland's cause was hopeless. According to Alford, Arundel 'said secretly to his friend, as I take it yourself [i.e. Cecil] or Sir William Petre, that he liked not the air', naming the plague as an excuse for the councillors' turrophobia. Whether this remark was made on the 19th or a few days earlier is not clear. At any rate, about noon, Winchester, Arundel, Shrewsbury, Bedford, Cheyne, Paget, Petre and Mason contrived to make their exit and hurried to Baynard's Castle to join Pembroke, ostensibly the duke's chief ally, who had already evaded the Tower guard. Safe in Pembroke's palace, the fugitive Council at once summoned the Lord Mayor and chief citizens. The leaders had made up their minds to transfer their allegiance to Mary. Northumberland's plot had collapsed with dramatic suddenness. Suffolk surrendered without resistance. Jane wished to return home, but the Tower gates were not open to her. Her nine days' reign was over.

Northumberland soon capitulated, with some show of crying 'God save Queen Mary'. That evening, at the Guildhall, the Lord Mayor entertained all the Lords of the Council except Arundel and Paget who had posted to Framlingham on the previous day, taking the Great Seal to Mary and seeking forgiveness on the Council's behalf. Their plea was granted, but the Tower held Northumberland, Suffolk, his four sons including Lord Guildford Dudley, Northampton, Huntingdon and Cheke.

---

* Strype, *Cranmer*, i, 433. The names as given in J. G. Nichols, *Chron. Queen Jane* (Camden Soc., 1850), 109, and by Froude, *op. cit.*, v, 205, are correctly given, but have been inaccurately read by C. Read, *op. cit.*, 477, n. 59. The original letter is in B.M., Lansdowne MS., 3, f.50.

4 Three Steadfast Catholics

In the general retreat of the Catholics during Edward's reign, three prominent adherents of the Old Faith—Gardiner, Bonner and the Princess Mary—had each fought with skill and vigour. Petre was personally involved throughout, and his bearing is interesting in view of his attitude during the next reign, when the same three Catholics were to lead the counter-attack against the Protestants.

Soon after Edward's accession, Somerset and his followers had felt strong enough to coerce their Catholic opponents. The only episcopal opposition came from Stephen Gardiner of Winchester and Edmund Bonner of London. Both were imprisoned through the influence of Cranmer, whom Gardiner had tried to crush in the previous reign. Bonner humbled himself, and was soon released; the signatories to the Council's pardon included Cranmer and Petre. Gardiner's liberty was not restored until the general amnesty at the end of 1547. In the following May the Protector found it imperative to send for him again. He made some pretence of submission, but was ordered to preach a sermon at Paul's Cross on 29 June. He was to assert the government's authority, to obey their clear instructions on how to deal with controversial issues and to refrain from speaking about Transubstantiation. Although conforming generally, he neglected to recognize the Council's control in religious matters during Edward's minority and maintained the doctrine of the Real Presence. The councillors decided to send Gardiner to the Tower. Sir Anthony Wingfield, the Vice-chamberlain, and Sir Ralph Sadler were deputed to go to the bishop's house in Southwark and execute the order; Petre's accounts reveal that he accompanied them. With elaborate justification the Council recorded their reasons for the committal. Gardiner lay in prison for a year. In vain he appealed for trial. About the end of June 1549 Somerset took action. He sent Rich and Petre to the Tower. They told the prisoner that, if he would signify his intention to conform after studying the new Prayer Book they had brought him, the Protector's influence would be used in his favour. Gardiner pointed out that he was not proved guilty of any offence and with a flash of his ready wit said he preferred not to turn scholar in prison. Rich did most of the arguing; with Petre there was some reasoning; but Gardiner remained in the Tower.

In July Bonner, neglecting to use the Prayer Book, was ordered to clear himself from suspicion of holding unorthodox views. Again, a public sermon was the device; a ready-made homily was in fact laid before him. He, too, omitted to declare that Edward's authority was not limited because of his minority, and in other ways signally failed to satisfy the Council. A commission was issued for his trial. The judges were Cranmer, Ridley, Bishop of Rochester, the Principal Secretaries, and Dr. May, Dean of St. Paul's.* Petre formally opened the proceedings on 10 September at Lambeth Palace. After Bonner had railed against his denouncers in strong Tudor language, Cranmer engaged him on Transubstantiation. 'My lord of London! Ye speak much of a presence in the sacrament; what presence?' asked Cranmer. 'The very true presence of the Body and Blood of Christ', Bonner replied; 'What believe you, my lord?' The champions of the Old and Reformed Faiths had reached the crucial point. At this moment, Petre, 'beholding and looking very earnestly upon the archbishop, but saying nothing to it', dissuaded Cranmer from the dangers of answering. Silence was ever one of Petre's cardinal virtues; here it was effectively eloquent.†

The judges adjourned for a few days to give Bonner time to study the denunciation. Secretary Smith was then also present. Bonner protested: 'Because he sat not at the beginning, he ought not so to do [now]; for by the law, they that begin, must continue the commission'. The court turned to Petre for a ruling. Addressing Bonner, Petre declared (according to Foxe):

'My lord, in good sooth I must say unto you, that although I have professed the law, yet, by discontinuance and disuse thereof, and having been occupied a long time in other matters, I have perhaps forgotten what the law will do precisely in this point. But, admit the law were so as you say, yet yourself know, my lord, that this is our certain rule in law, *Quod consuetudo est juris interpres optimus* [custom is the best interpreter of the law]; and I am sure you cannot deny that the custom is commonly in this realm in all judgments and commissions used to the contrary; and, in very deed, we all together at the court, having the commission presented unto us, took it upon us; and therefore, for you to stick in such trifling matters, you shall rather in my judgment hurt yourself and your matter, than otherwise.'

'Truly, Master Secretary!' said the bishop, 'I have also of long while been disused in the study of law, but having occasion, partly by reason of this matter, to turn to my books, I find the law to be as I say; and yet, as I said, I tell you hereof but by the way, not minding to stick much with you in that point.'‡

* The proceedings are set out at great length in Foxe's *Acts and Monuments* (the 'Book of Martyrs'), ed. S. R. Cattley and G. Townsend (1837–41, 8 vols.), which is virtually the sole source.

† The pregnant phrase about Petre's silent effort was omitted from the first edition of the 'Book of Martyrs' printed in England (1563), perhaps out of deference to him.

‡ Dixon's comment (*Hist. of Ch. of Eng.*, iii, 134): 'This was true enough; and none knew better than the veteran [Petre] who had been on every commission from the beginning of the Reformation, how the process was abused. Commissions of large numbers were issued, and then limited by clauses empowering two or three of all the persons named: and of these,

Smith railed at Bonner's 'quiddities and quirks invented to delay matters'; the bishop retorted; and Petre brought the court back to order. The defendent promptly produced a long document in his own handwriting. Further altercation with Cranmer followed as to whether his denouncers should be admitted. Petre could contain himself no longer:

'We are not so straited [restricted in freedom of action], but that we may proceed against you, either at their promotion [prosecution] or without them, at our pleasure.'

'A God's name, then', said Bonner, 'put them by, and then do as your pleasure shall be, so you do me right.'

'Nay', said Secretary Smith, 'you ask you wot not what: you would have use follow your mind in these quiddities and quirks, to be seen a cunning lawyer.'

'Indeed', quoth the bishop, 'I knew the law, ere you could read it.'

After this resounding crack at Smith's arrogance, Petre brought Bonner to order again, producing eleven questions.

The trial dragged on amid similar scenes of recrimination between Smith and Bonner. The bishop refused to abide by any judgment given by Smith, who was his 'notorious and manifest enemy'. At the sixth session Cranmer, with the concurrence of the others (unnamed, except for Smith), pronounced Bonner contumacious, and fixed the final session for 27 September, when the decree would be made. But the judges did not meet on that day, 'divers urgent causes letting [preventing] them': a political plot was suddenly of more concern than a theological battle. The court assembled at Lambeth on 1 October, when Bonner was declared guilty, and Cranmer read their sentence of deprivation from his bishopric. The trial had ended, and Bonner returned to prison. On the 7th he appealed to the Lord Chancellor and the Privy Council—unaware that England that day was in the throes of a bloodless revolution. The prisoner very soon heard of big changes in the government, and renewed his suit to the Council, adding significantly, 'Dr. Smith, being a minister to the Duke of Somerset, and they both my deadly enemies, hath sundry ways studied and laboured my ruin.' The 'supplication' is dated the 26th, by which time Somerset and Smith had themselves been in the Tower for nearly a fortnight—prisoners of the Council! There is nothing in Foxe to show that Petre appeared after the second session.*

one or other would be absent from time to time. Bonner must have known that three out of the five who were named in the commission might try him: but he wished to prevent them from relieving one another.'

* The marked omission of his name on 7 and 26 October confirms his absence from the closing stages. It is further borne out by his account-book, which gives boathire to Lambeth only twice—on the day of the second session and on that before the fourth; but there is then

It was not until twelve months after Rich and Petre had visited Gardiner in the Tower that his case was brought up again in the Council. Provided that he was ready to accept the new Prayer Book, his release was advocated by Somerset, temporarily restored to restricted power. A great religious battle was about to begin. The Duke, the Lord Treasurer (Wiltshire), the Lord Privy Seal (Bedford), the Lord Great Chamberlain (Northampton) and Secretary Petre were appointed to visit Gardiner the next day (9 June 1550). 'A boat from Greenwich to the Tower and so to Greenwich again; for the dinners of 8 servants, my master being at the Tower' (Petre's accounts) confirms their visit.[75] They reported his willingness to study the Prayer Book, which had again been sent to him. The Council only got an indefinite answer and asked their emissaries to secure a more direct response: river transport to and from the Tower on 14 June tallies with the known date of the second call. A month passed. Warwick, appearing after illness, was severe when the case was brought up again on 8 July in a less complaisant session, and it was resolved to present the bishop with certain articles for his subscription. This time the prison visitors were Warwick himself, the Treasurer, the Master of the Horse (Herbert) and Petre; but not Somerset. Although Gardiner refused to sign the guilt clause, declaring that 'he would sooner tumble himself desperately into the Thames', he was willing to subscribe to the articles of faith. At the Council meeting on the 10th there was further debate. Herbert and Petre were to visit Gardiner again. They were authorized to soften offending words and exhort him to submit. The persuasive language of this moderate ultimatum reads like Petre's drafting. But all he and Herbert got was a stubborn refusal. Warwick's party now gained the lead. It was the Council's turn to be stubborn. The 'Nineteen Articles', set out in the Council Register under 13 July, were taken next day by Herbert and Petre, but 'for the more authentic proceeding with him' they were accompanied by 'a divine and a temporal lawyer' (Ridley, Bishop of London, and Richard Goodrich). These phrases were doubly significant to Petre, himself both a civil and canon lawyer. His suave interrogation had been thought inadequate. What line of argument he took on his sixth visit to the Tower is not recorded, but a complete stalemate led to Gardiner's summons to the Chamber on the 19th. He was

an unusual gap in the accounts until 1 October (the date of Bonner's sentence) when he was definitely in Essex. And he was to be abroad in the following February when Bonner's unsuccessful appeal was heard. His inclusion on 1 October seems only to be formal, in so far as it was necessary to recite all the names; instead of being third, as in the commission, he appears last, and the construction of the record has the effect of detaching him from the rest (Foxe, *op. cit.*, v, 795).

warned that his bishopric would be sequestrated, but he stood firm before the assembled councillors. Petre thereupon read the sentence, doubtless prepared by himself. It took some time before the formidable statement of offences reached its climax. 'Your former disobediences and contempts, so long continued, so many times doubled, renewed and aggravated, do manifestly declare you to be a person without all hope of recovery and plainly incorrigible.' Petre read on, announcing deprivation unless the bishop conformed within three months.[76] He got, in fact, four months' grace, but to no purpose. In November, Goodrich, Bishop of Ely, Petre and two other 'learned' civilians were appointed to advise how to proceed with the contumacious cleric. As a result, the Council decided to concede him a full trial. The commissioners were Cranmer, Ridley, Goodrich, Holbeach, Bishop of Lincoln, Petre, Sir James Hales, a justice of the Common Pleas, and several lawyers. Petre was one of the quorum, and could therefore not absent himself as he did in the later stages of Bonner's trial.

The court opened on 15 December 1550 in the Great Hall at Lambeth, Cranmer presiding. The proceedings were even more lengthy than Bonner's trial.* At the fourth session, on 8 January, Gardiner produced his 'Matter Justificatory', in no fewer than eighty-five articles, a document of abnormal length and an important record. There were nearly a hundred witnesses. Paget's perfidious evidence against his old master later drew reproach from Gardiner for his ingratitude. The depositions add only one fact to Petre's biography. Dealing with their call at the Tower in the previous July, Warwick referred to his demanding Gardiner's views on the King's authority while under age. The bishop had promptly countered by seeking Petre's view. 'My opinion is', he declared, 'except a king in his tender years be bound to his doings, as well as at full man's estate, it would be impossible to have that realm well governed.' It reads like an advance passage from Smith's De Republica Anglorum. Had Petre been witness instead of judge, more of his religious convictions might possibly have appeared in court. Of these, once more, any explanation is denied. Next month (February 1551), Cranmer pronounced the sentence, at the twenty-second session. Gardiner was to be removed from his bishopric. On hearing it, he declared that his judges were 'heretics and sacramentaries'. The Council met in angry mood next day and deprived him of such liberty and comfort as he had been allowed to enjoy in the

---

* Few readers nowadays would be willing to read through the mass of material printed in Foxe, op. cit., vi, 93–274, even if they were able to grasp the technicalities of ecclesiastical law. Dixon's account (op. cit., iii, 258; cf. P. Hughes, The Reformation in England (1953), ii, 105), makes easier reading, but for the full details the student should refer to the martyrologist.

Tower. Gardiner had declaimed too long; they were tired of him. But it was a bitter order, and it was to have its repercussions in the next reign.*

The issue of the First Prayer Book had coincided with that of a fresh heresy commission of twenty-five members directed against opponents of the new order. The quorum was any three of five named members including Petre. Among the victims was the obstinate eccentric, Joan of Kent. Petre took no part in the session. He was to be nominated again when the commission was renewed in January 1551. Joan was small fry. The Act of Uniformity tracked down, as it was intended to do, another woman, a princess, but the law allowed her to be called only the Lady Mary. In an undated letter, Catherine's faithful daughter expressed her opinion of her questioners in plain language: 'My father put them in trust to execute his will: and they have broken his will, and made laws contrary to it. I will keep his laws, as he left them, until my brother come to years of discretion.'[77]

In 1549 the Protector went into action against Mary. Rich and Petre were dispatched to interview her at Kenninghall, another of her mansions. She got advance news of their mission and wrote for advice to Van der Delft in London, suspecting that they were coming to try to induce her to conform with the new regulations and forbid her to practise the ancient religion, 'which she would never forsake in her life'.[78] Previous knowledge of the councillors' visit to Kenninghall rested solely on Van der Delft's report of 13 June to the Emperor.[79] Petre left Greenwich on 2 June, arriving at Ingatestone that evening. How he spent the next few days is not clear, but rewards paid by his steward on the 6th (p. 223) suggest that he hunted with Rich at Leighs Priory before they set off that afternoon, though Petre's accounts of the journey make no mention of his companion. 'The same night [Thursday] at Braintree', only six miles from Leighs, seems strange, but they had plenty of time to spare.† Resting the following night at Sudbury, another short journey, they dined

---

* Among the Petre family archives (D/DP O56) is preserved a bulky manuscript volume containing a contemporary copy of the depositions in this famous case. A few marginal notes are in Sir William's handwriting but not the text. Careful collation of this with Foxe's account reveals only very minor differences. In two or three passages where Foxe or his editor has inserted an omitted word, Petre's copy is perfect but otherwise has a normal quota of trifling clerical errors. This is believed to be the only contemporary MS. of the trial, except for a somewhat incomplete copy in the library of Corpus Christi College, Cambridge (MS. 127).

† This is the very stretch of road which Will Kemp, one of Shakespeare's associates, was to curse on the occasion of his famous morris dance from London to Norwich in 1599 (*Kemp's Nine Daies Wonder* (1600), Camden Soc., O.S., xi, 1840).

next day at Bury. 'The Lady Mary's house at Kenninghall' was reached before dark after a forty-mile ride just over the border into Norfolk. Their instructions must have enjoined them to be with her on Whitsunday 9 June, when the English liturgy was to be read for the first time in all churches. Rich and Petre declared how the Council insisted that the King's laws bound her and her household. Mary refused to convey the order to her servants. On their return the Council was summoned to hear the news. Mary's resistance could not well be overlooked, and her Grace was enjoined to obey his Majesty's laws and to send her comptroller and her chaplain to learn the Government's views more fully. Mary's written reply was spirited enough.[80] Next month her fault-finders were nagging again. This time their complaint referred to certain of her retainers attending seditious assemblies; the letter was Petre's work.[81] Not long afterwards, however, she got a letter from the King himself. Edward 'marvelled' at his sister's refusal to accept the order of Common Prayer but granted her special leave to have private service in her own chamber. The dispensation was to extend to her household servants, but Petre stiffened the terms of the draft by limiting the number to twenty whose names were to be declared.[82]

Soon afterwards, Mary removed from Kenninghall to New Hall, Boreham, five miles east of Chelmsford.* It was another of the mansions bequeathed by Henry to her. Here she was among those who were sympathetic to herself and near to Petre. Her trusted lady-in-waiting, Mistress Susan Clarentius, or Clarenceux, daughter of Richard White of Hutton (between Ingatestone Hall and Heron Hall), was kinswoman to Anne Petre's first husband, John Tyrell, and an occasional visitor to Ingatestone (p. 124–7). Mary had become godmother to Catherine, the Petres' youngest daughter, born 1545, and her relations with Lady Petre, an undoubted Catholic, were known to be cordial. At this time in particular, and indeed throughout the negotiations with Mary, Petre displayed ability and delicacy in reconciling his public duties with his private inclinations.

Although Mary had refused to conform, she continued to fear that her spiritual life would be interfered with. Knowledge of this is derived from

---

* Henry had acquired New Hall in 1517 by exchange with Sir Thomas Boleyn, whose daughter Anne had been born ten years before and whose son George became Petre's pupil ten years after. Henry was so delighted with its situation that he renamed it Beaulieu. A year or two later he rebuilt it. Beaulieu became one of his summer residences and there the Court held masquerades and revels. After her marriage to Henry, Anne often visited the palace. Later it was young Mary's chief abode. For the history of the mansion, see *Essex Review*, xvii (1908), 57–66, 121–32. It has survived, though part of its fine early Tudor brick front with its stone-mullioned windows was seriously damaged by enemy action in the last war.

the dispatches of the Imperial ambassador, whose presence at Ingatestone Hall in Christmas week is confirmed by the Hall accounts. On 14 January 1550 Van der Delft reported: 'Dr. Petre, First Secretary, having required me to hold his child [at the baptismal font], I went, on her written invitation, to see the Lady Mary, who lives not more than eight miles from his house. Her servants are well-to-do people, and some of them men of means and noblemen too, whose boast is to be reputed her servants. She has six chaplains, who say mass in her presence every day.' The ambassador's request that she be allowed to keep her religious liberty was refused. Plans to help her escape to Flanders were then hatched. Under one scheme Mary was first to remove from New Hall to St. Osyth's Priory on the north-east Essex coast, because it had direct access to the sea; but there was a snag: 'a lord was residing there who had just been admitted to the Council' (Sir Thomas Darcy, the Vice-chamberlain). An alternative plot seemed to offer a better chance of success. In the first week of July 1550, the Flemish admiral Scepperus (d'Eecke) was secretly sailing off the Essex coast, acquainting himself with suitable landing-places. The estuaries and creeks, penetrating deeply inland, offered exceptional opportunities. A short ride from New Hall, under cover of darkness, would bring Mary to Maldon, at the head of the nearest estuary. A long report about the plan, contains all the elements of a dramatic story—disguise, dawn escape, high tide, ruse for rendezvous in waterside churchyard, traitorous go-between.[83] In the meantime Mary had gone to another of her houses, Woodham Walter Hall, which lay close to Maldon and several miles nearer the sea than New Hall. The envoy and the comptroller were at Woodham Walter discussing the plans for Mary's flight in two days' time from Stansgate a few miles below Maldon. The watch retired at dawn. She would ride thither at that hour on the 4th under the pretext of going to 'purge her stomach in the sea', as her ladies did daily. But as the plotters went into the details, their spy rushed in to warn them that the men of Maldon were already threatening to arrest the envoy's boat, suspecting 'some understanding with the warship' riding at anchor off Stansgate. It was feared that the beacon-fires would soon be blazing along the coast. Immediate escape was considered, but abandoned. The danger was too great, for Maldon was to double the watch that night. And Sir John Gates, the Sheriff, had been detailed to guard the many winding lanes between New Hall and Woodham Walter and the sea.[84] So the envoy hastened back to Maldon, down the steep street to the quayside.* The

---

* To Essex readers and others knowing the Blackwater estuary, the account in the *Spanish Calendar*, x, 124–37, is of absorbing interest (the book is in the E.R.O. library); H. M. F. Prescott, *Spanish Tudor* (1940), devotes Chapter ix to it.

desperate plan had failed. Although Scheyfve, the Imperial ambassador in England who succeeded Van der Delft, had been in blank ignorance of what was going on, the Council's own spies knew of it. Petre's accounts have a solitary, intriguing entry. Lady Petre journeyed up to London— on the 4th, when the London steward's accounts have, 'My lady's break- fast, 5d.', which is one of the very rare references to this meal and unique in its context. Had she received secret advice of the collapse of the escape plot, and, fearing to put the news in writing or entrust it to a servant, rid- den forth from Ingatestone at dawn, and broken her fast in a city tavern to avoid comment by the Aldersgate household at her early arrival? If only a coincidence in date, it is a remarkable one. Her return home several days later may confirm that she had come up specially to acquaint her husband, but this is of course mere guesswork. At any rate, there is not a shred of evidence to suggest his being personally involved.

A few days afterwards, Gates warned Mary's chaplains to cease saying mass, and on the 25th Rich and Petre visited her at Woodham Walter or New Hall, probably the former. They conveyed 'letters of credence' de- manding her conformity[85] and the King's summons to the Court. She excused herself through indisposition. The Emperor's plans for spiriting Mary out of the country were defeated; the sheriff's vigilance outwitted the admiral's craft; but the Council's ideas for securing her obedience were equally frustrated.

In October Mary wrote personally to Petre about the Council's un- kindness in 'revoking' one of her servants from Flanders, whither doubt- less he had been sent by her with a message to the Emperor. Evidently she looked to Sir William for influential help; evidently, too, he gave it— by reading the letter to 'the whole Board', which authorized him to answer privately that they would make redress.[86] The Council were al- ways anxious to pay their respects to the second lady in the land, where religion was not in dispute; and Petre was equally cautious not to indulge in clandestine correspondence with her.

Late in the winter of 1551, Mary went to another of her residences— Copped Hall near Waltham Abbey, twenty miles away in south-west Essex. Being summoned to Court to explain her suspicious move, she was harangued by the King and the councillors. Two days after this verbal contest between an array of worldly-wise men and a solitary, un- worldly woman, Petre presented himself, to request her in the King's name to remain in London a few days longer. He reiterated the Council's 'most cordial affection'. They would always be ready, he declared with all the guile at his command, to render her any service in their power. Coming to the unresolved problem, he reminded her that the King in-

THREE STEADFAST CATHOLICS

tended to have his laws inviolably obeyed, 'in which speech Dr. Petre used many exhortations and inducements to move her'. He had to listen to many of her arguments and statements over again. 'She preferred that the King and Council should take away her life rather than the practice of the old religion, in which she was resolved to live and die.' Utterly steadfast, she had once more vanquished the Secretary. 'After this, Dr. Petre departed without uttering any further reply.'[87] It was typical of him. Mary returned to New Hall.

Somerset had surrendered after the paper war of 1549, but the Council's attack by letters failed to breach Mary's defences, and she continued to attend mass. The last missive to reach New Hall from Greenwich was fired on 24 June. Thereafter there was a truce until a week after Petre's return to duty.*

It looks as though the change in tactics, which occurred shortly after Petre's rejoining the Board, was initiated on his advice. Their irritation had in fact become unbearable. At their meeting at Richmond on 9 August, twenty-four members were present. They resolved to have done with the trouble by expressly forbidding mass and charging her chief officers to execute this precept. A message was sent to Copped Hall to which Mary had again removed, summoning to Hampton Court Robert Rochester, Edward Waldegrave and Sir Francis Englefield, her servants, who were instructed to convey the order to the chaplains. A week later all three returned to the Council, declaring how the Lady Mary, with impassioned speech, had demanded their obedience under pain of instant dismissal and offered her own body for the third time. Her officers were interviewed individually on two consecutive days by the whole Council, but remained firm.

Foiled yet again, the Board on 23 August reverted to the course taken before, decreeing that Rich, Petre and Wingfield should repair to Copped Hall. The envoys took with them a short letter from the King, who sent her a trusty and skilled officer of his own household to look after her material needs.[88] Rich offered to name the councillors present when the instructions for the interview were given. 'I do not care to hear their names', she retorted. 'My father made the more part of you', whipped her

---

* Both she and Scheyfve, Van der Delft's successor as ambassador, returned time after time to the so-called promise made to the Emperor that Mary's religious practices would not be interfered with. The Council had subsequently equivocated, and on 6 April 1551 Scheyfve sent one of his massive reports to the Emperor on yet another attempt to persuade the Council to redeem their promise. Paget and Petre in turn had been the government's spokesmen in a number of interviews with him about Mary and a counter-complaint that Chamberlain, the English ambassador in the Low Countries, was not allowed to use the Communion service. (*Span. Cal.*, x, 204, 225, 234, 255–6; Froude, *op. cit.*, iv, 562–3.)

Tudor tongue, 'almost out of nothing.' She declared that she would most willingly obey the King's commandments in any thing save her conscience, and rather than renounce the mass she would go to the block. Declining to accept a royal substitute for Rochester, she withdrew to her chamber. The commissioners called in her chaplains, who reluctantly gave in. As the Council's emissaries passed out through the courtyard, Mary delivered a little epilogue in the guise of a housewife. Speaking down from her window, she begged their influence in restoring her comptroller, for, she said, 'sithence his departing I take the accounts myself of my expenses, and learn how many loaves of bread be made of a bushel of wheat;* and I-wis [certainly] my father and my mother never brought me up with baking and brewing; and, to be plain with you, I am weary with my office.'

Mary's three household officers were sent to the Tower, but allowed to return to her in the next year. The councillors remained dubious, however, of the spirit of the chaplains' conformity; and Copped Hall was to be watched. For that task, Rich and Petre, with the Lord Chamberlain and the Vice-chamberlain, were assigned. Mary's four religious inspectors were all Essex men.† They were to 'see by all means they could, whether she used the mass, and, if she did, that the laws should be executed on her chaplains'.[89] More trouble with his leg undoubtedly provided Petre with a genuine excuse for not prying on her. In actual fact, the Council sent no more formal deputations. Mary's intractable spirit had worn them down; the lonely woman had won the final round.

Petre was the only figure *always* included among the councillors selected for judicial or admonitory action in the determined campaign against the three Catholic stalwarts.

* The methodical Cecil of course noted this useful point (p. 134 n.)

† The last was Gates. Lord Darcy was Lord Chamberlain from April 1551 to the end of the reign, except for the short period 22 August–17 October 1551, when the Earl of Huntingdon held the office. It seems likely that Darcy, rather than Huntingdon, was intended. In August Petre was granted twenty timber oaks from a Crown wood in Essex—a reward for his efforts on the Council's behalf (Strype, *Mem.*, ii, pt. ii, 245).

CHAPTER VII

Life at Ingatestone Hall

1 Family and Guests

IN all Tudor households, Twelfth Day was the climax of Christmas.[1] At Ingatestone Hall, in the middle years of the century, it was, perhaps, a day of special significance: Secretary Petre could rarely leave the Court until after New Year's Day, but he always tried to get to his country home shortly afterwards. In 1548, for instance, he left the young King at Hampton Court on 3 January. The roads were hard, so the Court blacksmith shod his mount with 'frostnails'. Riding up Kingston Hill, he gave a groat in alms to two beggars. Accompanied by his steward, John Kyme, who had £20 in the privy purse, and by several servants, he reached London, crossing from the south bank at Paris Garden to Paul's Wharf in time for supper. After breakfast next day, wrote the steward, 'my master rode into Essex' to join his wife and children and the guests. They were entertained by several Welsh harpers, three minstrels and Gilder the tumbler, all of whom earned their 'rewards'. Eight years later several mummers performed before the household.

Throughout Christmastide the Great Hall was crowded every day. On Christmas Day 1551 many Ingatestone folk were invited to dinner, and at supper, 'a mess in the hall and three poor fellows that came from London'; a mess was four people served with meat cut for that number. Sunday dinner: more than twenty Ingatestone men, mostly with their womenfolk, seven couples from Mountnessing, and 'eight poor folks, besides two mess that came unbid'! Next day was the turn of the villagers of Buttsbury and Margaretting; from the latter also came 'four singers and players'. Tenants of other manors in the estate arrived in smaller numbers later in the week. Then, on New Year's Day 1552, a second lot of Ingatestone people were among the guests, and there sat down to dinner 'six mess of the town and of them that brought presents'; and there were four 'mess' for supper.

Usually at that stage of Christmas the festivities at Ingatestone were intensified. Family guests began to arrive in force. Predominant among them were Lady Petre's kinsmen, the Tyrells, with their wives. On Twelfth Day, 1552, Richard Baker, son and heir of Sir John Baker, Speaker of the House of Commons, arrived from Kent with six servants; he came to stay for nearly a week at the home of his betrothed, Catherine Tyrell, daughter of Lady Petre by her first marriage to Sir John Tyrell, who had appointed the elder Baker as supervisor of his will. Not all of the copious fare went to the family circle in the big Dining Chamber. On this final and chief feast day there was an animated crowd of humbler guests in the Great Hall below, fifty for dinner and as many or more for supper: 'eight mess of serving men of Ingatestone besides a great number of boys'. So, all told, rich and poor and servants, over a hundred mouths were fed twice that day.

During those four years in the middle of the century, the family changed in number and composition. At Twelfthtide 1548 Petre had come home to a family of girls. There were five of them, perhaps six. He was the father of four, aged from twelve to two—Dorothy and Elizabeth by his first wife, and Thomasine and Catherine by his second. Older than these were their half-sister Catherine Tyrell and apparently another half-sister Anne Tyrell.

On 16 September of that year Petre's second son was born (the first, John, did not survive infancy). He was named Edward after the King. Kyme gave 6s. 8d. in alms and posted back to Court with the tidings which he delivered 'to the King's Grace, my lord Protector, and others'. At the christening, five days later, there were present at dinner Sir Henry Tyrell and Sir John Mordaunt and their wives from East and West Horndon, 'Mr. White, Mr. Morris, Mr. Bean, Mr. Lentall, Mr. Pownsett, Mr. Berners', all of Essex, 'Mr. Petre' (Sir William's brother William or Robert), and '43 strangers in the hall'. The Earl of Arundel sent his servant with half a mark (6s. 8d.) as a christening gift. On 1 October Lady Petre was able to sit up and receive the congratulations of the gentlewomen living nearby: 'Monday dinner. Wives to see my lady at her upsetting, 14.' After that, there is no mention of the infant.* Probably he died (or was buried) on 18 October, when Sir Thomas Tyrell of Ramsden in Essex and 'eight women to see my lady' dined at Sir William's table.

Petre continued to give liberal hospitality until mid-November, when 'my master took his journey to the Court and before his going we had this resort of strangers'.

Sunday dinner   Sir John Mordaunt and his wife, Mrs. Clarentius, Mr. Clovell,
                  Mrs. Clovell vidua, the two Pascalls, 3 waiting gentlewomen.
                  14 strangers in the hall.

* The earliest Ingatestone parish register is not extant. The ancient book of hours which records births (next footnote) does not give him, but Lady Petre's funeral record refers to 'Edward Petre eldest son that died sans yssue' (J. J. Howard and H. F. Burke, *Genealogical Collections of Roman Catholic Families—Petre* (1887), 49, 55). The account-book has this entry for the week ending 18 Nov., 'To Pakes' wife for cakes made against the christening of master Edward and for the churching of my lady, 12d.'

Sunday supper Sir John Mordaunt and his wife, Mrs. Clarentius, 3 waiting
gentlewomen.
6 strangers in the hall.

Monday dinner Sir John Mordaunt and wife.
6 strangers in the hall.

Tuesday supper Mr. White, Mr. Man.
& Wednesday 3 strangers in the hall.
breakfast

On 20 December 1549, at Ingatestone Hall, occurred an important
event. It was the first link in the long chain of succession of the Essex
Petres. Sir William had sent £100 'in ready money' to his wife in anticipation. On that day she gave birth to a son, also named John, destined
to become the first Baron Petre. The lackey hastened to Court to earn a
whole sovereign from his master. Sir William, who soon rejoined his
family, took thirty sovereigns and thirty half-sovereigns, probably to distribute as largesse. John had two distinguished godfathers in the Earl of
Warwick and Van der Delft, the Spanish ambassador; and Lady Paget was
his godmother.*

Lady Petre did not nurse her son. His foster-nurse was Alice the wife of
Robert Humfrey of Crondon, a neighbouring demesne farm, who was
Petre's acater. The choice of a woman to be hired to suckle the baby de-
pended not only on her health but also on her moral qualities, which were
absorbed with the milk by the infant, according to current belief. Baby
Humfrey meanwhile was cared for by another wet-nurse, a not uncommon arrangement.

Humfrey's wife for nursing Mr. John 13 weeks, after 10*d.* the week, now due
25 March, 10s. 10*d.*

Mistress Bexwell that she laid out for 6 lb. of flax bought at Stock what time my
lady went to see Master John at Crondon, 2s. 6*d.*

Blakborn's wife of Stock for nursing Humfrey's child 12 weeks, 9s.

* The date of John's birth is recorded only in Lady Petre's fifteenth-century book of hours,
in which it is entered twice, the first time briefly in her own handwriting. The second note
occurs among the detailed entries, all written in a hand of c. 1575, and names the godparents.
This MS. is now in Mr. W. A. Foyle's possession at Beeleigh Abbey, Essex. Mr. Foyle kindly
lent it for the first annual exhibition (the subject being 'The Petre Family') at Ingatestone
Hall in 1954, when the entries were checked with the somewhat inaccurate transcript in
Geneal. Coll. of R.C. Families—Petre, 49–50. The same entry of c. 1575 also states that John
Petre was confirmed by Cardinal Pole, no date being given. Lady Petre bore another son
apparently named William in August or September 1551. The account-book in mid-
September notes '18 gallons of ale behind unpaid since my lady lay in of child bed'; her
funeral certificate, already cited for Edward's birth, gives 'William Petre third (*sic*) son that
died also sans issue', who was dead by 14 Sept. (p. 96). Two more children have been incorrectly assigned to Secretary Petre instead of to his grandson (*Geneal. Coll.*, 39; cf. 51).

Soon after his return from France at the end of March, Petre rode into Essex to inspect his son, when half a mark was produced from the steward's pouch for the nurse. A few months later the young heir was installed at Ingatestone Hall, his cot having been suitably covered with much frizado and embellished with six yards of parchment lace and two yards of ribbon. Goodwife Humfrey remained nurse to the young son and heir till he was five, and her husband was regularly paid for John's maintenance at the rate of 16d. a week. By February 1555 he had left her care, but he never forgot the Humfreys. He gave them handsome money presents, as for instance in 1568: 'To my nurse Humfrey's husband 3s. 4d.'; and of course they did not forget him, and he gave a groat later in the same year 'to Richard Humfrey my nurse's son for bringing a dish of wardens'.

'Two abses [ABCs] for Master John Petre to learn on' introduced him, when 5¼ years old, to the world of letters, and 'a grammar' six months later, to that of words. In the meantime his boyish pride was gratified when a live gift arrived (and he was old enough to be taught how to reward servants): 'Delivered to Master John Petre 12d. which he gave to Mr. Foster's servant for bringing unto him a little ambling spayed mare, with saddle, bridle and harness.'

John was by no means the only boy brought up in the household. Sir William decided, when his heir apparent reached adolescence, against placing him with another family, but he took at least one youth under his own care—George son of Sir John Fermor, M.P. for Northamptonshire, a distant cousin. It was of course a prevalent practice for gentlemen's sons (and less often, daughters) to be sent from the parental roof to a different establishment, where their discipline, manners and education might benefit: the origin of the English ideal of boarding at a 'public' school.

The periodic advent of boys from other families into Petre's home was due, however, to his acquiring wardships, which he began to do from 1546, and during the next fifteen years or so he always had several male wards of good family who had lost their fathers. In all, nine wardships were granted to him. With the exception of the two girls (co-heirs) and one boy, all came to live with the Petres. Under feudal law, if a tenant-in-chief died while his heir was still a minor, the sovereign became the guardian of the heir's body and lands. But the Crown almost invariably sold the wardship with the valuable right of controlling the marriage of the ward to a suitable spouse. There were always plenty of applicants for such a profitable investment. Thus it was that Petre obtained husbands of substance for two of his daughters. He treated his wards on the same basis as he did his own children, and their names are often linked together in the accounts. A little can be gathered about the wards' education whilst members of the Ingatestone household. There is no specific mention of a tutor, though one ward in March 1550 was bought some books, including the English psalms decreed in the previous year, and another was given a Latin primer. Good manners and manly virtues were generally considered at least as important as formal tuition, but it is unlikely that a man with Petre's academic background neglected his wards' early education. One was first sent to Cambridge and later joined another of his wards at Oxford. He provided a tutor at each university. Expenses for a year at Cambridge (1554-5), including tuition, food, books, clothes, laundry and fuel, amounted to about £9. The Court of Wards settled each ward's 'exhibition', or maintenance allowance, which was paid to the guardian. (See Appendix D.)

Meanwhile the Tyrell and Petre girls were growing up. In July 1548, Ingatestone Hall was full for the wedding feast of 'Mistress Anne' with Mr. Stonard of Luxborough in Chigwell, Essex. The bride was almost certainly Lady Petre's daughter by her first marriage.*

Strangers this week at the marriage of Mistress Anne

Sunday supper. My master, Mistress Clarencius, Mistress Stonard, Mistress Mildmay, Mistress Tyrell of Shenfield, Mistress Carrow and her sister.

Monday dinner and supper and Tuesday dinner and supper. My master, Mr. Mordaunt, Sir Harry Tyrell, Mr. Edmund Tyrell and Mr. Stonard, with their wives, with 8 mess of strangers besides.

Wednesday dinner. The most part of the same.

Catherine Tyrell was married in June 1552 to Richard Baker, the privy councillor's son. To take charge of the wedding feast, Sir William brought down from London a skilled master cook named Wilcocks, as well as four under-cooks. Ingatestone Hall was overflowing with the guests and their servants, and for once the household officer could not list them all.

Strangers at the marriage of Mistress Catherine Tyrell

Sir John Baker, Sir Martin Bowes, Sir Richard Lye, Mr. Cowlepapir [Culpepper], Mr. White, Mr. Tofton, Mr. Argall, and their wives, my Lady Barkley, Mr. Salinger [St. Leger], Mr. Barrett, Sir Harry Tyrell, Mr. Berners, Mr.

* She is not given in *Geneal. Coll. of R.C. Families—Petre*, 39, 55, nor does she seem to be otherwise recorded. In his will (he died in 1579), Stonard left his manor of Luxborough to his wife Anne and referred to 'Tyrell his brother'[-in-law].

Wilford, Mr. Anthony Browne, Mr. Edmund Tyrell, Mr. Clovell, Mr. Tyrell of Warley, Mr. Latham, Mr. Morris, Mr. Cooke, Mr. Beckingham, and their wives, Mr. William and Mr. Charles Tyrell, Mistress Sulyard, Mistress Pascall, with an hundred mess besides in the hall and other places in the house.

On the usual reckoning of four persons to a mess, there were about four hundred people. Most of the guests departed two days later, after dinner.

Girlhood was short in the sixteenth century. A daughter was taught by her parents to begin thinking early about marriage; that of Dorothy, Petre's own eldest daughter by Gertrude his first wife, at the age of twenty, would have been considered a late one. In September 1555 Dorothy was married to Nicholas Wadham, a Somerset man; it was a union that resulted in a great Oxford memorial. Her wedding was the most important domestic event in that year, and all the family journeyed to London. It cost Petre £73, mostly on clothes. Many pages are filled with the details of the materials bought for making her wedding garments and all the accessories, on which over £11 was spent, with more on jewellery. 'Jeremias the goldsmith' charged 18s. 6d. for her ring, 2s. being the cost of fashioning it and the balance that of the gold itself. As much as £37 was disbursed on 'apparel for the children and others'.

By 1555 Thomasine, the elder daughter of Sir William and Dame Anne and now ten years old, had reached the age for being educated in the duties of a lady. She was about to enter the house of one of the greatest families in the land, that of the 'Marquess' of Exeter, herself a lady-in-waiting to Queen Mary.* The Marchioness was the daughter of William Blount, fourth Baron Mountjoy (see p. 68), and was a sponsor at the 'bishoping' of Catherine Petre. Lady Petre fitted up Thomasine afresh in London with a black damask gown, a French hood, a very expensive hat and of course one of the new farthingales, as well as many more articles of apparel, at a cost of over £10. At last she was ready for the exalted finishing school for girls, and on 14 November she started off on the journey to Hampshire with a strong escort of servants.

Christmastide and family christenings and weddings were not the only occasions on which guests gathered at Ingatestone. In October 1548 Lord Rich, of Leighs Priory in north Essex, journeying towards London, arrived for dinner and probably slept at the Hall: 'My Lord Chancellor,

---

* Second wife of Henry Courtenay, Marquis of Exeter and Earl of Devonshire, she was a devout Roman Catholic, had been a prisoner in the Tower nearly twenty years earlier, and her attainder had not been reversed until Mary's accession. Her son, Edward Courtenay, 'the last direct heir of the noblest family in England', had recently begged in vain for permission to return home to pay his respects to his mother.

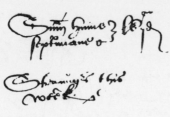

INGATESTONE HALL: PROVISION ACCOUNT BOOK

Part of the clerk of the kitchen's accounts for the week ending 24 November 1548; refers to Princess Mary's first visit.

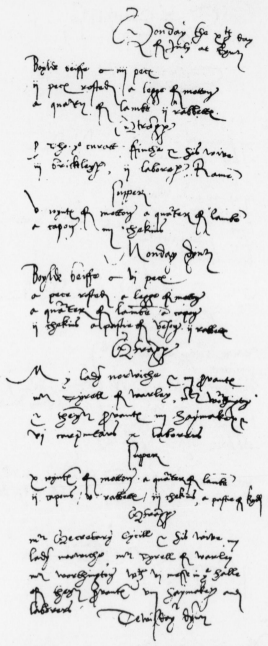

INGATESTONE HALL: PROVISION ACCOUNT BOOK

Part of the clerk of the kitchen's accounts for 11 and 12 July 1552; refers to Secretary Cecil's visit.

with the number of thirty persons of his train.' Next month a princess slept under Petre's roof.

> NOV. 22. *Thursday supper and Friday dinner.* My Lady Mary's Grace, with her train of two mess in the parlour, seven mess in the hall, besides other officers.

So the servants had to cope with nearly fifty guests, and while they did so Sir William entertained his distinguished visitor, the steward producing 5s. from the privy purse for his master 'to play at cards' on the second evening. She departed next day and Petre left for the Court on the following morning. A few days later Mary was at Ingatestone again, on her return.

> NOV. 28. *Wednesday supper.* My Lady Mary's Grace, with her train.

His parliamentary duties did not allow the Secretary to act as her host then, and she must have spent the winter night with Lady Petre on her journey to New Hall, Boreham, one of her chief residences, which was two hours' ride away. Early in February 1550, while the master was abroad, there was more commotion. The Lady Mary had sent word to Ingatestone that she would come over from New Hall. Fresh rushes were laid down and extra women were brought into the kitchen. Mary probably made the visit in order to offer her felicitations in person to Lady Petre on the birth of her son John. A month later she accepted an invitation to return the call at New Hall.

Quite often, in fact, it fell to Lady Petre to be the hostess. In July 1552, while Petre was with the King at Oatlands, she was entertaining Dorothy's godmother, Lady Norwich, and two neighbours, when the other Secretary also arrived on his way to London after a tour in his native Lincolnshire. It was Cecil's second visit in that year.

JULY 11—*Monday dinner*
My Lady Norwich and 4 servants, Mr. Tyrell of Warley, Mr. Worthington, and their servants.
4 haymakers, 6 carpenters and 6 labourers.

JULY 11—*Monday supper*
Mr. Secretary 'Cycill' and his wife; my Lady Norwich; Mr. Tyrell of Warley; Mr. Worthington.
With 6 mess in the hall of their servants, 8 haymakers and labourers.

JULY 12—*Tuesday dinner*
Mr. Secretary 'Cicell' and his wife; my Lady Norwich; Mr. Barrett and his wife.
With 8 mess in the hall.

The kitchen staff had thus met the coincident extra demands of harvest folk as well as notable visitors; all told, with the family and the servants, at least eighty persons to feed. On the last two days of August the Petres entertained Lady Darcy, wife of the privy councillor and owner of St. Osyth's Priory near Colchester, with a retinue of thirty or more; and next day there came Lady Gates, wife of another councillor and owner of Pleshey Castle near Chelmsford, with Sir Anthony and Lady Cooke.

Historians have written a good deal about the open houses of the nobility,* but there is little in print about the extent to which men of less exalted rank kept open table. The Petre archives give a clear answer to the question, who ate in the Great Hall on those ordinary days when the master and mistress were at the Court? The neighbouring gentry and relations rarely appeared then, though their servants came, with errands, enquiries or presents. For instance, in 1552, a small number of tenants were seen almost every week, no doubt on business. There were also local craftsmen—tiler, smith, glazier, wheelwright, sawyer—whose frequent appearances betoken final or minor building operations. With them were usually several bricklayers, carpenters and unskilled labourers. From August to October six carpenters fed at Petre's table; now and again, too, a tailor and a maltman. Occasionally there was a sudden influx, for example, a few years later, four carters with oats from East Horndon and ten carters 'that came with pale from Horsefrith Park' in Writtle. Itinerant paupers and passengers hopefully turned up. Once or twice a week a few 'poor folks' or 'poor fellows', as they were usually termed, are mentioned at the end of the 'strangers'. Poor women and pedlars also occur. In the mid-winter months of 1551–2 there was an average of forty 'strangers'; in the following summer and autumn, double that number; but it must be remembered that this term covers everyone not normally living in the house. On some days, however, nobody came from the outside world. As all food provided had to be accounted for, it may be assumed that the record of hospitality is a complete one, unless broken bread or the like was given to beggars and vagabonds outside the gatehouse.

2 Food and Drink

Some aspects of the provisioning and the cuisine of the great establishments of the Tudor period are well known.[2] For more ordinary households evidence is scarce. Sir William Petre's two kitchen books (or

* E.g. S. T. Bindoff, *Tudor England* (1950), 30, referring to the Duke of Buckingham's house at Thornbury, Gloucestershire, 'In its great hall there regularly dined, so we learn from a set of accounts for 1507–08, between 100 and 200 persons',

'week books') are among the very few surviving records of food and drink consumed in a mid-sixteenth century manor-house of moderate size.* Indeed, the 1552 book shows what passed through the Ingatestone Hall kitchen in serving all the 366 dinners and 300 suppers (Fridays and a few other fast-days saw no supper). In the twelvemonth from December 1551 to December 1552 some strange animals, fowls and fishes were received by the Ingatestone steward and cook. It also shows, even if sketchily, the food sent into the ordinary folk and servants in the great hall every day of the year; also, when the Petres (or Dame Anne only) resided at home, a twice-daily glimpse of the private dining parlour, or of the big dining chamber if their own guests were numerous. What was drunk each day is not recorded; but no matter, as the periodic checks of the beer and wine cellars reveal enough.

The feeding of the household, especially when much hospitality was being given, required an able organization. Petre and Edward Bell, his house-steward, seem to have created it. The disposition of the personnel was not unlike a broadly-based pyramid. Above the kitchen-boys and stable-lads were the cook and the horsekeeper; there was Robert Humfrey the part-time acater; and all three in turn and the other servants took their orders from Bell; but always at the top was Sir William—in spirit, if absent himself, when his wife was in command. And of the twenty indoor and outdoor servants in 1548-52, the majority were concerned directly or indirectly with providing the household with food and drink. Besides the produce of the Ingatestone demesne, some supplies were also drawn from the farms and parks at East Horndon and Crondon, which Petre also kept in his hands.

All the provisions were meticulously vouched for by tallies. 'I delivered the remain', the 1548 'week book' states, apparently on a kitchen maid's promotion, 'as may appear by tallies made betwixt her and me, to be accounted of the expenses weekly, and also of all other the like that shall come to her hands after the day, by way of emption, provision, present or otherwise.' The same check governed the grain; when deliveries were sent to the kitchen, the two servants who had threshed it got tallies, 'as

---

* In Appendices E and F are transcripts for the week after the close of Christmastide, 8-14 Jan. 1547-8, and of the three weeks of Christmas, 20 Dec. 1551 – 9 Jan. 1552, each of which had its own feast-day—Christmas Day, New Year's Day and Twelfth Day. The nearest equivalent seems to be the account-book of Paget's clerk of the kitchen, West Drayton House, Middlesex for Nov. 1547 – Feb.ʳ1548 (Midd. Rec. Off., 466/H12). Cecil's somewhat similar accounts in loose sheets (Hatfield House, 'Bills') are not detailed or orderly. Cf. *Cal. Middleton MSS.* (H.M.C.), 388 *et seq.* esp. 394 (1542 onwards, but few details) and *Cal. Rutland MSS.* (H.M.C.), iv, 260-387 for noblemen's houses. Of later date, Cecil's less detailed general book, 1575-7, is useful for comparison (C. Read, 'Lord Burghley's Household Accounts', in *Econ. Hist. Rev.*, 2nd series, ix (1957), 343-8).

may appear by their scores betwixt them and me'. Thus they followed the ancient accounting method of notching a stick or tally which was then cleft lengthwise, each party to the transaction keeping one of the halves against the next annual audit: an elementary but foolproof method. Each week the steward visited the granaries, millhouse, malthouse, bakehouse, dairy, dovecote and the various store-rooms for cheese, fish and so on. With the cook he inspected the larders and other kitchen stores, ending his tour with the butler in the butteries and the cellars. In his book was written each Saturday a statement of what provisions had been received a week earlier, how much was spent, and what remained.

The staple foods of course were bread and cheese. Three qualities were produced by the Ingatestone Hall baker, but some of his terms are obscure. During 1548 he turned out 'manchet', 'ravel bread', and 'tems bread'; in some weeks 'tems bread' became 'carter's bread'. The 1552 book also has three columns, headed 'manchet', 'yeoman's bread' and 'carter's bread'. Manchet was white bread of the finest quality, made from wheaten flour. Ravel bread, a rarer term, was made of whole meal or of flour with the bran left in. One of the other terms was used by Thomas Tusser, who was William Harrison's contemporary and also an Essex man:

> Some mixeth to miller the rye with the wheat
> Temmes loaf on his table to have for to eat.[3]

Wheat and rye mixed are known as maslin or meslin, and Tusser's marginal note reads 'myslen'.* Although rye as well as wheat was grown in south Essex, the steward records only wheat for baking and oats for the poultry; never rye or meslin. A later writer's notes on bread placed 'yeoman bread' next to the best, and explained that if the grossest part of the bran was extracted the baker could make 'a brown household bread agreeable enough for labourers', which corresponds with the 'carter's bread' baked at Ingatestone. In big households the servants were graded

---

* Cf. *Best's Farming Book* (Surtees Soc., 1857): 'massledine for our own tempsed bread baking'; the editor explains the verb 'tempsed' as 'passed through a tempse, or coarse hair sieve'. Cf. 'ravel', to sift through a coarse sieve, and '4 yards of ravelling for meal' (Petre's accounts, 1556). Harrison described the various grades of wheaten bread, from the manchet and 'ravelled bread' down to 'brown bread', which itself had two grades, the better having little of the bran extracted, the inferior having little or no flour in it. From a bushel of wheat the baker, according to contemporary documents, was expected to produce 25, 30 or 40 cast of bread. An unpublished household notebook of Cecil's states that a bushel yields 25 cast of white bread, the loaf weighing 16 oz.; also, earlier in the same book, that it produces 27 loaves of 23 oz. (B.M., Lans. MS. 118). (Paget's account-book (Midd. R.O.) also uses 'cast'.) For manchets, cf. *The . . . Household of . . . Earl of Northumberland, 1512* (1827), 134; and Cecil's household book (f. 38), '15 cast of manchet, 2 to a loaf, weighing out of the oven 16 oz.'

as gentlemen, yeomen and grooms; so 'yeoman's bread' was the middle quality.

The quantities baked were reckoned by the 'cast', which was equal to two or three loaves, depending on their size and the quality of the flour. Figures are complete for fifty-one weeks in 1551–2, but in Catherine's wedding week the harassed servant failed to keep count. The total works out thus:

Bread baked at Ingatestone Hall in 1552

Manchet	Yeoman's bread	Carter's bread
1,900 cast	5,560 cast	1,480 cast

Two manchets were roughly equal to a loaf. The Hall ovens therefore turned out the equivalent of about 20,000 loaves of bread. The presence of Sir William and his guests did not substantially alter the proportions of each kind, as there were also the guests' servants. It is evident that most of the Petre household were allowed bread of medium to good quality. The following table gives the five weeks in 1551–2 when the largest quantities were eaten, also a week in November when Sir William and Lady Petre were away and hospitality was limited to five local folk on one day only. The manchets referred to in the last line were probably eaten by the Petres' children and a few of the superior servants.

Week including	Manchet: cast	Yeoman's bread: cast	Carter's bread: cast
Christmas Day	26	100	22
New Year's Day	60	140	12
Twelfth Day	40	216	12
Cecil's second visit (July)	46	118	24
Lady Darcy's visit (August)	70	130	30
Lowest number of 'strangers'	20	60	30

Next in importance to the bakehouse came the dairy. Milk being perishable had no place in the accounts except for cream at weddings and the like, but they afford much information about cheese and butter, which were abundant and cheap. In the sixteenth century and a good deal later, cheeses were described by the district where they were made rather than by their quality. Camden, writing in the early 1580s, was amazed at the 'cheeses of an extraordinary bigness' made from ewes' milk in the marsh pastures of south-east Essex;[4] and a few years later John Norden commented on the 'great and huge cheeses, wondered at for their massiveness and thickness', which were produced in those parts.[5] Petre's accounts prove that the practice also obtained farther inland. In 1550 'three pails to milk ewes in' were bought, and the sheep-milker is mentioned twice in

1555. Ten milking sheep have been reckoned as equal to one cow.[6] John Skelton, the early Tudor poet, draws a crude picture:

> A cantle of Essex cheese
> Was well a foot thick
> Full of maggots quick:
> It was huge and great
> And mighty strong meat
> For the devil to eat,
> It was tart and punicate.

The consumption in Petre's country house was about two cheeses a week in the winter of 1551–2, after which lead was the term used, and the weekly amounts ranged between a half and three leads.* As Camden remarked, cheese was good for the servants and humbler guests 'to fill their bellies with', and the abnormally hard Essex cheeses were economical fare in the Ingatestone Hall budget.[7] In 1548 about 150 cheeses were eaten, and four years later the equivalent of well over 200, the latter working out at around 2,664 lb. In January 1552 there were 118 cheeses in store; thereafter from two to four a week were made.

The Ingatestone dairy produced three sorts of butter—fresh, for immediate use; salted and pressed into earthenware pots or into barrels; and clarified (melted) and potted for culinary use. Butter was in fact needed chiefly in cooking, being the cheapest sort of fat. The weekly stocktaking refers to various measures—dishes, pots and barrels.† Two sorts are mentioned only in one June week when the family, guests and servants used 3 quarts of cream butter and 5 quarts of crude butter. On New Year's Day 1552 there were 88 dishes in store. '[Fresh] butter spent this week 3 dishes, 2 dishes of salt butter spent this 3 weeks past, and a pot of clarified butter spent since Lent containing 14 dishes' is a typical weekly statement.

* A cantle was a thick cut or section. The Petre archives yield other details on cheese manufacture. They refer to cheese as 'weys', 'leads' and 'cheeses', never by avoirdupois weight. The Essex wey contained 336 lb. (the *O.E.D.* thus defines it, quoting a book of 1596; this is confirmed by St. Osyth's Priory accounts, 1512 (*Essex Review*, xxx, 1)). But lead is apparently a very rare term (not in *O.E.D.* or Halliwell's *Dict. of Archaic Words*, but cf. F. W. Steer, *Farm and Cottage Inventories of Mid-Essex* (1950), 39, 91 (10 lead = 5 cwt.), confirmed in Petre's accounts). The accounts show that a wey contained 6 leads, so a lead was therefore 56 lb. (this agrees with Elizabeth Middleton, 'Essex Records as Material for the Study of the English Language' (*Essex Review*, lxiii, 131)). A lead contained a varying number of cheeses, according to size, from nine 'small cheeses' to three large ones. On this estimated weight of about 20 lb., the 'great Essex cheeses' do not seem to have been phenomenally big.

† A dish has been defined as containing 24 oz. (E. Middleton, *op. cit.*, 131, quoting *Eng. Dial. Dict.* under Cheshire and Shropshire; not in *O.E.D.*). But a south-east Essex farmer was charged in 1709 with selling 'a dish of butter which ought to weigh 2½ lb.' (E.R.O., Q/SR 541/7).

The total consumption in 1552 was 388 dishes, or between 582 lb. and 970 lb. according to how 'dish' is computed. In addition, 6½ dishes were sent to the London house and 31 were sold at 5d. each during the spring. During 1552 (52 weeks) the cook used 2,657 eggs. The normal consumption was about two score a week, but Catherine Tyrell's wedding caused the figure to jump to 'vj hundred' (probably the long hundred).

The number of animals slaughtered seems high for a household of moderate size, and if, as contemporary writers said, the poor could not afford enough meat, the Ingatestone servants fared well. 'One ox (or one steer) cut out into livery pieces' (usually about 30) is the initial entry in a majority of the 1548 weekly lists. The number of liveries, or rations, is always given, and seems to correspond with the total number of household servants plus guests' servants, if any.

During 1548 the Petre family, nearly twenty servants and the guests consumed 55 oxen and calves, 2 cows, 133 sheep and lambs and 11 swine. The figures for 1552 were: 1 bull, 17 oxen, 14 steers, 4 cows, 29 calves; 129 sheep, 1 teg, 54 lambs; 3 boars, 9 porks, 5 hogs 'killed for bacon'; 3 goats, 7 kids; 1 stag, 13 bucks and 5 does; these are the calculated totals for 46 weeks (no meat in Lent, no figures for one week). Most of the deer came from Crondon Park, the rest as gifts; there were apparently no deer in Ingatestone Park, despite the Crown licence. In the poorer households, most of the beasts were killed around Martinmas (11 November) because of the shortage of winter feed, and the beef was salted for use during the winter months. It is no longer believed that the meat consumed in winter by the more substantial farmers was almost wholly salted, and Petre's two kitchen books certainly bear out the present theory.[8] While by far the largest quantities of meat eaten were the servants' 'livery pieces' of beef (1548) or 'boiled beef' (1552), both books reveal that in every week of the winter, except in Lent, some 'roasting pieces' (1548) or 'pieces of roasting beef' (1552) were served. These vary between twelve and one pieces a week, according to whether the Petres were at home and the number and quality of their guests. That any of this was de-salted beef can be disregarded. The roasting pieces were undoubtedly from freshly-killed cattle and sheep. And of course the kitchen was also well served in winter with fowls and occasionally with venison, as deer, unlike other animals, can forage for themselves in cold weather.

Among the wildfowl and fish that came to the table at Ingatestone Hall there were some strange varieties.* Mallards were plentiful; widgeons,

* Details are given in Appendix G. The Tudors reckoned all fowl and nearly all fish in the ordinary plural; the modern convention of the collective singular is disregarded in this chapter.

wild ducks, teals, cranes, shovelards, and shellfowls less common. The kitchen got an abundant supply of woodcocks in the winter, likewise of snipes, or snites, and marles. In the winter season, too, it received other small wildfowl called oxbirds. Among the smaller birds, curlews, praines (akin to curlews), plovers and redshanks were numerous, and a solitary goodwin came among a New Year's gift of wildfowl. Some supplies from the marshy coast Petre obtained by priced contracts.

Agreement with a fowler, 1552		Covenant by a tenant, 1570	
Curlew, each	8d.	Curlew, each	8d.
Plovers, the dozen	2s. 4d.	Plover, each	2d.
Praines, do.	2s. 4d.	Mallard, each	4d.
Snipes and tukes, do.	18d.	Snite, each	1d.
Teals, do.	2s. 0d.	Teal, each	2d.
Oxbirds, do.	4d.	Oxbirds, the dozen	3d.
Woodcocks, the piece	4d.	Redshanks, do.	8d.
Wigeon, do.	4d.	Duck, each	4d.
Heronshew, each	16d.		

To the 1552 list may be added an entry for October:

Paid to the partridge-taker for 15 partridges after 4d. the piece, 5s.

The supplies for several weeks included a few stockdoves, which were baked. These were wild pigeons, not taken, as the name would suggest, from the stock in the dovecote. Pigeons from the Hall cote were eaten regularly from April to late September. The heaviest drawing in 1552 took place early in August: 'Pigeons taken out of the dovehouse this week three score pair'. The total number of pigeons drawn between Easter and Michaelmas was 1,080: no mean source of food, even allowing for the preponderance of bone and wing. Pigeon pie, therefore, frequently appeared in these months.

Tudor folk, like their ancestors, regarded many kinds of birds as edible. The choicest birds were larks, several dozen of them coming now and again into the Petres' kitchen. Sir John Mordaunt of Thorndon (West Horndon) sent a crane, seven dozen larks and seven 'snites'. 'Blackbirds 12' of the 1548 Ingatestone book was the counterpart of 'four and twenty blackbirds baked in a pie' of the nursery. Often, however, the entry merely gave so many 'birds', which usually denoted blackbirds, starlings and sparrows. A 'birder', one William Wortley, was frequently paid for wildfowl and small birds, as for example '9 dozen sparrows 13½d.', or 1½d. a dozen. This was his regular rate, and his best effort was 18 dozen 'birds', 2s. 3d. He seems to have combined snaring and birdliming with wild-fowling (some birdlime was bought in 1555). Fifty years later five or six times his rate was to be recorded elsewhere in England,[9] so that even allowing for the depreciation of money values Petre seems to have made a good bargain.

Meat of all sorts, including poultry, was prohibited during the whole of Lent, every Friday and Saturday, and several other fast-days appointed by the Church and added to by the State because of the high price of meat and to support the navy and shipbuilding. The importance of these fish-days is emphasized throughout the kitchen books. There was not as great a variety as with wildfowl—and certainly not always the freshness. The chief distinction in everyone's minds was not so much between 'sea fish' and 'fresh [freshwater] fish' as between fresh and not so fresh fish; in other words, straight from the sea, stew or stream, or from the saltfish-store. The steward entered up freshwater fish only when it came as presents; in 1548, 12 carps, 9 breams, 5 roaches, 3 perches, 1 tench and 1 pike. He did not account for what was taken from the Hall fishponds.

Small purchases of 'sea fish' were made by Petre's acater at Brentwood and Chelmsford, occasionally at the decaying little market of Horndon-on-the-Hill, or a little farther afield at Barking, an important fish-market on a Thames creek. With some regularity he thus got supplies of soles, plaices, flounders, whitings and 'choyts', or 'cheyts'; less often, rochets, mullets, brets, smelts and cods; occasionally mackerels, gurnards and butts; once a bass, a fresh salmon and a thornback.*

Harrison's well-known remark that oysters were 'generally foreborne in the four hot months which are void of the letter R' could scarcely apply to the Ingatestone household, for whom the acater bought fairly regular supplies from early July to late March. Their weekly consumption ranged from two pecks to two bushels. They were abundant, in no way a luxury and in 1548 cost 8d. or 9d. a bushel, or as little as 12d. for 3 lb. if bought at Battlesbridge at the head of the creek which penetrates twenty miles inland to within twelve from Ingatestone. A few pence were very occasionally spent on other shellfish such as crabs, whelks and mussels.

The saltfish-store was no mean closet, and it held mostly big fish. Petre's orders were that ample stocks for emergencies as well as Lent and fishdays were always to be in hand. In mid-February 1548, immediately after the arrival of a cartload of 'Lenten stuff' from London, the quantity seems astonishing by modern standards. In addition to the 29½ couple lings recorded in January and untouched, there were 56 couple stockfish, 75½ couple haberdins and 17 couple lings. Week by week these were

* As with fowls, the Tudor plural was plaices, not plaice, and so on. See Appendix G for an explanatory note on the meaning and etymology of the names of some of these fish.

gradually reduced from exactly 300 fish in February to their lowest level in October, when the tally of 53 was made up of stockfish 1½ couple, old ling 11 couple, new ling 14 couple and haberdin nil. 'Stourbridge ling' were bought at the famous Cambridge fair.* In later years Petre got some direct from Harwich or even King's Lynn. In 1548 a big consignment of herrings came from London in February and lasted until May. Each week in Lent the household got through a barrel of white (pickled) herring and half a cade of red herring. These were the normal measures for white and red herring, cade being another name for a barrel holding six long hundreds of six score each. At the beginning of April the week's consumption was 'white herring 70, red herring 20'. The former were salted, not smoked.

Fresh fruit, vegetables and herbs from the orchard and the 'cook's garden' were not taken on charge by the steward. Fruit often figures in the lists of presents, but his accounts, like those of noble households, are silent about what vegetables and salads were eaten, except for a solitary entry for January in the 1550 household book. It noted that the gardener was supplied with 'colwort' seeds 4d., parsley seeds 4d., 'cersyell' seeds 2d., cucumber seeds 2d., parsnip seeds 2d., 'pompions' [large melons] 8d., white beets 1d., radish 2d. and a basket to carry herbs. These and other vegetables provided the ingredients for soups and salads, which are thought to have been preferred to cooked vegetables in Tudor days.[10]

A pleasant aim was the successful grafting of many fruits on to one tree. Of Petre's interest in such experiments nothing is known beyond the arrival of 'a bundle of apple grafts', after which the gardener got a grafting-knife and fetched fourteen peartree stocks to graft. Larke's survey of 1566 leaves no doubt about Petre's well-ordered orchard.

The large quantities of food consumed at Ingatestone Hall by the family, servants and wards, by the guests and their own servants, and by the craftsmen and tenants visiting the house on business were of course greatly augmented on special occasions, when gargantuan supplies of victuals were provided. The bill of fare, in fact, ranged between solid and sumptuous, monotonous and extraordinary. The 'strangers' who crowded the Great Hall over the Christmas of 1551–2 were not the only visitors; there

* The ling, found in the Northern seas, was a large codlike fish, three to four feet long. It had either been salted or split and dried. Tusser, the farmer-poet of Essex, Petre's junior by about twenty years, was to sing of 'Ling, saltfish and herring, for Lent to provide'. In its class ling was the best—after being soaked in water twelve hours before the cook prepared it for the meal. The haberdin was another kind of large cod, salt or sun-dried; its name of Dutch, not Scottish, origin. The stockfish, usually meaning the cod, had been cured by being split open and dried hard in the cold air, without salt; when it reached the kitchen it was beaten with a club, or stock (Petre's cook had a 'stockfish hammer'). Cf. ling bought at Stourbridge fair for Middleton Hall, Staffs., in 1524 (*Cal. Middleton MSS.* (H.M.C.), 372).

were also the specially invited guests. In the first days, these were only tenants; then, after Sir William's arrival on 4 January, there came the Petres' relations, friends and the eldest girl's future husband, with all his servants. In the first half of the week before Christmas Day, when the family was not in residence, normal dishes were served. For Sunday dinner, the servants had the company of twelve local folk. Between them all, they ate 3 pieces of boiled beef and 1 piece roasted, a neat's tongue, a baked leg of mutton, 2 coneys (rabbits) and a partridge; with 2 joints of mutton and 2 more coneys for supper. Lady Petre came home on Wednesday, on which there also appeared a huge venison pasty. On Christmas Day the servants carried in to the dinner tables 6 boiled and 3 roast pieces of beef, a neck of mutton, a loin and breast of pork, a goose, 4 coneys and 8 warden pies (baked warden pears, coloured by saffron grown at Walden in Essex, were deemed a dainty dish). Five joints of mutton, a neck of pork, 2 coneys, a woodcock and a venison pasty were served for supper.

Although Christmas had fallen on a Friday, which was a fast day, the Church allowed meat to appear in place of fish on this feast day. But New Year, also a Friday, was a minor festival in its eyes, and only fish and 'whitemeat' (eggs, butter and cheese) were permitted. At dinner the company ate a ling, an haberdin, 2 mudfishes, 6 plaices, 8 whitings, a cod, a salmon, 3 cakes of butter, 20 eggs and an unspecified quantity of cheese; and at supper half a ling, 2 mudfishes, 4 plaices, 4 whitings, 3 cakes of butter and 5 eggs. Two 'humble pasties' were in the dinner menu on the Wednesday after Christmas. Next day's dinner included 2 'humble pies'. These pasties contained venison enclosed in pastry and baked without a dish, umbles being the edible entrails and coarser parts of the deer. On Twelfth Day, when Richard Baker arrived, the kitchen staff served 9 pieces of boiled and 6 pieces of roast beef, a pestle (haunch) and leg of pork, 2 legs of veal, a young tender pig, a loin and breast of veal, 2 coneys, 10 beef pasties, 2 mutton pasties, 4 venison pasties, 3 geese, 2 capons, 2 partridges, a woodcock, 2 teals and a dozen larks. At supper were consumed a mutton (a whole sheep), 2 mutton joints, a shoulder of venison, a breast of pork, 6 coneys, a venison pasty, a duck, 2 capons, 2 partridges and 2 teals.

On Tuesday 2 March, near the end of the long winter, when the family was still away and the only strangers given hospitality were four local folk, they and the servants disposed of 4 pieces of boiled beef, a leg of veal and a hen for dinner, and 4 joints of mutton, a breast of veal, 2 capons, 2 hens and 6 eggs for supper. Much of the meat had probably been salted down for many weeks. It was the last meat to be tasted for a long while.

The following day—*Dies cineris*, as the account-book specially notes—was Ash Wednesday. The meal was prepared from the following, which the servants shared with five villagers:

Dinner. Half a ling, half a haberdin, 2 mudfishes, 36 white herrings, 26 red herrings, 4 cakes of butter, 4 eggs.

Supper. Nil.

Next day '3 poor men' sat at the open table with the same five:

Dinner. A jowl of ling, half a haberdin, 2 mudfishes, 40 white herrings, 50 red herrings, 2 cakes of butter.

Supper. A tail of ling, 3 mudfishes, 30 white herrings, 2 cakes of butter, 6 eggs.

Thus they finished off the first big Lenten ling, 'that noble fish', as the lovable Thomas Fuller of Waltham Abbey wrote a century later, 'corrival in his jowl with the surloin of beef'. Friday was all fish, including 2 'plaices', no supper. Saturday, much the same, with a stockfish added. Fish would have appeared, irrespective of Lent, on Fridays and Saturdays, which were fishdays. On Sunday, the usual salted fish, half a salt salmon, a jowl of conger, and 3 whitings. Monday, only fish, with 2 flounders added. Tuesday, lots of fish, as the local carters and their men were busy and twenty-five of them needed feeding. They ate a whole ling, a haberdin, 2 mudfishes, a stockfish, 120 white herrings, 30 red herrings and 2 cakes of butter. The acater went to market for an 'emption' of fresh fish consisting of 15 plaices, 5 fresh eels, 2 flounders and a peck of oysters. And so the first week of Lent ended, and the second week began, and ended, with fish. Not a taste of meat or fowl: much the same routine except for 2 salt eels. The third week, salt or dried fish most days, with a little fresh fish. Fourth week, fish salted and fresh, all the same varieties if such a word can be used, with a 'piece of green fish' (fresh cod) served for Sunday dinner. At that meal there also appeared half a salted salmon; they dined off its tail on Tuesday and off its jowl on Friday. Fifth week, the same fare, and on Friday, 'My lady came from London with Mr. Baker and her servants'. Some freshwater fish was also served, probably at her own table, consisting of 5 carps, 4 breams, a perch, half a thornback, a pickerell and another piece of greenfish. As none of these are recorded in the week's 'expense of provision' nor in the 'presents' or 'emptions', it may be assumed that the stewponds were drawn upon. Lent dragged on to the sixth week, when another salmon was seen at three meals. The seventh week began on Wednesday 13 April, with the same politico-religious prescription. The fast of Good Friday was strictly observed: the 2 flounders, 2 cakes of butter and 4 eggs were probably eaten by the younger children. Saturday, fish. Thus ended the forty-sixth fishday. The kitchen book has faithfully reflected the wearisome rigours of the Lenten diet. It was relieved a little by the abundant and cheap supplies of butter for fish-frying, which had been supplemented by a special pre-Lent purchase in London of four gallons of 'frying oil' at 2s. 2d. a gallon. The steward summed up: 'Spent this Lent in the house 4 barrels of white herrings, one given to the poor and one spent at London: 4 cades of red herrings, 2 of them spent in the house, one spent at London, and one given to the poor; 4 congers.' He then added a note of the sole departure from the fish diet: 'Spent this Lent 2 lambs, 3 capons, 4 partridges, 6 chickens on the children and them that were sick.' No relaxation occurred on Mid-Lent Sunday, called by some 'Refreshment Sunday', nor even on Lady Day, one of the great feasts, perhaps because it fell this year on a Friday. A recent writer stated, 'The enforcement of Lenten fasting raises a number of puzzling questions. Did people live by fish alone, and where did the fish come from?'[10A] Edward Bell gives clear answers for Petre's household.

Throughout the year, of course, there was no supper on Friday, but in some weeks the fast was relieved by a light meal in its place, judiciously called 'Drinking at night', which was probably a recognized term, as it is also found in place of Friday supper in Cecil's interesting but unpublished household book.[10B] For this a minimum of two cakes of butter and half a dozen eggs were used—a little more if there were guests—and a couple of plaices or soles also found their way to the table very occasionally. On other special fasts, such as St. Matthew's Day (Wednesday 20 September) and the Vigil of St. John (Thursday 23 June), a 'drinking' with the same ingredients replaced supper. Breakfast, so termed, is not mentioned in the kitchen-books; people broke their fast in the morning, if they wished, with cold meat (fish on fast-days), bread and cheese.

When Lent of 1552 had passed the scribe turned over a new leaf and wrote, not in low Latin but good English, 'Easter Day'. And with it, the reappearance of meat, given no doubt a vociferous welcome:

Dinner. Boiled beef 3 pieces, roasting beef 2 pieces, an hinderquarter of veal, a capon, 8 pigeons.

Supper. 4 joints of mutton, a rack of veal, 8 pigeons.

The week's consumption, a complete change, was an ox, 2 calves, a teg, 2 muttons, a lamb and a goodly number of pigeons. There was in truth a flutter in the dovecote, for '58 pigeons were taken'.

Despite the seemingly endless Lent, weekly fishdays continued. After each Thursday the meat vanished again until Sunday, so that when a distinguished visitor came to stay on the last Friday and Saturday in April the cook could serve him with no venison, no wildfowl, not even boiled beef. Yet there remained in the larder 2 joints of veal, one of mutton, 6 pigeon pies, 3 kid pasties and a lamb pasty, as well as 25 pieces of beef for the servants. And the denial was not due to the guest being the Bishop of Norwich (Petre's old friend Thirlby), but because secular laws had pronounced dire penalties on anyone who ate meat on a statutory fishday. Not long afterwards Ascension Week came round, and with it a further short period restricting the household to eat fish from Monday to Saturday, when they were relieved at last by Ascension Day.

By the eve of Catherine Tyrell's wedding in June, many of the more important guests had already arrived. The whole company consumed at Saturday's dinner 4 lings, 5 couple haberdins, 16 mackerels, 2 congers (one boiled, the other baked), 15 couple soles, a thornback, 2 pikes, 4 mullets, 40 flounders, 3 dishes of butter (4½ lb.), a lead of cheese (56 lb.) and a score of eggs. The marriage feast on Sunday is thus accounted for:

Wedding feast

Dinner. Beef boiled roasted and baked an ox and a quarter; veals 4, lambs 6, kids 2, bucks 2, geese 22, cygnets 2, capons boiled and roasted 25, pheasants 7, rabbits 16, chickens 2 dozen 4, 'brewers' 6, partridges 7, heronshews 8, quails 5 dozen.

Supper. Muttons 5, lambs 4, kids 1, bucks 1, capons 10, pheasants 3, chickens 3 dozen, rabbits 36, pigeons 20 pairs, peachickens 4, quails 2 dozen.

'Brewers' (brewes) were apparently a kind of snipe, and heronshews were young herons.

What the crowd ate came from three sources—the demesnes and parks as well as the granaries and store-houses at the Hall, the guests' gifts and the acater's purchases. Except the last, it is found in the usual, though swollen, list:

Expense of provision this week

3 oxen given by Sir John Mordaunt, Sir Harry Tyrell and Mr. Anthony Browne.
Calves 7, all Ingatestone bred.
Muttons 10.
Lambs 14, 10 of them given.
Kids 3, 2 of them Crondon bred, 1 given by Mr. Stanton.
Bucks 6, one from Sir John Gates, one from Mr. Stonard, the third from Mr. Honyons, 2 from Crondon Park, and one from Writtle.
A stag from Mr. Stonard.

Wheat 9 quarters 7 bushels; malt 44 bushels; oats to the yeoman's stable 4 bushels; oats to the poultry at Thorndon 3 bushels; oats to the poultry at Ingatestone 3 bushels; oats to strangers 1 quarter.

12. INGATESTONE HALL: THE LONG GALLERY

13. INGATESTONE HALL:
HERALDIC GLASS IN THE
LONG GALLERY

14. VIRGINAL DATED 1562 IN THE LONG GALLERY

15. TUDOR PANELLING IN THE GARDEN CHAMBER

Lings 2, haberdins 4, conger 1, stockfish 2 couple.
Butter 44 dishes.
Cheeses a lead containing 6 cheeses.
Geese 52, capons 58, pheasants 19, rabbits 3 score couple, chickens 12 dozen 8, heronshews 30, quails 14½ dozen, a firkin of sturgeon.
Eggs 6 hundred, cream 8 gallons.
Bread 'baken' this week [blank].

A glance at the contents of the larder at the end of the week shows that some venison was left over in the form of three pasties of fallow deer and one of red.

The acater made some extraordinary purchases for the wedding feast.

Paid by Wilcocks the cook for the baking a conger 5s., an hundred marchpane bread 6d., a quarter gold 16d., 1 lb. turnsole for jellies 2s., ½ lb. grain 9d.*

The flavours and hues of these delicacies deserve an appreciative under-standing of the fancy ingredients stirred and turned in the imported cook's array of skillets and posnets. Marchpane was the sugary, pounded almond confection, to be known later as marzipan, and 'wrought', as Harrison re-marked, 'with no small curiositie'. The ¼ oz. gold leaf was used for gild-ing the surface of one of the sweetmeats, perhaps the marchpane. The colour of the jellies, purple or violet, was the result of putting into the hot liquid some linen rags which had been steeped in turnsole plant juice. Grains, likewise, were a forerunner of cochineal.

'When Mr. Secretary Cecil and his wife were here', the acater augmented the ordinary supplies by paying 3s. at Chelmsford market for half a calf and 7½d. for strawberries. Lady Norwich (Dorothy Petre's godmother), the Cecils and other guests were visiting the Hall while haymaking was in full swing. Then, in turn, the harvesting of the corn reached its height on 16 August (old style, now reckoned as 26 August): Strangers. 6 score persons at Thorndon when my master's wheat was 'roppe'. That day the kitchen sent out to the East Horndon farm half a steer carved up for the 120 hungry reapers; half an ox had gone thither a few days before. The week's list of provisions also gives 'four muttons' and three hogsheads of beer (162 gallons) sent to the harvest folks there 'when my master had his wheat ropped', for the urgency of their work demanded that food and drink be brought to them. There is of course no question of crediting Petre as a generous employer with dispensing all these extra victuals to the harvesters. They, like most craftsmen and labourers, were paid at a lower

* Cf. the reference in the description of the Serjeants' Feast, 1555, in W. Dugdale, *Origines Judiciales* (1662): 'The serjeants made choice of one Wilcocks for their cook, whose office it was to furnish the kitchen with pots, pans, spits, racks, chafers and other like necessaries.'

rate when given 'meat and drink', as in the county justices' wages assessments of later date.

Except for Christmas and the June wedding, the most extensive hospitality given during 1552 was when Lady Darcy and her train came to Ingatestone:

Dinner. Boiled beef 16 pieces, 4 pieces roasted, half a calf, 2 pigs, 7 capons, 5 pasties of venison, 12 conies, 20 pigeons, an heronshew, 7 quails, 5 partridges, and 2 tarts.

Supper. 11 joints of mutton, half a lamb, 4 capons, 3 pasties of venison, 9 conies, an heronshew, a peahen, 18 pigeons, 6 chickens, 3 partridges, 2 tarts, and a florentine.

Pig, in Tudor language, referred only to the very young and tender animal. The florentine, a special kind of meat pie or tart, was perhaps the cook's *tour de force* for the benefit of the guests.

In October 1548, a present led to a unique entry: '10 pasties of wild boar'; its head, a delicacy, was also sent to grace the high table. The wild boar became virtually extinct in England within the next century. Presents in kind were not confined to relations and friends. By general custom, the tenants and the local tradesmen and craftsmen sent Petre wildfowl, poultry and fruit—nine oxbirds, for instance, or a basket of wardens, a pannier of pears, or a dish of quinces; half a dozen artichokes or a dish of walnuts were equally acceptable. A gammon of bacon, or a flitch, in true Essex style, arrived now and again with greetings. A few 'capons in grease', some geese (usually alive), and many domestic fowls, fattened capons, turkeys (guinea fowls), partridges, pheasants and quails came as offerings for the table. The weekly 'remain of the poultry', with such entries as 'quails four dozen, one dead', 'geese four and one dead', shows that they also arrived alive and were put into the fowl-coop by the orchard wall, where Petre had a contrivance for 'the better cherishing' of his own fowls. The steward seldom wrote 'Presents nihil'.

The time of universal present-giving was the New Year, not the Nativity. Very different from gifts at the Court were those in the country, where there was an abundant choice of edible offerings. As John Petre was born on 20 December, the New Year and the baptismal feasts almost coincided and there was a copious inflow of gifts. From Thorndon, Lady Mordaunt sent a guinea fowl, a mallard, a woodcock, 2 teals and a basket of 'wafers [biscuits] and other cakes for the christening of Master John'. The good wishes of relations and neighbours were accompanied by curlews, praines, plovers, oxbirds, mallards, redshanks, teals, woodcocks and small birds, such as 6 dozen larks. The humblest tenants proffered their respects, even if only with a fattened capon or two. Thomas Mildmay of Moulsham Hall, on the Ingatestone side of Chelmsford, sent 7 partridges and 10 'snipes'. It took two of Sir John Mordaunt's servants to bring a turkey hen, capons, mallards, woodcocks, teals, 'snytes' (a couple of each) and a dozen chickens. Those who failed to send a gift at the New Year had a final opportunity at the close of Christmas: 'Given to Mr. Worthington's man for bringing a lamb to my Lady upon Twelfth Even, 4d.' A delightful entry reads: 'Mr. Pascall's man bringing two couple capons from his master, with divers other presents, as in the week book at large appeareth, from the wives of Baddow'.* John Pascall of Great Baddow, close by Chelmsford, was a relation of Lady Petre through his marriage in 1549 with Mary Keble. Some food also came as rent in kind. The largest quantity was sent from the Thamesside marshes at South Benfleet, the tenant of which was obliged to deliver, either to Ingatestone or East Horndon, 60 wethers 'unshorn in their wool' between Christmas and 12 January, 20 ewes at Michaelmas and 3 'good fresh salmons of the largest sort taken within the waters of the marsh' between Candlemas and Bartholomewtide. In addition he had to deliver 3 more salmons for which Petre would pay 3s. 4d. each.[11]

Altogether, the 'week books' reveal an ordered, self-contained household, well-provisioned at all seasons largely by produce from the farms and parks held in demesne (Ingatestone, Crondon and East Horndon), supplemented by 'presents', rents in kind, and tithes from the two lay rectories. Wine, dried fruit and spices had to be bought at London, and saltfish at Stourbridge Fair or ports, but apart from such food, the housesteward relied on the outside world only for 'fresh acates' or 'emptions': he used both terms, and once the curious heading, 'Emptions of cates'.

In the second week of 1548† the emptions cost 24s. 5d., or double the average amount. The routine items were whitings, mackerels and oysters, a little fresh meat, some fowls, and yeast for baking and brewing. The small supplies of meat required nearly every week to help out the 'ox cut in livery pieces', lambs and so on, were mostly bought from Peter Preston, a local butcher. The emptions were made by the 'cater', a word which may be equated with the modern caterer just as the Tudor poulter became poulterer. Besides his visits to local markets on Tuesdays and Fridays, in rush periods before the arrival of notable visitors he rode forth with packhorse to buy extra necessaries and delicacies. 'Paid for eggs bought by the cater and the kitchen boy against my Lady Mary's coming,

* Cf. 'To sundry wives which bought presents on Twelfth Day', 1551 (*Cal. Ancaster MSS.* (H.M.C.), 463). See 'The Pascall Family' (*Trans. Essex Arch. Soc.*, xxiii, 54–65).
† See Appendix E.

3s. 1d.', is the first entry in an abnormally long list, made up largely of wildfowl and fish, butcher's meat including a tender piglet, also (for once) extra butter and candles; the total cost was 50s. 1d. Mary's call on her return journey meant another inflated list which included 240 eggs (3s. 10d.). Shortly before her third visit a few months later, a servant was dispatched 'to seek wild fowl', and the carter brought back from London 'a frail [rush basket] of figs 3s. 6d., half a piece of great raisins 5s. 8d., a box of "luxaun" 8s., 4 lb. currants 16d., 4 lb. almonds 16d., 4 lb. rice 10d., 100 oranges with a basket 14d., 2 lb. pepper 5s., 2 lb. prunes 8d.' The shop in the High Street also sold ninepennyworth of goods: '2 lb. prunes 5d. and 2 lb. great raisins 4d. bought at Ingatestone town against my Lady Mary's coming': country prices, despite the cost of carriage from London, could be competitive. Again in 1550 the village store got custom when Lady Petre had a sudden fancy: 'Laid out for sugar candy bought at Ingatestone for my lady, 2d.' John's birth also called for delicacies: 'Spices—Paid for bringing from London a box of biscuits 14d., a box of caraways 14d., 6 lb. damask prunes 12d., 6 lb. great raisins 12d.'

While the acater thus added variety to the victuals which the estate provided, food was occasionally dispatched from the Hall, when the family was at Aldersgate: 'Sent to London half a pork, 20 cast of yeoman's bread, 3 capons, 4 couple of coneys, 4 pieces of beef, 2 dozen larks, 3 snipes, 2 curlews, 1 duck, 3 wigeons, 36 eggs.'

In discovering the vast consumption of Petre's beer, it must of course be remembered that generally very little water was drunk. Although at Ingatestone Hall there were two rural phenomena—a piped supply of 'sweet' spring-water in the house and a drinking-tap in the yard—his servants were perhaps little disposed to patronize these new-fangled contraptions. 'Water', Dr. Boorde wrote a few years earlier, 'is not wholesome sole by itself for an Englishman', and he sang the praises of good ale brewed from malt and water alone.[12] Ale and beer seem originally to have been synonymous. But after the introduction of hops about 1525 beer denoted the liquor preserved and flavoured with them. According to one version of a well-known rhyme—

> Hops, Reformation, bays and beer,
> Came in to England all in one year.

But imported hops were certainly used in beer-brewing somewhat earlier. There was a 'hopgarden' at Ingatestone in 1548, probably the 'hopyard' of Larke's plan, just outside the orchard wall. In the Petre accounts it is clear that ale was only for the sick, the young, the ladies and a few others who preferred it to the slightly bitter beer. Brewing was normally the housewife's task, but Petre's establishment was large enough to employ a part-time brewer. How skilled his task was can be deduced from the equipment he used—rowers (in which to stir the barley), scavel (spade), jets (large ladles), mashing vat (in which hot water was added to the malt to form wort), sweet wort tun, copper for boiling wort, cooler, chunk (into which the wort ran), yealding vat (in which it was left to ferment), cowls (big water-carrying tubs), yeast-tubs, roundlets (yeast-casks), leaden troughs, skeps (baskets), iron-hooped stuke (handle) and pulley (for loading the casks to be carted to the buttery). The 'great' vats and all the rest could be seen in the brewhouse, at any rate in 1600, when there were also two hopkilns nearby.[13]

In the buttery there were two sizes of cask—the big hogsheads holding 54 gallons and the kilderkins of 18 gallons. After the 1547–8 Christmas hospitality, there remained 10 kilderkins of 'household beer,' or 'single beer', and half a hogshead of 'March beer', a stronger brew. Judging from the high and low figures of the weaker drink, which alternate fairly regularly in the weekly 'remain of the buttery', the brewer carried out his task almost every fortnight,* and his brew contained between 16 and 20 kilderkins (288 to 360 gallons). Evidently it was of very low alcoholic content—the single 'X' of monkish days. Apart from a single hogshead in February, no more March beer was received until May, when 8 hogsheads arrived. In August 3 quarters of malt were sent to the East Horndon farm, 'provided for Cornelis' brewing'; and a month later Cornelis delivered to the Ingatestone cellar another 8 hogsheads; this was gradually drunk in addition to the single beer, until only 1 kilderkin remained at the end of November. He evidently brewed the stronger stuff with plenty of hops, and it remained longer in good condition.

The 1552 book, unlike that of 1548, makes no distinction between the strengths. The fortnightly brew yielded about 32 kilderkins. During hay-making, harvest and festive periods it was necessary to brew every week. The buttery held 40 kilderkins (720 gallons) just before the New Year and the same quantity in readiness for the wedding. No March beer is mentioned, but 4 hogsheads (216 gallons) of the Ingatestone brew left the buttery for the Aldersgate house, and the brewer's cart that took it brought back a supply of Lenten fish. In October the store suddenly sank to 4 kilderkins, and perhaps because the Hall brewer was sick or the malt ran

---

* In 1599 brewing took place almost every week at Petworth, the Earl of Northumberland's house (Mr. G. R. Batho's unpublished London M.A. thesis, 'The household accounts of Henry Percy, ninth Earl of Northumberland (1564–1632)', p. 169).

out the next week's emptions were exceptional in including 14 'kilder-kins' of 'small beer' bought from Thomas Ramme, a local brewer, for 19s. 10d. (When brewing ten years later, his apprentice fell into the vat and was drowned in the hot liquid.[14])

About a decade later, Harrison's wife, who brewed their beer monthly at Radwinter, made 200 gallons for 20s., as against the Ingatestone brewer's charge for 252 gallons. It looks then as though Petre's small beer worked out at 1d. a gallon. Very approximately, the average consumption a head at the Hall on normal days was one gallon. The 32 normal brewings in 1552 produced 1,024 kilderkins, or 18,432 gallons. If allowance is made for extra heavy brewings before the jollifications and the mighty thirst during hay and corn harvests, the total consumption in 1552 is estimated at 20,000 gallons, or 160,000 pints! The net cost was probably no more than £75. The English, in truth, were a nation of 'maltbugs', as Harrison declared. At the royal palaces it was the same story. A Spanish eye-witness related that the courtiers and their servants drank more beer than would fill the river Valladolid;[15] and the Ingatestone household's consumption would fill the river Wid.

Petre's outlay on wine was also substantial. In the week after Twelfth Day 1548, the Ingatestone wine-cellar held half a hogshead of red wine, one and a half hogsheads of French wine, half a puncheon of Rhenish wine and half a butt of sack; white wine and claret nil. A week later his claret was replenished by a hogshead, white wine by a tierce and an extra hogshead of red wine arrived, all sent from London.* When Sir William and Lady Petre were both at Court, his house-steward kept the wine-cellar locked up. It was in the middle of August that the store in the cellar was at its highest level: Gascon claret 4 hogsheads; white wine, red wine and French wine, 1 hogshead of each; all 'these remain full and not broached'. The contents amounted to 378 gallons. The second book gives only the result of stocktaking at the beginning of the steward's financial year, shortly before Christmas.†

---

* The tun equalled 2 pipes (pieces, or butts) or 4 hogsheads, and contained 252 wine-gallons, the puncheon 84 gallons; the tierce was a third of a pipe. Petre's first recorded purchase was a puncheon of French wine which cost him 55s. in 1543. He twice bought a tun of Gascon wine at London in 1544, but it was not until 1560 that a cask of this size was carted to Ingatestone. The small roundlet or runlet was no fixed measure: 'a roundlet of Rhenish wine containing 21½ gallons' and 'rundelet of muscadel containing 6 gallons' occur in his accounts for 1549–50.

† Cf. the contents of Anne of Cleves' cellar in 1556: Gascon wine 3 hogsheads £9, malmsey 10 gallons 16s. 8d., muscadel 11 gallons 23s. 10d., sack 10 gallons 13s. 4d. (A. J. Kempe, *Loseley MSS.* (1835), 10–14). For contemporary prices of wines, see A. L. Simon, *History of the Wine Trade in England* (1907), ii, 280–5.

Wines remaining in the cellar 6 December 1551.

A butt of sack and 12 gallons.
2 puncheons of French wine and 20 gallons.
An hogshead of French wine.
An hogshead of Gascon wine with an half.
An hogshead of red wine with an half.
A piece of Rhenish wine.
4 gallons of malmsey.

These totalled 584 gallons. Despite the cheapness of wines—around 1s. a gallon—Petre had expended about £25 on laying in this quantity. The cellar also contained 3 hogsheads of verjuice and one of perry. The verjuice, a sort of very sharp cider, used in cooking or as a condiment, was probably the first produced at Ingatestone Hall; in the previous year Petre had ordered the making of a 'crab press', to crush the juice out of his apples. As perry-making scarcely differs in method from cider-making, the press was perhaps also used to produce the perry, rarely recorded in the eastern counties. Memories of a few successful monastic vineyards doubtless account for his hopefully spending 5s. in 1550 'for 14 vine roots bought at Charing Cross and sent to Ingatestone'. In the main, Petre's preference was evidently for the sweet French wines, mostly shipped from Bordeaux. 'In the difficult matter of foreign wine', according to one historian, the lord of the manor, even in Shakespeare's time, 'was often more ready to trust mine host's cellar than his own'.[16] Petre's wine-cellar may therefore be regarded as well stocked to meet the reasonable needs of his distinguished visitors and Christmas guests.

3 The Household

The country house required a large number of servants to maintain it. Several more were needed to wait upon Lady Petre, the children and the wards, though two wards before coming of age each had his own man-servant. A few officers were also employed to look after the estate.

It is in 1550 that the establishment can first be clearly seen. The *quarterly* wage-lists and other references show that the indoor and outdoor servants at Ingatestone alone increased from 17 to 21 in the course of the year. Edward Bell the house-steward and Robert Humfrey the acater received no wages but held neighbouring farms on lease at low rents. John West the law-steward had the highest sum, probably a retaining fee (13s. 4d.), except for one Haywood (15s.) whose duties are not known. There were also a gardener (10s. 6d.), cook (10s.), butler (10s.), part-time brewer (5s.), two horsekeepers, stable-boy, two carters, cart lad, lackey and six other menservants, one of whom must have been clerk of the kitchen. Lady Petre's servants were Mistress Percy the housekeeper, Mistress Mary who looked after the children (10s. each) and four maids, the youngest getting 5s. a quarter. 'Thomas Coke' was not the only servant to be colloquially known by his office. His real name occurs when he was engaged and given 3s. 4d. earnest money: 'in reward to Thomas Gryffith the cook at his going into Essex'. The book refers to 'John Gardyner', 'John Buttlare', 'Richard horsekeeper' (or more often 'Richard of the stable'). Quarterly stipends were also paid to 'Sir Thomas of Buttsbury 33s. 4d.' (increased to 40s. in 1555) and 'Sir Richard 13s. 4d.', their prefixes being courtesy titles extended to clerics. The latter was the household chaplain and had his own chamber at the Hall; Petre had obtained a Crown licence for a family chaplain in 1546. Buttsbury rectory belonged outright to Petre; the priest who served the cure was a superior servant removable at will, and eked out his scanty stipend as often as he could with free meals at his patron's house. They are not included in the figure of 21, nor are the warrener, the miller and the falconer, all of whom were otherwise remunerated. Living in the demesne farmhouse at East Horndon were a bailiff (11s. 8d.), 'the widow that keeps the house', a carter, a boy and a dairymaid. The annual wage payments in 1550 were £51, of which the small Horndon establishment cost £11.

As usual, the ordinary household servants were hired by the year. In addition to their wages, they got board and lodging and their livery allowance of clothing. Every spring and autumn a bulk purchase of grey cloth was made for the servants' 'summer liveries' and 'winter liveries'. The latter was bought in some years at the great Bartholomew Fair in London. In winter they wore 'grey frieze', a coarse woollen cloth, and in summer 'grey marble', a parti-coloured worsted interwoven so as to resemble the veining of marble,[17] which was a little finer in texture and is sometimes referred to in the accounts as 'fine marble cloth'. Blue was the more common colour of servants' liveries. Petre's servants in their summer mottled grey marble must have presented a striking appearance. Even the miller and the warrener had their marble livery cloth, but the household chaplain's '3½ yards of cloth for his livery' was presumably black.

Some of the servants occasionally got extras—'rewards' for heavy work and so on; when Mistress Mary knitted 'two pairs of hoses' for the children she got 3d. a pair, and the gardener's wife earned a little for casual weeding.

The servants attached to the town house, as seen in the London accounts for 1550, were Mistress Wells the housekeeper, a cook, a laundress and at least nine men, but the last were mostly his personal attendants at Court rather than domestic servants. In fact the housekeeper may have been the only permanent servant at Aldersgate.[18] 'Old John Cook' was followed in 1549 by 'Richard Cook', who accompanied his master to Boulogne in the following year. 'Edward and Dick of the stables', sometimes described as 'the two horsekeepers', were probably identical with their namesakes at Ingatestone. The wages of the housekeeper, laundress and most of the men were 10s. a quarter; the 'old' cook got 12s. 4d., his successor 16s. 8d. John Kyme, Petre's chief steward, does not appear in the lists, nor does Richard Stonley, his London acater and agent. More than once several of the servants won a bonus of up to 10s. In addition, there seem to have been one or two wageless boys and girls, who flit momentarily through the accounts, such as 'Tom of the kitchen for a pair of hose 3s. 8d.' In 1550 the London steward paid out £23 6s. 8d. in wages, together with money for 'rewards' and livery cloth. 'His board wages for 8 days after 5d. by the day' and 'Dinners of seven servants on three days at 3d. the piece every meal 5s. 3d.' are typical entries showing how they fared when unable to feed in the Aldersgate house. Their meals were usually paid for when Petre was being entertained. 'Servants' suppers when my master supped at my Lord Chancellor' shows that open house was not kept in London, and Petre as well as the servants frequently fed at one or other of the many respectable taverns and cookhouses near at hand.*

The 1556 audit-roll shows that the ordinary wages of the Ingatestone, East Horndon and Aldersgate servants and the personal attendants rose to £107.† This record does not state numbers and only names the higher servants, none of whom had left. Additions to the country lists were the keepers of Writtle and Crondon Parks. A London armourer employed to look after the armoury at Ingatestone Hall was included in Kyme's list. The item for 'wages of such servants as daily do attend upon my master and my mistress at the Court' distinguishes them from the small Aldersgate staff. 'The Court' entry thus shows annual wages of £29 15s. against £18 for 1550. The 1556 roll includes only the servants' summer cloth liveries costing £29, so that the adjusted figure for wages and clothes should be about £175. This sum does not take into account the few senior officers

* The well-to-do townsman's dinner was often eaten at a tavern or bought at the cookshop and taken home (J. C. Drummond and A. Wilbraham, *The Englishman's Food* (1939), 60).

† A quarter's wages of the servants of Sir Francis and Lady Willoughby at Wollaton Hall, Notts., in 1572, amounted to £40 (*Cal. Middleton MSS.*, H.M.C.), 541-2; this included £5 to the musicians. For Sir William's short-term musician, see p. 211.

who received their equivalent of wages in the form of low-rented farms and the like. It is evident, therefore, that in 1556 Petre was spending about £250 in keeping up his three houses and providing himself and his wife with officers, servants and attendants befitting their position.

More exact figures of the whole staff employed occur in an unexpected source. Petre's friend, William Pownsett, of Loxford Hall, Barking, a former steward of Barking Abbey and an Exchequer official, made his will in 1554.[19] He gave legacies to all Petre's servants: 'Mistress Mary Persey 10s., Mistress Joyce 7s., and Mistress Joan 5s., the gentlewomen of my lady Petre; John Kyme gentleman 20s., Richard Stonley gentleman 20s.; to the rest of the gentlemen of Sir William Petre 6s. 8d. being 9 in number, 60s.; Thomas Bishop his servant 6s. 8d.; to the rest of the servants of Sir William Petre men and women as well attending upon him at the Court (14) as elsewhere at his houses (31), being 45 in number at 5s. apiece, £11 5s.' So Petre's affluence by 1554 had extended to allow him to keep in his pay-roll sixty officers and servants.*

There were times when Sir William and Lady Petre needed a fairly large escort, well groomed and well equipped. Ceremonial occasions and diplomatic negotiations, too, required that the Secretary should be surrounded by a suitable entourage. As one of the New Men, his social standing with fellow councillors also demanded it. To this extent, the Petres' appearance at the various palaces where the Court lay may seem ostentatious, Sir William being accompanied by his steward and fourteen menservants and his wife by her 'gentlewoman' and several maids. Among them, however, his lackey and others were regularly employed between the palaces, law-courts, Aldersgate and Ingatestone with messages and so forth, and the journeys of the Court, especially the longer progresses, necessitated the carting about of a large amount of his baggage —at the Secretary's own expense.

The Ingatestone household with about thirty officers, indoor and outdoor servants certainly cannot be regarded as over-staffed. Their careful employer saw to that. It was only when he was in residence there that this number was increased by his personal attendants; his guests, if they had tried to count, would have noted about forty servants in all. †

* Cecil had twenty-five, including two farm-hands, in his Wimbledon household in 1555 (C. Read, *op. cit.*, 87).

† It is not easy to distinguish clearly between menial servants, who normally lived in the house or outbuildings, and retainers. The latter apparently included both the superior personal attendants and some tenants who were only servants in the sense that they had to attend on their lord on special occasions, wearing his distinctive livery (hat, badge or whole garment). Petre's miller and warrener were among his retainers. Under the Tudor law of 'livery and maintenance', the Crown granted licences to a limited number of magnates to

The normal establishment, in fact, was no more than was required in a country house of medium size; in noble mansions, as other records show, the number was much larger. The domestic and farm servants were expected to provide nearly all the needs, with little recourse to market. The maids, for instance, made the ordinary clothes for the family as well as their own. Even the raw material of the simpler garments was prepared, such as 'spinning 4 lb. tow, 8d.' and 'spinning 1 lb. fine flax, 6d.'; but 'weaving 37 ells fine canvas, 18s. 6d.' was a skilled job for which an outsider was paid, and as already mentioned cloth for the servants' liveries was purchased in bulk. Candles were bought by the acater from a Chelmsford chandler. In 1548, for example, '8 lb. small candle 16d., 4 lb. watch candle, and 6 lb. big candle 20d.'; and immediately before the visit of Lord Chancellor Rich, '12 lb. small and 6 lb. middle candle 3s.' But '2 lb. cotton wick for candles at 18d. the lb., sent to Ingatestone' in 1560 shows that they were then, if not earlier, being made there; an interesting description of the candle-making equipment is preserved.[20]

The estate furnished all the fuel for heating, cooking and brewing. Ample supplies for producing charcoal came from Petre's woods. In this ancient operation, split wood was placed in a conical pile, which was then mostly covered by turf. Such a 'hearth', built in a forest clearing, was burned very slowly; when cold, the black charcoal was packed into bags. The skilled charcoal-burner who worked in the lonely depths of Writtle Great Wood also kept bees and sold the honey to his landlord at the rate of two gallons for 5s. 5d. For his main labours he was paid thus:

To Robert Marshall my master's collier in Essex for hewing wood and coaling 7 loads of coals, every load containing 2 dozen 3 quarters, after 22d. for every dozen, whereof 2 loads went to London, 3 to Ingatestone, and 1 to Horndon, 35s.

At the time of Dorothy's wedding in London his products had to be supplemented by a purchase there of 'a load and 16 sacks of charcoals' for 24s. 8d. and '9 chalder of sea coals' which cost £3 6s. 8d., with 3s. 6d. for unloading, 2d. to the 'shiplads', 8s. for measuring and 14s. for carriage from the quay to Aldersgate. Other household fuel came in the form of faggots, talwood and billets. These three terms, with 'coals', stood for separate sizes laid down in the Act for the Assize of Fuel;[21] a sack of

have a specified number of liveried retainers, additional to regular attendants and household officers. In 1546 he was authorized 'to retain 20 men in his livery, over and besides household servants and daily attendants' (L. & P., xxi, pt. i, 302(38)). Queen Mary was somewhat generous in issuing such licences. Petre was allowed 60 retainers; among her other licensees were Gardiner and Arundel (200 each), Pembroke and Paget (100), Rochester (60), Bourne (40), Sir Henry Tyrell (20) and Boxall (10) (Cal. Pat. Rolls, Mary, i, 390; cf. Strype, Eccl. Mem., iii, pt. ii, 160).

charcoal had to contain 4 bushels (a century later a load is stated to have been 30 sacks of 3 bushels).[22] Petre paid 10s. for 'making 30 loads of tal-wood and billet' and 18s. for '15 hundred faggots'.

There was much other activity in the woods—felling, dressing and squaring—to supply the timber needed for the building operations at Ingatestone, East Horndon and Crondon, e.g., 'felling and bretning out [splitting] 44 loads of wood 11s.' Sawyers were sometimes paid 'by great' —a fixed price for the whole job—instead of by the day. 'Sawing 550 boards at 12d. the hundred 6s.', 'sawing 2,650 slitting work 30s. 11d.', and 'breaking timber at the park and sawing 4,200 slitting work at 14d. the hundred, cutting 8 timber logs overthwart 8d.' are typical payments. Sawpits were frequently made at a cost of 8s. each.

Ingatestone Hall gave employment to many local craftsmen, most of whom were Petre's tenants. Joiners, carpenters and turners all got plenty of orders in the house and the farm-buildings. Here are sample bills: 'William the joiner working 5 days including cupboards 3s. 4d., for his boy 20d.; making a new bedstead with a trucklebed, a press, and a form 4s. 4d.; 6 new cupboards 10s.; a large bedstead 10s.; laid out to the turner for turning 4 cupboard feet 12d.; 12 stools 9s.; a new square table, 2 frames for tables, and one for the map 3s. 4d.' Next time a turner was employed directly: 'for turning 8 dozen feet for stools 8d.' For a big job a carpenter had £40 by 'bargain', with 2s. earnest money. A new farm-cart was made by direct labour for 47s.: the body 7s.; the Ingatestone wheelwright for a pair of shod wheels 11s.; a Brentwood smith, for strakes (iron rims for the wheels), nails and other ironwork 29s. A plough, however, was bought for 3s. 8d. at Billericay.

Other wheelwrights and smiths got custom from the estate, such as 'Robert Ashby the wheeler for making 2 axletrees and mending both carts in divers places 3s. 4d.' Very long bills sent in by 'Foster the smith for iron work' each quarter were copied into the account-book. They give a valuable picture of the blacksmith's skill and abound in strange terms of his trade. He had various jobs to execute in the mansion and the outbuildings, such as making 'two great bars whereon the vice of the turnbroach [turnspit] standeth', 'a paring iron for the butler' and numerous keys and locks; gudgeons, spindles and a host of other useful iron accessories were also needed. Farm and garden tools and the iron parts of the heavy wooden farm implements—clouts, clout-pins and linch-pins for the carts, for instance—accounted for much of his work. For the plough-oxen he supplied 'a staple to an oxyoke in weight 2 lb. 6d.', '3 iron pins for oxbows 2d.' [the bow-shaped wooden collars fastened to the yoke] and 'a pair of ox-nails in weight 9 lb. 22½d.' The horses probably gave him the most work. As a farrier his bill ran thus: '126 geldings' shoes 21s., 56 removes of geldings' shoes 2s. 4d., 15 great horse shoes 5s., 36 cart horse shoes 6s., 76 hackney shoes 12s. 8d.' Cart harness was not made, but bought from Nash, a Chelmsford saddler, whose detailed bill for 32s. is set out. 'The trap of wire to take mice' which the butler asked for must clearly have been an elaborate cage to cost as much as 10d. 'Hankin the smith' who did much of the shoeing in the stables was regularly employed to make a good deal of iron-work in and about Ingatestone Hall. 'A new key and mending the lock of one of the park gates 8d.', 'a lock and key for a chest for Mistress Elizabeth [Petre's daughter] 8d.' and 'the pipe of the tunnel for the brewhouse 4d.' are typical of many entries. Only once was his skill unable to meet the occasion. Lady Petre asked her city merchant friend to find an expert, with this result: 'To a smith of London sent hither by Mr. Garrett to mend the turnspit and the clock at Ingatestone and at Horndon, working 9 days after 8d. the day, meat and drink, 6s.; 16 lb. iron 3s. 4d.; 2 bushel of coals 14d.; the use of the smith's files of Ingatestone 6d.' The cooper of Billericay was paid 20d. for 'setting on 18 hoops and cutting 2 hogsheads for fish'; the tanner got 4s. 2d. for 'tanning and curing 5 goat-skins'. Only one call by an itinerant tinker is recorded.

Bricks were made in clamps, that is, they were burned in stacks in the open, not in kilns. The best brick-earth on the estate was at East Horndon, where Walter Gye the brickmaker was paid in 1550 for '4,600 bricks at 4s. the thousand 18s. 4d.; 50,000 of earth to make brick in part payment for making the same brick at 20d. the thousand 10s.; 1,250 paving tile 50s.' Foster the tiler had a contract to tile the Horndon house for £9. He was paid the unearned balance while he lay 'very sick'; he died, and Petre had to pay £3 to others to get the work finished.

It is clear that the demands of the Hall were mainly for services rather than for goods. Wage-earners or contractors worked on materials which the owner provided. Among local exceptions to this generalization were the shoemaker and the potter. The former charged 10d. a pair for Lady Petre's shoes, 7d. for her children's and 9d. for the kitchen boy's that had to stand harder wear (he soled them for 6d., mended them for 1d.); but the youngest daughter's shoes were bought in London, and cost 9d. a pair. Petre's accounts take back the history of the pottery manufacture at Stock, near Ingatestone, a century earlier than was previously known. Although clay suitable for earthenware was available in most parts of Essex, the Stock kilns were among the few known to Essex historians.[23] In 1550 'Prentice the potter at Stock' supplied '4 pots for flowers 2d., a cream pot and a cheese pan 4d., a pan ½d., a dozen cups for the butler 12d.,

2 pots for herbs for the parlour 4*d*., 3 stone pots 18*d*., pottle glasses 12*d*., 8 quart glasses 16*d*., 4 stool pots 8*d*., 2 milk pans 2*d*., 2 stew pots 2*d*.', as well as a still with cups for it and 2 watering pans. For distilling herbs, a well-established Tudor art, Lady Petre bought '6 stilling glasses' at Chelmsford for 12*d*. (a still-house occurs in the inventory of 1600). Twenty earthen drinking cups, 11 stew pots and 4 close stools were ordered from two Stock potters in 1555, but Lady Petre obtained from London '9 pottle glasses after 3*d*. the piece for waters that were stilled this year' at Ingatestone.

One account describes what was bought at Ingatestone fair (20 November) in 1550:

> *Cloths for the dairy house.* 4 yards of ravelling for meal 10*d*., an ell of canvas for a cheese cloth 9*d*., 3 quarters of canvas for a cleansing cloth for milk 5½*d*., 2 ells of canvas to make boulting cloths 18*d*., bought by Elizabeth at Ingatestone fair.

> *Kitchen stuff.* The same time for a skummer bought by Mary 20*d*., a latten ladle 16*d*., for changing 4 dishes, 4 pottingers, 7 saucers, 2 platters and a platt 10*d*.

> *Nails.* 3 somes [a some was 12,000] of 2*d*. nails 29*s*., 200 double tenpenny nails 2*s*. 8*d*., 800 single 10*d*. nails 4*s*., 1000 roof nails 12*d*., bought at the fair.

> *Implements of husbandry for Horndon.* Paid to Robert James [the Horndon bailiff] for that he laid out at the fair for half an horse hide 2*s*. 8*d*., a calf skin 12*d*., an hatchet 10*d*., a bush hook 18*d*., 2 axes 2*s*. 9*d*., a bill 8*d*., a fan and a basket 2*s*. 1*d*.

> *Cart harness for Horndon.* Paid at Ingatestone fair, to Nash of Chelmsford, for 4 halters 2*s*., 4 bits 8*d*., a collar 16*d*., a panel for the full horse 12*d*., all these parcels bought for the horses that shall go to plough at Horndon.

By old custom, servants were given a day off to enjoy themselves at the local fair; two of the Petres' maids spent some shillings on useful articles before buying their own fairings and joining in the fun. As already seen, Petre also patronized Nash at his Chelmsford shop. A few household necessities were bought at another fair: 'Paid to the maids of the dairy at Ingatestone that they laid out at Chelmsford at May Fair, 2½ yards canvas for cheese cloths 17½*d*., 4 yards coarse ravel 14*d*., a basket to carry clothes in 5*d*., their expenses 3*d*.'

The Ingatestone accounts and a few payments in the London accounts show to what extent the Hall relied on London merchants. They supplied nearly all the salt, spices, dried fish and dried fruit, also pitch, hemp, cord (though rope was bought locally at so much a pound), most of the nails, 'an hundred of red ochre 20*d*.' and an occasional twopennyworth of ink.

In London, too, were obtained the costly plate and jewellery, fashionable clothes, most of the better fabrics and textiles and nearly all the ladies' embroidery material save the trifles they bought from pedlars at the gate. Writing paper came from London or Brentwood at 4d. a quire. But the records show admirably how Petre's servants, tenants and the craftsmen of the neighbourhood provided most of the other things required, making them with their own hands and their innate skill. By drawing liberally on his estate and his purely local resources the household, apart from the periodic need to replenish the big store of saltfish, was not far from being self-supporting.

These are the *minutiæ* of life in a mid-Essex manor, but it was a life which had greater depth and continuity than the uncertainties of high politics. An Essex writer, beloved of many, has penetrated to the heart of the matter: 'Whatever the passions and intrigues at the Court, whether services at the church were in Latin or English, the fields must needs be ploughed and sown, the hedges brushed, the ditches cleared, the crops harvested, and thrashed, and ground.' [24]

CHAPTER VIII

Secretary to Mary

1 Royal Marriage Plan and Rebellion

MARY saw the Protestant government collapse ignominiously very soon after Edward's death. England's lawful Queen made her way from Framlingham Castle towards the capital. On 29 July 1553 she reached her Essex home, New Hall, Boreham. There Cecil delivered his 'submission', and the Lord Mayor and Petre's rich merchant friend William Garrard, then Sheriff, presented her with an acceptable 'benevolence' in the form of a thousand half-sovereigns in a crimson velvet purse.

Despite his share in the deposition of the puppet-queen and her manager, Petre was momentarily without office for the second time in six years, and, for all he knew, permanently so. It is unlikely that Mary decided on the membership of her Council before consulting Gardiner and other victims of the Somerset and Northumberland régimes. Thousands of other anxious Englishmen awaited events, for a woman monarch was entirely alien to their ideas.

Petre was not in the company of the courtiers paying suit to the Queen at New Hall. 'On 28 July', Strype stated, 'most of the Lords of the Council repaired to her. Yet some few, for the necessary carrying on of business, tarried at Westminster; and among the rest, the Earl of Shrewsbury and Petre.'[1] It was probably a day or two afterwards that the Queen made him one of her two Principal Secretaries. In the notes of Council proceedings in Mary's first month are some interpolated entries of admission of nine members on various days between 28 July and 5 August, no places of meeting being given. 'Sir William Petre, knight, sworn of the Council' occurs under 30 July, when he must have been present to take the oath;[2] it was of course the logical occasion for his being appointed Secretary, the actual date not being on record. If Strype, that indefatigable record searcher, and this informal but precise register are both accurate, Petre had had the Queen's summons and ridden down into Essex that morning or the previous day, because Cecil 'kissed her hand at Sir William Petre's house at Ingatestone, before any other of the Council men'.[3] Almost certainly, therefore, he received the double mark of royal favour in his own house, and the Council probably met in his stately gallery. It seems that Cecil craved Mary's pardon importunately at the Court's first stopping-place after New Hall, and the warmth of her response may be judged by the fact that she left him out of the Council.

After resting a night or two at Wanstead House, where she was joined by Princess Elizabeth with her retinue, Mary arrived in London on 3 August. Her entry was notable for scenes of almost ecstatic triumph and joy. Lady Petre was among the ladies who accompanied her. Among the Tower prisoners at last released were the aged Duke of Norfolk, who had been saved from the scaffold by her father's death, Courtenay, to whom she restored the earldom of Devonshire, and Gardiner, the ex-Bishop of Winchester. The other incarcerated bishops, Bonner, Tunstall, Day and Heath, also regained their sees. Petre at once concentrated on pressing public affairs. In the state papers is preserved an important document, drawn up in these weeks, which indicates that his primary aims were to restore order and to abolish abuses. 'What is to be done after the death of King Edward' is a three-page memorandum, wholly in his hand.[4] 'First', Petre wrote, 'to the intent that God from whom all goodness descendeth may be truly preached and reverently served and obeyed, some grave men well learned in the scriptures and of good life and conversation are to be chosen to set an order in matters of religion.' There must be 'no bribers'; all licences for retainers should be revoked; and the royal household costs should be reduced. These notes 'speak nobly for the intentions with which Mary and himself were setting generally to work';[5] Froude's comment is marred only by his ascribing it to Gardiner. Petre was about to give arduous service to a sovereign who, without the least doubt, did not shirk hard work. According to the Venetian ambassador, she rose at daybreak and transacted business incessantly until midnight; she was always ready to give audiences to her councillors and required every detail of public affairs to be submitted to her.[6]

Besides Petre, Mary appointed only eleven of the former councillors, among them the Marquis of Winchester, the Earls of Bedford, Pembroke, Arundel, Shrewsbury and Westmorland, Baker and Mason. In addition to Northumberland and his chief henchmen, Suffolk, Northampton and Gates, sixteen lost their seats, including Cranmer, Huntingdon, Cecil and Cheke, the last after holding office for a month. Seven displaced members came back: Norfolk, Gardiner, now Lord Chancellor, Tunstall, Thirlby, Southwell, Rich and Paget. Among the newcomers were Mary's household officers, Rochester, now Comptroller, Waldegrave and Englefield. 'Within two months of her accession its members numbered well-nigh fifty. Of these almost three-fifths had never sat at the council board before; the majority had no claim to their position beyond religious sympathy and the promptitude and energy with which they had espoused her cause. In their counsel there was little wisdom and in their multitude no safety. Winchester and Pembroke were not retained by Mary without some hesitation; as late as 11 August they were in confinement, but on the 13th they were sworn of the privy council'.[7] Sadler, who had been Principal Secretary immediately before Paget and Petre, was also among those who temporarily suffered loss of liberty. Later in the month Sir Thomas Wharton, lessee of New Hall, and Sir John Mordaunt of Thorndon Hall took their places at the Board.

Once again Petre had bridged the broad torrent between opposing camps. He had already seen Cromwell and Somerset go to the scaffold; now Jane and Northumberland were in the Tower, while most of Edward's councillors were dismissed. Mary 'seemed to have to include the able Sir William Petre', says Gardiner's recent biographer,[8] echoing Froude's view that Petre was one of the councillors who, 'too powerful to affront, too uncertain to be trusted as subjects, Mary could only attach to herself, by maintaining them in their offices and emoluments'. That he would be useful in her government as a councillor goes without question. But as Queen's Secretary, he would need to work in close harmony with her. Was there some bond of friendship uniting these two dissimilar people: Mary, the least diplomatic of rulers, fervent, obstinate; and Petre, the supple, adroit lawyer, who had steered his political bark successfully through such rough seas? Secretary Petre was now serving his third sovereign (his fourth, if Jane is counted). The two rejected Secretaries were not to reappear in the political scene for some time— Cecil for one and a half years, Cheke for three (one spent in the Tower on a charge of treason). For the first time, the secretaryship was conferred by letters patent, and was to be held during the royal pleasure at the accustomed salary of £100 a year.[9] 'Mr. Secretary Bourne' was first entered in the Council book on 21 August. Sir John Bourne was the sixth Principal Secretary to share the appointment with Petre. The Council, thus reconstituted, soon proved itself to be too unwieldy, and an inner body managed the chief affairs. The chosen few were Gardiner, Arundel, Paget, Petre, Rochester and Thirlby; or, according to another source, the first four.[10] Here, in effect, was a plan for sound administration more thorough than that which Edward and Petre had prepared.

Early in August Petre was collaborating with Gardiner in surveying the nation's finances:[11] no easy task, but less embarrassing to Petre than his sitting in judgment upon the bishop a few years earlier. Like Paget, Petre was a fiscal expert. Throughout this reign and in the next, he often dealt with matters concerning foreign currency and loans,[12] into the intricacies of which he had been initiated as far back as 1545; and he was in close touch with Sir Thomas Gresham, England's shrewdest financial brain and the country's chief merchant representative at Antwerp. Gresham, who had succeeded Dansell as royal agent, was striving to save England's credit in face of ever-mounting debts to foreigners charging crippling rates of interest. Petre corresponded with and apparently patronized Christopher Dauntsey, another financial agent at Antwerp,[13] who was dismissed for inefficiency but remembered to send him more than one New Year's gift. He was also one of the five commissioners for confirming the Hanse merchants' privileges.[14] Some of the government's monetary problems may well have been assigned because of his proven probity. Perhaps his best testimonial from historians is that of Froude, commenting on a manuscript apparently prepared shortly after Mary's accession and detailing the value of all the properties that had passed from the Crown in Edward's reign, by gift, sale or exchange. 'After liberal deductions, there will remain on a computation most favourable to the Council, estates worth half a million which the ministers of the Minority with their friends had divided among themselves. . . . From the report Lord Paget and Sir William Petre would seem to have made the smallest use of their opportunities.'[15] The opportunities had been there during the last few years, when 'a corrupt court-circle reaped a golden harvest'.[16] Gardiner and Petre continued to work hard on the public accounts, and the Queen contributed by cutting down the royal expenses. For the next four years Petre was to be in almost sole control of foreign affairs, subject to Paget's concurrence on matters of major policy: witness the mass of his correspondence with England's resident ambassadors abroad—with Wotton now again at Paris, Thirlby and Mason at Brussels, Vannes at Venice—in the form of original incoming letters and drafts of outgoing letters.* His grasp is exemplified by a remark of Vannes, 'You sleeping know better than I waking', unless it is calculated flattery.

Despite the more pressing economic and political troubles, early attention was given to the universities, where there had been a continued decline in the number of students. The Queen directed both universities in no uncertain language to undertake their own reform. The initiative appears to have come from Petre. There exists his own draft of the injunction—to Oxford, of course, his *alma mater*.[17] The worst disorders had arisen because the ancient statutes had been 'altered, broken and almost utterly subverted to the great discredit of the university and no small hindrance of the commonwealth'. Reminding those in charge of

---

* It is all fully abstracted in print (*For. Cal.*, *Mary*), but has little relation to the story beyond emphasizing this part of the Secretary's heavy burden.

their duties to religion, the royal letter enjoins strict observance of the statutes. If they disobeyed, Petre added, they would forfeit office, but he had second thoughts and deleted the threat.*

He was again firmly established. Northumberland was tried by his peers and executed; Northampton, was condemned but reprieved; Suffolk, Lady Jane's father, and others suffered heavy fines; and Gates, who had shared with Petre the parliamentary representation of Essex, was put to death. In the brief aftermath of Jane's 'rebellion', Petre was among the nine commissioners charged with examining the prisoners and assessing their fines.[18] Cecil had evaded prison and fine, but the Queen commanded him to surrender the office of Chancellor of the Order of the Garter. Six days later, on 27 September, it was given to Petre, with the annual fee of £100 for life.[19] Cecil, Petre's junior in age and experience, had outstripped him by securing this dignified appointment five months earlier, but apparently never wore the robes at a formal meeting. Of the officers of the Order, whose status did not equal that of the Knights, Chancellor ranked below Prelate but above Register, Garter and Black Rod. The office was one 'of very great charge', to which a 'man of good estimation being a knight and a gentleman born and also of good experience and learning shall be chosen'.[20] The chapter decreed that the statutes ordained by Edward should be abrogated, as 'in no sort convenient, but impertinent, and tending to novelty'; and the new Chancellor was to have them speedily expunged from their records.[21] It was a grand assembly, which the Queen had summoned at St. James's Palace before her coronation. In the state journey to Westminster Abbey, the Queen's chariot was followed by Elizabeth's. After that bearing the 'ladies of estate' rode ten ladies dressed in crimson velvet, their horses likewise trapped; they included Lady Petre, a happy woman, riding behind her Queen and friend. The Secretaries' place of honour in the long procession was between the two Chief Justices and the Treasurer and the Comptroller.[22]

Petre evidently showed Wotton that he could see the lighter side of all the grand pomp in the Garter ceremonies, and his friend's response might have come from Lamb's pen.

I thank you much for the promotion whereto you have promoted me by your last letter, but I am sorry you forgot to send me my title and name whereby I should be called—whether it be Yellow Cross, or Green Mantle, or Obscuran-

---

* The visitation of Oxford of 1549 (in which Petre did not act) had been repeated in 1551; the visitors included Warwick, Northampton and Petre 'as of old' (R. W. Dixon, *op. cit.*, iii, 384), but nothing of Petre's share, if any, seems to be recorded. 'In September [1553] it was rumoured that he was out of office' (*D.N.B.*), must refer to September 1554 (see p. 182).

tius,* or such other; for that would have set me well forth *pardy*, and have made me welcome here, at least amongst my fellows the Heralds. And seeing you have made me a Herald, though you have poured no bowl of wine on my head, I intend to show you some part of my cunning; and therefore I send you a certain declaration, whereby may appear (as I take it) certain degrees of consanguinity and affinity wherein the Queen's Highness and the Prince of Spain are knit together.

But, remembering a saying of Will Somers (seemingly the jester to Henry VIII and Edward VI), Wotton referred the genealogical matter to those who understood pedigrees better. And so on in like vein.[23] By the time it reached Petre, he was too involved in grave events to relish Wotton's drollery.

The Parliament which met shortly after the coronation had been elected with little interference. But the reappearance of many Protestant members was a reminder that a minority had not gone back to the Roman faith. They included the former Secretary, Smith, one of the most advanced reformers behind Edward's first Act of Uniformity. Petre's fellow member for the county was Rochester, who could claim to be an Essex man as his grandfather lived at Terling, close to New Hall. Among its routine business, a bill 'for artificers in towns', reminiscent of that in the previous parliament, was committed to Petre.[24] On the vital question of religion, the Queen's intentions had recently been announced. 'Albeit her Grace's conscience is stayed, she meaneth graciously not to compel other men's consciences' was the crucial passage in a declaration which Petre in the company of nine others may have signed with relief and hopes of order.[25] Early decisions had to be made concerning nonconforming bishops and leading Protestants, and in these Mary showed little vindictiveness. Both archbishops, with Latimer Bishop of Worcester and Hooper Bishop of Gloucester, not without cause, were committed to prison. Cranmer, like Cheke and other reformers, had had the chance of leaving the country, but unlike them remained, prepared to face the consequences; Archbishop Holgate was now over seventy. Although London and some other cities, with Kent, Essex and East Anglia, remained predominantly Protestant, many Englishmen welcomed the impending return to Catholicism. Parliament ordained that the country should revert to the religion of Henry's last years. All Edward's reforms were swept away. But in certain respects the members were far from complaisant to Mary's wishes. They would neither denationalize the Church

* In reference of course to Rouge Croix, Bluemantle and Clarenceux (Clarentius); Wotton held no heraldic office.

of England—the Queen must remain its Supreme Head—nor restore the monastic and chantry estates in lay hands.

Parliament urged the Queen to drop her ideas for a Spanish marriage. This match was the central point around which the history of the reign was to turn, and Petre took an important part in the negotiations. An alliance with Prince Philip of Spain, the Emperor's son, would benefit England's trade with Flanders and have military advantages in the event of war with France. But a major objection was the Englishman's hatred of foreigners in general and subjugation to Spain and Rome in particular. So it was that the dearth of English nobles of ancient stock led to two men of royal lineage, who were otherwise most unsuitable, being considered eligible for the Queen. These were Edward Courtenay: handsome, but too young and dissolute; and Reginald Pole: only in minor orders (though a cardinal), which papal dispensation could overcome, but an elderly ascetic. Mary was indignant at the Commons' temerity. During October and November the intrigues between Renard the Emperor's ambassador and the inner Council were actively pursued.[26] Paget and Petre, 'the Queen's First Secretary', were always present, the others being Arundel, Shrewsbury, Rochester, Gardiner, Tunstall and Thirlby. Paget's private advice to the ambassador, that the Emperor should be asked to write personal letters to each, soliciting their support for the Spanish alliance, was accepted. Renard wrote, 'I have been to the Earl of Arundel's house and presented your Majesty's letters to him. I also said to Secretary Petre, who was in the earl's house, that I had letters to him to refresh his memory of what I had laid before the Council': a tactless remark to which Petre retorted, 'I shall act as a trusty servant and councillor may be expected to do'. Meantime the far-seeing Gardiner was consistently pressing for an English marriage: failing Courtenay, then Pole; never Philip. The Queen 'was very angry with the Chancellor; she went to consult those present of her Council, who were the Chancellor, Arundel, Thirlby, Paget, and Petre'. Arundel, Paget and Petre were informed before Gardiner of her final decision to marry Philip. Mary was convinced that union with Spain would further the return of England to the Catholic religion, a result for which she yearned. She also yearned with romantic impatience for the wedding. Philip was twenty-seven; she was ten years older.

At last the negotiations were nearly through; rewards to the influential councillors might clinch the matter. Another of Renard's extremely long reports to the Emperor ended: 'I have made no definite promises of rewards from your Majesty to anyone over here except Paget. Some present by way of recognition would encourage the Earl of Arundel,

Petre, and the Comptroller in their devotion.'[27] Soon 'the time-serving Gardiner succumbed to the leaders of the Spanish faction, Arundel, Paget and Petre',[28] a reproach which the patriotic Chancellor, accepting the inevitable, does not deserve, even if the others had been following a consistent policy. At the end of the year all four were given the task of preparing the marriage treaty that Petre himself had advocated provided that it would not allow Philip a free hand in English affairs.

During the Anglo-Spanish negotiations, Henry II King of France and Noailles his ambassador at the English court were striving to prevent a marriage which would ensure control of the seas by Philip and Mary. French and Imperial counter-plotting is illustrated by passages from Renard's report on 29 November: 'Last Sunday the French ambassador asked Paget to dinner alone, and when Paget excused himself on the ground that he was to be the only guest, also invited the Earl of Arundel, Dr. Petre, and the Privy Seal. The French will take the Lady Elizabeth out of the country. It would be well to shut her up in the Tower.'[29] Gardiner would also have the princess safely there, but Paget opposed the idea. Wotton was in despair. 'It will be very hard to avoid war between us and France', he wrote, begging Petre's aid to get him recalled to England. One vital question permeates the whole correspondence, with its reports, schemes and suggestions: was the Emperor or was the French King to lead Europe?

The marriage treaty was completed by the commissioners. It was a masterpiece in England's favour. All the nation's liberties were to be preserved; Mary was to be the sole ruler, though aided by Philip who was to be given the style of King but no rights of succession though she was to receive a dower of £60,000 if she survived him; England was not to be drawn into any war of his; only Englishmen were to occupy offices in Church and State; their heir, if any, was to inherit the Netherlands. For securing these honourable and advantageous terms, much of the credit rests with Petre, who, with Paget, and in the later stages Gardiner, had borne the brunt of the work. Petre kept in his custody a lasting memorial —his own fair draft with the sovereign's superscription, 'MARYE THE QUENE', signifying her approval. (p. 194)[30] Rochester complained that the Queen now trusted them first. In fact, Mary's favours temporarily excluded some of her other Catholic supporters, particularly Waldegrave and Englefield: 'the Queen now communicates her affairs to Paget or Petre instead'. Secretary Bourne is seldom mentioned.

Meantime Parliament had been dissolved. In December Petre's steward started a fresh account-book, which has survived. On the 20th, the Court removed to Richmond, Petre proceeding by hired barge with greater dignity (and expense) than in the usual wherry. Back to Westminster the Court went just before the New Year. 'Given to the Queen's Highness by my master in gold £10' has its counterpart, 'Wagstaff of the Guard bringing a gilt standing cup with cover from the Queen to my lady 13s. 4d.' If the bringer's reward was one-tenth of the value of the gift, Mary therefore gave Lady Anne plate worth about two-thirds of the gold which she accepted from Petre. Pembroke, who could well afford it, bestowed a similar piece of plate on the useful Secretary. The £5 in gold from Tunstall showed that long imprisonment had not alienated an old friend.*

Despite the terms extracted from Spain, few sections of the nation were won over. Suspense had been kept up by the trial, in November, of Cranmer,† Lady Jane Grey and several others in the Tower, all of whom were sentenced to death; and tension was only increased when their executions were postponed. By now, the Queen's scheme to ally England to Rome and Spain, with all its inherent dangers, had diminished her initial popularity. Even the pro-Philip party in the Council began to flinch in face of the country's rising dissatisfaction, diligently fostered by Noailles the French ambassador, which eventually boiled over. Not long after Twelfthtide, the malcontents' loosely concerted plans were put into action in the south-western and south-eastern corners of England. Their avowed object was to stop the marriage and loss of English independence. The underlying aims were to prevent the restoration of the mass, to dethrone Mary, to marry Courtenay and Elizabeth, and to murder Arundel, Paget and Petre; the last, incidentally, was among Arundel's frequent visitors about this time. The first plot was the ill-fated attempt by the Carews, the same brothers whose violence against the Western Catholic rebels in 1549 was still remembered; Courtenay's last-minute cowardice doomed their intended revolt to utter failure. No doubt Petre, having acquired an estate in South Devon in 1546, was one of the active councillors to smother it before military forces were needed. His January accounts noted 20s. to the armourer, whom he retained for 6s. 8d. a quarter, for riding to Ingatestone, repairing and oiling the armour and guns there: a wise precaution.

* Sir William and Lady Petre each received a royal New Year's gift, probably plate, in 1556 (20s. and 13s. 4d. gratuities), when he again gave the Queen £10.

† A little mystery surrounds removals from Lambeth to Aldersgate Street several weeks after Cranmer's trial: 'Carrying stuff by barge from Lambeth to Broken Wharf 2s. 4d.'; 3 'carres' that carried the same to my master's house in London 12d.; with two servants' expenses 'that day being occupied about the same stuff 16d.' Had Cranmer, condemned to die, given some of his furniture to his old colleague to prevent its passing to a Catholic archbishop?

Overthrow of the other plot was to require far more determined action. The impending marriage was formally announced on 15 January 1554. Ten days later Sir Thomas Wyatt, the poet's son, raised the standard of revolt at Rochester, and a number of bands under influential leaders in Kent joined him to defend England from foreign domination. Meantime a French invasion was feared. Rebellion led to urgent countermeasures, even to diplomatic highway robbery. Noailles' couriers en route for Dover were waylaid; their dispatches were rushed to Chancellor Gardiner. Cipher letters in front of him, he passionately unburdened himself to Secretary Petre. It was two days after the outbreak of Wyatt's rebellion. 'Such letters in times past I durst not have opened, but now, somewhat heated with these treasons, I waxed bolder.' Petre was given a hint that Elizabeth might possibly be implicated: a further letter would follow as soon as he had deciphered all the intercepted correspondence. A post-script added that Wharton 'shall tell you the rest'.[32] If the Chancellor received a reply it is not preserved.

By 1 February the insurrection had become formidable. The Council decided to tell Wyatt that the Queen was willing to listen to objections to the marriage. Paget and Petre were deputed to consult Renard about this ruse to gain time while her forces were coming up; he thought the plan 'excellently matured'.[33] But Wyatt wished to have the Queen and the Tower. His reply stirred Mary to appeal in person at the Guildhall to the loyalty of her subjects. It was a brave speech, comparable in its eloquent reasoning with the more renowned address that her younger sister delivered at Tilbury in 1588 to loyal soldiers instead of to half-hostile citizens; and it went a long way towards preserving England from civil war. Wyatt reached Southwark to find thousands of armed Londoners defending London Bridge against a declared traitor. A few days later he decided on a wide flanking movement with a forced march to Kingston, whence after crossing he advanced next afternoon to Ludgate. Again the Queen stood firm, resisting Gardiner's urgent plea to fly; again the citizens repelled him. Wyatt was forced to surrender to Pembroke, Lieutenant of her army. Mary's second show of cool courage had been vital in saving her capital city and all that its possession implied. Accommodation in the Tower and other prisons was soon over-taxed.*

---

* Temporary prisons for Wyatt's men were found by commandeering some of the city churches, including St. Botolph-without-Aldersgate (Petre's parish), the church-wardens' accounts of which confirm the chronicler's story about the use of churches in the emergency, 'For making clean the church and churchyard after the rebels there were enclosed, for perfume in airing the church, and for digging and levelling the procession way in the churchyard, 8s. 8d.' This expenditure follows immediately after heavy expenses incurred in restoring Catholic ritual. (Guildhall Lib., MS. 1454.)

Of more interest is the part that Petre played during the rebellion. There was of course no standing army; the county militia was still levied on a conscript basis; and although Henry VII and his son imposed severe limitations on the number of retainers in the nobles' establishments the large landholders were not relieved of the obligation in an emergency to find the quota of men according to their position. Petre's estate lay fairly near the scene of the revolt. The way in which he met his liability is described in his accounts in some detail (Appendix H).

He at once called several of his able-bodied Ingatestone Hall servants to arms; on the day after Wyatt raised his standard, six of them were journeying up to London, and fodder for fourteen of Petre's horses was accounted for from the previous day until a week after the insurrection had collapsed. In company with his personal attendants at Court and with a few of his tenants who had mounts, he had orders to report to Sir Thomas Wharton, who was prominent among those who suppressed the revolt. Petre had equipped them as 'light horsemen' with red broadcloth coats and white frieze jerkins. He also mustered from the villages on his Essex estate at least 142 footmen, and apparently one or two of his more substantial lessees sent their own men to join Petre's 'band'. It was of course composed mainly of archers, but some carried firearms, swords or pikes. The 'sergeant' in charge of the footmen was one of Petre's Court servants, and they had their own ensign, or standard. In the days before military uniforms, it was essential for soldiers to keep close to their own colours, for there was little to distinguish friend from foe. After all the bustle and hurry, Petre's band was ready to go into action.

In the final skirmish when Wyatt capitulated Pembroke was supported by Bedford, Paget, Clinton and 'divers other lords on horseback'.[34] Did the men from the Ingatestone estate fight in company with Wharton's soldiers under Pembroke? And did Petre lead his own men? The evidence is intriguing, but not conclusive. An item in his accounts, '6 links for the soldiers, being sent for in the night before they went to the field', refers to 2 or 3 February, but there is no other mention of their share, if any, in the actual fighting, except perhaps for his 'loss of armour and artillery'. One yeoman of Ingatestone, John Gilbert alias Hale, former tenant of the 'Dolphin' inn, got condign punishment. At the first manor court after his neighbours' return, they saw to it that he was presented for 'refusing utterly' to obey the order of the lord of the manor 'to serve the Queen in the last rebellion begun in parts of Kent'. The statutory penalty was confiscation of his property and its profits for his lifetime to the lord.[35] He pleaded guilty and craved the lord's pardon. Petre granted it, waiving his rights; but it was conditional on the offender paying steward Bell the very stiff sum of £20 within a month, 'to be distributed to such men-at-arms of the manor who served the Queen at London against the rebels'. He paid up.[36]

As for Petre, he certainly equipped himself. His mail shirt was lined with Milan fustian, the seat of his new saddle was stuffed with down, a pillion was made for his travelling casket; his coat of plate and dagger are mentioned; and 'Hans the armourer in reward when my master had on his harness 6s. 8d.' indicates active intentions. Finally, there is a tantalizing hint in Wotton's letter from Paris to him dated 23 February. 'Understanding how valiantly you have fought in the last battle', his friend wrote, 'I would advise the Queen's highness to take Mr. Dymocke's office from him and to appoint you to be her champion.'[37] (Sir Edward Dymoke held the hereditary office of royal champion at the coronation; in 1549, probably in acknowledgment of some service, he had sent Petre 'four boxes of marmalade small and a box of biscuit bread'.) Wotton's playful hyperbole need not be allowed to discount his reference to Petre's martial courage.

His expenses in raising this territorial unit amounted to £116 18s. 10d. 'or thereabouts, besides the loss of armour and artillery'. To Kyme, his careful accountant, such phrases went against the grain, and a dispute between him and Wagstaff, one of his fellow servants, was worse. Out of a bag of money containing £88 10s. 8d. which Kyme had received from Napper, Petre's Oxfordshire estate agent, to pay for the soldiers' wages and coats, £16 was handed to Wagstaff, Kyme alleged, 'which is denied by him'. Petre's deficit was trifling in comparison with the Tower armouries, investigated shortly after Elizabeth's accession, when a full statement of equipment handed out and of losses sustained in the rebellion was drawn up;[38] Petre's own allocation is known (see Appendix H). No doubt he wrote off the missing £16 and replenished his armoury. As a member of the government, he could afford to bear the whole cost of his 'band', for although 'the Tudor monarchy had faced the third, and in one sense the greatest, of its crises',[39] some degree of stability was quickly restored, and that was what mattered.

During the critical weekend when Wyatt's force stood at Southwark, the councillors' recriminations were in sorry contrast to the nation's needs. A week later a violent dispute occurred between Gardiner, 'the most hot-headed in the affairs of religion' in Renard's view, and Arundel, supported by Paget and Petre, 'who were all for religious moderation'.[40] After the real danger had passed, the Council decided to provide the Queen with a bodyguard, mostly supplied by its own members. The majority, like Petre, were appointed to procure a hundred footmen each.[41]

Although formal Council meetings had been abandoned, the Principal
Secretary could not lay down the pen for the sword at once. The latest
news must be given to Gresham at Antwerp, advising him not to send
any more money to London until after the rebels' defeat, though he was
probably aware of the rising, for his courier had been 'stayed by the way
with threatening words' from Wyatt's men in Kent.[42] Thirlby writing
from Brussels was anxious about affairs in England and about his old
colleague; he could arrange for the immediate dispatch of 4,000 German
mercenaries and three ensigns of horse in fourteen 'great ships', if required.
The offer was urgently repeated three days later. By then the danger was
over.

After the rebels' surrender, there were many interrogations. On
11 February Gardiner wrote to Petre: 'To-morrow, at your going to the
Tower, it shall be good ye be earnest with one little Wyatt [Edmund
Tremayne] there prisoner, who by all likelihood can tell all'; the Secretary
was to extract a confession 'by sharp punishment or promise of life'.[43]
That Petre ordered him a spell on the rack is confirmed from another
source.[44] The victim was a Devon man in Courtenay's service. Two
important prisoners, Lady Jane Grey and her husband, were beheaded
that day. Soon after this vicious revenge, Petre was the presiding judge
at a special session of justices of oyer and terminer for trying insurgents
who had been under Wyatt's banner at Brentford. They sent the rebels
to the Tyburn gallows, there to be hanged, drawn and quartered.[45]
Pollard's statement that Petre 'ingratiated himself with Mary by his zeal
in tracing the accomplices of Wyatt's rebellion'[46] is based only on Lloyd's
assertion that Petre 'searched the bottom of Wyatt's insurrection'.[47]
Renard, on the other hand, credited him with influencing Mary to show
clemency in discharging eight of the accused. Among those released was
Northampton, who was deprived of his rank and reverted to that of Sir
William Parr. Mary enjoined Petre, with his fellows, to apply themselves
even more diligently to finish off the trials of the prisoners.[48]

Meantime those intercepted letters of the French ambassador, when
decoded, had yielded their terrible secret. 'Gardiner felt the thrill of a
gambler whose throw has been marvellously successful.'[49] The princess
was to replace Mary on the throne. Wyatt is said to have implicated
Courtenay and Elizabeth. On 8 March Renard wrote that Elizabeth was
to be examined at Westminster 'that day by the Chancellor, Arundel,
Petre and Paget, and her fate should depend on her answers'.[50] So Petre
found himself involved in a dangerous task, that of interrogating the
woman who would be sovereign on Mary's death, unless her own were
demanded. The result was as barren as her elder sister's examinations in

Edward's time. Most of the councillors, including Petre, thought that Elizabeth should be closely guarded, but not imprisoned. The Queen shrewdly asked each in turn to accept the custody of the princess in his own house. Everyone refused the risky role, and on 18 March Elizabeth was imprisoned in the Tower. Petre's accounts during these days of suspense show that he had been at Arundel's mansion on 21 February, the Tower on 1 March, doubtless to examine Wyatt before his trial, Bedford's house on the 2nd and the 8th, and Baynard's Castle (Pembroke's) for supper on the 5th, 'thence to the Lord Chancellor's in the night and from thence to the Court'. Gardiner's hostility to Elizabeth was implacable and he was insisting that she must be removed. Could Petre's late call on Gardiner on the 5th have been to advise moderation? It will probably never be known whether Elizabeth was innocent or not. Wyatt's death had been postponed in the hope of eliciting more damaging evidence against her; but on the scaffold next month he declared her complete innocence. Suffolk, Jane's father, was now beheaded.

The mid-February day on which Petre and Baker sat in judgment on the rebels is the date of a lucrative grant to both men as compensation for loss of their offices in the recently abolished Court of First Fruits and Tenths. Treasurer Petre's salary of £120 for life was replaced by an annuity of £266 13s. 4d., which was given also in consideration of his service to Henry VIII, Edward VI and the Queen. (Next year Petre's annuity was reduced to £200 on his being granted certain lands in Devon, Somerset and Dorset.[51]) Early in March 1554 he received what was undoubtedly another mark of Mary's favour when she granted him the important lordship and manor of Writtle, near Ingatestone; it was too big to be given solely 'for services to the Crown', so he had to surrender a smaller estate (p. 267).

The rebellion had been broken; and letters of thanks arrived from the Emperor for twelve of the leading warriors and councillors, including Petre. They contained a hint of monetary reward. Renard's task was to find out whether the plot had affected the Queen's intention of marrying. He conferred with Gardiner, Petre, Paget and Rochester; then together they sought the Queen, urging her to lose no time.[52] She needed little persuasion. Even the rival factions in the Council were agreed that the marriage must go forward. On the 6th the Council and the Imperial ambassadors witnessed the proxy ceremony by which Mary became Philip's wife. A few days later, alarmed by the rumour of a French attack on the coast, she asked Renard to discuss the threat with Paget and Petre.

The same pair had come to the conclusion that the only way to overcome the brawling in the Council would be to raise the status of the existing unofficial inner body to a 'Council of State', thus excluding the uncontrollable crowd. Gardiner, Arundel, Thirlby, Paget, Rochester and Petre, Renard reported, would be deputed, and he was hopeful that Arundel and Paget could be persuaded to work with Gardiner; without such a drastic reduction the deep split in the Council would lead to civil war. About the end of March the over-anxious Queen spoke to five members of the oligarchy, including Petre, 'separately and together, and adjured them to be reconciled'; she is reported as having given her assent to limiting the Council 'to six members, as Paget and Petre had advised'. Uneasy harmony prevailed for three weeks; then discord sounded afresh.[53]

Mary's second Parliament assembled on 2 April 1554. She had promised to submit the marriage question to it, but there seemed no alternative but to pass the bill. Petre was appointed to a small but strong committee of the Council to consider the legislative programme.[54] Mary dissolved Parliament early in May on the Emperor's advice to proceed cautiously in restoring the Catholic religion.

At the end of April, when giving the personnel of the conciliar parties and incidentally disclosing that the two Secretaries were in opposite camps, Renard explained that the plan for a Council of State had broken down because the Chancellor's supporters resented their exclusion, except for Rochester: the Queen, he added, had overlooked that they were Catholics and the others, including Petre, were mostly heretics.[55] Their vociferous complaints caused her 'to take a dislike' to Paget and Petre.* The accusation of heresy was grounded upon Paget's influence in the Lords' recent rejection of Gardiner's bill, passed by the Commons, for reviving the Heresy Act. In the absence of details of the debates, the coupling of Petre's name with Paget's suggests that the former had also opposed the penalty of burning, a point of some later significance. Bitter rivalry in the Council, however, did not affect the choice of men for important meetings with the Imperial ambassador, and those with long experience were still selected; Petre was invariably associated with Gardiner, Paget and Rochester, to whom Arundel and Lord William Howard were sometimes added.[56] No confirmation from other sources that the omnipresent Petre was in disfavour with Mary can be traced, and it was not until the autumn that any further hint in that direction was heard. But there is no doubt about Paget's impending fall from grace. He informed Renard that affairs were going all awry through Gardiner's fault. 'I fear the result, and the man who usually confers with you and me fears it no less than I' (a clear reference to Petre). Wotton was pretty

* This is the version given in the printed calendar; a closer translation runs: 'They have so overwhelmed her Majesty that she is disgusted with Paget and Petre.' (Tytler, *op. cit.*, ii, 373.)

sure that his dispatches from Paris would be intercepted, and arranged for Petre to have a fresh cipher. Early in May Gardiner believed Paget, Arundel and Pembroke to be scheming to arrest him; they themselves knew that they stood in danger of committal.[57] Renard wrote on 20 June that the Queen would certainly have imprisoned Paget, had she dared to risk a commotion before Philip's coming. And so the Tower at this crisis received no victims of either party; its gates had been opened instead on 19 May to release Elizabeth because it was too dangerous to keep her there. Both leaders, Arundel and Gardiner, were visited by Petre on successive days, the 21st and the 22nd. The earlier of these entries in his accounts tallies in date with a passage in Renard's dispatch: ' We dined at the Earl of Arundel's house, and after dinner Petre told [me] that the councillors had consulted on the powers to be exercised in England by M. Briviesca', who was the Emperor's plenipotentiary for punishing any members of Philip's suite found guilty of crime.[58] Elizabeth was sent to Woodstock, while Courtenay was first transferred to Fotheringhay Castle and then exiled. His implication in the recent rebellion, even after bizarre stories of a cipher cut on a guitar have been discounted, is regarded as almost certain.

Frustrated by the delays in Philip's arrival and the absence of encouraging words from him, the Queen felt that she must escape from the Court feuds. She removed to Richmond at the end of May, taking only a few advisers with her. So, on the 30th, after a morning spent in the Star Chamber, Petre went upstream by barge to join her, a cartload of his 'stuff' having gone by road on the previous day to Richmond. On 19 June a Spanish envoy brought the news that Philip was on his way. On the same day the Court left Oatlands for Guildford: the first stage, according to historians, of her journey to meet Philip. But Petre's accountant made a special marginal note, 'Incipit progress', against his entries for the 16th, 'being the removing day from Richmond to Oatlands', which suggests that Mary, no longer able to contain herself, had already started. Mr. Secretary had had two very active days in London before returning to join the Court at Richmond on the 15th: going downstream by barge from Mortlake to London, he spent the evening or night of the 13th at Sir Anthony Cooke's town house.* Next morning he went to Westminster, doubtless to consult with the councillors left behind, down again to Blackfriars, thence to Garrard for supper, finally by barge

---

* Committed to the Tower on suspicion of complicity in Lady Jane Grey's affair, Cooke had recently arrived at Strasburg, where he remained in exile for the rest of the reign. Petre's accounts seem to show that Sir William and his wife kept in touch with Lady Cooke, whose gratitude was expressed, for example, in the following October, when she sent a hind calf to Ingatestone.

back to the Court. Leaving Richmond, he bought twentypenny-worth of strawberries (about two quarts) for his wife. Sir William and Dame Anne both presented a creditable appearance as they rode forth. For his robes the Secretary had been provided with some costly velvet, judging by the 10s. reward. He had been measured for a coat of plate armour by 'Hans the armourer, servant of Mr. Hoby', Master of the Ordnance. The trimming of his two crossbows was not overlooked. He furnished himself with two gowns, one of damask, the other of velvet satin-faced and silk-fringed, as well as two coats of velvet and damask adorned with parchment lace, for which the tailor's bill was over £5, Petre having first bought eighteen yards of black damask which cost him £7 13s. An embroiderer was paid for 'drawing my master's cognisance or badge' (either arms or crest). New marble cloth was bought for his servants' liveries. His train consisted of fourteen horses, of which apparently ten were mounts and the rest drew the baggage cart; Sir John Fermor had sent him two geldings, 'the one a sorrel trotting, the other a brown bay ambling', apparently as mounts for himself and his wife. He bought 'a covering for my lady's saddle of calves' leather 3s. 8d., a pair of gilt bosses for my lady's horse 6s. 8d., and a new bit and garnishing the bosses of my lady's bridle 20d.' And Gresham's warehouse supplied 2½ lb. 'silk fringe black for my lady, £3'. The merchant himself knew nothing of this trifling transaction, for he was on the high seas with the Spanish fleet that was bringing Philip and a vast sum in bullion, part of the cargo of the treasure ships which had recently reached Spain from the New World. Gresham had negotiated this urgently needed loan, which would go a long way towards ingratiating Philip with the government.

The Court stopped two nights at Guildford; there Winchester and Secretary Bourne appeared, the latter after a month's absence from the Council, which was still transacting business daily. Petre gave 10s. to his unnamed 'host for the use of her house and for servants' lodgings'. Then on to Farnham Castle, which belonged to Gardiner, where the Queen resolved to await news of Philip's approach. These were days of anxious suspense. Petre bore more than his usual amount of responsibility, as Paget was now not merely out of favour but under grave suspicion. That he was secretly engaged in frequent correspondence with Mason, the English ambassador at Brussels, lent countenance to his being involved in some deep-laid plot to get Elizabeth married, even to his securing French help. The Queen threatened to intercept the Mason–Paget letters, but Petre told her that they did not come in his mail-bag and were entrusted to tried servants.[59] He had to write many letters, for instance to the Lord High Admiral (Howard) about paying the navy at Southampton, for the sailors must be kept in good temper, and to Garrard with a handsome order for canvas to make toils (enclosing nets), for the courtiers must be given good hunting. Garrard reciprocated with a good supply of choice apples. Petre himself enjoyed some hawking. During the three weeks' stay at Farnham, a pair of greyhounds arrived from Sir Thomas Pope, who had been Sheriff of Essex and Hertfordshire in the previous year, a grey mule from Paget, a sorrel horse from Mr. Leigh the Auditor, a bay gelding from Dr. Oglethorpe the Dean of Windsor and two bucks from the keepers of Guildford and Odiham Parks. All the time his steward was accounting for every item; ranging from his satin night (evening) cap down to intimate requisites of personal hygiene such as 'my master's urinal, 2*d*., mending my master's close stool, 1*d*.' While at Farnham he had a summer-house put up, in the shade of which he did the work of the Latin secretary as well as his own; for example, a Latin letter in his hand to Renard, who had already gone ahead to Southampton: 'I am sending you letters that arrived last night from Spain which will give the ardently desired tidings of His Highness's arrival at Corunna.'

Nothing was previously known of the ten days after the last Council at Farnham on 10 July except that it met at Bishop's Waltham on the 13th to the 15th. The accounts help to fill in some of the details and confirm the facts already known about the rest of the journey. The 11th was 'the removing day from Farnham to Mr. Norton's',* but it was only a brief call, 2*s*. 6*d*. being 'the charges of my master and my lady's geldings standing at Mr. Norton's'; and that night Petre and his servants lay at Alton. Next day the Court reached Bishop's Waltham, the Queen no doubt staying at Gardiner's palace. 'That night at Waltham: horsemeat at Cheriton, the Queen dining at the Bishop of Lincoln's, 18*d*.' Then the steward was silent for nearly a week, a restless week for all. On the 18th, anxious perhaps not to overburden his host, Petre moved elsewhere for two or three days: 'My master going from Waltham to Meon Stoke.' That meant going back seven miles. At Stoke, where capons, chickens and cygnets reached him from Gardiner, he gave 30*s*. 'in reward to the gentlewomen of the house there', with 17*s*. 4*d*. in tips to servants, cook and turnbroach, the scale of which suggests generous hospitality. The 21st was 'removing day from Waltham to Winchester', where Petre's servants had lodged since the 12th. On the 20th the Spanish fleet anchored at Southampton. There Arundel invested Prince Philip in the Queen's name with the George and the Garter. Mary entered Winchester on the

---

* Perhaps the Hampshire justice mentioned in the Council register; but cf. Robert How's notes of the progress, 11 July, 'the Queen went to Norton' (*Chron. of Q. Jane & Q. Mary*, Cam. Soc. (1850), 77).

21st, taking up residence in the bishop's palace, where Philip met her three days later. The post-nuptial rejoicing lasted till the end of the month. The councillors resumed daily meetings on the 27th, when much business affecting the Principal Secretaries was transacted, such as the ordering of a double-signature royal stamp for state documents.[60]

Petre's attendants were augmented by his town house staff at Winchester, where he paid 'for servants' lodging, 4 beds', and departed on the 31st with the knowledge that his negotiations for the marriage treaty had finally materialized. It was removing day to Basing, the mansion of the Lord Treasurer, who bore the cost of entertaining the King and Queen and their retinues. To provide accommodation at nights for the great double cavalcade presented problems. One of Petre's men was 'appointed his harbinger' and rode ahead to secure a room for him at Basing, Reading and Windsor. Some of Petre's servants 'went before with my lady', while he lay at Reading in the house of an unnamed goodwife, who charged 5s. for the night's lodging. The axletree of one of his baggage carts broke, and a relief cart had to be hired. He arrived at Windsor on the evening of 4 August. Next morning a servant rode up with his master's Garter robes for the following day's ceremony, which Philip's investiture with the Mantle and Collar enhanced with a special grandeur.

2 Philip, Pope and Pole

The joint reign had scarcely begun before the dark clouds of conciliar disharmony gathered once more. Thirteen sat round the table at Windsor Castle on 6 August 1554: a good muster, including the Chancellor and both Secretaries. But there were some noticeable absences. Since the last full Council at Winchester, Gardiner's enemies had been sitting at their own privy board and they avoided the court of Philip and Mary during its week's sojourn at Windsor. Arundel, Pembroke, Darcy and Cobham had in fact withdrawn to Paget's house at Drayton; 'behaviour which is not to be interpreted otherwise than as a sign of evil intentions, for when Englishmen have a conspiracy on foot these meetings always take place': a remark which shows that Renard was well versed in recent history. His report continued: 'Paget is taken to be the author and abettor of all evil plans, and he has been the more ready to plot since he has seen that the Queen is indignant with him, and he no longer counts. Arundel aims at marrying Elizabeth to his son, and preventing the Chancellor and High Treasurer from governing.'[61] Petre made a journey on the day this letter was written:

178

Horsemeat at Uxbridge, my master being at the Master of the Horse one night,
4s. 10d.

Reward to Sir Maurice Barkley's servant being my master's guide to the Master
of the Horse, 2s.

The nurse that keepeth Mr. Barkley's child at Ditton [not Drayton], 2s.

It is impossible to say whether Petre's visit, limited to a one-night absence
between Council meetings on the days before and after the journey, was
connected with the intrigues against Gardiner; Sir Edward Hastings, the
Master of the Queen's Horse, was one of her staunch Catholic supporters.
(Uxbridge and West Drayton are equidistant from Windsor; Barkley was
a distant relation of Lady Petre.) Paget's place remained vacant until the
Court's arrival at Richmond on the 13th, and not until it reached Westminster a week later were three other seats filled, those of Arundel,
Pembroke and Hastings. There is a glimpse of Petre's train in the great
concourse on the 'removing day': 'the charges of 10 horses at Kingston
the night of the Queen's coming to Richmond, for that the horses could
not come that night over the water'. There a royal cook got 4d. for
roasting his partridges, and another groat went on posset ale for Sir
William who probably had a cold but did not stay away. His harbinger
and an attendant had fallen sick at Windsor, and when the Court proceeded to London they were taken in the cart, an ignominious way of
returning. 'To mistress Joyce my lady's gentlewoman towards the buying
of a verdingale 5s.' denotes a little token of gratitude for constant attendance during a tiring progress. Doubtless she had hankered to possess one
of these new Spanish farthingales—'verdingales and such fine gear', as
Latimer had dubbed them in a sermon two years earlier.[60] The other
servants got bonuses of over £2 between them.

Charges for 'my master's and my lady's suppers at London' on
17 August marked the end of their two months' journey. Philip and
Mary entered the capital as 'King and Queen of England, France, Naples,
Jerusalem, and Ireland, Defenders of the Faith, Princes of Spain and Sicily,
Archdukes of Austria, Dukes of Milan, Burgundy and Brabant, Counts
of Hapsburg, Flanders and Tyrol'. Even Petre, experienced diplomat as
he was, needed enlightenment on this jargon of extended sovereignty.
Wotton explained the difference between the Realm of Naples and the
Kingdom of the Two Sicilies.[62] He also expressed relief on learning that
the King was conducting himself 'so gently to all men'; Philip was in fact
making every courteous effort to placate his new subjects, even to drinking
their loathsome beer. The Queen's unpopularity, too, had temporarily
receded. The nation's attitude after the splendid marriage that Petre had

helped to bring about has been summed up thus: 'Mary's success had brought a glittering array of honours for England's sovereign; the promise of light taxation and of protection from France at Spain's expense, and the prospect, over which Mary was gloating already, of a male heir to combine in one great monarchy England and her market in the Netherlands.'[63]

The progress obligation had cost Secretary Petre over £30. It is unlikely that any of the Queen's officers received any travelling expenses. Was there not, however, some prospect of Imperial largesse to those who had been engaged in procuring the marriage treaty? Ever since the end of 1553, the ambassadors' reports from England had revealed their anxiety about this delicate matter. The recipients, the amounts, the method—all were carefully considered, for the potential benefits which the Hapsburgs hoped to gain by the Anglo-Spanish marriage treaty were substantial. Generosity was valuable, the Emperor was informed, in securing the goodwill of those who counted, because 'these people lay store by such presents', and a small one would be 'disdained'. At last he authorized his envoys to seek the Queen's own views on those who should be rewarded, observing that it would be preferable to bind the beneficiaries by pensions rather than to give lump sums, which would be forgotten as time went by![64] What appears to be the final version of the lists named thirty men to receive gold chains or money; Mistress Clarentius and thirty of the Queen's ladies, unnamed but doubtless including Lady Petre, were to be rewarded; and thirty-six nobles and high officers to have pensions or the like. Pensions of 2,000 'crowns English' were to go to some earls, of half that amount (£250) to twelve councillors, including Petre; of 600 crowns to a few others including Bourne. Paget was 'to be recompensed, as his Majesty knows'. Gardiner complained later that he had not been given a pension.*

Petre's efforts brought him a liberal addition to his fortune, but so far this year, except for two brief spells, he had not seen his Essex house. There had been parliamentary work, followed by Wyatt's rebellion, Council strife and the progress. On 23 August he travelled in the opposite direction to his fellows: 'Removing day from Westminster to Hampton Court, and my master that night into Essex'. At the same time he

---

* Not until recently was it established that the pensions were paid, at any rate for one or two years. Petre's accounts confirm. Those for 1556 prove that it was in fact received: 'King's pension due last day of June, £250' (E.R.O., D/DP A14, f.12). But his pension was behind by 1558. 'What is owing to his Majesty's English pensioners in respect of the last six months of 1557' shows that the Crown's debt to Petre was £125, and a few of his colleagues' pensions were a whole year overdue. By the beginning of 1559, most of the pensions were in heavier arrears; £375 to Petre for eighteen months (*Span. Cal.*, xiii, 373, (454–6). His first instalment (£145 16s. 8d.) came in Sept. 1554 (A5, f. 34).

dispatched a tasty load thither: 'A firkin of fresh sturgeon sent to Ingate-stone, 24s.; a barrel of olives, 2s.'

He resumed Court life on 6 September. 'The split in the Council', Renard wrote, 'is caused by the fact that the Chancellor is trying to subject the realm. There is a bitterness between Arundel and the Chancellor that will never disappear until one or the other has been discredited.'[65] Not being involved in the Anglo-Spanish intrigues, the Venetian ambassador was able to take a more detached view. 'The leading members', he described in one report, 'are lodged in the palace where her Majesty resides, some of them sleeping there, according to ancient custom, so that she may never be alone. They meet very early in the morning, and, provided the chiefs are present, although they may not be more than six or seven, the Council is understood to be assembled, and the president proposes the matters for discussion—though at present the Bishop of Winchester has the management of everything—and each member present is at liberty to give his opinion by word of mouth, the decision of the majority being presented for approval to the Queen, who, deferring in everything to the Council, approves accordingly. Next to him, those most in the Queen's favour are the Earl of Arundel, Lord Paget, and Secretary Petre; but Paget now, as an acknowledged anti-Catholic, is out of favour with her Majesty.'[66] Philip had begun to take part in the business of the Council almost at once. Although Paget was his chief English ally, it is probable that Petre was the intermediary between him and Mary on conciliar affairs.

Philip proving neither ardent lover nor sympathetic counsellor, Mary tried to sublimate her frustrated passion by concentrating on bringing back the whole nation to Catholic Christendom, enforced if necessary by severe penalties. She had already discussed it with Gardiner, Thirlby, now back in England, and Petre.[67] The agent she desired was Reginald Pole, whose royal blood, high morals and theological knowledge singled him out for the task. Mary's third Parliament was summoned for November. She persuaded the Council to issue injunctions to ensure that the electors were admonished to return men 'of the wise, grave and Catholic sort'. The leading men of Essex may have had doubts over Petre's religious views, but the first two epithets applied, so his steward entered 4s. 'to the servant of the Parliament House for the fees of my master being knight of the Shire of Essex'. Mary won the first round; her regained popularity and the pressure brought to bear on influential electors secured the virtual disappearance of Protestant members. As papal legate, Pole was given full powers to recognize the lay owners of monastic estates and to absolve the nation on its submission. Then, and not till then, did Parliament reverse his attainder, still outstanding from Henry's time, and the exile was free to come back. The Queen had obtained the Council's consent to dispatch Paget and Hastings (a nephew of Pole's) as commissioners to the Emperor at Brussels to arrange for Pole's return. Cecil accompanied them; but his reappearance is not significant, as he took no active share in the negotiations.[68] Charles made Paget his confidant in a private interview granted to him.

In the course of this, Paget could not resist bringing up the old question of limiting the membership of the Council, which Renard, Petre and he had failed to carry through in the previous spring. Again, the essential personnel of an inner executive was put on record: Gardiner, Paget, Thirlby and Petre 'are experienced statesmen whose services are indispensable'. But still nothing was done. Renard explained why on 23 November. 'As for the reduction of the excessive number of councillors, it has proved impossible to achieve this measure, for it created too much bad feeling between the old and recent members of the Privy Council', especially as the new list did not include Winchester and eight others, 'who consider themselves to be as deserving as those who, as they say, rebelled against the Queen'. Speaking somewhat freely, Paget gave the Emperor a detailed, if one-sided, description of affairs at Court, with illuminating comments on his own colleagues. 'If Secretary Petre wishes to retire', he remarked, 'he ought not to be allowed to do so, but kept in office, for he has been there so long that he is as good as a Council register and reminds the members of everything that has occurred in the past.'[69] Paget's felicitous phrase rings true.

But what of the hint of Petre's resignation? It is not an isolated one. Another source, early in September, refers to 'talk that Secretary Petre was out of his office'; its reliability is perhaps to be discounted because many rumours flew around in that week.[70] A whisper reached Mason at Brussels: 'We say here,' he wrote to Petre on 7 December, 'that it is possible that Mr. Cecil may succeed you, where good meaning must needs be commended of all good men. And surely if, in case you will needs be disburdened, you can devise to place so sufficient a successor, the world must needs think that in leaving the office you minded not to leave your commonwealth unfurnished of a convenient minister, whose match of those years I know not within the realm of England.'[71] There was a much later echo in an Elizabethan pamphlet against Cecil, then Lord Treasurer. 'Many still recollect', it stated, 'how he persuaded Sir William Petre to resign up his office of the Secretaryship unto him, if Queen Mary could have admitted the same, who never could be persuaded to believe him.'[72] In the light of Paget's recent encomium about the Secretary's knowledge, it seems that Philip and Mary were opposed to Petre's intention, whether inspired or not by Cecil. At any rate, the flow of 'foreign' state papers through the same Secretary's hands was no whit abated: the volume of letters addressed to him and drafted or corrected by him is indeed one of the chief memorials to his unremitting labours, which were reduced to a negligible extent by Bourne.[73] No wonder that Petre was 'sore offended' with Gregory Raylton, one of his Signet clerks, whose sick leave at Basle seemed to be unduly prolonged.[74]

When the Legate reached Canterbury, the first sign of religious ecstasy appeared. 'Thou art Pole,' he was addressed, 'and thou art our Polar star, to light us to the kingdom of the heavens.' This parody of Christ's Petrean metaphor probably displeased one Secretary, who was to tell Mary, when Pole's star had fallen, that papal legates were very dubious blessings to England. The Queen accorded a rapturous welcome to the Cardinal at Westminster. Emotionally disturbed, Mary declared she experienced John the Baptist's mother's prenatal joy, and the Council issued written instructions to Bishop Bonner for Te Deums to be sung in every London church as a general thanksgiving for the quickening of Mary's 'child'. Petre was not one of the ten signatories, who belonged chiefly to Gardiner's faction and included Rich, now in league with him.[75] Three days afterwards, Secretary Petre summoned the Lords and Commons to the Court to hear a declaration by the Legate.[76] There, in the Great Chamber, Pole addressed both Houses, the King and Queen being present at this extraordinary scene. On St. Andrew's Day the Lords and Commons gathered again at the palace to hear the Legate absolve the nation. The people of England were received again into the fold at the price of obedience to the Bishop of Rome. In contrast to the chroniclers' and ambassadors' picturesque narratives of a day which marked the climax of the ceremonies, and indeed the climax of the reign, the matter-of-fact entries in the steward's book run: 'Two boats for my master from Westminster to Paul's wharf, and so returning to Westminster; my master's boathire and the Bishop of Ely's from the Court to Lambeth, and returning.' Cranmer being in prison, Lambeth Palace had been assigned to the Cardinal. Other sources tell how Pole was conducted across the river in a royal barge by Arundel and six other peers. So Petre and Thirlby, recently translated from Norwich to Ely, were also among those who escorted the Legate to or from the great assembly.

Parliament resumed its proper work. But the unity of spirit in Westminster Abbey was not equalled in Westminster Hall. The ghost of persecution, which had been laid in the previous parliament, rose again and stalked through both Houses; its previous opponents had been reduced by the elections, and the remnants' attempts to block its path failed. In the middle of December it was given statutory authority to walk abroad through the whole country—the ancient heresy laws were re-enacted. Then Parliament debated the repeal of the anti-papal Acts of the Henrician Reformation and confirmed the laity's title to the former ecclesiastical possessions. The bill, of prodigious length, has often been praised for its orderly precision and graceful language; it is a monument to the industry of the drafting committee, whose membership almost certainly included Petre. Entries in his accounts show that he visited Pole many times between 1 and 24 December. Among them, the first quoted evidently refers to his steward's bringing back the draft bill after Pole's study of the latest amendments.

1554

DEC. 19. My boathire that night, being sent to Lambeth for the Act of Parliament.

22. My master's boathire from Westminster to Lambeth, and so returning, the boat waiting in the night.

23. The like boathire and like waiting in the night.

24. My boathire to Lambeth and returning, being to the Cardinal with a book touching the Parliament.

A corresponding entry in the Ingatestone account-book shows that Petre's present to the man in the ascendant came from one of his Essex parks, 19*d.* being paid to two servants 'going to London with a doe, capons, two cygnets and other things that my master gave to my Lord Cardinal'. The 'Great Bill' led to a struggle between Paget's small party and the Church majority, headed by his bitter enemy Gardiner, who secured the re-establishment of the ecclesiastical courts with their ancient privileges of arbitrary arrest and discretionary punishment: powers that were soon to be abused.

Very long debates revolved around the secularization of church property. To avoid the challenge of laymen's titles by succeeding popes or the bishops' courts, statutory confirmation was demanded. Sensing that the country's penitence was hollow, Pole threatened to go back to Rome. In the intensity of the speeches, Parliament allowed itself no Christmas recess apart from the one-day Feast of the Nativity. The Master of the Revels had made his usual preparations for Christmastide, including a masque of Venuses, cupids and torchbearers as well as Udall's plays,[77] but this year the minds of the Court were concentrated not on jovial but on a mixture of spiritual and material affairs. When it was clear that a majority in both Houses was adamant about monastic lands, an attempt was made by Bourne on Gardiner's behalf to hand back to the Church the pensions granted to laymen, but this also was defeated. Finally, the entire ecclesiastical legislation of Henry VIII was swept away and the Pope's supremacy was restored. Of other bills, several were committed to Petre;[78] no details are known except for one in which he was deeply involved. 'During the [Christmas] holidays Secretary Petre, the Queen's Comptroller [Rochester] and Englefield came to see me at my house', Renard related, 'and told me that a bill touching your Majesty's and the Queen's security had been passed by the Upper House and sent down to the Lower.' It was an attempt by the Court party to remove the restrictions on Philip's exercise of power during her life. The Commons substituted their own version. Renard strove hard to get a copy from its clam-like custodian: 'Secretary Petre burned a memoir in Latin which he began but refused to leave with me.'[79] The bill ultimately passed but declared Philip Regent only till his child should come of age and while he remained in England.

Petre's accounts perhaps reflect the religious changes. In October 1554 'a table of alabaster for my master's chapel' was set up in his Aldersgate house. It came from Compagni (p. 63). Apparently a gift, as the steward accounted only for a reward to Compagni's messenger, this tangible offering would not have pleased the Imperial ambassador, who denounced the influential merchant-banker as a pro-French spy. Compagni, a denizen of England, had been associated with Sir John Gresham, uncle of Thomas, from as early as 1542. Later, he figures much in ambassadorial correspondence between Petre, Thomas Gresham, Vannes, Mason and Wotton in connection with loans and other financial matters.[80]

The discerning Secretary and former Visitor did not feel personally satisfied about the recent legislation. He wished to make assurance doubly sure by securing a special private dispensation. So, during the following summer and autumn, Sir Edward Carne, the English envoy at Rome, obligingly worked to obtain this.[81] Paul IV's bull (28 November 1555) is unique, being the only papal muniment received by an individual owner of former Church property to confirm him and his heirs for ever in their possessions. It has been twice reproduced and is biographically important, because it enumerates the monastic lands then held by Sir William and explains how and from whom each property was acquired— by purchase, exchange or gift; the value, and if bought the price, are also stated.[82] For Church lands throughout England he had paid in cash to the Crown or lay vendors, market prices totalling £2,945 9s. 9d.; their annual value was £179 14s. 7d., giving him an average initial return on his investments of six per cent. The solitary gift from the Crown was the manor of South Brent in Devon formerly belonging to Buckfast Abbey; this he acquired from Henry, 'partly in exchange for other lands [Clatercote properties, p. 20] and partly in reward of the services rendered'. The gift represented only one-fourth of the value of Brent (p. 268). More than one writer has stated incorrectly that Dr. Petre was rewarded by Henry with huge gifts of monastic land; one went so far as to add, 'In Devonshire alone, 36,000 acres' of Church appropriations, a phrase which a standard authority copied without verification.* The bull refers to ten manors and several small properties, other than South Brent. As emphasized later Petre was in fact only a minor beneficiary of the Church. The Pope not only absolved him from every sort of ecclesiastical censure but also enjoined the Bishops of London and Exeter to promulgate the bull whenever he called on them so to do. Thus, his rights were legalized by the Roman Church in as binding a document as canon lawyers could devise. In seeking the dispensation, Petre had declared his readiness to apply the income from his rectories to spiritual purposes. Immediately after receiving the bull, he granted annuities worth £20 from the rectories of South Brent in Devon and Hawkhurst in Kent to the Dean and Chapter of Christ Church, Oxford.

3 Protestant Martyrs

From the zenith of Mary's rule the descent was unexpectedly rapid. The Heresy Act was put into force without delay. The Archbishop confidently believed that most of the offenders would save themselves from the awful penalties by recanting. Few could have foreseen how the land would be stirred into abhorrence of the Roman Church. Yet once the Queen had set her hand to the plough her conscience would not allow her to abandon it. The heresy commission first met towards the end of January 1555. It was presided over by Gardiner. Judge in Bonner's and Gardiner's trials, Petre was saved some coat-turning by being left out. Paget argued for lenient methods of repression. The accused men were three bishops and a few others. Five refused to recant and were condemned. The first to go to the stake at Smithfield, in the presence of two

* The Devon figures, first found in G. Oliver's *Collections* (1857), 197 (copied by A. F. Pollard in his *D.N.B.* article, but recognized as 'wild' by A. L. Rowse (*England of Elizabeth* (1950), 239 n.)), were taken from a mid-seventeenth century deed! Once again they appeared as '36,000 acres of abbey lands in Devon alone' in P. Hughes, *The Reformation in England*, ii (1953), 174 n. Canon C. T. Kuypers, honorary archivist to Lord Petre, first drew attention to Oliver's unfounded indictment in the *Brentwood Diocesan Magazine* in 1920. For Sir William's West Country estates, see p. 268.

councillors, Southwell and Rochester, was John Rogers, who had worked closely with Tyndale and Coverdale in translating the Bible.

Within a week three more burnings took place. Hooper was taken to his see of Gloucester, Saunders to Coventry and Dr. Taylor to Hadleigh in Suffolk. The last, who crossed swords with Bourne by defending Cranmer's Prayer Book at his preliminary examination, was met at Aldgate by the sheriff of Essex and his company. Recognized and encouraged by a townsman of his near Brentwood, he was forced by the angry sheriff to don a close hood, with eye-holes and mouth-hole. This ill-assorted company rode to Chelmsford, where the sheriff of Essex laboured unavailingly to win Taylor to conformity before handing him over to the sheriff of Suffolk. Constancy and courage marked the last hours of all these men.[83]

The next batch, of various callings, were south Essex men, and were executed in their home towns for more widespread effect. Anthony Browne (not the Henrician councillor, now Viscount Montague), who had bought Weald Hall in 1553, was the principal justice of the peace assigned to superintend executions in two neighbouring towns on the same day; the story of the youthful Hunter's martyrdom at Brentwood is well known. Next month (April 1555) the scene shifted to the Quarter Sessions at Chelmsford. Sitting on the Bench were prominent Catholic justices, Rich, Browne and Tyrell, who was Lady Petre's brother-in-law by her first husband. To Chelmsford Bonner had sent an offender; two months later, as he died in the flames, the folk of the county town heard him exclaim to Rich, 'You are the cause of my death.' So far, Bonner's diocese of London, comprising the city, Middlesex and Essex, had yielded by far the greatest number of the victims, of whom the majority went to the stake in Essex.

But the burnings led only to new strife in the Council. The Lords of the Council 'talked strangely', and their indignation at the violent exercise of episcopal domination was marked. The multitude of dispatches of the Imperial and French ambassadors reveals another series of conferences, mostly secret, in which Petre's figure is always discernible. Sometimes he took a leading part, sometimes he stayed silent in the background. During these weeks, his accounts note several visits to Lambeth, presumably to call on Pole; at the end of February he dined with the Venetian ambassador, with Arundel and with Baker; and there were more visits to Lambeth during March and early April, with one on Gardiner. On 18 March he attended 'the christening of Lord Paget's daughter's child', to whom he gave, probably as godfather, 'a gilt standing cup with a cover, glass fashion', which cost over £5. This domestic event fell in a period of two months when Paget avoided the Council almost entirely, preferring to consolidate his alliance with Philip, whose moderate views gave better grounds for hope. At the end of March Mary had summoned her 'leading councillors', Winchester, Petre, Rochester and Englefield, to whom she solemnly declared her resolve to restore all the Church lands remaining in Crown hands. She bade them jointly with the Cardinal and the Chancellor to announce her example to the nation. As a beginning, the Friary at Greenwich was set up again and monastic life was revived at Westminster Abbey. Two reminders occur in Petre's accounts for 1556: 'The baker at Charing Cross for bread for the friars, 2s.', and 'bread for the friars at Greenwich, 12d.'

The Court had spent the whole of the winter at Westminster. On 6 April 15s. 8d. was spent 'for a barge for my master and my lady from London to Hampton Court'. Mary was now preparing for the birth of her imagined child at Hampton Court. Lady Petre was among the ladies in constant attendance: a Spanish courtier expressly stated that the councillors' wives (and servants) also ate in the palace.[84] 'All the Court', says one chronicler, 'was full of midwives, nurses and rockers.'[85] Urgent business, apparently for the Queen, sent Petre hurrying to town and back between the Council meetings on 19 and 20 April. A few days earlier Mary had issued instructions for bringing Elizabeth from her virtual confinement at Woodstock. There was a demonstration in her favour at Colnbrook on the way, and it is not improbable that Petre's mission was to warn the city authorities to prevent any such popular rising. She arrived at Hampton on the 29th. The Queen did not see Elizabeth at once; on the day after her arrival Mary's 'pains' began—and subsided. But word reached London that day, though none knew how, of the birth of a prince. There was wild exultation until messengers arrived contradicting the news. A shilling reward to one of his servants 'for bringing letters from London' on 1 May perhaps records Petre's receipt of a friend's hasty account of the scenes there. By the following day the news (first and second versions) reached Brussels, Mason's laconic comment to Petre on 3 May being: 'We were merry for the time.'[86] Gresham, too, writing from Antwerp, told the Secretary how the Regent's reaction to the news was to distribute largesse to the English mariners to get drunk; the cautious financier was doubtful himself.[87] Left in guarded seclusion, Elizabeth wished to meet several influential councillors and sought the help of her great-uncle, Lord William Howard, who arranged for Gardiner, Arundel, Shrewsbury and Petre to visit her apartments a few days later. 'My Lords, I am glad to see you', she exclaimed, 'for, me-thinks, I have been kept a great while from you, desolately alone. Wherefore I would desire you to be a means to the King's and Queen's Majesties, that I may be delivered from prison.'[88] The Chancellor begged her to submit to the Queen's grace, but the princess maintained her injured innocence. A week later, she gained an interview with Mary. Yet another week, and she was free.

About this time two of the prominent Devon malcontents temporarily reappear in Petre's story. Edward Courtenay, Earl of Devonshire, had been exiled. The Chancellor's enemies declared that it was he who procured Courtenay's release, in agreement with Rochester, Englefield and Petre, 'so as to be able', Renard told the Emperor, 'to promote him to the crown in case the Queen were to die'.[89] Brussels was his first place of sojourn, and from there Mason wrote to Petre in May, describing the welcome given him at the Emperor's court.[90] Sir Gawain Carew had also been liberated in the previous January; he sent his man to Petre with a salmon pie and two lamprey pies, apparently outsize ones, judging from the gratuity: only a week later, the Council resolved on a further act of leniency towards him. A curious if not somewhat suspicious coincidence is that Sir Nicholas Arnold, another recently released prisoner, sent a present, to wit, a salmon pie and two lamprey pies. As it happened, Petre's accounts were punctuated during the spring of 1555 by entries about various gifts. Little offerings came, for example, from Lord Cobham (a heronshew and a gammon of bacon), to whom Petre had probably written a day or two beforehand telling him of the Council's decision in his dispute with another nobleman, and from Sir Maurice Denis the late Treasurer of Calais (strawberries and peas). Occasionally a strange name in the accounts can be traced in the Council register as a suitor or defendant. Lady Audley was in trouble for keeping her daughter from her husband, and the Council sent a stiff letter (even marital affairs were within their purview); a week later a 'white ambling gelding' arrived from the mother. Perhaps the clearest record of the Secretary's acceptance of a bribe, though harmless enough in its object, is found in the previous year. Lady Tailbois, wife of Sir Peter Carew, had made an earnest suit to the King and the Queen for leave to write to him and to send him some financial relief in prison. She appeared before the Council, Petre being among those present, on 22 September, to receive details of the royal clemency.[91] Five days earlier Kyme wrote, 'In reward to the Lady Tailbois' servant for bringing an ambling grey gelding to my master, 10s.' The Tudor sovereigns expected the Court magnates to augment their low salaries by such offerings as part of their recognized remuneration for services to the suitors.

Noailles, the French ambassador in England, writing in June 1555, referred to his having passed information to the Queen through her most intimate councillor (*'son plus famillier conseiller le secrétaire Pitre'*); and the mass of foreign correspondence with which he personally dealt grew no less. He managed to indulge in the joys of the chase at Nonsuch and Hanworth Parks at the end of May, and on both occasions Pembroke lent him a mount. Following a run of almost daily Council meetings from mid-May to mid-June, the register gives no business for five days, when the accounts show a sudden round of calls on colleagues. He supped with Wharton in London; next day, dinner with Gardiner and supper with Baker; third day, dinner with Arundel, whose barge took him back to Hampton Court. The political repercussions of Mary's apparent barrenness must have been among the main topics discussed. By now Renard thought that her pregnancy was simulated. 'The looks of men are grown strange and impenetrable', he wrote; and in the middle of July, 'The Council learned that a number of gentlemen were holding meetings in London; no one stays in London in summer who is able to go away, because of the heat and prevalent illness. They have been ordered to go away.'[92] Pembroke and Baker were ordered on 17 July 'to repair hither by Saturday next at the latest'. Such language is reminiscent of the darker days of Somerset and Northumberland. Baker immediately resumed his attendance, after six months' absence; Pembroke, after six weeks, not quite so promptly. The Queen sent her Secretary four gifts of game in July (she had rarely done so before), which were conceivably intended to strengthen his allegiance. He had written as late as 12 July from Hampton Court to the Earl of Devonshire that her delivery was expected daily. As a courtier he went about his business more sphinxlike than ever. On the 15th he dined with Cardinal Pole at Isleworth. A fortnight later, Lady Petre accompanied him to town, where he bought her an expensive present and a drink to slake her thirst, all on a summer's day:

JULY 28. My master and my lady going to London.

29. A goldsmith in Cheapside for a flagon chain of gold, weight 3½ oz. at 53s. 4d. the oz., £9 6s. 8d., and for the fashioning, £9 16s. 8d.; which chain was delivered to my lady.

Mistress Wells for the carriage of certain stuff of my lady's which was sent to the Court, 4d.

Boathire from Teddington to London, with 6d. for a wherry that was taken up and then returned, 3s. 2d.

Drink by the way for my lady, 2d.

Was this journey to the capital, ostensibly to buy jewellery for Dorothy Petre's wedding early in September, a cloak to cover a secret meeting? Sir William and his wife were back at the Court next day.

By now some of the Queen's ladies had diagnosed her condition as dropsy or tumour near the womb, but durst not tell her, and the royal physicians were hesitant in dealing with a patient who still insisted that she was with child. Not until the beginning of August did she admit that her 'pregnancy' had been a delusion.

Charles V, intending to abdicate in favour of his son Philip, required his presence in the Netherlands; and having lost hopes of an heir by Mary Philip prepared to leave England. Twice, then, in rapid succession, the statesmen had to adjust themselves to changed circumstances, and those including Petre who had striven hard to bring about the Spanish marriage and all that it entailed now knew that it had been to no purpose. 'The day of the Queen's removing to Greenwich' (26 August) was in effect the first stage in Philip's journey to Flanders—little more than a year since the Court had welcomed him with such splendour at Winchester. Rarely failing in his Council attendances, Petre hurried between Greenwich and the capital almost every day in a week which culminated in the wedding at London of his daughter Dorothy with Nicholas Wadham. On the same early September day as the wedding, the King departed, leaving Mary in Pole's charge. He entrusted the government to a select Privy Council composed of Gardiner, Paget, Arundel, Pembroke, Thirlby, Winchester and Petre, who were urged to lay aside internal quarrels, to manage Parliament, and to pay the royal debts.[93] Philip's wisdom in including two members of the clerical party silenced the opponents of the inner council oligarchy. Here, in the opinion of a recent historian, 'it is plain that one of the basic ideas of the cabinet system was already germinating; the result, like most constitutional development in England, of practical considerations rather than of any very exact theory'.[94] The Queen resolved to stay at Greenwich to await Philip's return. Petre's official life for the next three years was spent mainly there except when the Court removed to St. James's Palace or left the summer heat of London for the country.

In the same week as the wedding, a trial began at Oxford, where Cranmer, Ridley and Latimer had been incarcerated a long time—a trial of three Fathers of the Reformation. It was the most important round in the contest promoted by the arch-persecutors. As far back as March 1554 the trio had been removed from the Tower and sent to the University to undergo a test by way of theological disputation. Before a committee of Convocation to which the Council passed their cases, they had been condemned. At that time the heresy laws had not been re-enacted. Cardinal Pole had recently appointed a commission to re-try all three for obstinate nonconformity. The session opened on 7 September. The case of Cranmer, as an archbishop, had to be referred to Rome. The bishops were sentenced, and on 16 October they lit their historic candle. Petre's activities on the day they gave their lives at Oxford can be followed in some detail from three sources. He hired wherries from Greenwich to the Lion Quay, from the Old Swan to Westminster and from the Temple to the Lord Chancellor's. The steward paid 'for the servants' dinners, my master dining at the Serjeants' Feast', which explains his being at the Temple. The company had proceeded from Westminster Hall to the Inner Temple hall for the usual sumptuous dinner, at which the Lords of the Council were the principal guests.* After the feast, there was a procession to St. Paul's; but Petre, as his accounts disclose, did not take part in it.[95] Of Gardiner's behaviour that day a curious story is told.[96] While he was awaiting news, there came to his house the old Duke of Norfolk. The Chancellor postponed dinner from three to four o'clock, when one of his servants arrived, having posted from Oxford as the faggots were fired. 'Now', the bishop said to the duke with grim satisfaction, 'let us go to dinner', but no sooner had Gardiner begun to eat than he had a seizure. Norfolk's appearance is a fable of Foxe's, for he had died in the previous year; but the bishop's health was certainly failing through dropsy. Did Petre pay his call to console him in his last illness and to discuss the tragedy at Oxford which we know from more reliable sources gave Gardiner no joy? Or did word of his sudden relapse reach Petre at the Temple?

In the second half of 1555, stirred up by the Queen's circular letter to bishops in the inert dioceses, the inquisitors had been active mostly outside Bonner's sphere. Soon after the autumn Parliament had been dissolved the persecution raged again. Cranmer's case was pursued. Petre was spared the discomfort of sitting in counter-judgment to the great religious trials of Edward's reign and the shame of condemning him. After a long series of abject confessions had been wrung from Cranmer, he made an eleventh-hour withdrawal of his recantations and held the hand that had written them in the flames.† New commissions were issued to intensify the heresy-hunt everywhere. In 1556 many more faggots were fired in Bonner's diocese than in any other. Thirty-one men and women

---

* Among the eight new serjeants elected that day was Anthony Browne of Weald Hall.

† A mundane echo of this spiritual struggle was heard ten years later. The two Oxford city bailiffs who provided the three martyrs with food and drink during their long imprisonment had spent £63, as well as 12s. for 'woodfaggots to burn them'. 'Notwithstanding their endeavours to get themselves reimbursed, they could never get but £20 which they received by the means of Sir William Petre, Secretary of State.' Finally, in 1566, the bailiffs sent up a petition to Archbishop Parker and the bishops, begging them to join together and find the money to pay off the long outstanding debt (Strype, *Memorials of Cranmer*, i, 562–5).

went to the stake at Colchester, Stratford in West Ham and Smithfield. Not long after these spectacles of horror, Oxford, Darcy, Edmund Tyrell and Browne sent twenty-three men and women to walk from Colchester to London in a string of ropes. A rout of a thousand persons cheered the guarded gang's arrival in the city. Bonner hesitated in face of the dangerous demonstration. Pole advocated their release by an easy form of submission. This was done, and they returned home. The year 1557 saw no diminution in the persecutors' vehemence.

The bright light of spiritual devotion which illumines most of the burnings detracts attention from the submissions. Some months later, recantation saved another victim from a fiery death but sent him to an early grave. Sir John Cheke, Secretary of Edward's last days, had been released after a year to go abroad. In August 1554 Petre got a friendly letter from him written at Padua, but later heard from Mason of the poverty of Cheke's wife (Mason's step-daughter) at Brussels: 'Her husband by his folly is fallen from £600 per annum to less than nothing; had he followed advice, he had not fallen into the folly which for lack of grace he fell into.'[97] Mason and Petre, two efficient trimmers, could indulge in sympathy for a less adaptable friend. In 1556 Cheke was arrested; his seizure is said to have been due to treachery on the part of Paget and Mason, though the charge against Mason is not proven.[98] Cheke had committed no offence but had been too closely associated with Cranmer on liturgical matters. His courage failed him at the prospect of the stake. In October Cheke renounced his faith utterly before the Queen, Cardinal and Council; Pole wrested an even more humiliating submission from him before he was released. Pining away with shame, he died before long, only forty-three years of age. The country lost a beneficent scholar.

During 1555 and 1556, when the Council records can be supplemented by Petre's, visits to Ingatestone were extremely few. In 1555 they were limited to two October days; in the next year, to Twelfthtide, two days in June, and a fortnight in early autumn. How far this was due to his being chained to Court and Council, how far, if at all, to his determination to keep away from the Essex burnings, cannot be ascertained; a fair guess would attribute it to both. The remarkable fact remains, however, that his name is never linked with the long persecution in Essex or London. A search in the printed material and in the steward's accounts has yielded nothing to indicate his individual participation. Yet the Essex magnates figure many times in the story. Edmund Tyrell of Rawreth, Sir Henry Tyrell of East Horndon, Sir John Mordaunt of West Horndon, Anthony Browne of South Weald, Thomas Mildmay of Chelmsford and William Berners of Thoby Priory near Ingatestone, were the most energetic justices of the peace in prosecuting offenders; some possibly under orders, others, like Edmund Tyrell, anxious to lead heretics to the fire.[99] The great Essex landowners, Oxford, Darcy and Rich, were enjoined more than once to supervise the executions. Rich and Mordaunt, though infrequent attenders, were privy councillors. The majority of the justices named were neighbours and friends; the Tyrells were family connections (and Petre's Kent relation was so active as to be called 'Bloody Baker'). Only at the very end of the reign is there a minor reference to Petre—as a sort of guarantor for Lady Wentworth, who was apparently the daughter of Humphrey Tyrell of Little Warley; suspected of Protestant sympathies, she appeared in person before the Council, made submission, was sent to her mother's house in Essex, and was charged not to depart without first communicating with Petre.[100]

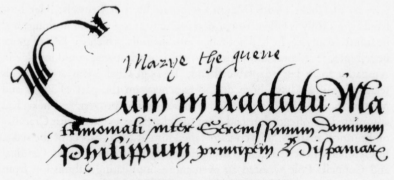

FROM PETRE'S MS. TREATIES BOOK

Despite this significant silence in the national archives, which speak so often of his other activities, he cannot be exonerated from the general condemnation, because he was one of those in authority. According to what is probably the fairest, undenominational statement of the guilt problem, Gardiner initiated the burnings, though he was quick to recognize their futility; Bonner was the most active; Pope and Pole must bear much of the odium; Parliament permitted the persecution; the ecclesiastical courts carried it out; but the ultimate charge lies against the Queen. 'The Council, had it been so minded', the same statement adds, 'could have prevented her from persecuting; it was not so minded, because members likely to adopt this view had been excluded by Mary from its ranks. The fact that the burnings ceased at once on Mary's death measures the extent of her responsibility.'[101] There remains one aspect of Petre's share of the blame. As lawyer and parliamentarian, he knew that the stake was the punishment for those convicted of heresy; but although men of his age were far from squeamish about physical pain the burning of his venerable friend Cranmer must have nauseated him. A man of uncommon moderation, Petre could not have been in accord with those whose passions were directed against the genuinely steadfast clerics who were prepared to sacrifice their lives. Like Paget, he was a *politique* (to anticipate a slightly later term), convinced that religious strife should be settled by peaceful politics; but he had a stronger sense of the rule of the law and was less opportunist than Paget.

CHAPTER IX

Resignation—but no Rest

1 *The Problem of the Secretary's Surrender*

IN October 1555 (to return to the broader track of political history), the
Queen's urgent need for money led to the calling of her fourth Parliament. In company with most councillors who were not peers, Petre was
again returned; but it included not more than fifty members of the last
body and it was antagonistic to Mary. Petre was prominent on the opening day and two days later, when he read in her presence a letter of goodwill in Latin and English from the King. After this, Gardiner spoke with
great eloquence. 'He had projected some additional security for Church
and Abbey lands; and this project was afterwards brought to bear by his
friend Mr. Secretary Petre',[1] who had paid frequent calls on him at
Lambeth shortly before Parliament assembled. But the speech overtaxed
his strength, and he died three weeks later. 'The time-serving Petre, who
tried to pour oil on the troubled waters', according to a modern historian,
'was a poor substitute.'[2] Of course Petre could not step into the place of
the indomitable Chancellor. For thirty years Gardiner had worked un-
weariedly for the state; his judgment as a councillor was shrewd; but he
was an adept at double-dealing, and he was vindictive and ruthless.

His death, following the departure of Philip and Renard, deprived the
country of leadership when in sore need of it. 'Petre might have filled the
role, but one of Noailles' informers had heard him complain bitterly
about the baneful results of the Spanish marriage only two weeks before
Parliament met. One who hated the Spaniards as heartily as Petre said he
did was no man to direct a programme which (in the Queen's mind at
least) included Philip's coronation.'[3] If the source of this comment is to
be trusted, Petre refrained from pressing for more personal power.
Although Philip recommended Mary to appoint Paget as Gardiner's
successor, he had to be content with becoming Lord Privy Seal. She was
averse from a lay Chancellor, and gave the Great Seal to Heath, now
Archbishop of York.

Tumultuous debate took place over the provision of funds, the bill for
which was not passed until the Queen told the Commons that she would
waive part of the sum required; Petre was her mouthpiece.[4] In other ways
he acted as intermediary between her and Parliament. Early in the session
a brief note, 'Mr. Comptroller, Mr. Secretary Petre, with 18 more
[unnamed], to devise articles for aid to the Queen', emphasizes his status;

and a bare entry, 'Arguments for execution of laws—Mr. S. Petre', seems to refer to his leading the debate, as the Journals very rarely name a speaker at this date.[5]

Mary's over-tender conscience led her to promote a bill for restoring first fruits and tenths to the Pope. Although fifty representative members responded to Petre's summons to the palace, where they had to listen to a royal sermon, her piety had little effect on the recalcitrant Commons.[6] The discussions on the impropriated estates and church goods were very lengthy. In the previous June, Paul IV had issued a bull ordering the restoration of all church and monastic lands. Whether it was directed against England, which was not referred to, is uncertain. At any rate, it was kept secret. 'No one', wrote Pole in August, 'knew as yet, save the Queen's Secretary, who was the person who spoke about it to the King.'[7] Pole was warned by Philip to lose no time in asking the Pope to withdraw it, and a new bull had arrived, before Parliament assembled, assuring secular possession.

In the debates on a bill to confiscate the Protestant refugees' estates Cecil suddenly emerged as their champion and as spokesman of an anti-government group, whom he entertained to dinner. Shortly afterwards, several members of this small opposition party were dispatched to the Tower. Cecil himself was examined by Paget and Petre. 'When he was brought before them he desired they would not do by him as by the rest, which he thought somewhat hard—that was, to commit them first and to hear them after. But prayed them first to hear him and then to commit him, if he were guilty.' The combined influence of his two colleagues saved him from prison and disgrace; but the incident, derived only from Cecil's early anonymous biographer, is obscure and enigmatical. The author of the most recent study concludes that Cecil, convinced that Elizabeth would be on the throne before long, was playing an astute part in thus identifying himself with the Protestants.[8] Perhaps the half haunch of a hind which Cecil sent to his influential friend on 24 November betokened gratitude; but whether that or favours to come accounted for the gelding from Arundel and the goshawk and couple of spaniels from Clinton can only be guessed.

To stave off her foreign creditors Mary had to rely partly on her financial expert, Gresham, with whom Petre kept in close touch. Writing to the Queen two days before Christmas, apparently from Leyton in Essex, Gresham had first refreshed her memory. She had commanded him to confer with Thirlby, Paget and Petre about her debts abroad; as it was dark when he left her presence, he did not like to trouble them that night, and a fit of burning ague intervened next day, so he sent his 'factor' to them with a message. He then embarked on a sea of figures, which Mary referred to Petre, whose notes on this and other letters of Gresham's bears witness.[9] The Queen remained at Greenwich. She tried to solace herself with work, sitting most afternoons with the Select Council. Most of the important letters that Philip received from them were written or drafted by Petre,[10] who was also responsible for co-ordination between the lawyer councillors at Westminster and the advisory body at Greenwich. But his role about this time was a strange and difficult one. Shrewd confidant of leaders, he was seldom a leader himself, and in this year of manifold uncertainties he was drawn by powerful forces in several directions.

The growing dissatisfaction with the Queen and all she stood for gave birth to a number of conspiracies which were loosely related. A formidable rebellion for deposing her was being planned in the early weeks of 1556. It was to be led by Sir Henry Dudley, a distant kinsman of the late Duke of Northumberland. After succeeding to the throne, Elizabeth was to marry Courtenay, Earl of Devonshire, and popery and Spaniards were to be driven out of the country. One criterion of the gravity of the plot, which did not mature, is the large number of parliament-men and other gentlemen who were implicated. During the previous year the exiled Devonshire and Petre had exchanged a number of letters, apparently of a cordial nature. In October, having obtained a licence to travel, Courtenay desired Mr. Secretary to seek the Queen's concurrence. Petre was also privately interested, as he was negotiating with him for buying his manor of Whitford near Axminster in Devon.[11] Later, at the time of the crisis, there is a possibly relevant entry in Petre's accounts. On 24 February 1556, 'the Earl of Devonshire's servant for bringing letters to my master' was given 40s., a large sum but explicable if he had travelled from Italy primarily about the proposed sale of the manor. Petre had initiated the matter, probably because Whitford lay next to Shute Park which he had bought in 1554 and because he knew that the earl was in need of money. Devonshire's agent had written four months earlier that 'the manor of Shute is a very stately thing, and Mr. Petre hath divers great and profitable things there', advising Courtenay to sell the estate to the influential Secretary, 'considering who he is', and adding surprisingly, 'He can dispend in that shire [Devon] about four or five hundred pounds a year, and saith that he beginneth to have a mind to leave Essex and settle in that shire.'[12] But Petre did not buy Whitford, perhaps because Mary was against the breaking-up of her cousin's estate. Courtenay died of a sudden illness at Padua a few months later.

None of the known sources for the Dudley plot mention Petre, but later in the summer he was involved in examining Peter Killigrew concerning piracy and an intended French invasion; also in argument over the pirates' best vessel, the return of which was demanded by Henry II on the ground that it had been lent to Killigrew only for the duration of the Franco-Imperial war. A nice point for a lawyer and a diplomat, and after being closeted with Mary Petre replied that she was anxious always to be known as 'Princesse de Justice'![13] The Secretary had vanished from the Court in the weeks of tension when the plot was being unravelled. A short illness coincided with the emergency. But he quickly recovered, and in the late spring and early summer his company was sought more than in any earlier period, judging from the round of visits. Accompanied by his wife and a train of eight servants he dined with Rich. The Master of the Horse (Hastings) at Chelsea, the Cofferer (Sir Richard Freston), Secretary Bourne, Dr. Thirlby and Sir Richard Sackville were also his hosts. His dinner at 'the Lord Mayor's' was only one of five occasions, including the mayoral feast in the previous October, when his friend Sir William Garrard entertained him during his year of office. It is clear that he continued to lodge at St. James's, as boathire to the wharf from Aldersgate was very infrequent.

Instead of the customary summer progress the Court made only a short journey, first to Eltham Palace, where the Queen gave Petre a buck from the park, and then on to the Archbishop's palace at Croydon. The change of air and scene is said to have helped the Queen to recover a modicum of health. But her Secretary was to remember Croydon as the place where the stone first gave him serious discomfort. He was obliged to return to London by litter, and was in the hands of two surgeons for three weeks (see p. 250). Appetizing food and remedies arrived from several friends, such as a side of venison from Lady Wharton at New Hall, whose husband had lent the horses for the litter. On 12 September the invalid struggled back to the Court, by boat up to Lambeth, thence to Croydon by litter, the 'harness' for which had been made by Sir Philip Hoby's servant. Two letters from the Select Council to the King in mid-September were drafted by Petre, who was able to journey to Ingatestone in the saddle, if 'my master's riding into Essex' on 23 September may be so construed. He was in London again on 1 October, but in the early winter he gave up his chamber at the Court, possibly because he was still convalescent. The Petres were living at home, but there is no hint of entertaining, although he was in constant attendance at Council. And there, at Aldersgate, John Kyme closed his account-book as usual on 30 November, and the one he started on the following day is not preserved. The entries for the last day prove that Petre did not forget his younger colleague of the previous régime, biding his time in the twilight before the next regnal dawn: 'Clerke the goldsmith for a gilt salt with a cover which was given at the christening of Lady Cecil's child, 71s. 6d.' This was Anne, and Lady Petre was one of her godparents. It affords ample proof that the Petre–Cecil friendship had extended into the family circles.

The Dudley plot had failed. The burnings continued. Yet the higher as well as the lower ranks were mostly opposed to active enforcement of the Heresy Acts. Why, then, asked Froude, did not the lords and gentlemen of England trample down the perpetrators of these devilish enormities?[14] The historian began to answer the rhetorical question by quoting a cipher letter of January 1557 to Petre from Wotton in France, concerning another conspiracy, graver than Dudley's, and 'devised by some of the best in England, and so many were agreed thereupon that it was impossible but that it must take effect', were it not for one man who 'stayed' it; they did not intend to murder Mary, 'but to deprive her of her estate, and then may she chance to be used as she used Queen Jane'. There was, it is true, some suspicion in the diplomat's mind as to the credibility of his news, but he placed on his correspondent's shoulders the burden of deciding when to disclose the alleged plot.[15] Petre's reaction is not on record. Yet a further ill-conceived and short-lived plot was led by Thomas Stafford, who captured Scarborough Castle at the end of April. Petre again got to hear of it in a long cipher dispatch of 14 April from Wotton telling how suspicion had fallen on Stafford.[16]

The same letter also expressed concern regarding his channel of communication; above all, Wotton was mystified by lack of word from his trusted friend at a critical time when he was in a position to forewarn the government. 'Within the last three or four months', he reminded the normally punctilious Petre, 'I have sent several letters, but having no reply from her Majesty or the Council I fear they have not been delivered.'[17] Yet Petre was not an absentee. A fortnight later Wotton must have been aware that Petre was no longer holding the secretarial office and directly addressed the Queen with hints of wounded pride at not being informed and of anxiety as to who had opened his letters intended for Petre. 'Five or six days ago,' he concluded, 'I sent one of my servants by Dieppe with a letter to Sir William Petre, whom I yet took to be one of your Majesty's Principal Secretaries.' His next report still betrayed his reluctance, even in cipher, to convey secret news for the Queen except through his old associate. He had apparently never corresponded with Bourne, and now there was another co-Secretary and a stranger. 'During the time Sir William Petre held office, I was in the habit of troubling him with letters containing such matters as might not be considered worthy of her Majesty's attention' (tactful Wotton), 'leaving it to his discretion to make such use of them as he deemed fitting. The like fashion I shall be glad to use with Dr. Boxall, trusting you will treat my communications as Sir William Petre did.'[18] This one is addressed to Secretaries Bourne and Boxall. John Boxall, Warden of Winchester College and Archdeacon of Ely, had been sworn as a councillor in the previous December.

Petre had at last given up the office of Principal Secretary; thus he was termed on 28 March 1557, but 'Sir William Petre' two days afterwards.[19] Had he been endowed with prophetic vision in 1544 when he took the reins from Wriothesley, could he have foreseen the rough road with its deep potholes and sharp bends, he would have doubted his ability to steer the secretarial chariot safely; yet far from being overturned he finished his journey, giving up the reins probably of his own accord. He had apparently contemplated such an act in the previous autumn. It had brought forth this comment from Wotton, writing privately to Petre on 8 October:

> As for your office, knowing the weakness of your body, and the pains and travail by you sustained therein already, I cannot but think that you do well to leave it. And for because the office is so easy and pleasant, and I so meet a man for it, you may be assured I must needs thank him as much as the thing deserveth that would wish me to it. I am now so broken through age since my coming hither that you shall not know me when you see me. And therefore 'tis time for me to get into a corner and take me to my beads; and to remember that we have not here *permanentem civitatem*, and therefore to begin to put on my boots and prepare myself to go to the other place where we look to rest.[20]

It is easy to dot the i's and cross the t's of 'the pains and travail sustained' and to see the contradiction as Wotton's whimsical humour. Both men had another decade of useful work ahead. Named in October as Petre's probable successor was Mason, ambassador at the Emperor's court, who according to the Venetian ambassador there had heard that the Queen would 'soon recall him with the title of Chief Secretary'. But Mason never became Secretary.[21]

To find the determining factor behind Petre's resignation is an interesting problem. The generally accepted view that it was due to sickness[22] is not borne out by his very infrequent Council absences before or after his ceasing to hold office, nor by the mass of his official work in the months to come. Three possible reasons can be offered; all three perhaps combined to influence him.

First, Mary's declining health and Elizabeth's imminent accession. It is inconceivable that Petre had not met the princess during 1556–7, especially when the Dudley and Stafford plots were being investigated. As Mary's barrenness and incurable disease became increasingly apparent he may have felt the need to relinquish the appointment which no longer gave him present satisfaction or future security.

The incessant burnings may have hastened the ending of his close connection with Mary, obsessed with her call to stamp out heresy. The total absence of his name in the well-documented persecutions, despite the setting up of stakes near his country home and the personal involvement of the other Essex magnates, is almost unaccountable unless partly intentional. Of Cecil, it is stated, 'He probably held himself aloof advisedly, and there is reason to believe that he regarded with something like horror the detestable cruelties of the persecution'.[23] Cecil and Petre were men of similar outlook, and it was more difficult for Petre to remain permanently aloof—the pen the Queen's Secretary held was not far removed from the brands the sheriff's men wielded. In ceding office, soon after another fierce outburst, he severed the intimate advisory link with a sovereign whose fanaticism he did not share.

The last is the most probable explanation. In January 1557 war had broken out in Flanders between France and Spain. The Papacy allied itself with France, and fighting between the Pope and Philip in Italy ensued. Letters to Petre from envoys abroad reveal that the French ambassador Noailles, under royal instructions, fomented discontent in England. Mary had shown reluctance to enter a war in which she would be opposing the Pope, but it vanished overnight under the emotional stress of Philip's coming back to Greenwich on 20 March. Philip had sought the government's support. At first 'led by Pole, Petre and Mason, they still clung to non-intervention'.[24] Two leading councillors confided in Noailles in the same week that 'their intention and their duty was to have no respect either for King or for Queen, but solely for the public good of the kingdom'.[25] Although Pole was a pacifist, it is unlikely that he would have made such a remark. Were they the words of Petre and Mason? It is impossible to say, but before the end of the month Petre was no longer Secretary. That resignation coincided with Philip's return seems tantamount to Petre's antagonism to war. Out of sympathy with the royal policy, he had no alternative but to give up an appointment demanding complete confidence between sovereign and minister. Indeed, Mary may have asked him to terminate it, for anger with the councillors' opposition to war led her, a week or two after Petre ceased to hold office, to summon two-thirds of their number individually to her presence, when they were threatened with dismissal, some even with loss of goods and estates, if they did not consent to the will of her husband. The mischief-making Noailles, reporting in the previous December on plots to disinherit Elizabeth, had opined that 'les Secretaires Pitre and Bornes sont autheurs et conducteurs de ceste menée'; but it would appear to be unlikely that the elderly Petre was involved in such a dangerous intrigue.

In the absence of definite evidence it is difficult to decide whether he had relinquished the helm of Mary's ship of state because of the impending war, ill health, nausea at her persecution, or the need to trim his sails before the next Court gale. It is however abundantly clear that he remained an active member of the crew. Ailing or merely tired, he did not leave them for more frequent or longer spells at Ingatestone.

The war crisis continued, but opposition suddenly evaporated at the end of April when Scarborough was attacked by Stafford with French support. Whatever doubts Petre may have had before this event, he continued to conduct most of the royal and conciliar correspondence. In this he was doubtless assisting Paget, chief of the war council. The ex-Secretary now accepted war as inevitable and loyally worked in the coalition government.

2 The First Anglo-Russian Trade Relations

The minister who had been addressed as 'Mr. Secretary Petre' since Henry's last years was now formally referred to as 'Sir William Petre, Chancellor of the Most Noble Order of the Garter'. As such he played his dignified part twice a year in the ceremonies commemorating the patron saint—St. George's Day (23 April) and St. George's Feast (in May or June). The former was held wherever the Court lay and included a splendid procession about the great hall; the latter took place at Windsor Castle, in or near the precincts of which the chancellor had a house for his own use. Petre was the first chancellor to be given a special badge. At a chapter held in October 1554, it was ordained that he and his successors 'should wear for a cognizance a Rose of gold about their neck, inclosed with the Garter'.[27] On several occasions 'silk ribbon for my master's Rose' was bought by his steward, who twice wrongly termed it the 'George', which was the jewel worn by the Knights. The Rose is seen on his portrait of 1567 (frontispiece).

It was in 1557 that Henry Machyn the diarist first described Petre in the chancellor's resplendent attire:

> The xxiij of April was St. George's Day, the King's Grace went in procession in his robes of the Garter . . . Petre wore a robe of crimson velvet with the Garter embroidered on his shoulder. And after the King and other Lords and Knights of the Garter went to evensong.[28]

Machyn then heralded in a strange figure:

And there was the Duke of Muskovea in chapel at evensong, and after he went and took his barge and went [from Westminster] to London, where three Knights of the Garter were chosen.

He conjures up scenes as colourful as those of the Garter ceremonies. Petre's name is peculiarly associated with this notability, more accurately known as Osep Napea, the first ambassador of the Tsar of Russia to visit England. Petre had recently played his part in the earliest trade relations between England and Russia.[29]

Since the days of his youth the Council had more than once discussed the problem of how to sell to India more English goods, especially cloth, without having to make the long southern voyage round the Cape. Men had sought to find a passage to the north of Europe which they hoped would lead to India and China. After one or two abortive proposals, a desperate expedition under Sir Hugh Willoughby set out in 1553; he and his crew were frozen to death, but Richard Chancellor eventually sailed his own ship into the White Sea and he was surprised to find that he had reached Russia. He journeyed on to Moscow, was received by Ivan the young Tsar (later to earn the name of 'the Terrible') and made arrangements for trade with England. Sebastian Cabot's Adventurers' funds financed the voyage; Garrard was one of the principal speculators. They were incorporated as the Muscovy or Russia Company in 1555.[30] Their monopoly charter listed all those who 'at their own adventure and cost' had furnished the ships, 'to attain' (with good Tudor mixture of idealism and realism) 'both the glory of God and the increase of the general wealth of the realm of the King and Queen and of their subjects'. Of the councillors, half a dozen nobles and about the same number of knights, including Petre and Cecil, gave their financial support to the venture; and so did over 150 London merchants. A little account-book of Cecil's records his five payments in 1553–6[31] totalling £100 to 'the Society of the Adventurers into Russia', but no items of this nature can be identified among Petre's disbursements. The 'ten couple of fish that came from Muscovia' which Garrard sent round to Aldersgate in December 1555 may however have been a fraction of the maiden dividend from an otherwise unrecorded voyage.

Chancellor undertook a second expedition to the White Sea and carried the Queen's letters to Moscow. He left Russia in July 1556, bringing the Tsar's ambassador, Osep Napea, but this time his ship was wrecked off Aberdeenshire and he perished in trying to save Napea's life; of the remaining three ships, two were never heard of again. The Council issued severe instructions to the sheriffs for the envoy's safe conduct on the long journey to London. On 25 March he was received with honours by the King and the Queen. Two days later, by their assignment, there 'repaired and conferred with him two grave counsellors, the Bishop of Ely [Thirlby] and Sir William Petre Knight, Chief Secretary, who after divers talks and conferences finally concluding upon such treaties and articles of amity, as by the letters of the King's and Queen's Majesties under their great Seal of England, to him by the said counsellors delivered, doth appear'.[32] Meantime the merchants had their first lesson in Anglo-Russian relations. Napea, they discovered with some ingenuousness, was

> not so conformable to reason as at first they would he should have been; being very mistrustful, and thinking every man would beguile him: which made them afterwards to advise their factors there, that they should take heed how they had to do with the Russes; to make their bargains plain, and to set them down in writing; for that they were subtle people, and did not always speak the truth, and thought other men to be like themselves.[33]

At Napea's departure on 1 May, a week after the Garter ceremonies, Thirlby and Petre, 'on behalf of the King and Queen, repaired to him, and with the Queen's letters delivered him noble presents for the Emperor, and gifts to himself'.[34]

To receive and look after ambassadors was a duty expected of a Principal Secretary (and it was Petre's last act in that capacity). England's two diplomatists, long tested in difficult negotiations, had had to re-orientate their ideas to meet those of the Russian ambassador and un-doubtedly used their own subtle methods.

That Philip would be excommunicated for warring against the Pope, that Pole would be recalled and his legateship revoked, were disasters which Mary never envisaged in the ecstatic days of the reunion with Rome. But now she had to face the unwelcome facts; and it is said that it was primarily due to Petre that Mary adopted the plan of forbidding the Pope's nuncio to land in England with Pole's summons to Rome.[35] Martial, not marital, needs had stimulated Philip's coming back to Mary. His mission achieved with England's declaration of war, he departed after a stay of only five months, never to return.

After the expeditionary force's initial success in France came the bitter news of the sudden fall of Calais (8 January 1558). Its loss saved the heavy costs of defence which had been out of proportion to its real value. But that view did not obtain then, and to many Englishmen the burner of Protestants had become the betrayer of Calais. The councillors had worked hard, but too late, to save the last foothold in France. With them, Petre was guilty of neglect of the fortifications. His share in the last-minute efforts is evident from the mass of correspondence concerning Calais endorsed by him. Though no longer Mary's Secretary, Petre seems to have been with her much at this time.

Had his accounts survived, they would probably have solved the mystery of his whereabouts at this disastrous New Year. On 4 January the Council, meeting at Greenwich, sent a letter bidding him 'to repair hither with all speed'. He had only been absent since 14 December, but he answered the call promptly and was with them on the 6th.[36] Yet the draft of a letter from the Queen to the Deputy at Calais (Lord Wentworth) dated 29 December finishes with passages in Petre's unmistakable hand-writing, and the same applies to another of 2 January.[37] It looks as though Petre remained behind in London to transact official business when the Court moved to Greenwich for the festival. One would have liked to find evidence for including Sir William and Lady Petre in company with Cecil,* Mason and Mildmay at a Christmas house-party in Berkshire, to which Hoby had also invited Lady Cecil and little Anne, goddaughter of Lady Petre.[38] Petre, Hoby and travel were however associated in another way. It was on 1 July 1556 that Hoby had sent his first invitation to Cecil to visit his country home. 'Peradventure my lady stayeth you, who, you will say, cannot ride [Anne Cecil was to be born five months later]. Thereto will I provide this remedy—to send her my coche: because she shall have the less travail thither. Let me know when I shall look for you at Bisham, that my coche come for her.'[39] This is apparently the earliest known reference to a coach in England. Five days later Petre's steward noted a handsome tip to 'Mr. Hoby's man for showing my master a waggon called a coche'. Petre was in London all that week, so evidently Cecil thought that his friend with leg and bladder trouble would like to take the opportunity of examining the new vehicle, which had originated in Hungary and was gradually being adopted throughout Europe. Petre acquired a coach four years later.

In January, the self-deluded Queen again claimed pregnancy, but by April it had come to nothing. 'Sterility', in fact, 'was the conclusive note of Mary's reign.'[40] Another Parliament assembled in January. The Queen had taken special measures to secure the return of 'discreet and

* C. Read (op. cit., 116) thought that Cecil was remaining in rural seclusion, but one of his few dated accounts of this period (noted by me in ploughing through 'Bills 1' at Hatfield House) records boathire to the town houses of Paget, Bedford and Cobham in the last week of January 1558. Some years later Cecil referred to favours which he had received from Petre during Mary's reign (E. M. and C. Read, Elizabeth of England: Observations . . . by John Clapham (1951), 74).

good catholic members', but with the result that 'the smallest proportion on record of old members secured re-election' (about one fourth).[41] Petre was returned again. Disaffected county as it was, Essex elected as its other member a man who also belonged to Mary's party. Waldegrave, thus following his uncle Rochester, who had recently died, was another of the trio who had withstood the inquisitions of Rich and Petre in the princess's retreats. After providing pittances for the defence of the country and for the exchequer, Parliament was prorogued. The subsidy, however, would not be collected until the summer, and the forced loans of 1556 had already vanished.* A French invasion was feared. In her dilemma the Queen had to find alternative methods for raising funds. Paget, Thirlby, Englefield, Waldegrave, Petre, Baker and Mildmay were formed into a permanent committee of ways and means, with instructions to sit daily 'till some device had been arrived at'; and Gresham was dispatched once more to Antwerp to borrow £200,000, if possible, at 14 per cent, so low had England's credit sunk.[42] Among other fiscal and mercantile matters recently referred to Petre and others was a major overhaul of the customs duties, which took over a year to complete.[43]

Petre seems to have enjoyed fair health again. His assiduous attention to Council affairs was in fact broken for quite short periods. More definite evidence of his work is seen in the ambassadorial correspondence, especially the outgoing letters. Of these, the number of minutes or drafts in Petre's hand showed no fall after his resignation. The Queen wrote to Lord Grey at Guisnes, to Lord Wentworth at Calais, to Mildmay at Dunkirk, to Gresham at Antwerp: her letters were drawn up by the ex-Secretary, not by Bourne or Boxall; the Council asked the Lord Mayor to seal certain bonds for the Queen's use: the minute was in Petre's autograph, and he wrote officially to Gresham in his own name on a similar matter; all this as late as midsummer 1558.[44] The councillors, if not the Queen, had presumably persuaded him to give the nation as of old the

---

* Mary's forced loan, an expedient not unknown in English history, met with much resistance. Petre's home county was the first to exhibit recalcitrance, sixteen Essex gentlemen receiving stern Council letters in October. Petre lent the maximum sum assessed (£100), and with exemplary promptitude (1 August) as behoved the Queen's Secretary and Custos Rotulorum of Essex: 'Paid to Mr. Rochester, Comptroller of the Queen's Majesty's Household, to the use of her Highness by way of loan, to be repaid at the Feast of All Saints which shall be in anno domini 1557, for the payment whereof my master hath a privy seal.' The mandates, or 'privy seals', were at first directed to the individual, but the dilatoriness in subscribing shown by some soon led to the appointment of commissioners for each county. The unorthodox channel for payment—the Comptroller rather than the Treasurer—increased the gentry's indignation. The forced loan was to be on the Council's agenda as late as February 1558, when Petre was one of the six selected to audit the accounts and scrutinize the arrears.

benefit of his knowledge of diplomatic correspondence; so the complicated threads remained in skilled hands. Not before April did the English ambassadors begin to address their letters to Boxall; not until then, a year after his resignation, was Petre released from writing Mary's own state letters.*

Petre's successor as Secretary has been termed 'the mediocre Boxall'.[45] In March 1558, Bourne, whose influence was not much greater, gave up office. Thereafter, unlike Petre, he rarely appeared at the Council. There is nothing in Petre's accounts to suggest that he had ever had any other relations with Boxall; nor do they afford more than slight evidence of friendship with Bourne. Boxall, too, was destined to lose his secretaryship before the end of the year. Their brief terms were in marked contrast with Petre's long tenure. But the relevant comparison is not with the two late Marian Secretaries, of whom little is known, but with his predecessors. Wolsey and Cromwell, and to a lesser degree Wriothesley and Paget, had exploited the lucrative opportunities which the office offered, following the tempting, rapidly climbing path to great affluence and power. Refusing to take it, Petre had ascended by a surer, less steep track. Even so, he had had to make his way through the tangled undergrowth of political plot and party prejudice, but the course he pursued earned him a high reputation which in turn became closely associated with the Crown office he had held for so long. The path was now well trodden and the way was open again to greater power; if less spectacular in its ascent than that discovered by the more adventurous Henrician Secretaries, it would satisfy the sounder, less grasping ambition of the man scheming to become Secretary to Elizabeth.

Philip had sent Count de Feria to England to discuss with the government the military situation following the loss of Calais. He contrived a meeting with Paget, Arundel and Petre before getting in touch with others. 'Your Majesty must realise', his uncompromising dispatch of March read, 'that from night to morning and morning to night they change every thing they have decided.' How often in the past years would this picture of conciliar dissension have been equally true. 'Those to whom you have shown the greatest favour are doing the least for you. Pembroke, Arundel, Paget, Petre, the Chancellor, the Bishop of Ely and the Comptroller are the leading members of the Council, and I am highly

---

* Evidence of Petre's work has also been found by me in the State Papers, Domestic. For example, the letter of 29 May 1557, calendared as 'Secretary of State to Lord Admiral Howard' is in fact a draft wholly by Petre; and the next letter, 'Secretary (Bourne?) to the Lord Admiral' is a draft in two parts, the latter being Petre's share (*Dom. Cal.*, 91–2; other drafts of Petre's are nos. 20–2 on p. 93, July 1557, and p. 101, March 1558).

dissatisfied with all of them. They do nothing but raise difficulties, whatever one proposes, and never find any remedy.'[46]

Mary succumbed at last to the Council's urgent plea to nominate her half-sister Elizabeth as successor. To this period belong the earliest of Elizabeth's many plans for marriage to Arundel's son, to the Duke of Savoy, to the King of Sweden, to Philip himself (should Mary die). The Swedish ambassador, in July, had seen her without Mary's knowledge, so 'the Queen reproved him in the presence of the councillors and Petre', an incident worthy of mention only because of de Feria's singling him out.[47]

When Parliament assembled to debate the promised second subsidy, Mary was on her deathbed. She died on 17 November at St. James's Palace. Across the river at Lambeth, Archbishop Pole, her cousin and closest friend in these last years, died later in the same day.* With their deaths papal dominion over England ended. It had been a St. Martin's summer for Catholics.

At Mary's funeral Petre had a prominent place in the small number of mourners nearest the 'chariot with the corpse'. In one of the mounted groups of ladies was Dame Alice Petre, her steed 'trapped to the postern with black cloth'. It was only five years ago since she had ridden in state, arrayed in crimson velvet, at her Queen's joyful coronation. The reign had been heralded by the nation's warm welcome to an injured princess, yet when this sincere and pious woman died she was almost universally hated. By her will, made several months earlier, Mary bestowed her charitable bequests mainly on the religious houses she had revived. She was generous, too, in her legacies: to her executors, some £500, the rest £333 13s. 4d. each, including Petre—testimony of her continued high regard. Among her assistant executors, who got £200 each, were Boxall, Baker and her household officers of Edward's days. This time, ironically enough, the significant exclusion from the legatees was not Petre, but Paget, although he was the only councillor on both the finance and war committees. But if the missing last token of her confidence grieved him, the pecuniary result mattered little—to Paget, Petre or the rest—because the will was ignored by Elizabeth, despite Mary's plea to her to allow it to be executed.[48]

---

* It was a season of deaths; among the dead, Maurice Griffin, Bishop of Rochester, of whose estates Petre was high steward, for which he drew an annual fee of £6 13s. 4d. Petre was 'chief mourner', Garrard being next in the list (Machyn's Diary, 180). Both were to be associated in 1562 in appointing the first master and usher of Bangor Grammar School: Dr. Glynne, Bishop of Bangor, bequeathed property for founding the school to Griffin, who, dying before carrying out the founder's wishes, in turn bequeathed it to Petre and Garrard for fulfilling the same intentions (Cal. Pat. Rolls, Eliz., ii, 158). A few years later Archbishop Holgate made Petre his senior executor for founding Hemsworth Hospital, Yorks.

CHAPTER X

Leisure and Pleasure

1 Music

INGATESTONE and the Petres have a special link with the golden age of English music. It is not always easy, however, to distinguish between patronage and performance. Henry VIII employed many court musicians, and he and the two princesses were accomplished performers. But it was the generation of the Secretary's son, not his own, which witnessed the astonishing growth of musical activity in England. Music figures prominently in Sir William's accounts and even more so in John's, which have recently yielded fresh and early evidence of John's friendship with William Byrd. Frequent mention of instruments in the father's accounts helps in reconstructing the musical background of the home in which John received tuition as a youth. To what extent the Secretary found time for playing his various instruments, whether indeed he could play any of them, the reader must judge for himself from the copious but subjective references.

The most common instruments in the sixteenth-century upper-class home were the virginal, the lute and the viol. Petre possessed all three. Of these, the virginal was a general name in England in that century for keyboard instruments including the spinet and harpsichord; its strings were plucked by quills operated by the keys, and it was placed on a table or stood on legs. In the lute, which had a flat belly and a pear-shaped back, the strings were plucked by the player, who held it. The term viol belongs to a family of bowed instruments which were distinct from the violin family. The first reference to 'wire for the virginals', just before Christmas 1548, is soon succeeded by 'bringing the virginals from the Court' to the Aldersgate Street house. Next year Petre bought a viol and a gittern. The latter instrument had a long neck, rounded back and oval-shaped body; it was in fact the medieval and Tudor guitar, 'usually strung with four gut strings and played with a plectrum'.[1] It was used to accompany the voice until it was largely ousted by the lute.

1550

JUNE. Instruments. For a small viol 13s. 4d., a 'gyttron'[2] 6s., a canvas bag to put the viol in 4d., viol strings 12d., the Frenchman's charges 4d.

Not unnaturally, these payments were made by the London steward, but the instruments were probably sent to Ingatestone, the next wages list for which included 'John the Frenchman that playeth on the instruments'. He got 10s., a sum equal to the higher servants' wages at the Hall for the whole Michaelmas quarter, but was not employed afterwards. Two entries in the same summer, '15 knots of lute strings 3s. 8d., a lute 8s., lace to the same lute 3d.', and 'lute strings bought at London 2s. 10d.', are followed four months later by a payment to an Ingatestone joiner for mending Dorothy's lute. The Frenchman may have been brought down to Ingatestone to teach her, though he probably also provided entertainment at meals, especially on those days when distinguished guests were present.*

After the three-year break in the accounts, virginals are mentioned again in 1555. Soon after the steward had paid 2s. for 'mending my master's virginals' at London, '2 knots of virginal strings 2d.' and four more knots (8d.) were bought there and were sent to Ingatestone. Then a maker of musical instruments patronized by Mary and Elizabeth figures in the London accounts:

1555
JUNE. In reward to William Treasorer's man for bringing a pair of virginals to my master 6s. 8d., and to one that played upon them 4s.

'A pair of virginals' meant only one instrument. Treasorer appears to have been unsuccessful in selling it, but seven years later no fewer than three pairs of virginals occur in the inventory of the London house.[3]

Sir William had already acquired an organ for his Essex house.

1556
JULY 14. To Gylham's man the organmaker for his charges being sent to Ingatestone to mend the organs, 5s.

1561
NOV. 30. A new instrument bought. To Gylham a maker of instruments for the making of an instrument for my master 40s., and in reward to his man 6s. 8d., besides another instrument which he had of my master, and to a carman for bringing home the new instrument 6d.

Both entries occur in the London accounts. The plural, or a pair of organs, was the normal term for a single instrument. The new one may have been intended to replace that repaired in 1556, though there is no reason why Petre should not have had an organ in each house. Many organs were sold at the Dissolution, such as that at Tilty Abbey in Essex for 33s. 4d. After Petre's purchase of Ingatestone manor in December 1539, very few

---

* Recent intensive research on this period has shown how extraordinarily little evidence there is of permanent household musicians even in nobleman's mansions (W. L. Woodfill, *Musicians in English Society from Elizabeth to Charles I* (1953), 59–73 and his appendix B).

monasteries remained; the last, Waltham Abbey, was dissolved by him, and it is tempting to conjecture that he bought the organ there which had been used by Tallis, later tutor of Byrd. The question is to decide what type of organ these entries refer to.* Gylham's taking the old organ or other instrument in part exchange veils the purchase price, but the net cost and the need for a cart to transport the new organ suggest that it was one of medium size or a regal, which was a smaller instrument provided with one or more reed-stops. If the latter, it was probably of the 'positive' or table type, not a little 'portative' regal, but as this term is not used, it seems more likely that both entries refer to organs proper.

Two small payments at Aldersgate in the winter of 1560–1 concerned the lid and the screw tuning-key of the virginals: 'To Ambrose the smith for a hinge for the virginals; for a wrest for them 22d.' On New Year's Eve, 1558, the London steward had paid 16d. 'for pennying and new stringing the virginals', with another 6d. for 'a box for the wires of the virginals'. In June 1560, 'mending and trimming of my master's virginals' cost 14s. including 6d. for a 'new key', presumably in the musical not the locking sense. 'Pennying', an unrecorded word, would seem by analogy with quillpen to refer to the quills (affixed to the jacks) which plucked the strings. The charge denotes a major overhaul, but evidently not needed through lack of use, for 10s. had been paid 'to Persey for teaching the gentlewomen to play on the virginals' in the previous winter, as well as a shilling for more virginal wire. The pupils would have been the unmarried daughters Thomasine and Catherine, the former just about to be wedded; their teacher was the senior female servant.

In May 1556, when Lady Petre was with her husband at London, a resident tutor had been employed, probably for the girls: 'To Thomas Jeffe for a dozen virginal strings 12d., for lute strings 16d., for viol strings 14d., and for his lodging three weeks 12d.'

Although the virginal is said to have been named from such damsels, it was not the ladies' sole prerogative. In Sir William's accounts it is twice referred to as 'my master's', never 'my lady's', a term which the steward often used and would have applied to the instrument, had it been hers. And a little later John had a virginal as well as a viol of his own. There is fairly clear evidence of his early musical training.

Ambrose the smith for a wrest for Mr. John Petre's virginals 16d. (1559.)

A Cullen lute bought for Mr. John Petre 13s. (1561.)

Mr. Lychefeild's man for bringing certain songs for Mr. John Petre 2s. (1562.)

* For a description of Tudor organs, see F. W. Galpin, *Old English Instruments of Music* (3rd edn., 1932).

The lute came from Cologne or was of a Cologne type, and the songs were presumably sold by Henry Lichfild, who has been described as 'one of the smaller figures among the English madrigalists' and composer of some pleasant songs;[4] his *First Set of Madrigals* was published in 1613.[5]

John's own account-book for 1567–70, when he was a law student at the Middle Temple, gives the impression that he was devoted to the lute, and he may indeed have been an accomplished lutenist. 'A song for the lute' came in 1567 from 'Mr. Litchfeld', but thereafter he gave his custom to a Mr. Pietro, whose 20s. bill for 'a book for the lute and pricking [writing] songs therein' was followed by several more, finishing with one for as much as 50s. for a new lute.[6]

The close friendship which developed later between John Petre and William Byrd may have originated in Sir William's last years at Ingatestone. The latter's name is attached to Byrd's Tenth Pavan and Galliard in the book of his compositions given in 1591 to Lady Nevill. This manuscript must have been seen by Byrd. 'It was a fashion to name pieces of this kind after personal friends';[7] the Pavan to the Earl of Salisbury (Cecil's son Robert) is one of the best known of Byrd's compositions. The pavan was a stately dance, the galliard a livelier one. Sir William's Pavan is 'grave and beautiful' and his galliard 'opens with a very graceful tune'.[8] How William befriended young Byrd, if at all, may never be found, but recent discoveries in John's accounts show that their own association was of earlier date than previously known. From at least 1586, if not before, Byrd was a frequent visitor to John's homes at Thorndon Hall and Ingatestone Hall, and his host usually dispatched a servant to 'fetch Mr. Byrd down from London'. The best details are for the Christmas of 1589–90. A month or so earlier, John had bought an unspecified musical instrument from Mr. Brough for £50—a substantial sum which must refer either to a new organ or to a fine virginal probably with a cover. He also got some new viol strings. On 26 December he sent a servant to London to escort Byrd to Ingatestone Hall, where he stayed for the rest of the Twelve Days, in fact until 8 January, when the steward paid £3 'to five musicians of London for playing upon the violins at Ingatestone by composition [contract] in the Christmas time'. In January, too, an Ingatestone blacksmith's bill for 'a pair of iron brackets to set the double virginals upon in the Great Chamber there' was paid by John Bolt, the Queen's virginal-player and Sir John's organist, whose Catholic connections later forced him to flee. 'Double' refers either to a two-manual virginal, or more likely to one with a longer, or lower, compass;[10] and the brackets for this instrument may have been set up in order to raise it above young children's reach when not in use. Whether it was to protect John's recent acquisition or a virginal brought down by Byrd can only be guessed, but there is no doubt about the musical Christmastide.* In 1593 Byrd was to come to live at Stondon Place, only five miles from Ingatestone and seven from Thorndon Hall, John's principal seat. Although a consistent Roman Catholic who was many times presented to the church and civil courts in Essex, he was saved from serious trouble by the combined influence and friendship of James I, who thought highly of him as organist of the Chapel Royal, and Sir John Petre.[11] Byrd reciprocated by dedicating to John, then Lord Petre, his second book of *Gradualia*, published in 1607. Besides John's Temple and later accounts, there have survived two manuscript song books, the covers of which are stamped 'John Petre'.†

In the upper ranks of Elizabethan and Jacobean society, the host expected his guests to take their share in madrigals, singing their part at sight from such song books, or accompanying their own songs on the lute. That John Petre was competent to do both is due partly to the instruction his father had provided; which leads back after this digression to the problem of Sir William's own musical attainments. 'My master's virginals', organ, viol, lute and gittern all occur in his accounts. He did not live in a period so sympathetic to musical skill as his son's. Nevertheless, the number and range of instruments at Ingatestone and Aldersgate Street belonging to Sir William compares most favourably with those mentioned in contemporary household accounts, some of which suggest that certain instruments had been bought to conform to fashion rather than to provide music.[12] It may be conjectured from the slight evidence that Petre could play the two keyboard instruments—virginal and organ—but not the other instruments.‡

But if Sir William was himself not a performer, he certainly patronized musicians of various grades. The boy choristers of St. Paul's, for instance,

* Byrd was already the 'Father of English Music' and the founder of the English virginal school; he was at this time 'busily occupied with the publication of his own compositions, and his output between 1588 and 1591 was very remarkable' (E. H. Fellowes, *William Byrd* (2nd edn., 1948), 17).

† Dr. E. H. Fellowes, Byrd's biographer, examined them in the Essex Record Office in 1939, describing them as 'exceptionally fine examples of their kind, very rare, and of priceless value to students of sixteenth century music' (D/DP Z6/1, 6/2). One contains the bass part of a large collection of Latin motets; Byrd's music predominates, but Fairfax, Taverner, Tallis, Tye and other composers are represented. The second book has the music of foreign composers and is unusual in giving both bass and alto parts.

‡ After a five-year quest, the Friends of Historic Essex in 1959 bought for display in the Long Gallery at Ingatestone Hall an Italian virginal dated 1562 (plate 14).

who were in great demand at society weddings and other festive events, came to his town house when he was convalescing:

1559
APR. 19. Money to musicians. To the children of Paul's for singing and playing before my master 6s. 8d.

He employed them at Thomasine's wedding:

1560
FEB. 10. The children of Paul's playing on the marriage day 6s. 8d. and to two men that carried the chests wherein their playing garments were and instruments 12d.

For weddings at Ingatestone he took a different course and brought down London musicians—four of them at Catherine Tyrell's in 1552, and more at Catherine Petre's:

1561
AUG. — Currance in reward for the having of his musicians at the marriage for space of four days £5; — two musicians here before the marriage 10s.

In London, on New Year's Eve 1559, 'three musicians that played before my master whereof Pyke was one' got 6s. 8d., and 'three minstrels playing at the door' 6d. 'Certain musicians' playing there on Christmas Day in the following year received 20d., and on one day in May 1562 'certain minstrels playing in Aldersgate Street' went away with 2s. Two months later, morris dancers got 3s. 4d. from him. He seems to have been generous to musical folk. He also gave occasional gratuities to waits, the small groups of wind instrumentalists maintained or sponsored by many towns, who originated as night watchmen in palaces and castles.[13] They usually played the shawm, or hautbois, which resembled the modern oboe. In order to augment their slender wages, some corporations allowed their waits to tour.

1548 SEPT. 20. The waits of St. Edmund's Bury 2s.
1550 MAY. My lord Talbot's waits 12s.
1554 JUNE. Guildford—the waits of the town 2s.

Guildford is accounted for by the presence of the Court. The visit of the nobleman's waits, probably so called because shawm-players, occurred while Petre was at Boulogne. He also gave a few shillings to the waits of London about New Year's Day 1559–60.

Musical entertainers of various categories who came to Ingatestone Hall also got their 'rewards':

1548 JAN. 6.   To the Welsh harpers 3s. 4d., three other minstrels 6s. 8d., one other harper 12d., Gylder the tumbler at two several times 3s. 4d.

1549 DEC.   To three minstrels of Chelmsford by my master's commandment in the Christmas holidays 5s. 4d.

1550 FEB. 9.   To 3 minstrels at my lady's commandment 20d. (Princess Mary's visit.)

1550 JUNE.   My lady gave to Blind More the harper 3s. 4d.*

1561 SEPT. 7.   To certain minstrels which came to Ingatestone 6s. 8d.

1562 APR. 5.   To the Earl of Oxford's man that played the flute and juggled at Ingatestone 3s. 4d.

Minstrels, who were sometimes distinguished from waits or official musicians, were not always limited in their repertoire to music. Some combined singing ballads with other entertainments. The tumbler and the flautist-juggler were typical of their class. The latter was upholding an ancient tradition, for Chaucer tells how 'Ther mightest thou see these floutors, minstrales, and eek iogelours'.[14]

2 Pastimes

Jocular and dramatic entertainments were given in many of the larger houses by wandering tumblers and by small bands of touring players. The laws against vagabonds, among whom strolling players, jugglers and minstrels were included, obliged the more respectable groups to obtain the patronage of a nobleman, by whose name they were then distinguished.[15] At Twelfthtide 1556, 'the mummers' were at Ingatestone Hall; and the town house was visited in 1562 by 'Nycolles a jester', possibly to cheer Petre after his illness. In 1555 'one being called Killcalf'

---

* William More the blind court harpist was a remarkable figure. Accused of being the medium for secret messages between some of the last remaining abbeys, he was cast into the Tower for treason in 1539, but was soon back in the royal service. Thrice in 1544 Petre gave him 3s. 4d. at Court; these quite large gratuities stand out in his first, very brief account-book, and one speculates if they imply genuine admiration for the harpist. One summer day in 1551 (?1552) More played before Princess Elizabeth at Hatfield and got 30s.; so did 'Farmor that played on the lute', and an identical entry in Petre's accounts shows that Farmor was at the Aldersgate house on Twelfth Night in 1561, when Petre gave him 3s. 4d. Eight years later 2s. 'to Mr. Secretary Cecil's man for so much given by him to More the harper by my master's commandment' may denote Petre's tip as a guest in Cecil's town house. More got a further 5s. from Petre in 1560. The blind musician, evidently a Welshman, certainly had a long career, for he is first found in Henry's service in 1525 and received the wages of royal musician until his death in 1565. (B. M., Egerton MS.2604; L. & P., Hen. VIII, xiv, pt. ii, p. xxx and xv, p. 217, etc.; Privy Purse Expenses of Princess Mary (1831), 104; P.P.E. of Hen. VIII (1827), 16; Household Expenses of Princess Elizabeth, 1551–52 (1853), 40.) As a courtier, Petre had to give New Year gifts to all the royal household, among them the company of musicians, who got 20s. between them in 1548 and 1550.

got a reward of 5s.; and at Thomasine's wedding-feast Lord Paget's man played the 'killcalf' to amuse the guests. In 1561 John Petre gave 3s. 4d. 'to the Lord Paget's servant that playeth the killcalf'; and it was evidently the same clown who appeared again a year later.*

Only once is there any record of a troupe of players at Ingatestone Hall. They were paid by one of the London servants, but the amount suggests that the owner was not present:

1560
NOV. 1. Reward paid to the Lord Robert's players at Ingatestone 20d.†

Many entertainments were associated with the religious feasts such as Twelfth Day (the Epiphany). The lovers' festival provided fun of a different sort. On St. Valentine's Eve the choice was by lot. Ironically, Cromwell was the Lady Mary's valentine in 1537, when his gift cost him £15.[16] Etiquette also obliged Petre to give a suitable present to the lady who had selected him. His wife bought the gift, and he paid her back a week later:

1556
FEB. 20. To my lady for so much money by her paid for six yards black satin given to the Lady Bulkeley, my master's valentine, 60s.

* This apparently unrecorded word is probably connected with killing the calf, 'a droll performance occasionally practised by vagrants in the North of England, perhaps of gypsy origin' (Halliwell's *Dict. of Archaic and Prov. Words*; not defined in *O.E.D.*); less likely, it may have much the same meaning as 'kill-cow' or 'kill-buck', a fierce-looking fellow or a mock ogre.

† Almost exactly a year later Lord Robert Dudley's players visited Grimsthorpe, when Richard Bertie's steward gave them 10s. although they 'offered themselves to play but did not', (*Ancaster MSS.* (H.M.C.), 465). When they acted before the Queen at Christmas 1562 they received £6 13s. 4d. for their play (*A.P.C.*, vii, 134). One or more of the professional touring companies performed at Maldon or Saffron Walden almost every year, their interludes being sponsored by the corporation, who usually gave each troupe about 5s. These small companies, generally of four to six men, included the chief houses in the area. Players' patrons with seats in Essex were the Earl of Oxford, Lord Rich and in Petre's last years the Earl of Sussex. In 1560, when Dudley's players came to Ingatestone Hall, they also visited Maldon, which received a visit from Lord Oxford's company in the same year. (The late W. A. Mepham's London Ph.D. thesis: copy in E.R.O.; much of it was re-written for the *Essex Review*, lv–lx.) Dudley's men, by then the Earl of Leicester's players, were to become the well-known company of professionals which included in its ranks James Burbage and a rising actor called William Shakespeare. The more fashionable interludes, however, had not entirely ousted the medieval morality plays, which represented 'native' drama in all its virility. 'Our forefathers', Dr. Mepham wrote (p. 159), 'saw nothing incongruous in mixing clowning and humorous scenes with the most solemn and serious Biblical episodes'; and the properties needed for these lively scenes were owned by the churchwardens of the more important parishes. Moralities, as these semi-religious, semi-popular plays are now called, flourished in Essex. Chelmsford had a well-established play. In a solitary instance, in 156(2?), the Chelmsford costumes were borrowed for private use—by Petre: 'Received for hire on the same garments of Sir William Petre knight 16s.' (E.R.O., D/P 94/5/1).

It is apparently young John who is next referred to:

1557
APR. For the fashion of a valentine in gold which was made for Mr. Petre, the
goldsmith having the gold again, 3s. 4d.[17]

One year, when the family were at Aldersgate, a servant of Lady Petre
drew a lucky card which was worth an extra quarter's wages:

1560
FEB. 20. To Mary the maid, who chose my master to be her valentine 6s. 8d.
(paid by my lady).

Did she manage to keep her half a mark till the autumn fair?

Petre enjoyed other indoor pastimes, at his own and his friends' houses
in Essex and London and at the Court. His favourite games were cards
and 'tables' (backgammon). Many of his class gambled to while away
the tedious winter evenings. Men of lower rank had also become addicts,
to the neglect of their skill with the longbow, and in 1541 Parliament had
tried to arrest this dangerous weakening of military strength by enforcing
archery practice. By the same statute, justices of the peace were to suppress all unlawful games in alehouses and the like, and artificers, labourers,
servants and such sort were prohibited altogether from playing except at
Christmastide; unlawful games included 'the tables, dice, and cards'.*
Petre's gambling habits are reflected in his accounts. 'Lent to my master
at Ingatestone when he played cards 5s.' is a typical but not very frequent
entry during periods when he was released from official duties. The
money advanced by the steward from the privy purse was relatively small,
ranging from 7s. 8d. to 8d., and the scale of his gambling is suggested by
the item of 3s. 'to my master in pence to play cards with'. Once, however,
in 1550, Lady Petre had to produce a sovereign for her lord 'to play at
cards' when Lady Norwich visited Ingatestone. His losses were correspondingly trifling—rarely more than 2s. 'Lost that night at cards 2d.',

* Although Sir William was such a devotee of gaming, he was an equally keen upholder of
the laws which forbade the lower orders of society to indulge in such pastimes. In an analysis
of the Elizabethan court rolls of six Essex manors, it is only within the manor of Ingatestone
during Sir William's lifetime that regular amercements of inhabitants for gaming are found
enrolled. In the presentments card-playing figures on a number of occasions and 'slyde grote'
once. In 1564 and 1565 no less than fourteen men were amerced on each occasion between 4d.
and 8d. for playing bowls. At a court held in 1568 three inhabitants were amerced 20d. each
for the triple offence of playing dice and bowls and for contravening the sumptuary laws by
wearing apparel beyond their status. It is interesting to note that after Sir William's death
only at one court during the remainder of Elizabeth's reign was there a presentment for
gaming.

at first when playing in 1555 with the 'Lord Steward' (Arundel) seems surprisingly small; 'lost at cards 1*d*.' even more so; but these sums are net losses for which the steward produced cash after deducting any winnings. There were times no doubt when Petre indulged in a little bout of gambling at Court, but the heaviest loss he confessed to his steward was insignificant compared with the scale of card-play in the heydays of the courts of Henry VIII and Elizabeth.

1553
DEC. 5. To my master in money which he lost at cards in the Chamber of Presence at Westminster 7*s*. 6*d*.

This probably tells of play with his fellow councillors while awaiting Mary's summons into the Privy Chamber. The low stakes for which Petre normally played are exemplified by 'money delivered to my master playing at cards at Hampton Court 18*d*. and at Greenwich 5*s*. 2*d*.', and recreation with his courtier or country friends in their own homes by 'play at cards with Mrs. Clarentius at Hutton 4*s*.', his hostess being Mary's intimate servant. What card games were being played can only be guessed; the contemporary fashion seems to have been primero, of Spanish origin and not unlike the later ombre.[18]

A game of backgammon was equally popular with Petre. 'Delivered to my master playing at tables with Sir John Mordaunt at Ingatestone 2*s*. 4*d*.' is typical of many entries. Again, the stakes were evidently small: 'Lost at tables with Mr. Cofferer 2*d*.' A game for two people, it was played with draughtsmen on a hinged board divided into four 'tables' furnished with fifteen white and fifteen black men and two dice-boxes. In 1560 'turning of the tablemen' cost 8*d*., and 'mending the playing tables' occurs twice. Chess perhaps also appealed to Petre, but as it was not played for money it did not figure in his expenses.

One day Mary chose her Secretary to entertain her at Hampton Court, and he hurriedly borrowed a mark from one of the household officers:

1554
SEPT. 13. To Mr. Rice for so much lent by him to my master to play at pass dice with the Queen, 13*s*. 4*d*.

Passdice was a game for two, played with dice, which led to its name being corrupted from French 'passe dix' (pass ten). The caster kept on throwing till he got 'doublets' (the same number turning up on both dice); if under ten he was out, if above ten he won. It is not disclosed whether Petre had to tender any money to his royal opponent. Princess Mary's personal accounts for 1536–44 show that she had indulged in cards freely when in her twenties, from 12s. 6d. to 40s. being drawn from the privy purse almost every month.

Once Sir William is noted playing cards with his son, then six years old, for a 4d. stake. All that can be gathered about Lady Petre's indoor amusements is a solitary loss of 6s. 8d. at cards and two references to 'tables'. It may be surmised that the family also played shove-ha'penny, as the inventory of Ingatestone Hall made in 1600 lists in the gallery an 'old shovelaboard of 4¾ yards in length' (perhaps a very long table with appropriate markings incised at the end, like the one which can be seen at Beeleigh Abbey, Essex).

Other leisure hours Petre spent in reading books. Of these, about thirty titles are given in his incomplete London accounts, but some purchases of books passed without names. It is almost impossible to distinguish between those bought for reference, study and entertainment. The European presses produced matter only of serious content, apart from the relatively few books on travel and adventure, and there was a flood of works on ecclesiastical history and current religious controversy. To public men with an academic training, such as Petre, the books of his age, mostly in Latin and largely unreadable nowadays, were read almost as a pastime. A typical purchase, *De veritate corporis et sanguinis Christi in Eucharistia contra Œcolampadium*, was entered in the accounts for 1547 as 'Rofensis contra Ecolampadium'; it was one of the anti-Lutheran treatises of John Fisher, Bishop of Rochester, and had been printed in Cologne in 1527. Other doctrinal and historical books Petre bought within a year of publication, such as Bishop Gregory's *Historiae Francorum*. The first edition of Froissart's *Chronicles* printed in London (1545) is evidently represented (1548) by 'Raynard the printer for a book called Frosard of a large volume, 18s.' It came from Reyner Wolfe, bookseller and King's Printer in Latin, Greek and Hebrew, at the sign of the Brazen Serpent in St. Paul's Churchyard. Next time Petre patronized this shop, in 1550, his interests included geography as well as history: 'Novis Orbis 6s., Ezebius with certain other old writers, 11s.'

Additions to his library came from English ambassadors abroad. In October 1553, for instance, his friend Wotton told him that the bearer would deliver a few books which he had previously mentioned. 'If I had been of late at Paris, as I have not, for the plague reigneth there', Wotton wrote, 'peradventure I might have found out some other book that might have pleased you; but that shall be for another time, and, God will, when Paris is clear of the plague. If you have not my Lord of Winchester's book called Marcus Anthonius Constantinus, I will send it to you.'[21] This was Gardiner's reply to Cranmer's answer to the former's *Explication of the True Catholic Faith*. Next year Wotton wrote that he had bought 'The new Old Pandects of Florence'; should his friend wish for any other book, he would do his best to procure it.[22] The arrival of 'the Pandects in quires in folio of Florence print' shows that books of this nature could be bought unbound. The new (1553) edition of the *Old Pandects of Florence*, a complete digest of the ancient laws, was probably of practical as well as antiquarian interest to a civilian. In 1559 Wotton bought 'certain new books' in France, which cost Petre 21s.

He possessed a few manuscript law books, which have been preserved (p. 41 n.), but very few printed law books figure in his accounts, probably because he had easy access to those he needed at Westminster. Petre's long-term ailments such as the stone led him to visit several other shops in St. Paul's Churchyard, the headquarters of the book trade, where he bought a number of medical treatises which had been recently printed in Basle and Venice, as well as more than one 'book of physic'.

The books which are thus known to have been acquired by Petre are among those that a man of his time and station in life would want. They reveal no special interest, such as the Latin and Greek classics, with which Cecil has been credited on the evidence of some booksellers' bills.[23] Some of Cecil's purchases, however, may have been for his son and his wards, as was definitely the case with Petre's children and wards, whose books are distinguished in his accounts from those obtained for himself. The number of children's books bought between 1544 and 1562 is in fact impressive. For instance, when he was nine, John was given Terence and in the next two years a Greek dictionary, Lucian's *Dialogues*, Vives's *Introduction to Wisdom*, Æsop's *Fables* in Greek and Latin, Ovid and Livy. It is interesting to find that when one ward was in his fourth year at Oxford Petre provided him with Sir Thomas Elyot's *Governor*, Robert Recorde's *Castle of Knowledge* and John Holywood's *Sphæra*.

There is no means of telling how large Petre's own library was. Some of his purchases of unspecified books may have been quite considerable. One lot cost him 47s., but books were relatively expensive (even a child's primer cost a shilling or two). While the 'chest wherein my master's books are carried' and the 'dryfat for my master's books' (1549–50) could refer to secretarial reference-books, the 'hogshead full of books' (1552) could not, as it was carried from London to Ingatestone. Unfortunately none of his printed books is known to have survived, apart from several that he gave to Exeter College in 1567[24] and a Latin Vulgate printed in Venice and superbly bound for the Earl of Arundel who gave it to Petre in 1563.* In the library of Gonville and Caius College, Cambridge, is Petre's 'Liber Peregrinacionum', which despite its clear ascription to Sir William, is a late fifteenth-century manuscript. A few of the annotations are in his hand. It is a religious allegory, mainly in the form of a dialogue between Imagination, Reason and Man.

3 Sports

'Hawks' bells for the tassel', 'three pair of couples', 'a lyelm for my master's dog', 'yeoman of the toils': such strange terms among Petre's expenses are relics of the outdoor sports of his day, when courtiers and country gentlemen pursued their pleasures in royal parks and their estates. The common beasts of the chase were the deer and the hare. Both were coursed. So when Petre, Baker and Bourne enjoyed some relaxation in Hampton Court Park, 'coursing there' in August 1555, they may not have been in full cry after deer. Greyhounds and spaniels were both employed to hunt deer and hares; spaniels were normally water-spaniels for forcing the quarry out of stream or lake. The pursuit of game being the big land-owner's sport, Petre's friends often sent him such gifts as a brace of grey-hounds or two couple of spaniels. In one apparently enigmatical entry, 'a couple of spaniels and a pair of couples for them', the latter couple refers to the brace for holding two spaniels (or hounds) together; and 'lyelm', an uncouth word from the French which has survived more generally as 'lien', was used for the leash of a keen-scented but mute hound, or blood-hound, whose task was to harbour the slowest deer by discovering its woodland lair. In 1550, the Lord Deputy of Ireland sent Petre two 'grewins', a rare early form of the word greyhound.†

There were few rigid rules of the chase governing the kind of dogs used or the method of killing. The fox, by the way, with badgers and the like, was classed as vermin and not accorded a run for its life. On occasion, when large quantities of venison were needed, the art of venery fell to a low level, very long nets called toils being used to give deer little chance of escape. Petre ordered great lengths of canvas for the yeoman of the toils when Mary was at Farnham Castle during the marriage progress,

---

* Now in the library at Arundel Castle; it must have been bought back at the sale of the Petre (Thorndon Hall) library in 1870. The book bears Arundel's signature on the title-page and is autographed by Petre on the flyleaf '1563—Gulielmi Petrei—ex dono Henrici Comitis Arundel'. This note has been supplied by my friend Francis Steer, F.S.A., County Archivist of West Sussex.

† Not in *O.E.D.*, but recorded in Halliwell's *Dict. of Archaic and Prov. Words* (1889) as found in Eastern England.

and on the return journey 'a great toil of four or five miles long' was supplied for 'the general hunting at Windsor Forest', when Cecil sent Petre a couple of spaniels.[25] On his own estate, Petre gave 50s. in the winter of 1555–6 to 'Mr. Powell yeoman of the toils for his pains taken about the taking of the deer in Horsefrith Park' in Writtle. Bucks and does were often delivered to the Ingatestone kitchen from Petre's parks of Ingatestone, Horsefrith, Crondon (disparked in 1551) and Writtle (acquired in 1554), but his accounts tell little of the chase over his lands, as it rarely involved expense, whereas hunting elsewhere meant the usual gratuities to keepers. At Whitsun 1549, for instance, the groat given to Sir Harry Tyrell's huntsman at Heron Park, and rewards of 5s. to 'the keeper of the Lord Chancellor's park at Leez' and 2s. to 'my master's servant for killing a buck' there show how Rich and Petre spent their time before setting off on their fruitless visit to Princess Mary in Norfolk (p. 117). In August 1554, when Petre had a short sojourn at New Hall, Boreham, a servant was sent in front with his greyhounds; in the following year, when Queen Mary and the Court were away from London, another servant reclaimed his charges for 'keeping my master's greyhounds this summer time and going with them to Windsor and other places'. The hard-working Secretary is occasionally found in the saddle at other royal parks not far from the capital, such as Nonsuch, Oatlands, Havering and Pyrgo.

Although hunting was a sport for the privileged few—the Crown saw to that—the product of the chase was enjoyed by more, as for instance in 1559 when the steward gave 'one half haunch of venison to Mr. Roydon my master's man to make merry with his neighbours at Ingatestone'.

'My master's goshawk' is often mentioned, and Petre employed a falconer, one Edmund Bell (probably his house-steward's brother), who bought the usual adjuncts of falconry in 1550, to wit, 'two pair of sparrowhawk bells 12d., three pair of couples 12d., and two hawks' hoods 6d.' The trained hawk, having been released from its hood, would soar off its master's gloved fist in pursuit of the rising quarry, which it would bring to ground, where it was located by the jingling bells attached to the hawk's legs. In 1555, on being given a goshawk by Arundel, not for the first time, Petre paid for 'a pair of hawk's bells for the tassel, and Drake's charges going to the Lord Steward's house for the tassel'. This was a male hawk, and in falconry tercel, or tassel, applied to the goshawk, the male peregrine falcon being a 'tercel gentle'. A week earlier, the Vice-chamberlain had sent Petre a goshawk, 'which the Queen gave my master, afterwards given to her Grace again'; why he returned the present is not clear.

223

Goshawks also arrived as gifts from Clinton and other courtiers, and a single sparrowhawk came from an Essex friend; both varieties were shorter-winged than the peregrine hawk and provided more profitable food, if less noble sport. In 1554 the Secretary took his hawk with him as far as Farnham, where he spent 2s. 11d. on a hawk's hood, glove, bag and bells. After some sport there, the hawk was sent back all the way to the mew at Ingatestone by one of his servants, who rejoined him at Bishop's Waltham just before the royal wedding.

Fowling appears rather as a utilitarian pursuit than as a sport, and the few entries no doubt reflect the contemporary view. The 'partridge-taker' and Malbrook, the wildfowl contractor of 1552, probably used firearms; duck-decoys were of slightly later date. In 1559, at any rate, one Boucheley, 'keeper of my master's park', got 5s. 'to buy him gunpowder to kill fowl with', and four years earlier 2s. was given to 'Thomas, Mr. Wadham's man, to buy gunpowder to shoot at crows about the house'. While in London, the Hall saddler had recently bought a pound of gunpowder for 12d. and a roll of match for 1d. The firearm which Thomas knew how to handle was as yet in its very early stage. Rabbits were still caught in nets around their holes or haunts, so in 1555 4d. was 'paid by Roger the warrener for thread to mend the hays and other nets'.

The owner of fishponds which could easily be drawn had little reason to be interested in angling, then a fairly new word, except to seek tranquil relief from cares of office. Drawing nets is probably implied in 1555, when 22d. was paid 'to those men that did help to fish the river in Waltham Forest being there with Mr. Browne of Fyddellars [Fithlers in Writtle] and bringing home four pikes, a great carp, and a dish of roaches', and twice later, when a few groats were given to several poor men of Buttsbury 'that did help to fish the river at Ingatestone'.

There is nothing to show that Petre indulged in the aristocratic sport of tennis as the Earl of Oxford may have done at his north Essex castle.* But Petre enjoyed an occasional game of bowls at Ingatestone; and 'making a frame in the end of the bowling alley' in 1555 is a reminder that it was played in a covered space; the alley was in the orchard behind the mansion. Entries relating to archery and fencing refer to Petre's son and his wards; in 1555, for instance: '2 bows for Mr. Talbot and Mr. Gostwick with 6 bowstrings 2s. 8d.' Bows and arrows were frequently provided for them from a tender age. In 1559, when he was 9½ years old, 'a bracer and shooting-glove for Mr. John Petre' were bought for his archery practice.

---

* 'Soap ashes for le tennisplay' occurs in a Hedingham Castle account-roll of 1488–9 (E.R.O., D/DPr 139).

From about the age of fifty, Petre was pained by the stone, which led him to give up the more arduous sports. By sixty he was deaf and perhaps denied the pleasure of listening to music. But there were always the bowling alley and in bad weather the gallery, where he may have played at shovelboard with the numerous grandchildren who were living at the Hall in his last years.

CHAPTER XI

Counsellor to Elizabeth

1 Secretary Cecil

ELIZABETH ascended the throne soon after her twenty-fifth birthday. For the third time in eleven years England had a new ruler. The Queen's first duty was to choose her ministers. Petre's standing with her was alluded to by Count de Feria, the Spanish ambassador, while Mary lay on her deathbed. In an interview given to him, the princess had spoken of Heath (the Lord Chancellor and Archbishop of York), Paget and Petre as 'most in her favour'.[1] The last two had been leaders of Elizabeth's 'protectors' when Gardiner had wanted to behead her, but need of their sound judgment is more likely to have influenced her than gratitude. Of these remarks they were probably unaware, but there was another who had received a signal mark of her confidence and knew how to act without delay. Sir William Cecil, joint Secretary with Petre in Northumberland's government and now thirty-eight years of age, had already been secretly selected by the future sovereign as her sole Secretary. Elizabeth was proclaimed Queen on the day of her half-sister's death (17 November); bearing this date is a memorandum in Cecil's hand of matters needing attention, not unlike that drawn up by Petre on Mary's accession. By the 19th, many of Mary's privy councillors and other magnates had collected at Hatfield. The Queen nominated only a few officers that day, but she made it clear that her Secretary was to hold an appointment of supreme importance. Overnight, as it were, the Secretary's office had been raised to a higher status. The words of her charge have now assumed the wonder of a prophetic utterance, for her confidence was to be justified over a period of forty years. 'This judgment I have of you, that you will not be corrupted with any manner of gift and that you will be faithful to the state; and that without respect of my private will you will give me that counsel which you think best: and if you shall know anything necessary to be declared to me of secrecy you shall show it to my self only, and assure yourself I will not fail to keep taciturnity therein.'[2] A famous speech and a shrewd estimate of character, the like of which Mary might have bestowed on Petre five years earlier, had her mind dwelt less on the religious and more on the political welfare of the country. The Lord Chancellor, Petre and Mason were appointed in the interim to transact urgent business.[3] But as yet Petre held no Crown office. Whether he was present at Hatfield cannot be traced: the fact that he was assigned for immediate work is not conclusive, since next day the Council had to write from Hatfield to Mason, who was similarly commissioned.

On arrival in London Elizabeth determined upon a Privy Council of eighteen. Only eleven of Mary's advisers were recalled to the Board. The big majority excluded, mostly Catholic extremists, were replaced by seven new men, including Cecil's brother-in-law Sir Nicholas Bacon. A week after the accession, the fourth Council meeting was held in Lord North's mansion at the Charterhouse, where the Queen was lodging. Petre was present. The attendance is entered in this order: Heath, the Earls of Shrewsbury, Derby, Pembroke, Bedford (the second earl, who had been an exile in Mary's reign), Lord Clinton, Lord Howard of Effingham, Sir Thomas Cheyne, Sir Thomas Parry (Elizabeth's faithful steward and now Comptroller), Sir Edward Rogers, Cecil, Petre, Mason and Sir Ambrose Cave. Sir Richard Sackville, cousin of the Queen's mother, was the only admitted councillor absent. Before the end of the year the aged Marquis of Winchester was reappointed Lord Treasurer and resumed his seat, together with the Marquis of Northampton, restored to noble rank, and the Earl of Arundel, too powerful to leave out; and soon afterwards Sir Francis Knollys, the Queen's cousin, joined them. Baker had recently died, and his place was taken by the new Chancellor of the Exchequer, Sir Walter Mildmay.[4] Despite the favourable remarks reported by de Feria, neither Lord Paget nor the Archbishop of York continued in high office. The former's latitudinarian opinions did not sway the Queen to retain him as her Lord Privy Seal and he was not admitted to the new body. Bacon became Lord Keeper of the Great Seal in succession to Lord Chancellor Heath, who also ceased to serve on the Council, which thus became a body of laymen only. There were then only eight Marian survivors. The story of Petre's public life, like Paget's, might well have ended in 1558. But Elizabeth chose him, and he was in office for yet a further term: 'he behaved as if it were not in the power of fortune to jostle him out of position'.[5] Of his old diplomatic colleagues, Wotton was to be readmitted after the conclusion of peace with France, but Bishop Thirlby was left out. Except for Cecil, 'few others of the Council counted for much in determining Elizabeth's policy'. Winchester, Arundel, Petre, Wotton, Pembroke, Clinton and Mason, who had served under Edward and Mary, the first four under Henry as well, were 'officials rather than statesmen':[6] another way of explaining some further coat-turning.

On 1 January 1559, Petre's preparations for a coming event were set down: 'Mr. Lamme of the Wardrobe by way of my master's reward for delivery of 6 yards crimson satin for a gown against the Coronation, 6s. 4d.; and 10s. to the tailor for making and furring it.' By ancient coronation custom the sovereign was in residence at the Tower. Three days beforehand the Knights of the Garter met to discuss final arrangements for the ceremony; and a minor defect was rectified: 'For a staff torch provided at the Tower, my master being late there at a Chapter touching the Order, 18*d*.; a goldsmith for mending the clasp of the register book of the Order, 6*d*.' (probably the double-clasped book shown in Petre's portrait of 1567). The Queen went in procession to Westminster on the eve of the coronation; Cecil and Petre were side by side, following immediately behind the great officers of state.[7]

Petre was a member of the small Council committee charged with ascertaining Elizabeth's annual revenue;[8] she was the third monarch for whom he undertook this necessary first task. His legal and fiscal experience was in demand again early in 1559, when he was chosen first commissioner, with Sackville, Mason and Mildmay, to investigate the Irish accounts, audit of which had led to the imprisonment of the Vice-Treasurer of Ireland.[9] (Petre's opinion on this state of affairs was to be sought six years later.) In January, Bedford, Cecil, Petre and Parry were appointed to confer with the Merchants of the Staple 'touching their incorporation which they claim'. The Staplers were lamenting their financial losses following the fall of Calais. Anxious to withstand the severe competition of their old rivals, the Merchant Adventurers, they had submitted a weighty petition supporting their claim. The four commissioners had to read a mass of statements bearing on it. The Staplers were granted the coveted charter in 1561. The Adventurers had an even more formidable competitor in the Hanseatic League. In 1556 the Ambassadors of the Hanse Towns, addressing a long petition in Latin to Petre ('Magnifico ac Ornatissimo Viro Domino Gulielmo Petre Militi'), complained of the restraints placed upon their export and import of cloths. He was commissioned, with Paget and Thirlby, to consider the dispute, and his long report to Philip, as well as his conference jottings, is preserved. In July 1560 Bacon, Winchester, Petre and Wotton signed a commercial treaty with the Hanseatic states, which was a satisfactory achievement after much effort.[10]

While Petre's knowledge of foreign diplomacy and commerce was thus being employed by Cecil, the older man did not hesitate to offer his advice on terms for negotiating peace with France. In January he wrote that he had read his own notes taken 'yesternight', the treaties and Thirlby's and Wotton's letters. He thought that Cecil should reply that a fuller answer would follow shortly or wait to see what news would come from France; he hoped to wait upon Cecil next morning, and enclosed his comments on certain customs proposals: a friendly letter between people on easy terms. He was closeted with the Secretary next day and the day after, when they sat late over their papers. The 'yesternight' notes have been preserved. They formed the draft of a proposed address by Elizabeth to the French King, expressing the view that the problems connected with the restoration of Calais were not insurmountable. Howard of Effingham, Thirlby and Wotton tried to secure its restitution.[11] Their failure was a good thing for England, as gratification of empty pride would have further impoverished the country, and the shame of cession was almost removed by denying France formal ownership unless she paid 500,000 crowns in eight years' time. It was part of the Peace of Cateau-Cambrésis (April 1559), the three-power treaty which put a term to the struggle between France and Spain.

Elizabeth opened Parliament at the end of January. On the 6th Petre's steward had paid £6 13s. 4d. to 'Lord Rich's man towards the charges of the dinner at the election of the Knights for Essex'.[12] About one-third of the members of Mary's last Parliament were re-elected; of these, Petre, Mildmay and Mason were outstanding. 'The leadership was provided by those privy councillors who secured seats by election, notably Cecil, Knollys, Parry, and the ubiquitous Petre.'[13] Among members who re-appeared were two Protestant champions, Sir Thomas Smith and Sir Anthony Cooke. The former, Petre's Edwardian colleague, had lived in retirement, busy with his studies. A profitable second marriage had brought him Mount Hall, Theydon, with a fair Essex estate, and he was also much occupied with rebuilding the house, which lay ten miles from Ingatestone and five from Gidea Hall. Cooke had only just returned to England from his religious exile; his two daughters Mildred and Anne were married to Cecil and Bacon. He now sat for Essex, having perhaps been recommended to the electors in preference to Waldegrave.*

It is not known if Petre had any share in the renowned religious settlement which Parliament's labours achieved.[14] A memorandum compiled by Armagill Waad, the former clerk of the Council, probably just before the session, may have influenced the Queen. It advocated caution. 'Glasses with small necks', Waad wrote, 'if you pour into them any liquor suddenly or violently, will not be filled. Howbeit, if you instil water into them by a little and little, they are soon replenished.'[15] Boxall seems to have momentarily led the small Catholic opposition party.[16] The Acts of Supremacy and Uniformity passed after a long session were at once the

---

* But the view, based on the Council's letter to Thomas Mildmay, sheriff of Essex, concerning the election (A.P.C., vii, 39), that this Parliament was packed, has been exploded (C. G. Bayne, 'The First House of Commons of Queen Elizabeth' (Eng. Hist. Rev., xxiii, 462, quoted by J. E. Neale, Elizabeth I and her Parliaments, 1559–1581 (1953), 40).

sepulchral monument of papal authority in England and the rebuilt gate-house of the Anglican Church. Cranmer's Second Prayer Book of 1552, with some modifications, became the sole liturgy. All the bishops except one refused to take the oath of supremacy and were deprived. Boxall soon got into trouble under the Acts and was sent to the Tower, where he joined Thirlby; Archbishop Heath had recently spent a short time there; Bonner was in the Marshalsea Prison; and Tunstall, in milder custody, died in November, aged eighty-five. But John Woodward, Petre's private chaplain, who had been rector of Ingatestone since 1556, continued to buy wax tapers for the Hall on Candlemas Day, as he had been buying ½ lb. 'sizes' (candles) several weeks before. Elsewhere there was no sudden abolition of the mass, but in May 1559 it was said in the royal chapel in English. In October Petre bought 'a book of the new service', and a year later the acquittal at the Essex assizes of a man who described it as 'paltry', a new English word, is typical of the prevailing leniency towards the ordinary Catholics.[17]

Three months after Elizabeth's accession he was a sick man. Divided between surrendering to his malady and supporting his friends, he wrote to Cecil from Aldersgate Street on 4 March 1559:

> I do understand from you by my servant whom I sent this morning to make my excuse that you would have me at the Court tomorrow in the morning by 8 of the clock. If my being there shall serve to any purpose for her Majesty's service I will not fail to attend you at that hour, otherwise I would gladly be spared. The humour [sic] which of long time hath troubled me is now fallen again into my leg in such sort as I am not able to go from one chamber to another, and yet if you shall think it necessary I will come as well as I may.[18]

He did not return to Court until the 20th, when he was commissioned, with Sussex, Bedford, Pembroke and Clinton, being 'persons of honour', to look into the dispute between the Irish Earls of Desmond and Or-monde.[19] After being in harness for two or three days he succumbed and was gravely ill. For the first time since the Dissolution the flow of his drafts, reports and letters stops entirely. His chances of survival, in one week at any rate, may have been tenuous (p. 251). Not until June was he fit enough to be conveyed to Ingatestone by litter. During his slow convalescence there his slender connection with public affairs was apparently limited to answering a few letters which a messenger brought from the Court at the end of July.

He marked his recovery a month later by a thank-offering of £5, to be distributed by his chaplain to the inmates of his newly founded alms-houses at Ingatestone (p. 278). He rode with his servants to London, and took a barge next morning to Kingston. Again it was only a short spell of work. A hired tilt-boat brought him back to London; he gave £1 in alms, and proceeded to Ingatestone. On returning in October, he lived with his wife in the town house, not at Court, and Mason, now back in England, was apparently his only guest. But the accounts and Council letters prove that he was dealing with public business, while struggling against poor health.[20] He spent the winter quietly.

The mutual compliments on 1 January included 'the Queen's New Year's gift to my master, being a standing gilt cup with a cover', and 'the Queen's Majesty, for a New Year's gift given by my master in angelets, £10'.* It is a noteworthy year in the annals of clothing, for the first pair of black silk stockings worn by Elizabeth was presented by her silk-woman. At the end of April Petre was suddenly in control of the secretariat again.

2 *Acting Secretary Petre*

Petre's emergence as Cecil's *locum tenens* was due to trouble in Scotland. Anglo-Scottish relations were indeed to prove the dominant factor in Elizabeth's first decade. In the summer of 1559 the Reforming Lords of the Congregation appealed to her for help in ousting the French from Scotland, under the Regent, Mary of Guise, mother of Mary Queen of Scots. Philip II's Spanish forces would doubtless land to support Elizabeth if she were threatened by an invasion in the north from a united Franco-Scottish kingdom; but the idea of Philip triumphant in England was anathema. Great-granddaughter of Henry VII, the Queen of Scots was the nearest heir to the English throne, should Elizabeth die without off-spring. Catherine Grey, Jane's younger sister, had the better title in law, but she also was unacceptable, and in the event of her succession 'faction would infallibly raise its head'.[21]

For good reasons, therefore, Elizabeth hesitated. The Scots were rebels and heretics: to aid them might result in a struggle with France, would be a breach of the recent treaty of Cateau-Cambrésis and would court papal enmity. Faced with such momentous problems, Cecil, too, had been worried but declared himself wholly in favour of armed intervention against the Regent. For several months the government vacillated.

---

* The Earl and Countess of Oxford between them gave £15 to the Queen on this occasion (Hedingham Castle accounts, E.R.O., D/DPr 142); the bishops gave an average of £20. Similar gifts were exchanged by the Queen and Petre in 1562, when his only other gift at Court was £3 to Secretary Cecil.

Winchester, Arundel, Wotton and Mason were dubious. Bacon and Petre advised only secret sympathy. On Christmas Eve, a week's debate ended with a resolution, which Cecil had striven to secure, urging the Queen to start a campaign in the north, but she was still firmly opposed to war.[22] Cecil was in a dilemma. Charged on appointment to offer the Queen his reasoned advice, he had done so in no uncertain manner on a point of major policy: 'thus Cecil's victory in the Council did not avail, and he resorted to the only means that he had of coercing his mistress—resignation'.[23] Elizabeth yielded, and threw in her lot with the Lords of the Congregation. Sir Ralph Sadler, former Secretary, and a veteran on Scottish affairs, was called from his long seclusion and was sent to the border to negotiate with the Lords. In February 1560 the Treaty of Berwick was achieved. It bound Elizabeth to dispatch an army to drive the French out of Scotland, and the Lords gave reciprocal undertakings in the event of an invasion of England. Next month the combined forces besieged Leith, held by the French, while Cecil and Petre drew up a royal proclamation disavowing any hostility towards France.[24]

In April Cecil received two letters composed in vigorous language at Pyrgo, a mansion close to Gidea Hall and six miles from Ingatestone.[25] They came from Lord John Grey, a leading Protestant, who emphasized the dangerous intentions of the pro-Spanish party, of which Paget was the recognized head; the best place for them was prison. The second letter branded Petre as well. 'As to the Philippians', Grey wrote, 'her Majesty must either disperse them to their own houses or else wipe them quite out of her Council; in the which number I reckon my Lord of Arundel, Petre and Mason.' Complex negotiations were taking place this month: the King of Spain, through his ambassador de Quadra, was trying to dissuade Elizabeth and Cecil from war with France. From Grey's strictures, it seems likely that Petre had dealings with de Quadra.

The assault on Leith in May was a dismal failure. The Secretary was the victim of the Queen's wrath. Decisions were taken to send reinforcements for a longer siege, and meantime Cecil and Wotton were ordered by the Queen to join Sadler in the north and negotiate.

It was at this juncture that an acting Principal Secretary in London was needed, and the duties fell on the man whose qualifications were perhaps unequalled. There is nothing to show if the choice was the Queen's or if Petre volunteered to deputize for his friend: so much, at any rate, for Grey's effort to rusticate him. Apparently he was still convalescent, but there is no doubt about the energy he displayed. Daily payments for wherries to and from the Court occur, as of old, in the first week in May. On the 6th twopennyworth of ale was brought 'when he was sick', and the fact that no groats were expended on the river in the following week might have indicated a relapse, were it not for a note of Petre supping with Garrard, who had constantly sent him delicacies during the winter. Petre was now godfather to young Peter Garrard, on whom he often bestowed little gifts.

Cecil gave Petre an up-to-date account of current affairs, warning him of the pitfalls, in much the same way as the senior man had enlightened Cecil on his succeeding Wotton as Secretary ten years earlier. Petre was handed the keys of the secret chests and the keys to the ciphers for correspondence with Cecil and the ambassadors, especially Sir Nicholas Throckmorton at the French court.* On 23 May Petre left the comfort and quiet of his Aldersgate house for the jealousies and noise of the Court.

He was temporarily installed, in fact though not in name, as Secretary to Elizabeth. To what extent he enjoyed her confidence it is impossible to deduce. Within a week, at any rate, he was the medium for all her messages to Cecil, who kept Petre well posted about his own movements.[26] The long journey with Wotton began at the end of May. Cecil had not fully recovered from a fever, so it was no surprise to Petre when he wrote two days later from his house at Burleigh near Stamford, 'I am rubbing on between health and sickness, yet my heart serving me to get the mastery.' The weary travellers arrived at Newcastle in the evening of 7 June. Next morning they met the French commissioners. Cecil and Wotton addressed a formal report to the Privy Council that night. A few days later Petre and Parry sent the Queen's instructions.

The conference soon adjourned to Edinburgh. While they were on their way, Mary of Guise died there, a severe blow to French aspirations. The tripartite negotiations of the English, the Scots and the French dragged on. Cecil, self-righteous, told the Queen he was doing most of the work: 'Mr. Wotton is very wise, and loveth quietness, but this matter requires travail'; and in the same strain to Petre: 'The hardest knot will prove the league betwixt England and Scotland.' If Petre could help them to a plainer explanation of one article, it would facilitate matters. Cecil was on the point of achieving the withdrawal of the French. If the Queen concurred, he was hopeful of concluding. Her letter of the 24th was delivered by courier from Greenwich to Edinburgh three days later, an astonishing feat, but her qualified approval failed to comfort Cecil, who demanded Petre's opinion. 'It is a pity to trouble you with our

* This was the only time when Petre was associated with Throckmorton, who was a first cousin of the Queen and a Protestant. He had entered public life in 1545 as a member of Parliament for Maldon in Essex, had a year in the Tower following Wyatt's rebellion and now held a vital post.

troubles', he wrote on the same day, 'and yet the Queen's Majesty's letters maketh me the bolder to impart the same to you.' Cecil was evidently not in unison with Wotton, who 'doubteth and dare not adventure; but we be but ministers', he added, still smarting under the Queen's rejection of his plans last Christmas, 'to do as we be commanded'. Petre, too, was troubled: Throckmorton's news told of preparations for transporting further French troops to Scotland being hastened, though, Petre assured Cecil, the Queen's navy at Portsmouth was ready for action.

At last, after dusk on 5 July, Cecil and Wotton were able to write to Petre: 'Our whole treaty be ready to be signed and sealed. We think the same shall prove very honourable for the Queen's Majesty and profitable for her realm.' The articles for the demolition of Leith, they added, had just been signed in a separate treaty; Petre had better keep it to himself and the Queen until their full dispatch arrived. Cecil had good reason to feel proud of his signal success. The French were to evacuate Scotland, and Mary was to drop her claim to the English crown.

Petre had also been busy with many other dispatches from abroad and with keeping Sussex, who had been sent to Ireland to combat Shane O'Neill, well informed of current events: all this was additional to Council attendances; and as Acting Secretary he was responsible for its agenda. Throckmorton had had enough of Paris and sought Petre's influence with the Queen for his recall. Petre, too, was hoping for early release. On 19 July Cecil's ailing deputy ended a long dispatch to him with the news that the Queen was proposing to go on progress in ten days' time to Portsmouth. 'I do much wish', he confessed, 'that you might be here before her Majesty's remove, for that I am utterly unable to follow unless I should go in a litter, and yet not able so to do without some danger and pain.'[27]

Nobody could describe the Cecil–Petre correspondence as lively, and Petre's letters are wholly objective apart from disclosing his dread of the progress. But nobody could deny that Petre had been an effective deputy, despite the pessimistic prophesies of some courtiers about Cecil's absence, 'Who will speedily resolve the delays? Who will make dispatch of anything?'[28]

After this plentiful, if pale, official harvest, a few private gleanings may be made. Thrice in June Petre had found it necessary to go up to London, but he stayed throughout July with the Queen at Greenwich. The accounts testify to hard work with no entertainment. Petre was accustomed to that way of life and could have taken it in his stride, had he been physically fit. But his back had been giving trouble again, and plasters were administered. He may have had an accident early in July, when $1\frac{1}{2}$ yards of broad ribbon was bought 'to stay my master's arm in', and 'Wright the surgeon at the Court' dressed the arm several times.

Petre was in the Queen's suite on 29 July when she dined with Archbishop Parker at Lambeth.* Cecil returned to London on the previous day to find that he had not fully regained the Queen's confidence, nor was he assigned to accompany her on the progress. Worse still, her relations with Lord Robert Dudley, Northumberland's fifth son, had reached the borderline of scandal. He was all-powerful at Court, and she would give scant attention to public affairs. Cecil planned to withdraw again into private life, though not quite forty. Had Petre's health been more robust, it is conceivable that Elizabeth would have invited him to resume his old office. Cecil thought of recommending Throckmorton, but did not resign. On 13 August Petre finished with the toil of state business and travelled to his country home, not by litter but by coach. His vehicle was one of the earliest coaches in this country (p. 206).

Next month Cecil's status was suddenly improved by a tragedy which obliged Dudley to quit the Court. His childless wife, Amy Robsart, was found dead at the foot of the stairs at Cumnor Hall, near Oxford, where she had been living alone for some years. Petre hastened to Court as fast as his health allowed, reaching Windsor on the second evening, the 16th, to join in the Council's anxious discussions whether Elizabeth would risk the throne to marry Dudley. The people were 'full of dangerous suspicions'. Quoth old Mother Dowe of Brentwood, according to Essex folk's depositions sent to Cecil by Rich and Mildmay, 'Dudley and the Queen played legerdemayne together, for he hath given her a child'.[29] Her commonsense prevailed; Cecil was restored to favour, and she told him of her decision against marriage. Petre had been at Cecil's side during the crisis.[30]

A renewal of his conciliar activities and unremitting support to Cecil extended to the end of May 1561. His steward's accounts, resumed again on 5 December, give forty-eight river journeys between Court and

---

* Matthew Parker had gone into obscurity rather than exile during Mary's reign. He was an erudite antiquary who had accepted high preferment reluctantly and was to be distinguished in the annals of the Church for his moderation, modesty and morals. While Acting Secretary, Petre had been in touch with Parker several times. It was probably with some disappointment that Petre had to forgo taking any share in the task of revising the statutes of Christ Church, Oxford. 'Although I be named in the commission,' he wrote to Parker on 6 June, 'yet for that I shall not be able to attend. I pray your Grace to take order therein.' Next month he transmitted to the Archbishop the opinions of some German divines 'which her Majesty prayeth you to consider, and to be at the Court tomorrow', not to advise Elizabeth, but to receive her own views! And a few days later Petre dealt with the supply of preachers as a temporary expedient in the numerous dioceses which the Queen had left bishopless. (*Works of Archbishop Parker* (Parker Society, 1846), 118–19.)

Aldersgate, or between London, Westminster and Greenwich: a useful record as the Council minutes are lost. Even during a spell at Ingatestone in April he was writing to Clinton (Lord High Admiral) and Cecil with his opinion on the articles exhibited by the King of Portugal's ambassador for restraining the traffic of English merchants to the Indies. Later in the month, the Chancellor of the Garter in crimson velvet mantle preceded the Queen in the procession of knights to St. George's Chapel, and he was present at the Feast at Windsor Castle on 18 May.[31] Then, on the 29th, he and Lady Petre returned to Ingatestone, but not for well deserved leisure.

CHAPTER XII

Queen Elizabeth at Ingatestone Hall

1 *The Royal Progress*

O N 31 May 1561, Sir William Petre's steward paid 10s. 'in reward to two of the Queen's Majesty's servants that brought the jesse to my master declaring the progress' (the 'jesse', or geste, was the document notifying the royal itinerary); and 5s. spent on cards suggests that the Queen's Usher responsible for arranging progresses stayed the night at the Hall. The house on which Petre had bestowed so much thought and money was to receive Elizabeth during her intended summer journey through several eastern counties. The full story of her visit to Ingatestone Hall will never be discovered. The known facts were meagre. The new evidence is in the book kept by Petre's chief officer, John Kyme. After some pre-liminary items, nine pages are headed:

> A Declaration of all such provision of victuals and other necessaries as was bought and provided against the Queen's Majesty coming to my master's house at Ingatestone, being the xixth day of July, the third year of her Majesty's reign, and there tarrying until the xxijth of the same, both days included.

The picture which these pages give is like an incomplete painting by the elder Brueghel. Large areas of the canvas are missing; the remainder is vivid and detailed.

The main preparations were crowded into the twelve days before the Queen's arrival. On 7 July, after a month's official work in London, Petre rode down to Ingatestone taking with him 'Mr. Wilcocks the cook', who had supervised the wedding feast in 1552. Petre had just added a few desirable items to his considerable store of plate, which included a pair of silver flagons acquired in 1544 for £30, six pieces of silver-gilt given by the King of France as well as much fine silver bought from Thomas Gresham and a Calais merchant in 1550, the two gilt standing-cups which Mary and Elizabeth had given on New Year's Days, 1554 and 1559:

> Danby a goldsmith for making and gilding a basin, weight 53¾ oz. at 2s. 6d the oz., £6 13s. 1d.
> Making and gilding 4 gilt cups chased, weight 51⅝ oz. at 22d. the oz., 113s. 2½d.
> Making and gilding one jug, weight 17½ oz. at 20d. the oz., 28s. 4d.
> The overweight in silver being ⅝ oz. at 5s. the oz., 3s. 1d.
> Silver to make a basin, weight 50¼ oz. at 4s. 9d. the oz., £11 18s. 8d.
> The fashion of the same, with my master's arms graven in the bottom, 20s.

It was thirteen years since Kyme had noted the acquisition of 'a salt with a cover gilt having my master's arms', perhaps his first piece of armorial plate.

Lady Petre supervised the preparation of the royal suite. She got thirteen ells of green taffeta sarcenet for £4 11s. to line the curtains, the best 'hangings' were brought down from the Aldersgate house, and 'a ¼ lb. of fusses for perfuming of chambers' was bought for 20d. Around the house, bricklayers, carpenters and labourers were busy 'making ranges, sheds and other necessaries against the Queen's Majesty's coming', which cost £3 8s. 2d. These were probably to house all except the most important of the Queen's retinue. Possibly the '6 staff torches at 8d. the piece' were for their use. Additional space in the cellars, always well stocked for normal needs, was found.

2 hogsheads March beer sent to Ingatestone, 20s.

2 tun of beer and ale at 33s. 4d. a tun, with 6s. 8d. for the carriage thereof from London, £3 13s. 4d.

4 barrels of beer at 5s., 20s.

An unspecified amount of wine was also brought down from the town house. Servants were dispatched to London to make last-minute purchases and to arrange for them and for other goods to be sent direct from Aldersgate or by carriers from the inns at the beginning of the Essex Great Road at Aldgate.

½ dozen stone cruses sent to Ingatestone, 12d.

Two baskets wherein the spice and vessels were trussed that was sent to Ingatestone, 9d.

A 'carre' from Aldersgate Street to Aldgate sent with certain stuff, 8d.

Mr. Wilcocks for 6 trays of wood at 14d. the piece 7s. and 6 flaskets at 10d. the piece 5s.

A 'carre' from Mr. Garrard's to my master's house which brought trays, flaskets and spice, 4d.

Three black jacks at 2s. 8d. the piece 8s., two pottle pots of pewter, silver fashion, weighing 10 lb., 10s., a cope basket and a trussing basket 14d., corn for the poultry 2d., a barrel for the lard 12d., a cart to Aldgate 12d.

3 dozen trenchers 18d., for 200 tainter hooks 16d.

1 dozen wax lights weight 3 lb., 2s. 6d.

6 baskets of sundry sorts sent from London with necessary things, 3s. 7d.

2 quire of paper spent in the kitchen, 8d.

Carrying of fruit from London to Ingatestone, 6d.

Carriage of 2 load of stuff from London to Ingatestone, 6s. 8d.

Holland the horsekeeper for his charges at two several times in riding to London with 2 horses, 23d., and for Arthur's charges in riding to London with Mr. Wilcocks, 8d.

Other servants were sent a long way to buy direct from Fenland fowlers. In the days immediately before the royal visit, contributions came from a steady procession of tenants on the estate and servants of Petre's friends, such as North, who many years ago had signed the receipts for the instalments of the purchase-money for Ingatestone, and Sir Gilbert Dethick, Garter King-of-Arms.

The charges of John Wagstaff in riding to Ely for fowl, 4s. 8d.
The charges of Richard Lunn in riding to Cambridge for fowl with 2 horses, 8s. 2d.
A man that did help to seek fowl in Cambridgeshire, 12d.
My Lord North's man in reward 10s. for bringing 6 cygnets from Huntingdon to London and so to Ingatestone 18s., which was for the carriage of them.
Mr. Stonarde's man for bringing a stag, 20s.
Mr. Swann's man for bringing fowl out of Kent, 10s.
Becke's maid 2s., Mr. Bradbury and Mr. Rutter's man 5s., Mr. Worthington's man 12d., Luckin's man 4d., Whitelocke's man 8d., Wm. Pascall's man 12d.
Haines' man the fishmonger for carriage of fish, 12d.
Mr. Gouge's man for bringing 20 caponets, 2 pigs, 2 dozen pigeons, and old apples, 16d.
Bexwell's man for bringing a lamb 4d., Dulcett's man for bringing a lamb, 4d.
Jeffreis' man for fish and oysters, 20d.
Mr. Edmund Tyrell's man for bringing 6 'shoulvlers' and 3 bushel oysters, 3s. 4d.
Mr. Dethike's man for bringing 6 egrets, 6 'brewes' and 6 'pewetts', 3s. 4d.
Driwoode's man for 6 quails and one dozen pigeons, 8d.
Mr. Pawne's man 4d., Mr. John Tyrell's man 2d., and Mr. George Tyrell's man 4d.
Wm. Fynche's man for bringing of peas, 2d.
Dale's daughter of Stock for bringing one dozen chickens, 4d.
'Bodeis' man for bringing 2 capons and 2 dozen chickens, 8d.
Mr. Browne's man of Kent for bringing 4 'heronshewes' and apples, 12d.
Apleton's man for a fresh salmon, 3s. 4d.
Yonge's man of Willesdon for bringing a turkey cock and ½ dozen pea chickens, 8d.
A bushel of hempseed for the quails sent to Ingatestone, 3s.
A basket for the pea chickens coopwise, 6d.

Well before the final preparations at Ingatestone were complete, the Queen had set off on her progress. On 13 July she had supped with Secretary Cecil at his house. She started next morning. The next few days were spent in leisurely travel into the heart of Essex by way of Wanstead, Loughton Hall, Havering and Pyrgo, but the record of these early stages is slightly confusing. In the Cofferer's account for that part which includes Ingatestone the sums refer to his own disbursements, which were additional to the hospitality given to the Queen and her train.[1]

	£	s.	d.
Havering			
Friday 18th July, ibidem Havering	95	12	7
Ingerston			
Saturday 19th, ibidem [i.e. Havering] and Hingerstone	102	8	7½
Sunday 20th, ibidem Ingerstone	114	7	9½
Newhall			
Monday 21st, ibidem [i.e. Ingatestone] and Newhall	105	1	6
Tuesday 22nd, ibidem Newhall	114	19	3½

As Petre's steward, however, definitely stated that the Queen stayed at Ingatestone until the 22nd, the probable explanation is that the advance party left for New Hall on Monday and Elizabeth with her main retinue followed next morning.*

Sir William and Lady Petre with the servants in their grey marble liveries awaited Elizabeth's arrival on 19 July. A large proportion of the Court accompanied her on progesses, but owing to the gap in the Council register in 1561 the personnel is unknown apart from Cecil and negatively the councillors who remained in London—Winchester, Sackville, Mason and Wotton—and also Gresham, who was just off to Antwerp.

About noon the long cavalcade turned off the Essex Great Road at 'London gate' into the lane leading to the Hall, having passed through rich, undulating country. The tree-lined boundaries of the fields which Elizabeth saw are unchanged today and were possibly 300 years old in 1561. The royal coach, cumbersome and springless, with its carved canopy and waving plumes, came through the outer gates, under the gate-house, through the base court and drew up before the Great Hall of which John Walker's little sketch of 1605 is the only reliable reminder. The real moment had arrived.

What followed, the sayings and doings of the next three or four days, cannot be recalled, with one notable exception. The anticlimax is sharp. Even the rooms which Elizabeth occupied are not known but deduction makes it fairly certain that her suite was on the first floor in the north side

---

* For these days three state documents have been preserved: (1) holograph letter from Cecil to Throckmorton dated at Ingatestone, 21 July (*For. Cal., Eliz.*, iv, 180, 193–4); (2) letter, preserved at Hatfield House in the form of a draft by Cecil, also dated 21 July, but without place (H.M.C., *Salisbury MSS.*, i, 261, printed in full in Haynes, *State Papers*, 368; absence of place verified by me); (3) instruction to all Vice-Admirals, dated 22 July at 'Beawliewe in Essex' [New Hall, Boreham] and signed by Elizabeth, the dating clause added in the same hand but a different ink, which suggests that it was written out at Ingatestone and subscribed by the Queen on arrival at New Hall (S.P. 12/18/23).

16. QUEEN ELIZABETH ENTERTAINED AT INGATESTONE HALL,
JULY 1561
     The first page of the special account of the food, drink and other expenses

of the quadrangle, including the present Garden Chamber * and the former Passage Room as her principal rooms (p. 33). This would give her easy access to the (now demolished) big private Dining Chamber in one direction and the Gallery and the closet overlooking the Chapel in the other. If a Council was held at Ingatestone, it may be assumed that it took place in the Gallery.

It is ironic that the silence of the records is broken only by Petre's eloquent accounts of the food provided for the visit. Elizabeth was personally the most frugal and abstemious of monarchs; but prodigality was a mark of honour and respect, her retinue was large, and most of their appetites were enormous. Much of the food, valued at approximately one-third of the whole cost, came from the estate, rabbit-warren, dovecote, fishponds and store-rooms, or was otherwise 'of my master's own provision'. The total is staggering, and even this does not include the presents brought by Petre's tenants and friends.† (Plate 16.)

4 qtrs. 2 bushels wheat at 20s. the qtr., £4 5s., 9 qtrs. malt at 12s. the qtr., £5 8s., 3 qtrs. oats at 6s. 8d. the qtr., 20s., 3 bushels barley at 14d. the bushel, 3s. 6d.

2½ qtrs. white wheat at 22s. the qtr., 55s.

4 dozen of bread bought, 4s.

3 oxen at £4 the piece, £12, 2 veals at 10s. the piece, 20s., 6 muttons at 7s. the piece, 42s.

30 couple coneys at 6d. the couple, 15s., 7 dozen pigeons at 18d. the dozen, 10s. 6d.

Soles, flounders, plaice, gurnards, conger and other sea fish, besides certain sea fish given to my master, £4 3s.

2 firkins of sturgeon at 23s. 4d. the piece, 46s. 8d., carriage from London, 5d.

12 lings at 2s. 6d. the piece, 30s., 14 haberdins at 8d. the piece, 9s. 4d., 8 carps and 8 breams, 10s. 8d.

6 cygnets at 10s. the piece, 60s.

6 dozen 'pewetts' whereof 2 dozen at 18s., the rest at 16s., £5.

1 dozen gulls at 3s. 4d. the piece, 40s.

2 dozen 'brewes' at 2s. the piece, 48s.

2 dozen 'egretts' at 2s. the piece, 48s.

Carriage of the said fowl from London, 6s. 8d.

12 herons and 12 'shoulvlers' bought at London at 2s. 6d. the piece, £3.

18 herons at 22d. the piece bought in Kent, 33s.

12 'shoulvlers' at 12d. the piece bought in Kent, 12s.

12 dozen quails at 4s. the dozen bought at London, 48s.

* Note for visitors: this is the first-floor room in which the Elizabethan tester bed stands.
† As usual, spelling is modernized except where noted. The order of the entries has been slightly rearranged by the insertion of a few items from earlier pages of the accounts.

4 cygnets bought at Cambridge at 7s. the piece, 6d. in the whole abated, 27s. 6d.
6 'bitters' bought there at 18d. the piece, with 2d. over in the whole, 9s. 2d.
27 geese at 5d. the piece, 11s. 3d.
26 caponets at 16d. the piece, 34s. 8d.
14 caponets at 8d. the piece, 9s. 4d.
1 dozen pullets at 4d. the piece, 4s.
4 dozen chickens at 3s. the dozen, 12s.
1 dozen chickens at 2½d. the piece, 2s. 6d.
6 caponets bought at London, 2 at 3s. the piece, the rest 2s. 8d., 16s. 8d.
1 dozen caponets, 2 couple whereof at 16d. the couple, the rest at 2s. 8d. the
    couple, 13s. 4d., and for 2 dozen chickens at 3½d. the piece, 7s., which were
    bought by one Felde of Fingest in 'Buck:', 22s. 4d. (Not paid, nor charged.)
Bullocks' livers to feed fowl, 16d.
Hempseed, viz. 4½ bushels at 3s. 4d. the bushel, 1d. over in the whole, 15s. 1d.
Barley to feed the poultry at London, 5d.
A quail cage with 3 troughs, 3s. 5d.
A bushel of hempseed for the quails sent to Ingatestone, 3s.
A basket for the pea chickens coopwise, 6d.

Gascon wine 2 hogsheads, £5, French wine 10 gallons, 13s. 4d., Rhenish wine
    4 gallons, 6s. 8d., sack 6 gallons, 10s.

693 eggs, 15s. 7d.
44 dishes of butter at 7d. the dish, 25s. 8d.
7 gallons of cream at 8d. the gallon, 4s. 8d.
Yeast and herbs for the kitchen, 18d.
A barrel of 'sampere', 12d., 1 barrel olives cont. 1 gallon and a pint with 4d.
    for the barrel, 3s., one barrel of capers cont. 3 lb. with 2d. for the barrel, 3s. 8d.
200 oranges, 19¼d.
Comfits of sundry sorts ut patet per billam, 28s. 6d.
Sugar, cloves, mace, pepper and sundry other kind of spice ut patet per billam,
    £7 15s.
More for 12 lb. prunes sent to my lady, 16d.
½ peck of fine white salt, 2½d.
Fruit, viz. pears, plums and 'genetings', 2s.

Spent in wood, coal and candle, 40s.

When the Queen left, Petre's steward rewarded some of her retinue
and those who had toiled in the kitchen.

Mr. Winkefelde the Queen's gentleman usher to be distributed amongst the
    grooms of the Queen's chamber, 40s., Mr. Webster master cook to be given
    amongst the children of the kitchen, 26s. 8d., the Queen's footmen, 26s. 8d.,
    and the porters, 10s.; £5 3s. 4d.

In reward to Mr. Wilcocks the cook at two several times, the one at Ingatestone before the Queen's Majesty's coming, the other at my master's house at London, 20s., more to him for working in the kitchen at Ingatestone 7 days, and for occupying his stuff there, with 2s. in reward to his man, £4 2s., Stephen a cook for working like time, 13s. 4d., Silvester a cook for working 10 days, 20s., Medcalf a cook and Whiteholmes for working 6 days, 24s., George Cook, Mr. Garrard's man, for his pains, 10s., 3 scalders, 8s., 2 turn-broaches, 2s., and a woman for washing the vessels, 8d.; £9.

Elizabeth had probably arrived about noon. Being Saturday, it was a fishday and dinner would be the only main meal served. Secretary Cecil was a staunch believer in maintaining the number of days in order to encourage the sea fisheries, which helped to man the navy in times of emergency. The occasion demanded and was met with sturgeon, a royal fish. Of the wildfowl, the brewe was probably a kind of snipe and the shoveller was the spoonbill duck; the egret was the lesser white heron, and heronshews were young herons—a very dainty dish. Other dishes for the high table can be visualized. Some of the herbs and spices, with the generous supply of cream, were doubtless required by Wilcocks to make sauces for garnishing the meat and the fish and the delicacies served afterwards. Sampere, later samphire (*herbe de St. Pierre*), was a maritime rock plant, the aromatic leaves of which were used in pickling, while mace was needed for spicing ale as well as food. The jenneting (*pomme de St. Jean*) was a variety of early apple, ripe by June. Tudor comfits were sweet-meats usually made of fruits or roots preserved with sugar. The two main courses, except on Saturday, would have been meat and game, followed by the banquet or equivalent of the modern sweet and dessert, though it is unlikely that Sir William led the Queen from the formal dining chamber to his little banqueting-house outside.

Petre had provided her with good eating, but how he entertained her is not revealed. There is no word of a professional touring company such as Lord Dudley's Players staging a performance in the inner court, nor of the chase over Petre's lands.

The host was then left to count the cost. His steward calculated the actual expenditure at £83 1s. 10¾d., priced the provisions drawn from the estate and stores at £39 2s. 10d., added his valuation of the presents in kind and produced the total figure of over £136. His cast was 2d. short.

Summa totalis of the whole charges of the Queen's Majesty's being at my master's house at 'Yngatstone', with £14 5s. 6d. for victuals given to my master for presents and valued at several prices, the particulars whereof are not in this book mentioned, £136 10s. ¾d.

Continuing along the Roman road, the Queen would reach Moulsham Hall, the home of Thomas Mildmay (elder brother of Sir Walter), who had succeeded his father in 1557.* The church bells were ringing as she rode through Chelmsford² towards New Hall, visited by her mother Anne when she was being wooed by Henry, and more recently the home of Sir Thomas Wharton.† After a four or five days' sojourn there, Elizabeth proceeded to Colchester, where the Corporation bore the expense. So greatly did she relish the oysters, perhaps for the first time, that they were afterwards sent for in immense quantities by the royal purveyors. On the last two days of July the Queen honoured Lord Darcy at St. Osyth's Priory. At Harwich she was so gratified as to ask the Corporation, who had entertained her, if she could reciprocate. Thanking her, they said they needed no more. 'A pretty town', she remarked, 'and wants nothing.'³ After remaining at Ipswich until 10 August, the Queen proceeded to Shelley Hall‡ near Hadleigh in Suffolk, thence to Small-bridge Hall in Bures, the old family seat of the main branch of the Waldegraves. (The home of Sir Edward, the second son, was at Borley Hall, a few miles away.) Crossing the Stour, she was back in Essex on the 14th, and a ten-mile journey brought her to Hedingham, the ancestral castle of the de Veres, where she spent four or five days as Oxford's guest.§

* For the details of this progress the historian has been dependant chiefly upon the Cofferer's account of the Queen's own expenses (B.M., Cotton MS. Vesp., C, xiv, 481, in J. Nichols, *The Progresses . . . of Queen Elizabeth*, 3 vols., 1823). This gives a fairly detailed itinerary; and the datings of letters at several stopping-places (see *Dom. Cal.* and *For. Cal.*) and other odd references all corroborate the Cofferer's record, for which there is no parallel as the Privy Council minutes are missing. Although not based on all the material then available, Miller Christy, 'The Progresses of Queen Elizabeth through Essex' (*Essex Review*, xxvi, 115–29, 181–97, also 97) is useful, also for the later Essex progresses of 1568–88.

† Mary had rewarded him with a lease of New Hall, but on Elizabeth's accession he was excluded from Parliament and Council. Only three months before she reached his house, he and Lord Hastings of Loughborough had been in serious trouble for saying mass there. On the Council's orders John de Vere, Earl of Oxford and Lord Lieutenant, had ridden over from Hedingham Castle to search New Hall, where he found many 'instruments of superstition'. He repeated the privy search in Sir Edward Waldegrave's house in north Essex. Wharton, Hastings and Sir Edward and Lady Waldegrave were tried at the Essex Assizes on 3 June, and all were sent to the Tower. Wharton was apparently freed, but Waldegrave died there on 1 September.

‡ Not the house of that name near Ongar in Essex, as imagined by Nichols.

§ Nichols' misreading of Henningham (an old form) as Hemingham caused him to identify it as Helmingham in Suffolk, but there is no doubt that she stayed at Hedingham Castle. Between 15 and 17 August Cecil dated several documents at 'Henyngham', which clinches the matter, although one of the printed calendars made a similar error to that of Nichols in reading the place as Hemingham (*For. Cal., Eliz.*, 251, 258–9; *Dom. Cal., 1547–80*, 183). A few days earlier a Havering man had been driving a heavily laden cart towards Hedingham Castle in the Queen's service, when his mount fell, killing him; this confirmatory identification is in the record of the coroner's inquest (P.R.O., Queen's Bench Indictments (Ancient), 603/114).

A short stage brought her to Gosfield Hall, where the host was Sir John Wentworth. After a two-day halt there, the royal party went on to Leighs Priory, to which Lord Rich had finally retired. She remained under his roof until the 25th. The train then moved to Hallingbury Morley (now Great Hallingbury), the house of Lord Morley.* Entering Hertfordshire, the Queen stayed at Sir Ralph Sadler's seat, Standon Hall near Ware. The last two halts were at Hertford Castle and Enfield. Elizabeth was back in London on 8 September, having been away for nearly two months, during which time her resting-places had included at least thirteen private houses in a journey of over two hundred miles.†

All the families, with one exception, whom she had honoured had come to the fore since the Dissolution. The first de Vere accompanied William the Conqueror and the family had held the earldom of Oxford since the reign of Stephen. On the basis of Petre's own expenditure, the Queen and her retinue must have cost the hosts about £2,500 in food and drink, quite apart from her Cofferer's expenses averaging £100 a day. Her stay with Rich cost him £389, that with Oxford £273, each for four or five days, which makes it clear that the burden of Petre's hospitality for two or perhaps three days was on the scale expected of him.[4] They were luckier in 1561 than the royal hosts of later years. In 1577 Elizabeth's four-day stay cost Sir Nicholas Bacon £577; her three-day visit to Lord Keeper Egerton in 1602 as much as £2,000; while the most fantastic hospitality was dispensed by Leicester (Dudley) during three weeks of princely entertainment at Kenilworth Castle in 1575.[5] The journey of 1561 was the first of Elizabeth's long progresses in which she stayed in courtiers' country houses, and Petre's household book is the oldest surviving record of a subject's own share of the expenses. The Queen did not yet expect extravagant receptions. But Petre only just escaped. Elizabeth's visits to Theobalds, Cecil's rising palace on the Hertfordshire–Essex border, began in 1564, and each cost him £1,000 or more.

There is nothing to show whether Petre joined the Queen's train when she left his house. It seems improbable, on account of his health and because his youngest daughter Catherine was married to John Talbot at Ingatestone on 18 August (p. 287).

* Father of the future Lord Monteagle of Gunpowder Plot fame. There is no evidence of any social links between the Petres and the Parkers, Barons Morley, although they lived less than twenty miles apart.

† The places visited are given in the expenses of the three gentlemen-ushers who organized the accommodation (P.R.O., E351/541, m.28). Several houses visited, e.g. 'Sir William Petre's', are named only from their owner. Sir John Wentworth (not Lady Maltravers, as in Nichols) is named at Gosfield, but no help in this respect is given for the houses visited before Ingatestone was reached. 'Henynghame' is named, if yet further confirmation is needed.

2 Lady Catherine Grey

Elizabeth's train at Ingatestone in July 1561 almost certainly included an impetuous lady in her mid-twenties wondering how much longer she could hide her double deceit from the Queen. Since the execution of Lady Jane Grey, her sister Lady Catherine ranked next in the succession by Henry VIII's will, should Elizabeth die childless. But Catherine had secretly married the Earl of Hertford, Protector Somerset's eldest son. It was treason for a person of royal blood to wed without the sovereign's consent; and now she was pregnant. The storm broke at Ipswich in August, following her confession when no longer able to conceal her state. A week later, the other rival claimant to the English throne, Mary Stuart, reached Leith from France, having eluded Elizabeth's ships. Sir William and Lady Petre had narrowly escaped two abnormal tides of the Queen's wrath which swept through the Court.

Catherine was dispatched to the Tower. Hertford, who was disporting himself in Paris, followed her on 5 September. Next day he was summoned before Winchester and Petre. Their son was born later in the month. In January Archbishop Parker, Petre and others were charged with the duty of re-examining the circumstances of the marriage between Hertford and Catherine.[6] On 12 May 1562, when Petre was sick, the commission pronounced the marriage invalid owing to the absence of witnesses. The discipline imposed on the prisoners was not severe, and Catherine gave birth to a second son early in 1563. Hertford was fined £10,000 for his further insult to the Queen.

In August Catherine was transferred from the plague-infected Tower to the custody of her uncle, Lord John Grey, at Pyrgo, which the Queen had granted him in 1559. Catherine's warder was the Duke of Suffolk's brother, who himself had experienced the austerities of the Tower through participating in the rebellion in favour of Lady Jane. Grey's moated medieval mansion spelt neither freedom nor friendship to Catherine, for he was no better disposed towards her than towards Petre. On 21 November 1564 Grey died at Pyrgo.* Writing five days later to Sir Thomas Smith, Cecil expressly stated that Lady Catherine was already in the custody of Sir William Petre.[7]

Elizabeth's confidence in him is shown by her committing a potential usurper of the throne to his care, a trust which he would have preferred in this instance not to have earned. John Hales had recently written a pamphlet urging Catherine's right over that of Mary Queen of Scots, for

---

* A later owner of Pyrgo was Sir Thomas Cheke (grandson of Secretary Cheke), whose descendants retained it until near the end of the eighteenth century, when it was pulled down.

which he got a sentence in the Tower.* Rumours got around that Cecil,
too, was inclined to favour Catherine's claim. He tried to clear himself of
suspicion. 'I will go upright, neither ad dextram nor ad sinistram', he
wrote; which would have been a suitable motto also for Petre.[8] A few
weeks after her arrival, Lady Catherine honoured Thomasine Petre who
had married Ludovick Greville (p. 287) by standing godmother to her
second son, born at Ingatestone.[9]

It is quite possible that the Council's plea to Elizabeth on 4 June 1565 to
show 'some remission of her displeasure' towards the unfortunate lady was
initiated by Petre, who was present that day.[10] Among the family archives
has been found a letter, addressed to him in London probably by his
steward or chaplain.† Catherine, it appears, had managed to let her
husband know that she was ill. Petre had been taxed with this, and his
Ingatestone officer excused himself.

> Your letters sent touching my Lady Catherine was delivered me on Sunday after
> eight o'clock, to the which I made no answer as yet, for that I had mentioned the
> same thing in your letters sent to your honour that morning. If there had been
> such danger in her sickness as was reported to you, your honour should have
> known of it. I am not able to say how sick she was but only by report, for that
> I came not at her, yet this I am able to say, that she had her breakfast, dinner and
> supper, as she hath been accustomed to have, whereupon I judged her not to be
> so sick as peradventure was signified to my Lord of Hertford. If her sickness had
> been such as a physician should have been requisite, I would have letten your
> honour have had knowledge. It was not in me to stay either her letters or her
> messengers sent to my lord, or to any other, for that I was not privy to them.
> My lady (as you do know) may send and doth at her pleasure, the which thing
> can not be remedied unless her servants should be inhibited going to the town.
> This day my Lady Catherine was a walking in your closes, and was in your
> parlour both dinner and supper. She is now very well, praised be God, with all
> the rest of your household here.[11]

It may be surmised that Lady Petre was advised by her lord to see that
their distinguished guest's servants were in fact 'inhibited' from slipping
away to Ingatestone and the great road except in company responsible to
Sir William.

One other relic of Catherine's sojourn under his roof was recently

---

* Bacon seems to have been in agreement with Hales, and was out of favour in 1564–5.
Anthony Browne, Petre's neighbour at Weald Hall, is said to have been proposed as Lord
Chancellor in his place. Browne himself a year or so later was the author of a pamphlet
advocating Mary's claims as heir apparent, which suited Elizabeth, who knighted him.

† Its fortuitous preservation among Petre's papers about his financial provision for Exeter
College (ch. xiv) is due to his having used the back of the letter for jotting down some rough
notes about the college.

discovered. Scratched on the carved stone chimney-piece in the room at the north-west corner of the main quadrangle, known as the Garden Chamber, are a few words which may be read as:

grayed goodnes getteth grace cath graye.

It is not known if Petre was reimbursed the cost of maintaining the noble lady, which amounted to about £5 a week. While Catherine was at Pyrgo, Dudley and Cecil had written to Hertford, whom Mason had under guard in his own house, stating that Lord John Grey was unable to bear the expenses of his niece 'and her train' and asking him to send £114 to defray her charges there, a curious request to a man whose marriage had been nullified.[12] On 21 May 1566 Petre thanked Cecil[13] about his 'late suit', which may refer to release from the guardianship (and charges) of the undesired guest in that month, when she was removed to the custody of Sir John Wentworth, a distant relation of Petre's first wife, at Gosfield Hall. Catherine seemed doomed to retrace part of the 1561 progress. Wentworth begged the Council to 'consider how unmeet a man' he was 'to receive such a charge being of years above threescore and sixteen, and of late much visited with sickness'.[14] His excuses were unavailing. Again, Catherine's warder went to his grave; and after being at Gosfield for a year and a half the ailing woman was removed in a coach to Cockfield Hall near Saxmundham in Suffolk, where her guardian was Sir Owen Hopton. There she died three months later, aged only twenty-seven, victim of the unabated anger of a queen who was pathologically jealous of all rivals. Catherine had never cast eyes on her husband since she left the Tower.*

* The youngest of the most unlucky sisters, Lady Mary Grey, a dwarf, apparently learned nothing from Catherine's fate. In 1565 she secretly married Thomas Keyes, the giant sergeant-porter of White Hall Palace. (He figured once in Petre's accounts, having got a groat reward, probably for opening the gates late one night, and Petre must have often exchanged a greeting with him in his countless comings and goings.) Lady Mary also was banished, first to the Chequers in the Chilterns, then to the care of Sir Thomas Gresham, who asked to be released from his responsibility more than once. She died at the age of thirty-three. Cecil had a share in her examination (S.P. 12/37/8), but evidently not Petre.

CHAPTER XIII

Elder Statesman

1 The Battle against Ill Health

PETRE's illnesses gave rise to many items of expense, from which it is apparent that he was attended by the leading members of the medical profession. Some were in the royal service; some earned renown in the chronicles of English medicine. The names of nearly twenty physicians and surgeons are found (the dates in parentheses refer to entries in his accounts). The majority of the physicians named were Doctors of Medicine of Oxford or Cambridge and Fellows of the College of Physicians. Those who held the office of President were the erudite John Clement (1555–9), Richard Master (1561), John Symings, or Symons (1559–60) and Richard Caldwell (1559–62) who founded the Lumleian Surgery Lecture jointly with Lord Lumley in 1581. Thomas Wendy (1555–9) was Physician to Henry VIII, Mary and Elizabeth; Alban Hill (1559) had graduated at Bologna; and Christopher Langton (1559) published several medical treatises. Petre was a patient of Richard Ferris, or Ferrers (1549), and of Thomas Vicary (1555–61), both royal serjeant-surgeons. Other surgeons who figure in the accounts were George Holland (1555–6), John Yates (1559) and William Crowe (1562), all of whom held offices of distinction in the Company of Barber-Surgeons, and 'Mr. Baltroppe' (1561). In later years, Yates and Crowe examined two notable Elizabethan surgeons, William Clowes and William Gale, before their admission to that Company; and Balthorp attended at the Queen's request 'Doctor' John Dee, the mathematician and royal astrologer.*

Medical knowledge and practice as yet showed little progress beyond the low medieval standards. Medicines prescribed by the physician were made up by the apothecary, who might give simple remedial treatment under the former's orders. The apothecaries belonged to the Grocers' Company and had to serve apprenticeship. The Court apothecary was an ancient office and continued to Tudor times. In 1544 Petre paid 8s. to 'Mr. Carleton the prince's apothecary', and at least one other royal apothecary, Alsopp, occurs in his accounts.

The seeds of Petre's ill-health may have been sown in those years when, as a commissioner for the Dissolution of the Monasteries, he

* Little or nothing seems to be known of the remaining surgeons, Andrews (1559–61), Gathe (1556), Sethe (1556) (perhaps identical with Gathe, but the original is clear), Wright (1560) and Wylde (1555), or of 'Dr. Cotton the physician' (1559–61).

249

journeyed hundreds of miles, often in midwinter, riding hard to keep up to the Vicar-general's stiff itineraries. The fee of 3s. 4d. 'to the surgeon that looked after my master's leg' at Ingatestone in 1548 was the prelude to many more, revealing that he probably suffered from a varicose ulcer which was treated over a period of years with ointments. That winter, in London, he became a patient of 'Forest the King's surgeon', whose charge for 'looking to my master's leg' was 33s. 4d., with a final 53s. 4d. for 'healing' it, sums which indicate many attendances. The 'flux' in his leg in 1551 was apparently a recurrence. It forced him to go in a litter into Essex, where he took several months to recuperate, and its legacy is the little series of intimate letters to Cecil (pp. 90-96). Early in 1555, physicians, surgeons and apothecaries tried to cure the Queen's Secretary: 'To Alsopp the poticary for a purgation for my master devised by Mr. Wendy 3s. 4d.'; 'To Wylde a surgeon for two boxes of ointment devised by Mr. Clement 2s.'; 'To Vycars the serjeant surgeon 3s. 4d.' More boxes of camphorated ointment came from the apothecary who also supplied much rose-water for the leg; once also white vinegar and rose leaves for making into rose-vinegar. A servant's expenses in April 1555 'riding to Sir Philip Parys in Cambridgeshire about my master's disease in his legs' testifies to the invalid's anxious quest for a remedy from one who had been a Dissolution commissioner and is described as 'an amateur surgeon whose cures deserve praise'.[1]

Petre was about thirty at the time of his first recorded illness—the sudden attack at Court just before Christmas 1545, from which he quickly recovered. In the following September he had 'back' pains which may have been rheumatism, but more probably were the first symptoms of a kidney-stone. He had further sporadic attacks, and ointments and plasters were applied. He was taken ill with kidney or bladder trouble at Croydon in the summer of 1556, when he had to abandon his duties and make a painful journey by litter to London, where several surgeons attended him. 'Poticary stuff' included camomile flowers, cummin seed, elder water and a clyster. The Bishop of Rochester sent him 'a powder for the stone'. Peter Vannes, the English ambassador, wrote from Venice on 10 October, 'I am sorry to hear that you are at times somewhat distressed with a spice [touch] of the strangolione [strangury].* Minding to go to Padua within these three days, I shall somewhat counsel with my friends

---

* 'Strangolione' is not quinsey, as identified by the editor of the For. Cal., but strangury, a painful urinary complaint the symptoms of which would occur during the passage of a kidney-stone down the ureter to the bladder. The O.E.D. explains that strangury was often incorrectly called strangullion (quinsey). Vannes' next letter to his friend from Padua, which was the greatest medical school in Europe, failed to mention any remedy and was the last before his recall to England.

what kind of remedy might be the more propice [propitious] for you'.[2]

Soon after Elizabeth came to the throne Petre had to combat three ailments—the stone, an ulcerated leg and a rupture. The account-book starting at that time after a two-year break mentions 'a lace for my master's truss', a phrase which suggests that it was no novel companion. A little later his rupture led to a 5s. payment 'to Yates a surgeon for making a new truss of jene fustian',* and 'buttons for my master's truss' shortly before the Queen's visit to Ingatestone is a further reminder of physical discomforts.

His letter to Cecil in March 1559 and payments to Andrews the surgeon for dressing his leg show that the ulcer had broken out afresh, but despite considerable pain Petre did not flinch from duty in the new Council to which Elizabeth had appointed him. In that month payments to surgeons, physicians and apothecaries resumed in earnest. Friends sent their own remedies—'a glass of rose water, a glass of cherries preserved, and a glass of damsons preserved' from Sir William Garrard, more rose-water from Lady Mordaunt and ale from Lord Rich.

Soon afterwards Petre collapsed. Andrews visited him seven times between 5 and 16 April, when physicians took over. Clement and Hills appeared on the 16th, Clement and Symons† from the 19th to the 22nd (the latter twice in one day), then Symons alone but almost daily till 10 May. In the next few days more physicians were called in—Caldwell, Wendy and Langton. The patient's condition must have been grave. The crisis seems to have passed after the 25th, when only Caldwell and Symons continued to attend. Convalescence in the country was agreed upon, and a saddler made 'a large double harness for the litter horse of neat's leather, with eight great rings of iron, three staples of iron for the sumpter saddles' and ancillary equipment elaborately described. Then, on 5 June, 13s. 8d. was paid 'to the litter man for the hire of himself and his two horses carrying my master to his house at Ingatestone'. He was safely home. The fight for his life in 1559 had succeeded. The story fills many lines of the anxious steward's script. It is evident that the stone, or

---

* Cloth, perhaps cotton velvet, made in Genoa (cf. 'fustian of Naples, apparently a kind of cotton velvet', O.E.D.). A sixteenth-century truss is illustrated in F. N. L. Poynter, *Selected Writings of William Clowes* (1948), plate v.

† Symons was apparently stepfather to John Donne, the poet, and was related to Clement (*Notes and Queries* (1954), 199, 412–14, 465–7). The author, Mr. Baird Whitlock, replying to Mr. Swain, stated that the Petre entries verified that the Symons–Clement association was closer than he had believed and they showed that Clement did not go into exile as a Catholic for at least a year after Elizabeth's accession. It was apparently the same Symons who attended Lady Catherine Grey on her deathbed in Hopton's house in Suffolk (*Dom. Cal.*, 1547–80, 304).

urinary lithiasis, from which Petre had long suffered, was suddenly aggravated, as a result of which many herbal mixtures and palliative remedies were prescribed. The April bill from the apothecary (one Ryche) is set out in detail. The items range from 5 April to 31 May, the majority being sent during the dangerous middle period: 'Maidenhair 2d., scolopender 2d., a box of unguentum album 8d., hartstongue 3d., alum 1d., a purgation and my pains for bringing it 6s. 8d., mercury 2d., syrup of vinegar 11d., white sugar candy 2d., six urinals 15d., a skin of red leather 6d., a clyster and for my pains 6s. 8d., a box of conserved cherries 6d., a box of ointment 2s., a lb. of barley 12d., a quart glass with water made with barley and certain other roots to make almond milk 12d., allocium to gargle with 12d., a box of white lozenges 12d., a sponge 6d., plantain water and honeysuckle water 6d., a box of perfume 2s., half stick of cassia 9d.'* In addition, more barley water and syrup of vinegar was sent on several days. The second and final bill, also copied out by the steward, covers the period to 3 June. Remedies which did not appear in the earlier bill include: 4 oz. syrup for the rheum 12d., 9 oz. syrup of succory with rhubarb 5s. 2d., a box of peppers 20d., a box of 'dia citoniton' 2s., a plaster for the stomach 5s., a plaster for the side 2s. 8d.; stuff prepared to carry into Essex, viz. 6 oz. syrup of white vinegar 16d., 2 lb. barley 16d., 4 oz. 'ceny alexandrie' 12d., 2 oz. galingale 8d., 2 oz. eryngus dry 8d., ½ lb. aniseeds 10d., ½ lb. 'colyander' seeds 4d., ½ lb. liquorice 2d. On 30 May Symons sent his own personal palliative: 'an herb called paspere being good for the stone'.

The apothecary's two bills, which amounted to 62s. 6d., illustrate prevailing reliance on polypharmacy, the mixing of many allied ingredients in a prescription with the hope that at least one would cure or relieve. From this plethora of herbs, oils, liquids and ointments prescribed for plaster and purges, it is clear that the Court surgeons shunned the only way of curing Petre's condition, by cutting for the stone, then a dangerous but not at all necessarily fatal operation; it was practised by peripatetic specialists, some of whom achieved great manual dexterity but were unqualified.†

Petre was back at work early in September. The malady continued to victimize him in the winter, though physicians' and surgeons' fees were lighter. Edmund Tyrell brought 'certain roots calls eryngus, good for the stone'; another neighbour sent 'a powder good to break the stone'; 5d.

---

* For some of the lesser known pharmaceutical terms, see Appendix I.

† 'Cutting for the stone' was known from early times. A pupil of Vigo of Padua described a modification of the operation in 1524 (Z. Cope, *William Cheselden* (1953), 19). Would it be that Vannes sought information there about this procedure (p. 250)?

was spent on buying 'hogsclaws to make powder for my master' (and later 'a mortar to stamp hogsclaws'); the apothecary supplied 'a box of ointment for the stone'; 10s. was given to 'one of Braynford [Brentford] by my master's commandment in reward for teaching my master certain medicines for the stone and brought certain things with him'. In the summer of 1560 Mr. Justice Browne of South Weald sent 'a medicine for the stone in a bottle', and 'a box filled with dried sampere' (samphire), believed to be a remedy for it, came from Lord Cobham, son of the former Deputy of Calais. In the last weeks of the previous winter Sir William had applied for an invalid's licence to eat flesh during Lent: 'the Lord Mayor's officers for a bill to suffer my master's Lenten stuff to pass'.

With the advent of the winter of 1560–1 he was again in medical hands; on 17 November he was visited by Caldwell and three unnamed surgeons, after which two electuaries arrived from an apothecary. Although soon active again, he marked the festive Twelfth Day in sober fashion by giving 10s. to 'one Toye a printer for a book of physic called Opera Montani bound in board'.* On the same day he paid Andrews 26s. 8d. for 'a box of unguentum album rasi 8d., a box of wood filled with feni cheni and a box of tin therewith filled 5s., a plaster called Jacob's plaster 12d., all which were sent to Ingatestone'. The invalid was making certain that he could treat himself next time he was down in Essex, and he went a stage further some weeks later in persuading Vicary to 'show him how to make the plaster called the Ceres plaster', which despite the mythological touch was in fact made of ceruse, or white lead: prudent man, to take such precautions in advance of the royal progress. In the event, the Queen's visit and Catherine Petre's marriage seemed to pass off without his requiring further medical help.

Although he often remained in London during the dangerous summer months to transact business in the law courts, he was apparently never a victim of smallpox or other infectious diseases which were the scourge of the overcrowded capital. He possessed spectacles from at least 1559, but there is nothing later to suggest that his sight was failing. The first hint of deafness had occurred during Mary's progress in 1554: 'Mr Paris' man, a plaster to lay to my master's feet, being good to preserve his hearing; to the poticary for frankincense and certain oils delivered at Winchester and Windsor for my master's ears'. The shilling paid in 1562 to a barber 'for things brought by him for my master's teeth' is a solitary item (the barber often undertook crude dentistry). Surprisingly, perhaps, Petre never

---

* The writer, Giovanni Battista da Monte (1498–1551), had also been a sufferer from 'les douleurs de pierre' and a section of his work is devoted to urinary disorders.

seems to have been bled, for this treatment was regarded almost as a general panacea.*

A single attendance usually cost 5s. or 6s. 8d. There apparently was little distinction between physicians' and surgeons' fees, whether they were in the royal service or not. The grave illness in 1559 cost him £20, of which £17 was for professional fees and the balance for pharmaceutical stuff.

Petre's intermittent struggle against ill health shows him in a creditable light. Physical discomfort, alternating with severe pain, was often his lot, and riding with the peregrinating Court must sometimes have racked him. Most of his complaints, while perhaps alleviated, probably remained uncured. The slightly pinched look in his portraits, according to medical experts, bears testimony to many years' suffering with the maladies which have been mentioned.

He had now reached mellow years despite precarious health. The Queen had stayed at his 'poor house', as the Elizabethan magnate habitually described his home. The half year after Petre's return to official duties on 9 October was one of the busiest periods of his life according to the steward's record of journeys between Aldersgate and the Court and the Star Chamber weekly diet accounts.† He was appointed, with Bacon, Cecil, Mason and Wotton, to investigate the Merchant Adventurers' petition about their declining business and other foreign trade affairs.[3] There was no Christmas visit to Ingatestone and Council sessions were interrupted only for a few days. In the last week of January 1562 he was sick again. 'Mr. Baltroppe the surgeon' attended him on five days and Vicary once. He may have been the last patient of Vicary, who died a few days afterwards. The final entry for this illness runs: 'The surgeon and the apothecary. For 4 oz. oil of vetres [vitriol] 3s. 4d., 2 oz. oil of roses 12d., 4 oz. letarche [litharge] 12d., 1½ oz. serous [ceruse] 8d., 2 oz. wax 6d., 4 oz. venecreke [fenugreek] 4d., 4 oz. linseed 4d., marsh mallows 2d. To the surgeon for making a plaster of the aforesaid parcels 2s. 8d., and for

---

* 'To a surgeon letting Mistress Dorothy's blood 3s. 4d.' is the sole reference to the practice. Drs. Owen, Wendy and Huick bled Princess Elizabeth (Elizabeth Jenkins, *Elizabeth the Great* (1958), 54).

† The latter (P.R.O., E407/53) begin properly this year and name those present. Although the names include some judges who were not privy councillors and several of the dates when Petre sat in the court were non-council days, further research would be needed to ascertain if his appearances were in the capacity of councillor or judge. He was in constant attendance in Michaelmas 1561 and Easter 1562 terms, but not in Hilary 1562. Thereafter his appearances were less regular. If they represent judicial work, his last attendance as a judge in the Court of Star Chamber was on 12 July 1565, the concluding session of Trinity term.

four earthen pans to make the salve 6*d*.' Back to work, he had as many as eighteen meetings at Lambeth between 13 February and 21 March, with as many visits to the Court. Apart perhaps for one or two days spent on the small commission on Catherine Grey's marriage, he was probably advising Parker and the 'Commissioners in Causes Ecclesiastical' —the notorious Court of High Commission which had been nominated by the Queen under the Act of Supremacy. Most of its sessions were held at Lambeth, but the records of its early proceedings are lost. It would be logical that Petre, canon lawyer and still custodian of the ecclesiastical seal, should have held some unrecorded appointment with the commission, to which he was formally added a few weeks later.[4] He was reaching the climax of work. On St. George's Eve (22 April) his itinerary was 'to Westminster, thence to Lambeth, thence to the Court, thence to London'. Leaving the Archbishop's Palace, after a morning session in the Council or Star Chamber,[5] he took part in the usual preliminary meetings of the Order of the Garter. Machyn recorded him as present on St. George's Day,[6] but a reliable narrative of the proceedings for 1561–4 named him present on the 22nd though ill on the next two days.[7] Caldwell (who became Petre's next-door tenant in Aldersgate Street) and two apothecaries administered a variety of clysters, oils and ointments. The patient recovered sufficiently to take a change of air at Ingatestone near the end of May. The round of duties was soon resumed, e.g. on 5 June, 'to Westminster, thence to the Court, and so to the Temple'.

Shortly afterwards he went on a secret mission to Durham Place in the Strand, the residence of de Quadra, the Spanish ambassador, whose insinuation into Elizabeth's confidence had been alarming Cecil for some time. De Quadra's house was a rendezvous of conspirators who came and went by the back watergate. And he himself was the arch-plotter. Cecil however held his own by counter-espionage. On 20 March de Quadra had written to the King: 'Yesterday Mason and Petre came to see me from the Queen, and told me that she had sent an ambassador to your Majesty's Court to maintain friendship, but that he and his servants had received such rough treatment in Spain, their trunks being broken open and some imprisoned, that she thinks her honour will not permit her to suffer it. Although I fancy Mason and Petre thought the occasion hardly one to take so much to heart.'[8] Petre's accounts show that he had also been at Durham Place on the previous day. Events took a dramatic turn early in June when de Quadra's secretary betrayed his master's diplomatic dealings to Cecil. It disclosed the identity of Catholic noblemen who had been conspiring with de Quadra. On the 20th 'boathire to Durham Place' occurs again. Elizabeth and Dudley were incensed that their secret

intrigues with de Quadra were now known to the councillors, who demanded his recall. Cecil and Petre were nauseated with the whole affair.
With his long experience in handling awkward situations, Petre probably
advised de Quadra to lie low if he wished to soften the Secretary's wrath.
He remained at the Court, but was discredited with Elizabeth, and Cecil's
position was strengthened. A buck came from the royal park at Woodstock, which could be construed as a tribute to Petre's diplomacy.

His old enemy evidently intervened after the Council at Greenwich
on 21 June. The pain led him to tip the boatman to row faster upstream.
He had recourse to apothecary's pills next day, shortly after which he
was in Essex. His journey back to London on 16 July was not spontaneous. Northampton, Arundel, Bedford, Petre and Wotton were summoned to Court 'for such causes as the Queen's Majesty would have them
consult of'.[9] This group was deputed a fortnight later to consult together
on some weighty matter about which the record is silent but probably
concerned naval and military action to be taken as a result of the savage
outbreak of civil war between Catholics and Huguenots in France.
Petre was wanted as one of those recently nominated to advise the
Queen because the situation there had suddenly deteriorated. 'Her
Majesty', Cecil had recorded, 'did choose the Lord Keeper Bacon, the Earls
of Arundel and Pembroke, Mr. Petre, Mr. Mason and me. This choice
was her own.'[10] The Protestant cause was desperate, and England was
asked for aid, Le Havre and Dieppe being offered as securities for Calais.
Petre was one of several advisers at home assigned to the commander-in-
chief, the Earl of Warwick (Lord Robert Dudley's elder brother).[11]

On 14 August he again had to exchange Council chair for bed. Crowe
the surgeon paid him three visits in the next few days. Back at Ingatestone
soon afterwards, the invalid dealt with some official correspondence from
the sickroom. In October the Queen fell critically ill with smallpox. Her
councillors in London were urgently summoned to Hampton Court. She
recovered, to the relief of the nation. Within a few days Petre returned to
London in physical discomfort, a chair and ironwork for his litter having
been hastily made. After a week's work he collapsed again at Westminster and his old friend Mason brought him home to Aldersgate, but he
resumed duties three weeks later, when the French ambassador's complaints were 'satisfied' by Clinton, Petre and Mason.[12]

The cost of the French war forced Elizabeth to summon her second
Parliament. The writs were issued early in November, whereupon Lord
Rich had ideas of his own about the representation of Essex. He sought to
procure the election of his eldest son in place of Petre. Rich had written
to Petre to enquire if 'he was minded to stand in this election', but he was

17. TOMB OF SIR WILLIAM AND LADY PETRE IN
INGATESTONE CHURCH

Sᵗ John Petre; Created
Baron Petre of Writle in Essex
Iᵗ 41. Obᵗ ÿ 11 of Octᵇʳ 1613

18. SIR JOHN PETRE
circa 1590

'not minded', deciding perhaps to retire in dignified fashion rather than be ousted by a younger man. Characteristically, he 'gave a modest answer' that he had never 'laboured' to win the seat. Incensed by Rich's tactless canvassing of family interests, the Council sent a stern remonstrance to Leighs Priory on 27 November. 'Although nature may move you to prefer your son, yet seeing he hath a place as your heir apparent in the higher house, and may also if you would by other good means be in the lower house', they censured the old peer for intervening against their 'reasonable desires'. Cecil had enjoyed himself making caustic amendments to the draft. So Petre, still *persona grata* with the magnates, was returned once more for Essex, with Cecil's father-in-law as his partner again; and Rich, two years later, provided an *alma mater* for other people's sons by founding Felsted School on his Essex estate.[13]

On 6 December 1562 Kyme entered Petre's study in the town house with the account-book. The steward watched him scan the pages for the previous month, run his quill down each, and add 'Payd—William Petre' at the foot: fourteen pages to examine, far more than usual. An item at the end caught his eye: 'Essex. Disbursed for my master's part of the charges in the Election of the Knights for that Shire, besides certain of my master's own provision, £4 8s. 3d.' Perhaps he uttered a low chuckle and with pen poised let his thoughts dwell on the rebuff Rich had earned. At any rate, he absent-mindedly scored through the two last entries in error. Writing 'stet', he certified his approval. The audit was done and Kyme left the room. Petre sat alone, reflecting for a while on the satisfactory state of his finances. But the evening was chilly. He closed the book, put it in the chest, snuffed out the candles and joined his wife in the parlour.*

2 Last Years at Court

In an age when prudent men guarded their tongues closely, Petre was outstanding in practising the virtue of silence. Positive expressions of opinion by him are rare survivals; they are characteristically absent from his own archives. But one has been preserved in literature and comes from the pen of Roger Ascham, who had entered Cambridge at fifteen and became one of Cheke's notable scholars. Then for two years he was

---

* The writer may perhaps be excused for momentarily combining fancy with fact, as this marks the end of the fine series of account-books. Kyme returned a few years later to Lewes, where he had bought the Greyfriars in 1557 and rebuilt it as the Friars; his will, dated 1570, reveals him as man of substance and mentions a room 'called Lady Garrard's chamber' in his chief house in Lewes. He wa buried at All Saints, Lewes, in 1585 (see p. 51n.). Kyme was succeeded by William Hudson.

tutor to the maiden Elizabeth. At the end of 1549 he abruptly resigned this post and returned to Cambridge. Before Edward's death he had been nominated as Latin secretary through the combined influence of Cheke and Cecil. On Mary's accession his chief concern was to recover the appointment which an avowed Protestant had little hope of obtaining except by the intervention of friends. He sought help from both Gardiner and Petre. Despite Ascham's strong adherence to the reformed religion, his literary abilities had earned Gardiner's kindly interest. In a long Latin letter to Petre he dwelt on the modest level of his own talents, likewise on the success with which they might be crowned through Petre's counsel, and expressed thanks for his promise of the salary of 40 marks a year which Vannes had received as Latin secretary.

On Christmas Day Ascham wrote to Petre for financial aid. He might well be anxious about importuning a man whose 'care for common affairs' gave little leisure for his own. Ascham also approached the Chancellor again, sending him an unusual New Year's gift in the form of a Roman gold coin and concluding hopefully that he believed Petre would soon try to settle him in his Court duties. Addressing Gardiner once more in January 1554, he harped on Petre's unmistakable signs of friendly influence. But neither office nor fee had materialized and the scholar was desolate. 'Since the time that your lordship', he wrote to Gardiner, 'did commend me unto the Queen's majesty, Mr. Petre hath conceived such good will towards me, that he hath many times said unto me that he would stay me in this court, and would therefore speak to the Queen's majesty.'[14]

About the same time he sent Petre another lengthy Latin epistle about Osorius, the author of De Nobilitate civili Christiana, a copy of which, printed at Lisbon twelve years earlier, he presented to his patron: a nice compliment from a Cambridge latinist to an Oxford legalist. But, as it happened, it was not reserved solely for him, for two very similar letters of Ascham's reveal how copies of Osorius were also offered to Paget and Pole during these weary months of waiting.[15] Probably Petre was unaware of the other copies and he evidently did his best when opportunity allowed for his less fortunate friend, who at last secured from Mary the Latin secretaryship. He had been a persistent petitioner, drawn by penury to sycophancy. Ascham's patent of office, when written out, had a somewhat long blank for insertion of the annual fee. 'The space which is left by chance', he wrote beseechingly to the Chancellor, 'doth seem to crave by good luck some words of length, as viginti or triginta, yea, with the help of a little dash quadraginta would serve best of all.' And decem, he added, was impossibly short. Gardiner, to whom the impoverished scholar's grim humour doubtless appealed, saw to it that the scrivener filled in the coveted *quadraginta*, which procured Ascham an annual salary of 40 marks. In 1557 Petre also obtained for him from the Queen at a low rent the reversion of a lease of the manor of Salisbury Hall in Walthamstow, Essex, for forty years to begin in 1564.[16]

Ascham had few friends at Court, but dining at the Principal Secretaries' table must have given him ample opportunity for congenial talk of books. 'Lent to Mr. Ascham by my master to be repaid at Michaelmas next, £5' is entered by Petre's steward on 20 June 1556 (as well as a note of the discharge of the loan on time), and on 30 June, 'Paid to Mr. Askeham for a book called The Nature of Metals bought, 12s.' This has not been identified and may have been a manuscript, possibly Richard Eden's translation of *De Natura Magneti*, published eighteen years later. Was Ascham in need of more money? On Elizabeth's accession there were more clamorous letters; he regained the Latin post and was installed anew as the Queen's tutor.

In the late summer of 1563 London had been scourged by the plague, to which Cecil referred on 27 August. 'I am glad, right glad', he wrote to Petre, 'that being so much afraid, God hath comforted [strengthened] you so well, as notwithstanding the appearance of so much danger, you, my lady, and all yours have been so well preserved, and so I wish you long continuance of God's favour.'[17] The Court had left the infested capital for Windsor Castle. There on 10 December Cecil entertained his friends to dinner and a topic of their discussion is preserved in literary annals by one of them. The guests were, Ascham related, Petre, Mason, Wotton, Sackville Treasurer of the Exchequer, Sir Walter Mildmay Chancellor of the Exchequer, Mr. Haddon Master of Requests, Mr. John Astley Master of the Jewel House, Mr. Bernard Hampton, Mr. Nicasius, 'and I'. He deemed himself fortunate to be 'in the company of so many wise and good men together, as hardly then could have been picked out again in all England', a modest remark from one who had been his host's senior at Cambridge over twenty years ago. There was strange news, Cecil remarked, that some boys of Eton had run away for fear of beating. He thought that excessive corporal punishment drove scholars to hate learning before they understood its meaning. 'Mr. Petre, as one somewhat severe of nature, said plainly that the rod only was the sword that must keep the school in obedience and the scholar in good order.' Wotton, however, agreed with Cecil. Haddon, a notable Cambridge scholar and like Petre a civilian, concurred with him and quoted 'the best schoolmaster of their time', who was also 'the greatest beater'. This was the renowned Nicholas Udall, a former headmaster of Eton. Then Ascham gave his own opinion, Cecil drawing him on as a good host should: children, he felt, should be attracted to learning, and that by love rather than the rod. After dinner Ascham read Greek with the Queen. Later in the evening Sackville came to him. 'I would not for a good deal of money', he declared, 'have been this day absent at dinner.' He recalled how his flogging schoolmaster had driven out all love of learning, and urged Ascham to write a book on the subject. And so it is this dinner party which gave rise to *The Scholemaster*. He completed it in 1566, but it was not published until 1570, two years after his death.

In the treatment of their eldest sons, what is now known of the two Sir Williams does not accord with their remarks on chastisement of scholars. The youthful delinquencies of Thomas Cecil whilst abroad in 1561-2 may perhaps be excused by the present-day psychologist as resulting from his father's narrow-minded discipline. So unrelenting were Cecil's feelings that he even contemplated asking Throckmorton to commit Thomas secretly to some 'sharp' prison in Paris.[18] In contrast, when the stern Petre of the Ascham story seven years later gave his own son free choice of a wife, his attitude was remarkably liberal for the period; and Petre was an older man than Cecil.

From 1563 onwards Petre's gradually decreasing activities are not easy to follow, and there are further long gaps in the Council minutes. In May he was appointed with Winchester and Mildmay on yet another commission for the sale of Crown lands, a reminder that the monastic estates were still crumbling away under the unceasing pressure of debt. Ironically, the selected salesmen were active agents of the days when the royal chest was being filled with church treasure. They were engaged for two years in further disposals.[19] Petre's advice and that of old Wotton was called for in connection with the half-hearted demand for the return of Calais.[20] In 1564 he was busy at Westminster on one of his numerous commissions in the early part of the long vacation,[21] and he was among the five councillors who remained in London while the Queen stayed at Greenwich and Cambridge.[22]

In the autumn Petre, Mason and Cecil (in that order) were chosen to settle with the Spanish ambassador a new Anglo-Flemish commercial treaty concerning in particular the vital cloth exports,[23] and he was still involved in the negotiations in July 1565.[24] The Council referred a petition from the 'poor artificers' of the Company of Clothworkers to Petre, Cave, Mason and Sackville; their complaint was that many of them had been thrown out of work because the Merchant Adventurers were selling more and more undressed cloths abroad.[25] He sat with the Council fairly constantly from September 1564 to July 1565.

A curious, anonymous missive was addressed to him in March 1566. Tearing it open, he found inside another letter which the nameless sender declared he had discovered 'very early in the morning as I went from Paul's church by Paul's wharf to the water by the tavern there. It was sewn with black Paris silk. No creature was by, so I took and read it and was never so afraid in my life.' He besought Petre to deliver it to the Queen. Petre took the right course in handing it to Cecil, as his endorsement, dated two days later, bears witness: 'This writing was delivered to me by Sir William Petre. I read it to the Queen at Greenwich.' There doubtless it was destroyed, and what so terrified the citizen remains unknown.[26]

The intermittent evidence of the defective Council Register shows that Petre had now irrevocably withdrawn from the centre of public life, but his advice was still valued.[27] By May he realized that he could no longer support even the role of Elder Statesman, and he wrote on the 21st from his town house to Cecil, the opening phrase referring perhaps to Catherine Grey (p. 248):

Because I find myself not able to go abroad, I am bold by these few lines both to give you my most hearty thanks for your assured good friendship in my late suit, for the which I do and shall during my life think myself most bounden unto you, and also to let you understand that albeit I find myself well recovered (I thank God) of my fever, yet there remaineth my old deafness. I account myself unfit to be in any company. I propose (as soon as I shall feel myself able) to go in a litter to Ingatestone with such remedies as the physicians do prepare for me as well for that as for a rheum falling from my head to my shoulders; I am persuaded that the open air will do me good as I think it would also do you if you might be spared. Of this my propose I thought only to let you understand, trusting you will use it as you shall see cause.[28]

The old, undemonstrative level-headedness remained: there were no reflections, no complaints, no regrets in this valediction. He reckoned himself unfit for company. It was almost exactly thirty years since that summer's day when Convocation had conceded his right to preside over their assembly. After three decades of political, economic and religious revolutions, the ageing official was revealing his innate modesty and sound sense by proposing to retire. A little later he was resting at his country manor, where he was visited by the Rector of Exeter College (p. 283); and Larke's detailed survey of the mansion and the great estate survey were made while Petre was there. But he did not give up immediately. By October, when the Council minutes were resumed, he was in the accustomed seat, though only once that month. Had he been tempted to return because two of his Henrician colleagues were among the company

—Sir Walter Mildmay, admitted for the first time, and Sir Ralph Sadler, back at Court after three years' absence? Recorded meetings during the next six months were at much longer intervals than in recent years; in the scrappy minutes his name occurs again in December.

In October 1566 he was appointed a member of the House of Commons committee on the succession question. A few weeks later he was concerned with the Duke of Norfolk and Cecil in the renewed negotiations between Elizabeth and Charles Archduke of Austria; but in the end she rejected every suitor and so avoided the matrimonial tragedies of the two Maries.[29]

Petre's last known attendance at the Privy Council was on 12 February 1567. Three months later there begins a three-year hiatus in the register, but it was probably in February that he decided to terminate his conciliar service, which he had given to the State continuously under four sovereigns for twenty-four years. On that winter day the man who had always assiduously cultivated the art of survival was the sole relic of Henry VIII's advisers present. Those with him at Westminster were younger men—Bacon, Bedford, Dudley (now Earl of Leicester), Knollys, Howard of Effingham, Cecil; all except the last two had been appointed since Elizabeth's accession. Most of Petre's colleagues in Henry's and Edward's Councils were dead—the great churchmen Cranmer, Gardiner, Tunstall and Thirlby; Secretaries Wriothesley and Paget; the diplomats Wotton, Mason and Hoby; the lawyers Baker and North (Rich was to live only till the summer). Some of Petre's Catholic colleagues of Mary's time had also died, including Rochester, Waldegrave, Southwell and Sackville; others, like Heath and Englefield, had been obliged to go into obscurity or exile. Of the few survivors from earlier years, Northampton and Pembroke were both absent in the winter of 1567. Arundel had been under house arrest, and his dangerous intrigues later led to further imprisonment. The octogenarian Winchester, the Lord Treasurer, appeared at the Board in March, after a long absence; he, too, then seems to have succumbed to advancing years. Smith had temporarily returned from France but was sent out again in that month. At this February meeting it is doubtful whether Petre had any bond of friendship with the others, apart from Cecil. A similar picture of a lonely Secretary, dated the previous summer (1566), has recently been drawn. It portrays Cecil seated among young strangers except for a few friends and those mostly in decay: 'Winchester was a doddering old man, Northampton almost a nonentity; Arundel was out of favour; Petre deaf as a post and though he remained titular Secretary until 1566 he had long ceased to function. Cecil, in short, though he was only forty-six years old, was one of the veterans.'[30] It was probably he who, on receiving Petre's letter of the preceding May, had persuaded him to return for another spell.

After a second session, the Parliament elected in 1563 and prorogued, was dissolved in January 1567, and Petre's release from duties in the Commons may well have been the final factor in his decision to retire from the government. He had served in Parliament without a break since 1542, possibly from 1536. No other sitting member had been elected so many times. Sir Francis Knollys's long tenure from at least 1542 (he said he sat in the Reformation Parliament in 1534) was broken by exile under Mary. Sadler, too, had sat since 1542 but not in Mary's Parliaments. Petre was undoubtedly the Father of the House in their eyes. Owing to the paucity of parliamentary papers, his share in drafting Tudor Acts can never be traced. His long administrative experience and knowledge of tactics had proved 'invaluable to the Queen in the House' during the Parliament of 1563–7.[31]

If he was no longer at Court he was still a privy councillor and he had not finished with public affairs. In June 1567 he was one of several commissioned by the Council to decide a matrimonial cause.[32] Early in the next year the Chapter of Wells wrote to Petre that their absentee dean refused to compound for non-residence. As a Wells annuitant of thirty years, albeit a trifling £2, Petre's influence in redressing their grievance was sought. He acted promptly, and in confirming the dean's offence recommended Cecil to intervene. Although wishing the Secretary continued health, Petre did not refer to his own.[33]

In May 1568 Mary Queen of Scots fled across the border to seek refuge in England. To discuss her case Elizabeth appointed Norfolk, Sussex and Sadler to meet commissioners from Scotland at York. Norfolk, first convinced of Mary's complicity in Darnley's murder, later began to scheme to marry her. The Queen transferred the enquiry to Westminster. The grave situation led to the decision on 30 October that 'the rest of the Council absent be sent for', Petre being among the seven named.[34] The assembly did not number him among them, when they met next month.

Exactly a year later, on 25 November 1569, he appeared at a special session of the Essex justices of the peace at Chelmsford. It was at least twenty-five years since he had first been included in the commission of the peace for his adopted county; as councillor-landowner his name was fourth, even in October 1544, only the Earl of Oxford, Lord Morley and Sir Richard Rich ranking in front of him.[35] Six months before this appointment he had received his earliest official recognition in Essex, when he became a county commissioner for sewers for the river later known as the Roding, a tributary of the Thames in south-west Essex.[36]

In May 1547 Petre became Custos Rotulorum for Essex,[37] and he retained the office till his death. This honourable appointment, said to date from 1390, was to be held, according to an Act of 1545, by a justice of the peace with knowledge and learning, described in 1581 as 'a very special justice, especially picked out either for wisdom, countenance or credit'.[38] With a solitary exception, Petre's name never occurs, even after his final retirement to Essex, in the many lists of justices present at the ordinary quarter sessions or assizes,* and there is no hint in his accounts or in other records that he attended these courts. 'In times past', John Carrowe the Clerk of the Peace wrote to him in 1555, 'you have been offended with me that I have not immediately after the sessions repaired to you with report of the doings there', tactfully adding that he did not forget he owed his appointment to Petre as Custos Rotulorum.[39] Carrowe enclosed an account of fines assessed at the quarter sessions at Chelmsford, and complained of the corrupt conduct of William Bendlowes of Great Bardfield, who became a serjeant-at-law in that year. By his will, proved in 1564, Carrowe bequeathed the (law) 'books appertaining to my office' to Petre.[40] Petre's name is writ large in national politics, but like others he regarded the office of Custos Rotulorum as a sinecure and he neglected his duties as a county justice; in contrast, his son John was an active member of the Essex Bench in later years.

It is curious, therefore, that almost the sole evidence of Sir William's attendance as a justice of the peace should be his last recorded public appearance. The special sessions held in many counties in November 1569 to secure the subscription of every justice to the Act of Uniformity were convened on the government's instructions after the serious rising of the Northern Earls. It was an anti-Catholic test. That the aged Petre felt it imperative to journey to Chelmsford is a criterion of the gravity of the national alarm.[41] The Essex subscription list is headed by Robert Lord Rich and John Lord Darcy, joint Lords Lieutenant, and by Petre on a line of his own doubtless as Custos Rotulorum. It is a very shaky signature (page 265). Among the others present, Cooke later followed him as Custos, Smith and Mildmay replaced Petre and Cooke as the Essex M.P.s and Smith succeeded as Chancellor of the Garter.

---

* The exception is that for Easter quarter sessions, April 1564 (Lord Mordaunt, Lord Rich, Lord Darcy, Petre, Anthony Browne, Cooke, Serjeant Bendlowes, Thomas Mildmay and eight others); a recognisance for appearance at sessions was taken before Petre in Oct. 1564 (E.R.O., Q/SR 10/32, 12/12). The Essex sessions rolls survive for 1556–7, 1562–3, thence almost complete from 1564; the Essex assize files, from 1558 almost complete (typescript calendars of both series are available in E.R.O.).

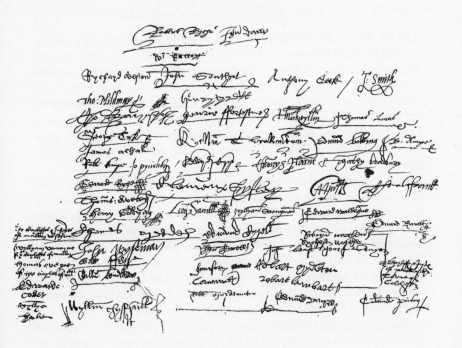

ESSEX JUSTICES OF THE PEACE, 1569

Signatures at a Special Sessions at Chelmsford for subscribing obedience to the Act of Uniformity.

CHAPTER XIV

Man of Fortune and Charity

1 The Building-up of Two Great Estates

ALL Dr. Petre owned in Essex at the time of his second marriage in 1541 or 1542 to Anne Browne, widow of John Tyrell of Heron Hall, was the original nucleus of the Ingatestone estate, together with his earlier acquisition, the small manor of Bayhouse in West Thurrock. Anne had several manors and some money. Soon afterwards Petre began to invest heavily in the land market, mainly though not exclusively in the Ingatestone area. How he continued over a period of thirty years to build up two great estates in Essex and Devon is a story in itself, and only a brief outline follows.*

In the middle of the sixteenth century land, wardships, farming stock and plate were still the main channels for the surplus capital of a man not engaged in commerce (Petre's share in the Muscovy Company in 1555 was a very minor stake). Ownership of an estate was also the key to social ascendancy, and Essex was an attractive field for investment. John Norden, near the end of the century, was to acclaim it 'most fat, fruitful and full of profitable things exceeding any other shires for the general commodities',[1] and the result of recent research is in keeping with Norden's high praise of the fertility and prosperity of the county.[2]

The first substantial addition was the manor of East Horndon, adjacent to the Tyrell manor of Heron Hall.[3] The new estate, once belonging to Waltham Abbey, had become one of Cromwell's many properties. On his attainder it was granted, among other manors, to Anne of Cleves for life. Petre soon obtained the reversion for £412. In 1544 he persuaded her to lease it to him for £30 a year. Rent paid to her occurs regularly in his accounts until her death in 1557, when he became the owner. He kept East Horndon Hall in his own hands and the family occasionally lived there, but the farm served mainly to supply Ingatestone. The house itself formed three sides of a quadrangle, had inner and base courts, apparently not walled in, and gardens, dovecote and two big barns.[4] In 1544-5 the manor of Bluntswalls in Mountnessing, to the south of Ingatestone, was purchased for £192 from the Crown, which also granted the manor and park of Crondon in Stock, near Ingatestone, together with the manor of

* This aspect has been fully covered by W. R. Emerson's unpublished Oxford D.Phil. thesis (1951), 'The Economic Development of the Estates of the Petre Family in Essex, 1540-1640', based on the Petre archives in the E.R.O., to which he presented a copy.

266

Peldon near Colchester and three manors in Gloucestershire and Kent, Petre having given up several small non-Essex properties and paid £303 in money. In 1546 he acquired from Rich the manor of Cowbridge in Mountnessing for £453, and from the Crown the rectory of that parish with the nearby demesnes of Thoby Priory, together with a Devon manor, paying £177 in cash and surrendering Peldon and £17 in monastic annuities. Also in Mountnessing was the manor of Bacons, which was divided from that of Ingatestone by the stream running close to the Hall; on the opposite side of his seat lay the manor of Margaretting; both manors were added in 1548 at a cost of £1,262. With these and some smaller properties, many fair acres around the former Barking Abbey manor were now in Petre's possession; but not all had been monastic lands.

He continued to consolidate the extensive estate in the heart of the county. The great manor and lordship of Writtle, with the manor of Boyton, Writtle and Horsefrith Parks, and a weekly market and two annual fairs were received in 1554 in consideration of his services to the Crown and of his surrender of some Glastonbury Abbey lands in Somerset and Devon,[5] for which he had paid the Crown £1,555 some months before Edward's death;[6] the low Crown valuation of Writtle was very favourable to Petre (p. 270). He was in a privileged position to secure this substantial estate—that from which his son's peerage was to take its name. He had been commissioned to look into the decayed revenues of the Writtle lordship, and only six months before acquiring it he had obtained the Crown offices of chief steward, receiver, bailiff and park-keeper, which gave him £17 15s. a year.

In 1554 he purchased for £440 the manors of Mashbury and Matching, three and ten miles respectively beyond Writtle. In 1562-3 the manors of Chignal St. Mary and St. James, linking the Writtle and Mashbury lands, were bought for £1,200, and the manor of Friern in Nevendon, which had belonged to St. Mary's-without-Bishopsgate, dissolved by Petre in 1539. The last was an isolated property, well beyond East Horndon and farther from his main seat: when an advantageous investment arose he took it even if it was outside the periphery of his existing estate. Another such property, bought for £840 in 1568, comprised two manors in Clavering and Langley in the north-west corner of Essex. Finally, only a month before his own death, Petre paid Sir Lewis, third Lord Mordaunt (son of Sir John, second Lord Mordaunt, who died in 1571), £2,000 for a scattered estate in the south of the county containing the manors of Ingrave (between Ingatestone and East Horndon), Cranham and Great Bromfords in Nevendon.

Such were Petre's chief Essex properties. He had thus risen rapidly to be one of the largest landowners in the county (only the Earl of Oxford, Lord Darcy and Lord Rich had somewhat bigger estates).[7] But that was not all. In the course of years he had also laid the foundations of a very large independent estate in Devon. The important and lucrative manor of South Brent and that of Churchstow, both Buckfast Abbey properties, were secured from the Crown in 1546 partly in exchange for his Clatercote and Peldon lands (p. 186) partly by purchase and partly by gift; the last element only amounted to £35 out of £138, the annual value of Brent.[8] An outlay of £1,106 in 1554 brought him the manors of Shute and Southleigh, the first instalment of his buying up almost the entire Devon estates of the Duke of Suffolk, attainted after Wyatt's rebellion. By the time of his death, Petre's investments in Devon, Somerset and Dorset had cost him over £7,000, and he then held seventeen manors and some smaller properties in his native county and the West, as well as a few other manors in the counties of Gloucester, Hertford, Cambridge, Suffolk and Norfolk. In the thirty-four years between the date of his original purchase of Bayhouse in 1537 and his last acquisition in 1571, Petre's net expenditure on lands was approximately £22,000, an average of £638 a year. He owned at the end of his life, in round figures, nearly 20,000 acres in Essex and well over 20,000 acres in the West; a total of about 45,000 acres, if the isolated properties are also included.*

The combined salaries, fees and perquisites of his public offices had furnished Sir William with a satisfactory income. While his perquisites were small in comparison with those of more avaricious associates, his position in successive governments gave him advance knowledge of the property-market, and this knowledge he had put to full and profitable use, setting aside most of his available balance each year to buy more land. A man of few, if any, extravagant habits, he was able through his judicious, long-term investment to leave his son a heritage of no mean order. Inevitably, one asks how Petre avoided falling into debt with such a heavy and continuous outlay. That he did so is abundantly clear; and it is unnecessary to recount a multitude of tedious financial transactions. His solvency is proved from his own archives, which tell a consistent story of prudent control of all his activities.

Details of the management of his extensive estates lie outside the scope

* His personal archives (Crown grants, original title-deeds, deeds register, accounts, valuations) provide in exemplary fashion the material from which a complete statement including prices can be produced; and the total figures quoted agree exactly with those on the Patent Rolls, in the case of purchases from the Crown. A few calculations have been made to cover exchanges, royal grants that were partly gifts, partly sales, and once or twice the capital value has been estimated on the usual basis of twenty years' purchase. The great register of deeds is D/DP E29.

of this book. It is possible, however, to answer categorically two major questions about the new owner. Was he a harsh landlord? Did he manage his estates efficiently?

The first was one of the chief problems recently solved by Dr. Emerson. After examining the great mass of leases and cognate material, he showed that Petre's treatment of his tenants was much less harsh than that of many Tudor 'New Men', whose conduct was condemned by some earlier writers. 'Not only did [Petre's leaseholders and copyholders] remain undisturbed', he declared, 'but leases which fell in almost without exception were renewed upon the old terms granted by previous owners, and in some cases upon easier terms. Rather than evicting tenants, the proportion of lease land to demesne land retained in the lord's occupation was increased slightly through additional leases granted.' [9] Sir William's conservative but liberal-minded attitude is all the more remarkable because the two decades following the Dissolution were a period of abnormal inflation when most landlords were forced, even if not anxious, to recoup themselves by raising rents. It is clear, at any rate, that the rapid enlargement of the Petre estates was not thus financed. (His 'goodness' towards his Essex and Devon tenants is also reflected in a number of documents,[10] though there is nothing to show that he ever returned to his native county after the Dissolution.)

It would be patently absurd to deduce from the almost complete absence of rack-renting that Petre was benevolent. To explain why he did not exploit his tenants to the full is also to give a partial answer about the soundness of his management. While his main policy had been to farm as far as possible an integrated estate, his secondary aim was to keep down expenditure, so far as rising prices allowed, rather than to increase income. This is evident from his careful watch over the ways of provisioning the household. To limit the acater's expenditure in the local markets, Petre almost invariably introduced some form of rent in kind with a reduction in the money rent when renewing leases; from the 1560s onwards this was persistently maintained, especially by way of corn rents.

In one way, it is true, he had determined to increase income without recourse to rent-raising. It is not surprising that the new lawyer-owner gave directions that manorial revenues should be investigated by perusal of the records, which disclosed 'decayed rents' and led to a general tightening up. But the extra receipts from the copyholders and other curial fees was small compared with what he could have extracted by increased rents from his leasehold tenants. Sir William's assured return by 1556 on his Essex acquisitions was only 5 per cent (on the usual valuation basis Crown grants gave the same yield); to which another 1 or 2 per cent was added on account of 'casualties', such as income from manor courts and sale of timber. To this modest yield on his capital expenditure there were a few exceptions. When he disparked Crondon Old Park in 1551, cutting up the demesne into five new holdings, he let them at rents of 1s. 8d. an acre, almost one and half times the figure obtaining in most of his other properties. Writtle was a more important exception. Granted to Petre on the basis of twenty years' purchase (in Mary's reign the average rate was twenty-four years[11]), the Crown valuation of £76 a year was much below its true figure. His own income, augmented by strict supervision of the manorial courts, soon amounted to £200, and much more in 1563 after he had leased parts of the demesnes. On the other hand, his custom of letting some properties near the Hall to several of his household officers and higher servants on easy terms resulted in a reduced income from these holdings. Not until his last years were rents giving him a 7 per cent return on his original capital and manorial court receipts and sales of timber another 3 per cent. In 1568 a valuation of all his estates disclosed a net assured income from rents of £1,332.[11A]

2 Getting and Spending

The only year after Petre's appointment to high office for which there is a complete record both of income from all sources and of expenditure at Court, Aldergate Street and Ingatestone is 1556. This is preserved in an audit-roll of twenty-four folios.[12] It shows what Sir William had achieved, after twenty years' public service, in establishing himself as a man of affluence, what he spent in accordance with his social status, and how he ended the year with a substantial surplus. A short summary has been compiled from the roll (Table 1 opposite).

Petre's very extensive investment in lands, especially in 1554-5, had produced a correspondingly higher income from this source. Even his increased official income had been well outstripped by revenue from his estates in Essex and Devon. Of the numerous annuities granted by anxious abbots in the last days of their houses, Petre's share had been partly commuted and now yielded £56,* but he still received the £100 from the estates of the bishopric of Winchester. Philip's handsome pension brought him £250, and compensation for his First Fruits office another £200. The Secretary's and the Garter appointments each carried

* From the first five houses listed on p. 21; the remainder were surrendered in 1546 as part consideration, with the manor of Peldon, for the Crown grant to him of Churchstow, Devon, and Mountnessing rectory.

the annual fee of £100. His half-share of the dividends from the Signet offices gave him £106. 'Homage of divers bishops this year, £6 6s. 8d.' proves that he still held the ecclesiastical seal. From offices and annuities Petre should have drawn £930, but some payments were slightly overdue.

There is no close relationship between figures for cattle bought and sold within a twelvemonth, but Petre was evidently making good profits from

TABLE I

Petre's income and expenditure, 1556

	£
Rents, manor court profits, timber sales:	
Essex estate	662
West Country estate	573
Estates held on lease and sub-leased	441
Crown wards' estates	196
Sales of cattle and other produce	610
Salaries and fees from offices, King Philip's pension, episcopal and monastic annuities	871
	3,353
Wardships, rents for leased estates, tithes	437
Payments and repayments of Crown dues and debts	523
Husbandry costs	44
Cattle bought	298
Food and other household costs	162
Clothes for family and wards	41
Servants' wages and liveries	144
Travel costs	73
Gifts and poor relief	124
Exhibitions to scholars	96
Buildings, including almshouses and repairs	253
Armoury	48
Miscellaneous	101
	2,344
Surplus	1,009

rearing cattle, which were sold for £468; as in his early years, the sale of wool at only £27 shows that his sheep-farming was not on a large scale. He took a quick profit of £49 from timber sales on his new Writtle estate.

The largest item in Petre's outgoings, £383, is the final payment towards £500 due to the Exchequer by a bond of March 1553, probably for the Glastonbury lands; he also paid £100 as his own 'forced loan' to the Queen, £40 for the first payment of the recent subsidy and repaid Napper's £100 loan. Husbandry costs are divided between the Ingatestone and East Horndon demesnes. The household provisions both at

Ingatestone and Aldersgate were relatively low, with bulk purchases of salt fish for the servants and others totalling £64 and wine a mere 55s.; his infrequent residence in Essex in 1556 involved him in little charge for hospitality.

It is important to estimate how far the surplus of £1,009 is representative of other years in Petre's most active period. Philip's pension was received only in this and the previous year. The loss of the secretarial salary in 1557 was made up by the Garter salary which he did not begin to draw until 1554. The Signet, etc., fees had been much higher in earlier years (see Appendix J). Among the outgoings, the Crown bond, forced loan, subsidy and debt, also the cost of building the Ingatestone almshouses, were all exceptional, and amounted to as much as £780; against this big sum should be offset a smaller figure for abnormally low entertaining costs. His very heavy capital outlay in the two previous years explains the complete absence of further acquisitions in this year. Of the total expenses in 1556, the sum attributable to Ingatestone Hall was £760, of which £298 was for cattle bought and £178 for the almshouses. Cattle transactions are not recorded in any other years after 1543, so that the adjusted figure for ordinary expenses at Ingatestone should be £305.

Apart from 1543 and 1556, Petre's total expenses have also been established for 1555, because the account-books of his personal and Ingatestone stewards have both been preserved. They show disbursements of £1,538 and £386 respectively, excluding lands. The two years 1555 and 1556, as already remarked, were those during which Petre probably spent less time at Ingatestone than in any other period. On the other hand, in 1555 Petre produced in cash no less than £1,181 in purchasing land, considerably more than his average; but it is not possible to ascertain his real revenue in 1555 as the steward covers up several of the quarterly payments as 'ready money received', although he meticulously gives the Signet monthly dividends.

For a third year, 1550, there are also detailed accounts giving the complete costs for Ingatestone Hall household and the Ingatestone and East Horndon demesnes, which include heavy building charges especially at the Horndon farm-house. The total outlay was £468, and the sole omission, apart from the cattle purchases, is the acater's expenses. These are given as £34 in 1555 and £21 in 1556, so the full figure for 1550 might be put at £500. On this basis, the average for Ingatestone, 1550, 1555 and 1556, was £393; a round sum of £400 probably therefore represents the expenditure in a normal year (the costs of Elizabeth's visit and Catherine's wedding at Ingatestone in 1561 are both included in the personal, not the Ingatestone, steward's accounts).

There are eight years as well as 1556 for which fairly accurate figures of Petre's income exist; and in addition to the three years mentioned the expenses for seven years are known, except for the Ingatestone costs.

In Table 2 below, the income totals for several years, as given in the accounts, have been adjusted by deducting items which cannot necessarily be deemed income. The very high estate receipts for 1556, it may be re-

TABLE 2

Petre's income and expenditure, 1540–1570

Income		1540 £	1542 £	1543 £	1548 £	1549 £	1554 £	1556 £	1564 £	1570 £
Estates (rents, manor courts, timber sales)		408	787	668	749	653	999	2,482	2,007	2,274
Offices (salaries, fees, annuities)		109	102	101	406	580	929	871	451	445
		517*	889	769*	1,155*	1,233*	1,928*	3,353	2,458	2,719

Expenditure		1543 £	1548 £	1549 £	1554 £	1555 £	1556 £	1559 £	1560 £	1561 £	1562 £
Purchase of lands		Nil	1,367	67	1,591	1,181	380‡	55	67	1,293	1,150
Other costs		815	476†	602†	762†	1,924	1,964	610†	925†	1,317†	1,223†
		815	1,843	669	2,353	3,105	2,344	665	992	2,610	2,373

* The steward's figures have been adjusted as follows: 1540—excludes £32 being part repayment by Wriothesley of a bond for £100; 1543—excludes £158 from sales of lands; 1548—excludes receipts by steward of £44 'in ready money', £300 'by the hands of William Garrard and William Pownsett'; 1549—excludes £158 'in ready money'; 1554—excludes £759 in various sums 'in ready money'.

† The figures for 1548, 1549, 1554, 1559, 1560, 1561 and 1562 exclude the unknown cost of running Ingatestone Hall and the estate; that for 1561 also omits £1,000 which Petre advanced on two mortgages.

‡ Repayment of £380 to Crown for a debt incurred in 1553, probably for purchase of lands.

peated, are due not only to the new acquisitions but also to sales of cattle, not normally recorded. The growth in Petre's expenditure is partly the result of the abnormal rise in prices—approximately 100 per cent between 1541 and 1561.

As a complete statement of the cost of the building-up of Petre's estates has been produced from his deed registers and other sources (p. 268n.), the 'purchase of lands' figures in this table may be ignored for the moment in calculating his average outlay. If the income figures for 1540 (before his second marriage) and for the isolated late year 1570 are also left out because there are no corresponding expenses, the remaining sums of income and expenses are seen to be closely linked in date. Receipts for 1542 and

1543 may therefore be averaged to correspond with expenses for 1543; expenses for 1555 and 1556 averaged with income for 1556; and expenses for 1559–62, with income for 1564; the other years are identical. The six figures for income are thus £829, £1,155, £1,233, £1,928, £3,353 and £2,458; total £10,956; average £1,826. The corresponding expenses (excluding land purchases) are £815, £476, £602, £762, £1,944 and £1,019; the average of £400 a year should be added to four of these figures for Ingatestone, the known cost of which is included in the others; total £7,218; average £1,203. The surplus for investment almost wholly in lands works out therefore at £623. While this result is only approximate, it is a sufficiently clear indication of Petre's satisfactory balance throughout the second half of his life. As some of the big 'ready money' items excluded from the receipts in the table are probably normal income rather than cash from the chest, and as the profits from cattle-rearing are very incomplete, the average annual surplus arrived at may be an understatement; on the other hand, a few special expenses escaped the steward's net, such as the 1,000 marks for Thomasine's dowry in 1560. But the figure of £623 is very close to that of Petre's average outlay on lands between 1537 and 1571, which was found to be £638 and is believed to be accurate.

The result is well in line with the assumption that all his available cash resources went into land, apart from what he invested in plate, jewellery and daughters' marriages. It is of course unfortunate that precise figures cannot be obtained and that those existing have to be used with caution; even so, it would be difficult to produce more reliable or complete figures for another mid-Tudor courtier-landowner of Petre's class.

To what extent, if any, did Petre add to his fortune through 'gifts' received at Court, especially in the period when he held the influential office of Secretary? The question applies to all Tudor Secretaries and some other office-holders. With Petre it is particularly relevant to seek an answer, because his reputation for official honesty cannot be allowed to pass without further scrutiny and because his legacy of private financial records provides a rare opportunity of making such an examination. A recent writer, faced with a similar problem in Cecil's allegedly vast unofficial income as Master of the Court of Wards, made every effort to furnish such an answer. Official salaries and fees present no difficulty. But, he wrote, 'Can the same be said about perquisities, gifts, rewards, bribes, and the whole collection of *douceurs* which oiled the wheels of Tudor administration? All men took them. Since, however, both donor and recipient hid the gift in a maze of euphemism and ambiguity, since such evidence as existed was often destroyed as quickly as possible, what numerical value is the historian to set upon rumour, hearsay, and slander? If, in the case of Burghley [Sir William Cecil], we knew the extent of the private fortune he inherited, and his income from his estates, we should know how far his high cost of living was met from these legitimate sources. Burghley, in fact, argued that it was from these revenues—not from public office—that he sustained his three houses, his family, and the way of life of a great courtier and statesman.'[13]

The accounts which Petre's steward kept are extant for nearly half the period in which he was Secretary. The record of receipts is as detailed and specific as that of expenditure, so often quoted. Each month the steward noted, in addition to all rents, timber sales, annuities and the like, Petre's half-share of the dividends from the signet, hanaper and petty bag offices. Everything is clear, except for an occasional entry of the steward's receipt of stated sums 'in ready money' from his master, but the term signifies nothing unusual and is sometimes explained, e.g. 'received of my master in ready money which was paid by Foster of Willington for 120 quarters of malt' (1555). Only in that year is there anything out of the ordinary, i.e. 'received of my master in 40 pistolets, £12 6s. 8d.' (after the proclamation of 1553 each Spanish pistolet was worth 6s. 2d. of English money). And of course cash was sometimes passed the other way, e.g. 'ready money delivered to my master in his chamber at Hampton Court'. In his expenses there is plenty of evidence of his receiving gifts in kind because of the usual reward to the bringer. Setting aside the many New Year's gifts, offering of game and the like from fellow courtiers, friends, neighbours and relations, the nearest suggestion of private perquisites is found in 1554–5 (p. 189). One further instance, not previously mentioned, was in July 1555, when Cornwallis thanked Petre for obtaining Heron's suit for the treasurership of Berwick. In September Petre paid for the carriage of three barrels of salmon sent by Heron; exactly a year later, under 'Salmon provided for the household', is a similar entry, and it cost Petre 7s. 8d. for carriage and freight. The most careful search through Kyme's orderly, informative books discloses nothing more questionable than these trifles, nothing more than a gelding or an outsize lamprey pie (unless it concealed a valuable gift!), nothing beyond ordinary tangible appreciation as understood nowadays. Nor is there a single reward to a servant bringing money without the purpose being stated.*

A final check may be made from the figures of Petre's income and

---

* A very sweet *douceur* arrived from Devon in 1552 when church plate was being requisitioned: 'Both the Earl of Bedford and Sir William Petre the Secretary received suitable gifts of sugar loaves—they had to be conciliated' (W. T. MacCaffrey, *Exeter, 1540–1640*, Cambridge, U.S.A., 1958), 217).

expenditure over a long period. These show that he was well able to pay for new estates out of current balances and they give no grounds for suspicion that he had a large undisclosed source of revenue by way of unofficial perquisites. Apart from his revealed ambition to become a great landowner, he never indulged extravagantly in building, entertaining, gambling, drinking and other ways of draining capital; and being a lawyer he did not waste money like some laymen in endless litigation. While it would have been more intriguing to discover in his well-documented finances some evidence or even suspicion of shady transactions, he must instead be given credit for conducting his public offices, as closely as any Tudor politician could be expected to do, in accordance with his own policy memorandum entitled 'What is to be done after the death of King Edward', which contained the pithy precept, 'There must be no bribers'.

3 Ingatestone Almshouses and Oxford Colleges

Getting is a more normal aim in life than giving; but the ways in which a man gives away part of what he has striven to get are among the keys to his character. There are several to Petre's.

The middle third of the sixteenth century was a transitional time for the charitably disposed Englishman. His mind was adjusted to new forms of benevolence, the Reformation having swept away so many of the accustomed objects. Petre's benefactions reflect these changes. He was one of the 'generous men who were creating a society in the image of their own aspirations'.[15]

At the time of the Dissolution, monastic almsgiving had relatively little effect in ameliorating poverty.[15A] The widespread distress gave rise to semi-compulsory parochial poor relief, with regard to which Petre's personal accounts have several items of exceptionally early date:

1555
MAY 31. My master's charity to the poor of Ingatestone. Paid to the collectors of the poor of Ingatestone since the 18th day of November last past for 28 weeks ended on Sunday next coming being Whitsunday after 20d. for every week of my master's charity, 46s. 8d.

This is followed by similar entries for Stock and Buttsbury for 26 weeks at 12d. a week for each. So far as is known, they are the earliest record of the actual operation in rural parishes of the Act of 1552, which began to convert voluntary relief into an indirect obligation. Thus, for these three parishes, assessments for the very first quasi-rate are preserved, replacing voluntary giving exemplified by:

1554
DEC. 24. Reward by the way of alms to the poor. Gave on Christmas eve to the
poor folks of Ingatestone, Buttsbury and Stock at my master's and my
lady's appointment, £4.

It is not unlikely that he had a share in drafting the 1552 legislation. In any case, as knight of the shire and privy councillor, Secretary Petre would have seen to it that his own parishes set a good example locally. By 1556 his steward substituted 'relief of the poor' for 'charity to the poor', a shilling or more for each of the parishes weekly. Compulsory rates were introduced in 1563, although the Act still termed the contributions 'charitable alms'.*

Much information is preserved about Petre's private almsgiving and domestic charity, an intimate if minor aspect of his life. Many small sums went 'in alms', 'to a poor man', and so forth. As early as 1544 he was giving 4s. 4d. a quarter 'to mother Pegge in alms', which was apparently a sizeable pension to the widow of his first Ingatestone bailiff; it was paid regularly, as was 10s. a quarter in the next decade to Mistress Wells, 'his bedeswoman', who had been his London housekeeper. Now and again several shillings or even a sovereign went to his humbler tenants or local craftsmen who had fallen sick, or to faithful servants leaving his employment or deciding to get married. 'Given to Horde at his marriage £10 and to Randall at his marriage 53s. 4d.', found in 1561, is the mark of a generous master; Horde had been with him for seven years. In 1559 over £5 was shared by three servants 'for their pains taken about him in his sickness, to buy them apparel'. In 1555 Veale got 2s. 'being fallen in poverty', and a few months later 20s. 'for charity sake to bring him into Devonshire being sick'. Gifts to individuals in distress portray a donor's kindliness perhaps even more than major endowments and are usually much more difficult to trace.

In the meantime he had evidently decided that the lay successor to the abbesses of Barking ought to give more help to the poor of Ingatestone

* The Acts cited are 5 & 6 Edw. VI, c.2, and 5 Eliz., c.3. References to the effect of the Act of 1552 are very rare. (See my 'Poor Relief Accounts of Two Rural Parishes in Bedfordshire, 1563–1598', *Econ. Hist. Rev.*, iii (1931), 102–16, and 'The Care of the Poor in Elizabethan Essex', *Essex Review*, lxii (1953), 7–28, where these entries were first published.) An even earlier record has since been found. The official contemporary copy of an Ingatestone will, July 1554, was written on the dorse of a discarded undated account beginning, 'The relief of the poor of the parish of Yng Petre—June: Sir Wm. Petre knight and lord of the town, 6s. 8d.; Mr. Cliff, 16d.'; this was clearly intended to be the parish assessment (E.R.O., D/ABW 31/87).

than his share of the embryo parochial poor rate. The scale of his charitable donation was liberal. He obtained a Crown licence in July 1556 to found 'a hospital or almshouse' within his manor of Ingatestone to house seven poor persons with a priest in charge and to make ordinances for the foundation; he was also licensed under the mortmain laws to endow it with lands to the value of £50 a year.[16] It was to be known as the Ginge Petre Charity. No time was lost. The audit-roll for 1556 has a section, 'Buildings at Ingatestone upon the chapel and almshouse'. The former clearly refers, not to the chapel at the Hall but to what Petre describes in the almshouse statutes as 'my chapel adjoining to the quire of the parish church'; it is in fact the existing brick south chapel of Ingatestone church. Architectural and documentary evidence confirms that it was rebuilt in the middle of the century, almost certainly on the site of an earlier chapel. Petre provided it as the chapel for his almspeople.

The priest and the poor (five women and two men) became a body corporate. The foundation deed and the ordinances are dated July–August 1557.[17] After Petre's death, the appointment of inmates was to vest in his widow, and after her death in his heirs, lords of the manor. The very detailed ordinances declared that he had already begun to build three additional dwellings so that ten almsfolk could be housed in all. Each got 2d. a day, with 6s. 8d. for wood and a livery of cloth worth 12s. at Christmas, when a further 6s. 8d. was shared by twenty poor folk of Ingatestone. The chaplain received £4 yearly wages, 10s. wood, 15s. livery and pasture for two cows.

In 1564 Petre gave further property producing an extra £16 a year, to be distributed among ten poor folk living in any part of his Essex estates.[18] His statutes did not make clear whether the rector of Ingatestone would normally be chaplain of the almshouse. John Woodward, who refused to conform and resigned the rectory in 1565, continued as Petre's chaplain at the Hall. Receipts for rents to the hospital bear the signature of his Protestant successor at the parish church.*

Petre had thus carried out his plan for the spiritual and bodily care of the poor near his Essex seat. He then turned his mind to All Souls College, Oxford, which had conferred a fellowship on him in 1523.[19] He was one of several donors whose gifts built the Warden's lodgings. In the same

---

* Later rectors also acted as almshouse priests until after the Catholic Emancipation Act, when new rules were made under which the almshouses were reserved for Roman Catholics (E.R.O., D/DP Q11/1; also E. E. Wilde, *Ingatestone and the Essex Great Road* (1913), 226-7). Petre's almshouses were close to the church and fronted Stock Lane (Walker's map of Ingatestone, 1605, E.R.O., P8A). Two cottages remain, those adjoining having been swept away by the railway in 1840, when the 11th Baron Petre built the new almshouses with their central chapel.

year All Souls received two endowments, the first through his goodwill, which in turn probably gave rise to his own. New scholarships were founded under each. Petre's old friend Pownsett, formerly chief steward of Barking Abbey and lessee of its demesnes, who lived at Loxford Hall near the abbey, left the residue of his property to be partly applied in 'other good deeds of charity'.[20] The testator had complete faith in his executors, who were Petre, William Cooke and Edward Napper.* Pownsett, like all three executors, had been a fellow of All Souls. Whether he mentioned his old college on his deathbed is unknown; at any rate, to All Souls the executors gave the legacy. They purchased the rectory of Barking and conveyed it to the Warden and Fellows by deed of 1 July 1557. The annual income was to provide 26s. 8d. for college uses and exhibitions for two poor scholars, being fellows, each of the annual value of 53s. 4d.[21] By another deed of the same date, Petre charged his own Gloucestershire manor of Toddenham and his lay rectory of Mountnessing each with an annuity of £6 13s. 4d. for identical purposes.† If his own scholars were not priests, they were to take orders within six months. Petre left the nomination of his three scholars to the Warden.[22] In 1559 he gave the bursars five marks (£3 6s. 8d.) He also purchased the 'Rose' inn and gave it to the college; the site was to become the Warden's garden in 1573.[23]

A little later his thoughts returned with affection to Exeter College, where he had been a commoner. Within a few years his benefactions were to be munificent enough to earn him the title of its 'second founder'. The story of his endowment can be amplified from fresh documentary evidence.‡ As already known from the college accounts, his chaplain began negotiations in the summer of 1564, when 14d. was paid 'for wine and sugar at the reception of Mr. Woodward, with whom we talked over the plan and design of Dr. Petre'.[24] John Kennall, the Vice-chancellor of the university, was persuaded by Petre to act as an intermediary in the next stages. The donor's primary aim was to provide facilities for the maintenance of additional scholars. Next March Kennall wrote that the

---

* Cooke, an ecclesiastical judge, was also the non-resident warden of Ilford Hospital in Essex, to which Pownsett gave a small legacy. Napper was also to be a benefactor to the college.

† Cardinal Pole gave the tithes of Stanton Harcourt near Oxford to augment the maintenance of the scholars of All Souls. His grant, dated 1558, states that it was made with the consent of Petre as patron of the vicarage (E.R.O., D/DP Q13/2). The college historian credits Petre with help in securing this gift (C. G. Robertson, *All Souls College* (1899), 91).

‡ Forty contemporary documents recently deposited by Lord Petre (E.R.O., D/DP Q13/1/1, catalogued by Miss Nancy Briggs, M.A., Assistant Archivist, E.R.O., who drafted most of this section). These documents have not been compared with the unpublished college archives.

college was most happy to accept his offer to increase their small company, and 'to take your appointed number into their fellowship to enjoy all the commodities of their college with such order for the election of your number for a certain time, or for ever, either for the country whereof you will have them chosen, or otherwise, as you shall appoint'.* Kennall pointed out that the seven fellowships Petre proposed to endow could not be maintained on £50 a year as each fellow was allowed £7 5s., in addition to the £5 chamber-rent due to the college. Since the college would lose £5 15s. annually by this arrangement, Kennall suggested only six scholars, thereby giving the college a yearly profit of 30s. A note in Petre's hand was clearly based on the lower number, with allowance of 40s. for 'one to read a continual lecture of philosophy or logic'. A week later Kennall sent Petre further particulars, with which the Rector personally hoped to wait upon him at Aldersgate. He received a Latin letter in the newly-imported Italic calligraphy (the 'cancellaresca' hand). Full of gracious, humanistic sentiments, it referred gratefully to the intended gifts to their little college, 'collegiolum nostrum', and was accompanied by the gift of a pair of gloves, no doubt made locally.

Petre was busily engaged in working out his ideas in detail. Many of his own memoranda are among the new documents. As a preliminary step, the cautious lawyer felt that the college should sue for a charter, the lack of which was a serious defect. At the same time the statutes 'made long sithence by Walter Stapledon then Bishop of Exeter' should be revised. This ought to be done, Petre considered, by himself with the advice and consent of the bishop. 'One thing that (in my opinion) is chiefly to be reformed is that the Rector's office is annual, by reason whereof he shall never be able to rule, and his small stipend for his living taketh away his estimation.' Petre made up his mind at once to enlarge his projected endowment to allow for an increase in the Rector's stipend which would give him more permanence and power as in other colleges. So ran Petre's thoughts on 1 May 1565.

Three days later he wrote several letters and his proposed 'articles', the drafts of which are in his descendant's archives. The articles provided for not more than seven scholars, to be named by Petre, from a grant of lands which would yield nearly £80 a year and be worth £100 when the leases fell in. He invited the Rector and scholars to propose any other necessary reforms and to make as speedily as possible a formal 'submission' to him for the reformation of the ancient statutes. This they did by a Latin docu-

* The attitude of the college is of interest, as can be seen from the later endorsement referring to the lawsuit over the right of nomination to the Petrean fellowships after the death of John, Lord Petre in 1613.

ment sealed on 18 May. In the meantime the Rector had sent Petre a note of fifteen points 'worthy to be redressed'. It was suggested that the Rector's authority would be enhanced through 'a longer continuance' of the office and by making his consent necessary for the departure of fellows to another college or for bachelors and scholars to leave the town. Among other *desiderata* were prohibitions against keeping hawks and hounds within the college or 'feasting' women of ill repute therein. The Rector also enquired whether in future senior scholars might be licensed to study civil law or physic instead of divinity.

Petre's own copy of his letter of 16 July, written from London, is of much interest. After acknowledging receipt of extracts from the statutes of Trinity College as well as Exeter, he expressed his own attitude. It adds a little to existing knowledge of the contemporary views of academic benefactors.

> Your travail in these matters do well declare to me your good wills to have your statutes reduced directly to such order as may be most to God's honour, increase of learning, maintenance of honest manners and conversation, and preservation of such lands as is or shall be hereafter bestowed upon you. If you continue to walk this way with due respect to God, assure yourselves God will assist all your doings and from time to time succour and provide for you. And the more you bend your endeavours this way the more comfort shall I have to do that I have determined, and perchance more if God make me able and continue my life . . . I think it very necessary your Rector's office be made perpetual. I would also gladly have a sub-rector and will provide for it. . . . And if you think good to have one of the scholars to be placed by me to be licensed to study the civil law I will not mislike of it. My scholars shall be ordered by your common statutes saving that in some few things I have mind to note three or four special ordinances whereupon I will determine when I shall see your common book. . . . And if any of you go to the west parts this summer, it shall be well you do write to my lord the Bishop of Exeter to make him privy of your doings so as at his coming to this next Parliament I may confer with my said lord for reducing things to a short conclusion.* I require no long book of your statutes nor straiter than is meet. There must be established some good discipline for order and good education of youth. All that I desire is that God may be well known and served.

The college, Petre added, could expect an advance payment of twenty nobles (£6 13s. 4d.), 'to be distributed, Mr. Rector, with the assent of the more part of eight of your most ancient fellows, as shall be thought best'.

The revised Exeter statutes, with their stress for example on college teaching, were clearly based in part on those of Trinity.[25] Unfortunately

---

* The prorogued Parliament did not meet again until 30 Sept. 1566.

Petre does not indicate whether he (or the Rector) selected Trinity merely as a new (1554) foundation, or whether he wished to try out the ideas of its founder, his friend Sir Thomas Pope. Another memorandum in his hand, undated but belonging to this summer, shows that he did not favour his fellows remaining laymen: 'The said scholars to be such as like to profit in learning, poor and unable to live of their friends and such as will determine their minds to the study of divinity and to be of the clergy.'

Petre's motives for endowing additional fellowships, therefore, were to give greater honour to God, to restore discipline and to raise educational standards; he also wished to provide recruits for the priesthood, like his contemporary Sir Thomas White, who had founded St. John's in 1555. The objects of Pope's foundation, on the other hand, were not primarily religious.[26] Petre's letter could be interpreted as confirming his latitudinarian attitude towards religion and his interest in the civil law, but the exact nature of his philanthropic aims remain obscure.*

John Neale, the rector, gave his sincerest thanks and named thirteen scholars deemed to be most worthy of help and 'fittest for us'.† The letter, addressed to Ingatestone, describes each, e.g. 'John Howlett born in Rutlandshire, 18 years of age, very honest, very quiet, sober and tractable, marvellous poor and toward, studious, a pretty scholar, for one year lay in our college, relieved partly with us and partly at Magdalen College, now a pensioner in Merton College.' He was one of the first seven Petrean fellows to be elected and later became an active Jesuit.

In the autumn Petre pushed on with the legal formalities, and the college notified him of their approval of the draft charter. At last, on 22 March 1566, the Queen issued her letters patent for incorporating Petre's scholars and for drawing up new statutes, not by Petre with the Bishop of Exeter's advice but the other way round subject to Petre's assent. (Although the nomination was vested in Petre and his son, the college was afterwards to elect them.) Handing over a further £26 8s. 4d., he appointed the first seven fellows, who sent him a Latin epistle, expressing their gratitude with classical allusions; it is dated 4 July and is subscribed by all.[27] The long line of Petrean fellows, who were to include so

* Some Petrean fellows were among those who left Oxford for Douai to become Jesuits; these included Ralph Sherwin, nephew of John Woodward, Petre's chaplain.

† Neale also solicited help in favour of his old school, Week St. Mary in Cornwall, 'a notable nurse unto hundreds of Devon and Cornish men, and always a ready (and now a needful) nursery for Exeter College. The school is dissolved, the lands gone away, because Jesus Mass was there weekly said. The fair walls remain, craving as it were some help of them whom she hath holpen, desirous to live and nourish.' Neale was deprived in 1570 because of his tenets and also went to Douai.

many men of distinction, had begun. The college wrote to 'their especial good patron' proposing names for the offices of sub-rector, dean and lector. The rector, sub-rector and an ordinary fellow visited Ingatestone during the summer of 1566 (the date is not given), receiving from Petre £3 for their expenses. They sent other representatives to the Bishop of Exeter, probably with a copy of the statutes, which cost 36s. 8d. to write out. All these disbursements they accounted for to Petre; there remained from his recent payment a balance of £19 0s. 5d. 'reposed in the common hutch to such uses as shall best like your honour'.

The income for Petre's re-foundation of Exeter College came mostly from properties which he had already purchased from the Crown by letters patent issued in the previous May. They comprised the rectories of Kidlington, Merton, Yarnton and South Newington, with the tithes, and some small properties, all in Oxfordshire. The cost, £1,376, involved a big outlay, even for a man of Petre's wealth. On 8 November 1566 Petre executed his deed of gift, which enumerated several additional properties; none was in Essex. In the articles of agreement, bearing the same date, it was stipulated that the vicar of Kidlington should give house-room to scholars of the college in time of sickness, a sensible provision which was acted upon more than once in later years when plague raged at Oxford. The estates settled on the college yielded £79 12s. 2d. a year. The greater part of this sum was to be expended in setting up the seven new fellow-ships for scholars from counties in which Petre or his heirs should have lands (originally Devon, Somerset, Dorset, Oxford and Essex); the balance was for the officers and the college funds. The rector's office was to be for life, the new offices of dean and sub-rector were endowed, and there were detailed provisions for teaching in the college. The lengthy statutes, signed by Petre and the Bishop of Exeter, have survived in the college and the family archives only as copies belonging to the next century.[28] In the opinion of a more recent college historian, the statutes, like those of Trinity, 'show the influence of the new learning and the new faith in almost every line', but views on religion were in fact not very prominent.[29]

Signal recognition of Petre's philanthropy came unexpectedly, even before his formal ratification in November. In September 1566 Elizabeth visited Oxford. One of Petre's original fellows, John Bereblock,* who had become dean in July, was something of an artist and drew what would now be called bird's-eye views of the colleges. The Queen examined them.[30] Every drawing was accompanied by Latin verses by Thomas Neal, Hebrew reader at Oxford, in the form of a dialogue between the Queen

---

* Signed the letter of July 1566 as 'Berblock'. In 1570 Petre gave him special leave to study abroad.

and the Chancellor (Leicester), in which the earl describes each college, Her Majesty replying suitably. Bereblock put these words about Petre's munificence into Leicester's mouth.[31]

But first to Exeter within the walls
  A proud addition I have yet to show.
And William Petre, for this gift is his,
  Will to his Queen a meed of honour pay,
Whose loyal words to hear thy will it is
  Among thy counsellors from day to day.
Our Oxford taught him to revere the Muse,
  Fair Devon bore him in her Western land:
To each for nurture he repays his dues
  And stretches out to each an aiding hand.
So thanks to him, this house, which once was poor,
  Shall now full chambers and full coffers own,
Increased in students and increased in store,
  A jewel, Princess, in thy glorious crown.
How great the scholars who these halls shall fill
  From one example clearly is displayed:
He shall be Bereblock (whose surpassing skill
  The pictures for these doggerel rhymes portrayed).
Then prosper, Petre, and untiring still
  Foster thy children with thy bounteous aid.

As he was then convalescing, it is doubtful if he journeyed to Oxford; even so, he would have been gratified with the panegyric. 'Increased in store' may refer to his having also enriched the college library with an important manuscript, perhaps itself a gift to him from Elizabeth, and some books, to which he added more later.*

He must have been pleased with the first academic results, for in 1568 he endowed an eighth fellowship with three tenements in Thorpe near Kidlington, which produced £5 2s. a year. This was the subject of a letter written in May by Mildmay to Cecil; the Queen, 'weighing the good use

* The treasure was a Latin psalter with fine gilding and illumination which had belonged to the Lancastrian and Tudor Houses. 'It was probably written for Humphrey de Bohun, Earl of Hereford, grandson of Edward I, and may have passed to the royal family through his grandniece Mary, who married Henry IV.' Later it belonged to Elizabeth of York, Henry VII's queen, and to Catherine of Aragon. 'It may have been the book from which the royal children learnt their Latin. In the calendar are births, deaths and marriages of the royal family up to the time of Henry VIII, and no doubt it passed to Elizabeth, who gave it to Sir William Petre, and he gave it to the College which he refounded. . . . Among the printed books given by Petre in May 1567 was John Benedict's Latin *Concordantiæ utriusque Testamenti*, Paris, 1562; and bound with it F. Hectoris Pinti Lusitani *in Esaiam Commentaria*, Lyons, 1561; so that Petre had the latest books from Paris and Lyons.' (C. W. Boase, *Register of Exeter College* (2nd edn., 1894), clxv–clxvii.)

he would employ it unto', had agreed to sell some small properties in Oxfordshire.[32] Petre had endowed a hospital and refounded an Oxford college; in later years, Cecil endowed a hospital and Mildmay founded Emmanuel College, Cambridge.

Not content with his various benefactions Petre left the college £40 by his will. A similar legacy was included in his widow's will, and his son John gave £15 6s. 8d. to augment the old fellowships, adding £20 under his own will. By that time the entire Petrean foundation was computed to yield £111 a year, more than double the college income before 1565. After Sir William's death, John continued to take an active interest in the affairs of the college. His relations with Exeter were generally amicable, although in 1583 one of the fellows disputed his right to nominate to his father's fellowships. On John's death, the college refused to accept a nomination made by his own son. In the subsequent lawsuit Exeter successfully claimed the right to elect the Petrean fellows.[33]

A sense of moral obligation, not as a scholar but as a landowner, led Petre to make a minor gift to New College, Oxford, which, with Winchester College, had been founded in 1378-9 by William of Wykeham, Bishop of Winchester. Among the endowments that the bishop settled on New College were the peculiar and the rectory of Writtle. Petre had acquired the liberty and manor of Writtle including Roxwell, and in 1565 he bestowed a small income for the benefit of both the manor and the college. He granted to the college two tenements in Writtle formerly belonging to Carpenter's chantry there. The rents of 13s. 4d. a year were to go towards the exhibition of any poor boy of Writtle or Roxwell who went to Wykeham's school or college; when no such youth, then to twenty poor parishioners on Christmas Eve.

Petre's daughter Dorothy married Nicholas Wadham in 1555. Before his death in 1609 Wadham had made plans for founding a college. His widow and executrix, then well over seventy, carried them out with singular devotion and with the promptitude and vigour to be expected of a Petre. Sir William's benefactions to Oxford probably influenced the Wadhams in their munificent endowment of the college which rightly bears their name.*

In 1568 Petre made two rather unusual charitable donations. Crondon had been an ancient possession of the bishops of London, and the park

---

* Some newly discovered letters in the Petre archives which throw interesting light on the negotiations of the foundress between 1610 and 1614 have recently been printed by my colleague Miss N. Briggs, 'The Foundation of Wadham College, Oxford' *Oxoniensia*, xxi, 1956); for the foundress's contribution, see also L. Stone, 'The Original Endowment of Wadham College' (*Wadham Gazette*, 1959, 118-19).

which they held in demesne helped to supply their table. Bonner seems to have been obliged in 1545 to transfer Crondon (as well as the manor of Chelmsford) to Henry VIII, who granted it to Petre later in that year. 'Albeit he is not bounden neither by law nor conscience to have any consideration towards the bishopric of London in respect of the manor and park of Crondon, yet of his good will and benevolence which he beareth to the see': so began his deed of gift of £100 to the Dean and Chapter of St. Paul's, dated 10 November. Despite his legal denial, Petre evidently felt, nearly a quarter of a century afterwards, that the episcopal loss had been his gain, so the income from his gift was to be used by future bishops for their household provisions or hospitality.[34] The leading position which Petre had held as an ecclesiastical lawyer doubtless explains his gift in 1568 of £20 to the Company of Advocates of the Court of Arches 'to be employed about the furniture and charges of your new purchased house lately called Monjoy House for their habitation and commons.'[35] The receipt was signed by the Dean of the Arches (p. 8) and nine other doctors.*

4 The Next Generation

A Tudor knight, obliged to meet the heavy expense of daughters' dowries, did not normally indulge in philanthropy at the same time. When Petre began his series of endowments, in 1556, none of his daughters except Dorothy was married. A closer look, however, reveals that he had already planned their future marriages in the manner of the age, in which custom compelled propertied men to make settlements on sons and provide dowries for girls, so that they started married life with an income.

In 1546 he contracted with William Gostwick of Willington, Bedfordshire, for the latter's estate to pass on his death to Elizabeth Petre or any other daughter whom Petre should appoint to marry John or Robert, Gostwick's sons; Petre could recover 1,000 marks if no marriage took place.[35A] John and Elizabeth were then both six years of age. William died at the end of 1549, when Petre secured John's wardship. Elizabeth married John Gostwick on 27 April 1558 at London. Until he became of

---

* Mountjoy House was a large stone building belonging to the Dean and Chapter and formerly let to the Blounts, Lords Mountjoy. It lay on the west side of St. Benet's Hill, the lane leading from St. Paul's to Paul's Wharf, and had been acquired by certain doctors of law in the previous year (Stow's *Survey of London*). Doctors' Commons was to be destroyed in the Great Fire and was later rebuilt. For the relationship between Lady Petre and the Blounts, see p. 26 n. I have to thank the archivist of St. Paul's Cathedral for this note.

age in August 1560 Petre maintained them and they lived in the town house.

In 1555, when Thomasine was twelve, Petre negotiated articles for her marriage to Ludovick, son and heir of Sir Edward Greville of Milcott, Warwickshire. By a settlement of 1557 between the fathers, they were to wed before midsummer 1560, if both children agreed.[36] They were married at St. Botolph's, Aldersgate, on 10 February in that year. The bride was given a splendid trousseau costing Petre £140, many details of which are in the steward's accounts. He had contracted in 1555 'to procure some advancement or preferment' for Sir Edward's younger children or to increase her dowry from 600 to 1,000 marks. In the event he eschewed nepotism and paid the extra cash. Greville on his part settled several manors in Gloucestershire and Oxfordshire on them. Each father bound himself to keep the couple with three menservants, one maid and six horses for two years in his home, if they so wished to accept free board and lodging. They chose to live at Ingatestone Hall, and no less than eight children were born and baptized there in 1563–77. Sir William was godfather to the first, his son John, to the second, both boys. Judged by later happenings, Petre cannot be credited with arranging successful marriages for Elizabeth and Thomasine, but these were not more disastrous failures than the marriage of Anne Cecil to her father's ward, the Earl of Oxford.* The wedding of Catherine, also at sixteen, to John Talbot esquire of Grafton, Worcestershire, took place at Ingatestone on 18 August 1561, shortly after the Queen's visit. The bride's and bridegroom's wedding apparel cost Petre £170 and the bills fill several pages of the accounts. Three of their children were born there, the last in 1571. In the years after Petre's final retirement, Ingatestone Hall was therefore not an elderly couple's quiet, solitary home but almost a patriarchal establishment. Though hard of hearing—at times a consolation with so many grandchildren around—he could seldom have been lonely.

* In 1568 Gostwick was described as 'a man of great simplicity, with very little or no understanding', who had entered into various incompatible leases. He seems to have tried to get the better of his father-in-law, the astute lawyer, by leasing in 1562 part of his Bedfordshire estate, although mortgaged by his father to Petre in 1545 for 2,000 marks. Petre sued him in Chancery in 1567, winning the case (*V.C.H., Beds.*, iii, 203). Greville's career was inglorious and ended tragically. His violent assault on Sir John Conway led to his imprisonment by the Privy Council's orders. On release he came to his mother-in-law at Ingatestone. Ten years afterwards he was again summoned before the Council, for fraud. Finally, in 1589, he was indicted at the Warwickshire Assizes as an accomplice in two separate murders. Ludovick was sentenced to the *peine forte et dure*, that is, to being pressed to death under heavy weights, which was the penalty for refusing to plead to an indictment. A defendant who thus 'stood mute' avoided the forfeiture of his estate to the Crown, so Ludovick's last act was at any rate heroic. (Cf. J. C. Jeaffreson, *Middlesex County Records* (1886–88), i–iii, for notes on the penalty.)

His thoughts no doubt were chiefly directed towards his heir apparent. When only five, John had been brought up to London for Dorothy's wedding, and he was then taken to Greenwich and presented to Philip and Mary. At Ingatestone his boyhood companions, though somewhat older, were mostly his father's wards; and their tutor was apparently Woodward, the family chaplain. John spent 1567–70 as a law student at the Middle Temple, where he kept an account-book,[37] which tells how he sampled life in town, practised music and fencing, and picked up a smattering of the law that would fit him for the County Bench and the management of the estate. The Inns of Court virtually formed a Third University for rich landowners' sons. Whether the Temple in preference to Oxford was his father's or his own choice is not known, but his marriage was not prearranged by the parents. On 17 April 1570, at Ingatestone, he wedded Mary daughter of Sir Edward Waldegrave of Borley (on the Suffolk border of Essex), who had died in the Tower nine years earlier (p. 244n.). Currance's musicians (p. 215) played under John's window on his wedding eve and at the marriage feast. 'Lady Waldegrave's eldest daughter', wrote Sir Francis Englefield, Queen Mary's faithful officer, from Louvain, 'is married to Sir William Petre's son and heir, whose parents gave him free choice of a wife, and now they joy much in his choice, for as they care not for his wealthy match, so they are glad that he made choice in a family of such estimation. Her mother gives with her but what she pleases, for to nothing at all is she bound or strained by his friends.'[38] Her dowry was £500.[39] Petre made them an annual allowance of £135 10s. Their early married life was spent at Writtle Park; about 1575 they moved to Thorndon Hall, which John bought from Lord Mordaunt in 1573.

In April 1571 Sir William Petre made his will.[40] It reflects the deep and well-considered charity which illuminates his previous benefactions. Alms to the poor of the parishes in which his chief properties lay amounted to £60, of which £40 was to be distributed in and around Ingatestone, 10 marks (£6 13s. 4d.) in St. Botolph's, Aldersgate, and the remainder mostly in the West. To provide five years' supply of firewood for the poor of Ingatestone and Fryerning he set aside 100 marks, and to aid eight poor maids at marriage another 40. He left £40 to the poorest inmates of the London and Southwark prisons and hospitals. The churchwardens got a token £10 for the repair of the 'parish church of Ingatstone alias Ging Petre' (he had paid the whole cost of building the south chapel). Finally, he entrusted £200 to his wife to 'bestow in alms and other charitable deeds in such sort as by me she is already instructed'. Some may declare that this clause, despite Petre's use of two separate philanthropic terms, conceals a bequest to the Roman Church, but such a claim would be pure hypothesis.

His servants were well rewarded. Five got £21 between them; the rest, not numbered, a year's wages; and his executors were to consider further gifts for long service. Widow Percy, his old Ingatestone house-keeper, had an annuity of four marks; John Woodward, his chaplain, a legacy of £40. Richard Stonley, John Cliffe and Edward Bell, his officers, for past service to him and future counsel and help to his wife and son, were each given an annuity of five marks. Four servants, including his cook, received life leases of farms, free of rent.

Of Petre's Court cronies a few were still alive, but only one was re-membered in his will: 'I do give to Sir William Cecil knight, now Lord of Burleigh, Chief Secretary to the Queen's Majesty, £20.' Here is final confirmation, were it needed, of their lasting friendship; but it is not known if Petre ever visited Theobalds (twenty miles from Ingatestone), the great Hertfordshire house that Cecil had bought in 1561.

Petre's relations fared in diverse fashion. Nicholas and Dorothy Wadham were bequeathed the £100 which he (Nicholas) 'hath already had by my order of my brother John Petre, late Customer of Exeter', who had died in the previous year. Greville and Talbot each received a silver basin and ewer. Petre had stood godfather to their first-born, so he gave a gold chain worth £40 to William Greville and £100 to Gertrude Talbot. The four other Talbot grandchildren each had 100 marks. The mothers, Thomasine and Catherine, were both left £100, to be paid when their own mother 'thought good'. The other son-in-law was accorded nothing, but Petre gave £100 to Elizabeth Gostwick and 100 marks to his godson William their son and heir. Gostwick's delinquencies, in fact, occasioned by far the longest clause in the will. John Petre was enjoined to complete the restoring of Gostwick's disordered properties and Elizabeth was to have no further monetary help if she vexed John in his unenviable task. Petre's stepdaughter Catherine Baker had died; it looks as though Anne her youngest child was a favourite as she was left a jewel worth £20.

It was understood that Lady Petre, who was to have Ingatestone Hall for life, would continue to reside there. The bequests to her were the usual medley of domestic and personal chattels; among them, all the clothes, jewels and gold chains she normally wore, except a gold ring set with diamond 'given me by the queen of good memory, Queen Mary' (possibly that seen in Lady Petre's portrait in the Long Gallery) and a gold girdle, which were bequeathed to John's wife. Dame Anne had ten featherbeds after John's choosing the four best beds. She was also to have her lord's horses, and all the oxen, cows and sheep in the Ingatestone demesnes and farms. He gave her a rent-free life interest in the town house. One half of the napery and linen stuff and of the pewter and kitchen stuff at Ingatestone and London was bequeathed outright to her, and she could have the use of all of it with the more valuable plate for life, if she did not remarry. The son and heir apparent was the residuary legatee of the goods and chattels, and of course all the estates were to pass to him and his heirs male.

Petre had founded a new county family, but twelve months after John's marriage, with no sign of Mary being pregnant, the testator had to allow for the possibility of there being no male heir. (William, apparently their firstborn, did not arrive till four years later.) Sir William's provision is significant only in showing how his wealth would have been distributed had John died without issue before his father's death. Petre entailed five manors in the West; one was to go to 'William Petre the son and heir of my brother John Petre the elder of Tor Brian deceased';* two to John the younger son of John Talbot; two to Edward, second son of Ludovick Greville, and in default to John, the third son. In the same event, one fourth of the testator's personal chattels not otherwise bequeathed were to go to his wife, another fourth was to be subdivided between his daughters and their children, and the remaining half was to pass to the poor and 'for other good deeds of charity' at the executors' discretion.

He named as executors his wife, his son, and John Cliffe of Ingatestone, his law steward and former Signet clerk, who was given an extra £20. It was normal for a testator to appoint overseers to supervise or assist the executors, and Petre chose a powerful business friend and a relative of his wife: 'I do pray Sir William Garrard knight, alderman of London, and Mr. Edmund Tyrell esquire to be overseers, and I do give them for their pains and for a remembrance of old friendship £10 apiece.' Finally, he added a third line of defence against anything going awry, 'requiring' his brother Robert, the Exchequer official, who had his own chamber in Sir William's town house, John Kyme and Edward Bell,† his two stewards of such long standing, to aid his wife, son and executors; and he rewarded all three with £10. The experienced lawyer, knowing the lamentable frequency of probate disputes, tried to safeguard his beneficiaries from

---

* The only other mention of his Devon relations is a legacy of £10 to each of his (unnamed) sisters' children. In 1560 his accounts refer to a loan of £4 to 'John Petre my master's nephew' to pay the bills of one Jacomyn a surgeon 'for healing his wound' and of an innkeeper, 'to be repaid by Mr. Petre his father' (evidently the same John, who died in 1568).

† Bell was now also Coroner of the Liberty of Writtle. He died in 1577. For his brass in Writtle church and his family, see *Trans. Ess. Arch. Soc.*, ix, 59–61, and *Ess. Rev.*, xvii, 15–18.

being involved in such trouble by begging his executors to interpret his bequests liberally.

The annual value of Petre's estates in Essex, Devon and elsewhere, according to the usual schedule attached to the inquisition *post mortem*, totalled £792 15s. 9¾d., a sum which agrees fairly closely with the capital he had expended in lands.

'He was a good master and neighbour, and remarkably charitable to the poor.' These were the words of a Catholic historian, not favourably disposed to one who had deviated from the strait way, but they ring true. A simple calculation bears out his comment. Petre's endowments were worth £178 a year—the equivalent of about £3,500 in capital. In his lifetime and by his will he gave away a further £563 in money for charitable purposes; he also built the almshouses and the south chapel of Ingatestone church. All this must have raised his total outlay to about £5,000.

The main phases of his philanthropy accord fairly well with the general picture of his age and class. Around the middle of the century the marked 'secularization of the charitable impulse', directed chiefly towards the poor and education, was a genuine sign of the 'changing pattern of aspirations' of men in the upper and middle social ranks.[42] The difficulties of understanding the charitable motives of so reticent a man as Petre are of course greatest if his spiritual, let alone doctrinal, ideas are sought. As so often before, there is little evidence, and that is baffling. It is better to dwell on his more tangible endowments. Their scale was munificent, and their results were lasting.

Petre had concealed his doctrinal views throughout his life, and it was not to be expected that he would disclose them in his will. But nothing he said, nothing others said of him, justifies any categorical statement on his faith. His actions over a quarter of a century confirm the almost unanimous contemporary view that his religious opinions were moderate. Rarely was this attitude more clearly expressed than during Bonner's trial, when, directing his earnest gaze on Cranmer, he had stopped the archbishop from penetrating further into fundamentals beyond human comprehension. Petre's bearing at the trial was very different from Smith's intransigence (incidentally, Smith and Mason among other colleagues had been ordained priests in earlier years). The retention of John Woodward as the family chaplain after his resignation of the rectory of Ingatestone suggests that the Petre household was Catholic, but it is no proof of Sir William's own tenets. Woodward had served him for some years in more than one capacity in the household, and Lady Petre, an uncompromising Catholic, would have been distressed had he dismissed the chaplain. Sir William was growing old, he had been a loyal minister of the Crown for many years, Cecil was his friend, and nobody would have been anxious to pry into his chaplain's position so long as the law was not openly disobeyed. Petre may not have been deeply religious, but some of his letters and his charitable deeds reveal spiritual convictions which indicate an attitude towards religion which was conservative; yet it may never be possible to pierce the barrier of his natural and deliberately cultivated reticence. That he was a pragmatist and a philanthropist is good enough.

Sir William Petre died at his Essex home on 13 January 1572. Nothing is known of his last illness. His will was proved on 31 January. He was buried in Ingatestone parish church on 1 February. The mourners, according to the certificate of the three heralds present at the funeral, included his son John, Sir Henry Tyrell, Sir Thomas Mildmay, Robert Petre his brother the Auditor of the Exchequer, and Edmund Tyrell of Rawreth.[43] 'His death was lamented by many', the laconic remark of a later historian, is probably true.[44]

In his will he asked to be buried 'in the new aisle of the parish church and there be made and builded some honest monument with the names of me and my two wives'. He left details to his executors, who erected a fine monument, in alabaster and marble, under the arch between the chancel and his aisle (plate 17). It was probably the work of Cornelius Cure, who designed the tomb of Mary Queen of Scots in Westminster Abbey, and bears effigies of Sir William and Dame Anne, but none of Gertrude his first wife. He is arrayed in plate armour, elaborately worked; over the monument, suspended from the arch in an iron grille, is the heraldic achievement.[45]

Lady Petre survived him by just over ten years. Her own will declared that she had lived and would die 'a true member and in the unity of the Catholic Church'.[46] Indeed, during her widowhood she sheltered the priest, John Payne, who lived at Ingatestone Hall under the guise of her steward. (Two, possibly three, ingenious priests' hiding-holes have been discovered in different parts of the building.) Payne was arrested at the Hall, imprisoned early in 1577 and soon afterwards exiled. The time of his return was not previously known, but he has been found as a witness to Lady Petre's will, dated June 1578. In 1581 he was betrayed by George Eliot, a servant at the Hall, was arrested in Warwickshire, and was indicted for high treason in plotting to assassinate the Queen, a trumped-up charge. He was put to death at Chelmsford on 2 April 1582—the only Catholic to be executed in Essex during Elizabeth's reign.[47]

Lady Petre's final will, made less than a month before her death, is in line with the charitable reputation she had earned during her lifetime. She died at Ingatestone Hall on 10 March 1582, and was buried in the church on 10 April.[48]

In the meantime, the mansion on which Sir William had lavished so much thought had already become the dower house. John was already at Writtle. About four years after his father's death he moved to Thorndon Hall, which he had acquired from Lord Mordaunt, and with it an estate in West Horndon and Ingrave that rounded off the large block of lands to the south of Ingatestone. He was soon to reap the economic benefits of this major piece of consolidation.[49] Thorndon was to become the main family seat for three centuries. In 1576 he was knighted and became Sheriff of Essex;[50] and in 1603 he was created the first Baron Petre of Writtle (plate 18).

And it is with his heir, not with his widow, that the story of Sir William Petre rightly ends. Giving his paternal blessing, he wisely refrained from moral advice. But he specially charged John to use 'good will and favour' in executing his will:

> So doing, God Almighty, by whose only goodness I have obtained all that I have had or shall leave, shall and will bless, direct and assist him to pass the course of this vain and uncertain life to his pleasure.

In this valediction he was only expanding the motto which he had chosen for the family—SANS DIEU RIEN.

5 Epilogue

Any attempt to assess Sir William Petre's place in Tudor political history is linked with the problem of deciding how far his advice swayed the leaders, at whose deliberations he was so often present, and how much his labours helped the administration of the state at its highest levels.

Petre became Secretary soon after the status of the office had been raised from a mediocre appointment in the royal household to the most powerful one in the government—that used by Cromwell as the chief means of wielding power, and therefore suspect at his fall. There followed a long decline in good government during a decade punctuated by political, fiscal and religious revolutions in which orderly progress became increasingly difficult.

No sooner had Petre been promoted as Secretary in 1544 than he took his share in the small Regency Council's responsibilities. Not long after returning from martial adventures Henry gradually lost his strong hold.

On his death the nation was staggered by violent changes in rapid succession: a boy King under a well-meaning dictator was later dominated by another dictator; the second, ruthless and perfidious, treasonably put on the throne a girl, but only for nine days; then the rightful Queen reversed the extreme Protestant reforms and restored Papal supremacy before she, like her brother, died prematurely; finally, another Queen succeeded, with ideas in great contrast to those of her predecessor. All these events were an unprecedented sequence for Englishmen.

The years of Petre's greatest potential effort coincided with the worst period of chaos in the sixteenth century. The amount of constructive planning which could be put into force was limited. In almost every branch of central administration, the magnates' rivalries forced the highest officials to concentrate on the immediate future. He was seldom a maker of policy in that age of opportunism. No Secretary had much chance to show creative capacity. Petre's retention of high office through the upheavals demonstrates his ability, which in the often treacherous and sordid circumstances could rarely be used positively and purposefully.

England's notable statesmen have earned reputations by their reforms or conduct of foreign policies. In Petre's time, however, progressive action was so frustrated by internecine duels in the Council that the best service which he could give to a country ruled by dictators (1547-53) and by declining monarchs (1545-7 and 1556-8) was to maintain whatever administrative continuity was possible amid the mounting confusion, and to keep a cool head and a quiet tongue. His work was thus necessarily unspectacular and has to be traced by delving deeply into the state papers. It is only after the testimony of many small items has been brought together that contemporary references to his ability can be fully understood. His industry is more apparent. The public records alone reveal the astonishing amount of business which was initiated or executed by him. His labours were in fact almost incessant, anticipating in large measure that devotion to the nation's needs which was later personified by Cecil.

It is not easy to define the relationship at any given time between the civil servants and the factious politicians in whom the power rested, because the pattern changed so often. But in calmer moments, the scheming leaders realized how much the country owed to such level-headed though versatile men as Treasurer Winchester, Comptroller Paget and Secretary Petre. They, and a few others, bore the real burden of central government before the partnership between Elizabeth and Cecil.

There is of course no question of comparing Petre's achievements with those of Cromwell, Gardiner or Cecil. He never rose to the front rank; nor did his long-term colleagues Winchester, Pembroke, Arundel,

Wotton or Mason; in Pollard's opinion they were all officials rather than statesmen. In Mary's first years he nearly attained the higher status, only to withdraw of his own accord. No pre-eminent statesman appeared in his most active period. When his energy was not being dissipated in avoiding Court feuds, the religious and economic troubles absorbed a disproportionate amount of what remained. He was also a leading Parliament man, as the Journals show; but in a period of upheavals little sound legislation emerged before Elizabeth's second Parliament.

He was known as 'a man of moderation' to many besides Sir Thomas Smith. Constant advocate of order, his public career exemplified Smith's ideals. Indeed, *De Republica Anglorum*, with its reasoning and its logical pleas for order in political affairs, might almost have come from Petre's pen.

In all this, Petre had infinitely more in common with his junior, Cecil, than his master, Cromwell, or his senior, Wriothesley. So swiftly did Cromwell and Wriothesley climb to power that they antagonized the other magnates, who pulled down each of them at the first opportunity. The lesson, soon to be repeated in the persons of other ministers, was not lost on Petre. Had Mary's spiritual balance and health not suffered, her industry and sincerity would have called forth Petre's sustained effort in what might have been a notable partnership. Equally he might have reached greater heights if, in the prime of his life, he had been Secretary to Elizabeth. He had the qualifications and the personal qualities she required. He had, too, one asset which Cecil strangely lacked—the knowledge and experience gained from foreign travel, which broadens the insular outlook.

The secrets of Petre's success in maintaining his place are found not so much in events as in his own character. In his capacity to turn to the veering winds of national politics, he was only one of several contemporaries to whom could be applied Winchester's oft-quoted epigram, 'I am sprung from the willow, not the oak', in response to his being asked how he managed to serve Henry, Edward and Mary in turn. But a later historian's remark, that Winchester 'was famous for his dexterity in shifting sides, always to his own credit', does not fit Petre so aptly; witness, for example, the small reward he got after each *coup d'état* in which he was a member of the victorious party.

Other traits which helped him to win security of tenure were a sober disposition, a polite personality, a natural reticence and above all, honesty. The last virtue, rare enough in Tudor court circles, is seen most often in the negative form of abstaining from dishonesty, and to give positive proof is difficult. However, some instances of Petre's unquestionable honesty have been noted in the course of the story. The Principal Secretaries had ample opportunity for enriching themselves by means of gifts and offerings from the mighty and the humble seeking their support in matters coming before the Crown or the Council. Despite the comparative profusion of documentary evidence of Petre's own finances, which has been very fully examined, there is not the slightest hint of his receiving lucrative income from this source.

It is a remarkable testimony to his reputation that records of his time do not yield a single harsh epithet about him, despite his numerous associates including ambassadors, whose dispatches abound with uninhibited abuse of royal officials. To avoid all forms of punishment and disgrace is enough to distinguish him; to remain completely free from vituperation by his contemporaries through so long a period is extraordinary. There is never the slightest hint of brutality or ruthlessness. The verdict of the older historians is also almost unanimous that he was not guilty of any of the common political offences, not even peculation. The earliest, only seven years after his death, is in Holinshed. The chronicler attributes Petre's long tenure of office to his 'judgment and pregnant wit' (i.e. intellectual ability). A generation later, Camden called him a 'man of approved wisdom and exquisite learning'. The eighteenth-century historian Strype, who was vicar of Leyton not far from Petre's Essex home, deals with his qualities in his 'Animadversions upon Sir John Hayward's Life and Reign of King Edward VI' (1630), a judgment of Sir William vitiated by fancy. 'Of Secretary Petre', Strype remarked, 'Hayward gives the character, "who under pretence of gravity, covered much untrustworthiness of heart"'; and then declared, 'An unfair character of a very wise and honest man and long experience in the public affairs, without any spot that ever I could find; except that he did comply with the changes of religion under the princes in whose reigns he served: which was a practice of a great number more besides himself.' Few historians of the Dissolution have been noted for their leniency towards the visitors; but Dixon, for instance, found no stronger term for Petre than 'omnivorous'—for the Crown, not for himself; and recent works based on closer research reveal nothing worse. That he 'deserted' Somerset in the crisis of 1549 is untrue of one who was prevented by the rebel Council from returning to the Protector. While his 'time-serving' actions cannot be denied, his aim seems to have been to serve Henry, Edward, Mary and Elizabeth with equal fidelity. Cecil's recent biographer makes the same point when he says that his subject 'was consistently loyal to the legitimate Tudor sovereign'. 'I shall act as a trusty servant and councillor may be expected to do' was Petre's way of fending off a crafty approach by the

Spanish ambassador, but there is no trace of hypocrisy; he meant what he said.

When the few mild censures of Petre are compared with those against other respectable councillors (some of his colleagues are beyond defence), the result is equally creditable. Historians' indictments of Paget for treachery and corruption, of Cecil for dissimulation and cringing at Mary's accession, of Smith's unscrupulousness and ill-temper, for example, are matched by Bourne's own admission of flagrant misdemeanour.

Another of Petre's few remarks about himself is in his letter to Cecil in 1551 on the sin of covetousness, or 'fishing in the tempestuous seas for gain and wicked mammon'. 'The confession is unique', Pollard remarked, 'but the vice was universal.' Judged by the black voracity of others, Petre's greed was pale grey. Oliver's charge that Petre secured great spoils from the Suppression of the Monasteries has been shown to be false.

His charitable endowments were substantial enough to earn him the title of philanthropist. The frequency with which letters mention his 'gentleness' (in the sense of courtesy and affability) is noticeable; and while some may be dismissed as sycophantic others have the ring of sincerity. References to his clemency towards prisoners appear occasionally, for instance, after Wyatt's rebellion. His accounts afford many glimpses of his kindly disposition, seen through the matter-of-fact entries of his two stewards. He took small advantage, as compared with men of his generation, of the landlord's opportunities for raising tenants' rents. While Ascham's story revealed Petre as a disciplinarian, he seems to have been slightly ahead of his time in giving his heir 'free choice of a wife'. His grave, slightly forbidding appearance evidently masked a good deal of innate benevolence.

Ten years ago, in *The England of Elizabeth*, Dr. A. L. Rowse, another West Countryman at Oxford, wrote of Petre: 'He was a humane man, with a sensible latitudinarianism of mind; a patron of learning and a benefactor to both his colleges at Oxford'. It is fitting that the present book should have been written by a man who, like Petre, adopted Essex as his county and has seen a wing of Sir William's own house devoted, as he intended Exeter College to be, to the 'good education of youth'.

Appendices

Appendix A

PETRE'S ACCOUNTS, 1539–1562

E.R.O.

D/DP *General, kept by Petre himself*

A1.   Nov. 1539–Oct. 1544.   Receipts of rents, annuities, offices, 1539–44; brief summary of expenses, Dec. 1542–Nov. 1543 (see Appendix B). Some entries in his wife's hand.

Personal, Court and London books, kept by John Kyme, chief steward

A2.   Jan. 1544–Nov. 1544   Detailed expenses and receipts. (Includes brief expenses during Queen Regent's progress, Aug.–Oct.)

A3.   Dec. 1547–Nov. 1548.   Do.

A4.   Dec. 1548–July 1550.   Do.

A5.   Dec. 1553–Nov. 1554.   Do. (Includes detailed expenses during Wyatt's rebellion and Queen's marriage progress, Feb. and June–Aug.)

A6.   Dec. 1554–Nov. 1555.   Do. (Includes Lady Petre's detailed clothing expenses for Dorothy's wedding and Thomasine's going to Marchioness of Exeter.)

A7.   Dec. 1555–Nov. 1556.   Do.

A8.   Dec. 1558–Nov. 1560.   Detailed expenses only. (Includes detailed clothing expenses for Thomasine's wedding.)

A9.   Dec. 1560–Nov. 1562.   Do. (Includes detailed provisions expenses for Queen's visit to Ingatestone Hall and clothing expenses for Catherine's wedding, July and Aug. 1561.)

Ingatestone Hall General books, kept by Edward Bell, house steward

A10.   Dec. 1549–Nov. 1550.   Detailed expenses.

A11.   Dec. 1554–Nov. 1555.   Detailed expenses, arranged under twenty heads.

APPENDICES

Contents of D/DP A11

Accounts of receipts and expenditure, Dec. 1554–Nov. 1555, arranged in the following sections, each section covering the whole year:

(i) Money received 'of my lady', chiefly for payment of wages [brief monthly statements]; (ii) Money spent (over £60) on clothing, including 'apparell for M'res Dorothye Petre ayenst her maryage' [detailed];(iii) Spices and fruit; (iv) Salt and fish ('lynges and habyrdens bowght at Harwhich'); (v) Malt; (vi) Carriage and travelling expenses; (vii) Servant's wages and liveries (includes curate of Buttsbury); (viii) Stable expenses (horseshoes, saddles, bridles); (ix) Repairs of carts and carters' expenses; (x) 'Rewards'; (xi) Tithes; (xii) Wood-cutting and fuel; (xiii) Hedging and ditching; (xiv) Metal repairs and payments to smiths; (xv) Building expenses (bricks and carpentry, including 240,000 bricks made); (xvi) Extraordinary payments (e.g. 'a pownde of gonepowder', 'iiij knottes of vyrgynall strynge', 'sope', 'yncke', 'collectors for the pore'); (xvii) Garden and orchard; (xviii) Husbandry at East Horndon; (xix) Annuities; (xx) Total payments, balanced against receipts in (i).

[Preparations for the marriage are referred to in several sections]

Ingatestone Hall Provision books ('week books'), kept by the clerk of the kitchen

A12. Jan. 1548–Dec. 1548. Detailed weekly statements (see Appendix E for week including Twelfth Day). (Includes names of guests and full list of presents received.)

A13. Dec. 1551–Dec. 1552. Detailed weekly statements, also food consumed at dinner and supper daily and at Catherine Tyrell's wedding (see Appendix F for three weeks including Christmas, New Year and Twelfth Days). (Includes names of guests and list of presents received.)

Various Accounts

A14. Dec. 1555–Nov. 1556. Complete audit roll of receipts and expenses, including Ingatestone (see pp. 270–72).

299

A15. Nov. 1556–Dec. 1557. Children's clothing expenses, kept by Lady Petre. (1 vol.)

A16. Jan. 1539–Oct. 1540. Detailed receipts and expenses of John Tyrell of Heron Hall, Essex, and his widow Anne, who married Petre, 1541–2. (1 vol.)

A17. Oct. 1567–Sep. 1570. Detailed receipts of John Petre when a student at the Middle Temple. (1 vol.)

Estate Receipts books

A83. Michaelmas 1563–Michaelmas 1564. Detailed receipts from all estates.

A84. Michaelmas 1564–Michaelmas 1565. Do.

A85. Michaelmas 1569–Michaelmas 1570. Do.

A86. Michaelmas 1570–Michaelmas 1571. Do.

General Note. Apart from the audit-roll for the accounting year December 1555–November 1556 (D/DP A14), there is no complete account of Petre's income and expenditure, and it is doubtful if such statements were prepared for him in earlier years. Similar accounts for the Tudor period are extremely rare, and the profit and loss account and balance sheet, as understood nowadays, were virtually non-existent. The main purpose of the accounts kept by Petre's chief and Ingatestone stewards was to record the items for which they were liable for discharge at the end of the accounting year (30 November). Some follow the contemporary 'charge and discharge' form; some do not even attempt this elementary form of balancing. 'There was no charge', Petre's chief steward wrote at the end of one account, 'made of the receipt thereof in any book declared before me.' The subject is discussed in *Studies in the History of Accounting*, ed. A. C. Littleton and B. S. Yamey (1956), and by G. R. Batho, 'The Finances of an Elizabethan Nobleman: Henry Percy, Ninth Earl of Northumberland, 1564–1632' (*Econ. Hist. Rev.*, 2nd series, ix (1957), 433–50); see also *Catalogue of Exhibition of Accounting Records* (Pub. Rec. Off., 1950).

APPENDICES

Appendix B

PETRE'S EXPENDITURE, DEC. 1542 – NOV. 1543

	£	s.	d.
Payments ordinary, wages and liveries	197	13	7¾
Buildings and reparations	153	11	9
Payments extraordinary	298	10	0½
Apparel and making thereof	17	11	1½
Expenses of the stable, besides provision of hay and oats	16	16	11
Laid out in the household for fresh 'cates' [acates, purchases]	15	17	4½
Wheat, 39 qtrs. at 10s. the qtr.	19	10	0
Malt, 54 qtrs. at 4s. 8d. the qtr.	17	12	0
Salt fish—ling half a hundred at £3, haberdin half a hundred and a quarter 30s., stockfish a quarter 6s. 8d., salt eels a firkin 12s., white herring 2 barrels 30s., red herring 1 cade 6s. 8d., sprats 1 cade 2s.	7	7	4
Sugar and spice—sugar 60 lb. at 7d. a lb., 35s.; great raisins 50 lbs. at 1½d., 6s. 3d.; pepper 6 lb. at 23d., 11s. 6d.; 8 oz. cloves at 2s. 4d.; 9 oz. mace 3s. 9d.; small raisins 24 lb., 4s.; prunes 40 lb., 6s. 8d.; nutmegs, cinnamon and ginger, 6s. 8d.	3	16	2
Wine—a puncheon of French wine 55s. 5d., besides ½ butt of 'muskedell' sent me by my brother	2	15	5
Linen cloth—a piece of 'sowtwyche' 11s. 4d., a piece of holland cont. 24 ells 18s., ½ piece of dowlas cont. 47 ells 26s. 8d.	2	16	0
Oats 51 qtrs. at 2s. 8d., hay 50 loads at 4s.	16	14	4
Wood bought with the making of the same, besides my provision at London and the carriage	12	13	7
Beeves 15 at 18s. the piece and muttons 54 at 2s. 8d. the piece	20	16	8
Veals 17 at 3s. 4d., 50s. [sic]; lambs 20 at 14d., 23s. 4d.; porkets 12 at 2s., 24s.; 2 boars at 6s. 8d., 13s. 4d.	5	10	8
Hops 3 hundred at 16s.	2	8	0
Salt—bay salt 8 qtrs. at 5s. 4d., 42s. 8d., white salt 1 qtr. at 6s. 8d.	2	9	4
Total expenses this year	814	10	4¼

Appendix C

PETRE'S ARMS

Sir William Petre was granted armorial bearings by Christopher Barker, Garter from 1536 to 1550 (College of Arms archives). The date of the grant is not given but must have been between that of his knighthood in 1544 and the earliest mention of his arms—a 1548 New Year's gift of a 'salt having my master's arms'. In 1549 Petre agreed to pay £20 to Peter Nycolson of Southwark, a glazier, for glazing East Horndon Hall and 'setting up there such several arms as shall be by the said Sir William appointed' (E.R.O., D/DP A4). His personal attendants wore his 'badge' on their livery. He used three armorial seals: (1) a large one, without crest but with the legend SANS DIEU RIEN—RIEN SANS DIEU, e.g. D/DP T1/1861 (1560), T1/582 (1569); (2) one of medium size, with helmet and crest but no legend, e.g. D/DP T1/1511 (1567); (3) one of medium size, crest only, apparently reserved for official papers, e.g. S.P. 10/13/43 (1551).

His arms were: *gules on a bend or between two escallops argent a Cornish chough sable, beak and legs gules, between two cinquefoils azure, on a chief or a rose between two fleurs de lis dimidiated issuing from the dexter and sinister flank of the shield respectively, gules*; crest: *two lions' heads erased and addorsed, the dexter azure, the sinister or, gorged with three barrulets counterchanged* (ex inf. College of Arms).

The three original quarries of heraldic stained glass in the Long Gallery at Ingatestone Hall show the arms of Petre and those of his two wives: his own as above (plate 13); the Tyrell arms, *argent, two chevrons azure within a bordure engrailed gules, an annulet for difference*; and the Browne arms, *azure, a chevron between three escallops, all within a bordure engrailed or*.

Sir William's arms were later known as 'Petre, ancient', in distinction to the simplified arms, *gules, a bend or between two escallops argent*, as borne by his son ('Petre, modern').

Appendix D

PETRE'S WARDS

Wards and wardships have recently been covered by two detailed studies, *An Introduction to the History and Records of the Court of Wards and Liveries* (1953), by Mr. H. E. Bell, and *The Queen's Wards: Wardship and Marriage under Elizabeth I* (1958), by Professor J. Hurstfield. The latter deals so fully with the financial aspects that only the cost of education of Petre's wards is referred to below in any detail. His accounts have many entries of expenditure and income concerning his wards, but no reliable figures of profit can be drawn, as the accounts have gaps.

The chief aim of the suitor to the Court of Wards and Liveries for the grant of a wardship was the valuable future right of arranging the ward's marriage. The grantee had the choice of marrying the ward to his own child or relation, who thus acquired the ward's lands, or of selling the right to the best bidder. How two of Petre's wards married his daughters is described on pp. 286–87. The guardian usually also secured from the Crown a lease of the lands during the minority at profitable terms. Petre was in a privileged place for seeking such grants.

In 1550 he was allowed to purchase the right of wardship and marriage of his own heir John and of the four daughters of his wife's first and second marriages and to vest it in his friend William Pownsett of Barking as trustee. The legal machinery designed to achieve this family safeguard worked in reverse: it was Pownsett who nominally bought the Crown grant for 100 marks and then released it to Petre eight days later (*Cal. Pat.*, *Edw. VI*, iii, 302, cited by H. E. Bell, *op. cit.*, 117 n.; E.R.O., D/DP F145).

Of his first three wards, the grant of Edward Sulyard's wardship has not been found. His other early excursions into the market concerned John Eiston and Thomas Leigh, granted in 1546–47 (*L. & P., Hen. VIII*, xxi, pt. i, p. 472 and *Cal. Pat., Edw. VI*, i, 100). In 1550 he obtained the wardship of John, son of William Gostwick, who owned a large estate at Willington in Bedfordshire but apparently lived at Cauldwell Priory, Bedford, of which he had a lease (*Cal. Pat., Edw. VI*, iii, 303). Petre had a good reason to be the best bidder (p. 286). In 1555 he also secured Anne and Juliana, daughters of John Drake, an Exeter merchant (*Cal. Pat., Phil. & Mary*, ii, 281). Petre had petitioned for this six months earlier, one month in fact before their father's death. Such unseemly anticipation was by no means uncommon (H. E. Bell, *op. cit.*, 115). His accounts give: 'The Clerk of the Wards for the writing of Mr. Drake's wards, 2*s*. 6*d*.; the Master of the Wards' servant for the letter to seize [take legal custody of] the wards, 20*d*.' The girls did not come to Ingatestone; a bond was given in 1556 by John Petre of Tor Brian to Sir William for delivering one of them to her guardian if she did not shortly marry a son of John.

In that year Petre bought the wardship of John son and heir of Sir John Talbot of Grafton in Worcestershire. With this grant his annual gross income from wards' estates totalled £196 according to his accounts for 1556 (E.R.O., D/DP A14). The last two purchases were in 1560 and the new wards were William son of Edward Napper, who had been his Oxford land agent, and Thomas son of William Berners of Thoby in Mountnessing, a government official (*Cal. Pat., Phil. & Mary*, iii, 165; *Eliz.*, i, 421); later Petre also became guardian of Griselda Berners.

With the exception of Eiston and the Drake girls, they all lived as members of the Ingatestone household. At least two of the wards received a university education. In November 1554 Sulyard was sent to Cambridge with Thomas Tyrell, who was presumably Lady Petre's brother-in-law. He was not a ward, but Petre paid for the youth's education. Their tutor was Richard Smith, M.A., who received £3 for his pains and a further £10 5s. 'for their meat and drink for 41 weeks (Nov. 1554–Sept. 1555) at 5s. weekly for both their tables'; with books, clothes, mending, washing, fuel, and 'reading', the total was £18 3s. 11d. Bell noted his own travelling expenses in riding over to Cambridge twice, in April and September, 'to dispatch with their tutor for all manner of things'. Sulyard and Tyrell were brought down from Cambridge to Ingatestone by Bell on 20 September. The former probably remained there until mid-October, when he was sent to London in the company of Talbot, both being attended by Petre's servant. They joined Tyrell at Aldersgate, all three departing on 15 October for Oxford 'to school' (i.e. as 'scholars' or undergraduates) in the charge of Napper, who was given £10 to provide their 'furniture'.

Although Petre was not formally granted Talbot's wardship until February 1556, it is clear that he had been assured of it well before that date, as the accounts show that Talbot arrived at Hampton Court to be placed in his care on 11 July 1555 (four weeks after the death of the boy's father): 'Master Talbot came to my master—cherries for the Lady Talbot bringing her son, 3d.'; followed next day by: 'A cap for Master Talbot 2s. 4d., 2 dozen buttons for his leather jerkin 8d., thread 1d., closing of the jerkin at the shoemakers 8d.' A few days later, attended by five servants, Talbot and Gostwick journeyed towards Ingatestone.

Sulyard, Tyrell and Talbot must have arrived to find Oxford in a state of turmoil, for Ridley and Latimer were burned there on that same October day. All three youths were at Oxford in 1556 and may have witnessed Cranmer's death at the stake. Napper was repaid £20 in May 1556 'upon a reckoning towards the finding of Talbot, Tyrell and Sulyard at Oxford', and a further £10 later that year. Sulyard completed his studies by at least 1559. On Talbot's return from Ingatestone to Oxford in February 1559, he was provided with new clothes, set down in great detail, furred gown, dagger, lute, and four books, at a total cost of nearly £10. He got 20s. 'in reward at his going', evidently pocket-money. Mr.

Delahyde, presumably a tutor, was given £10 towards Talbot's and Tyrell's 'diets' and a further 20s. for himself. In June 1559 £12 was 'delivered to Mr. Delahyde at Oxford towards the charges of Mr. Talbot and towards the charges of meat, drink and teaching of Mr. Thomas Tyrell'; and they got 13s. 4d. more pocket-money. The two apparently came down in March 1560, when the tutor received a further £10 16s. 2d. Petre had discharged his duties to the full. His accounts also reveal that he paid for the education of several poor scholars at Oxford; for example, in 1556, Richard Fountains, who became vicar of Brent in Devon, and Richard Percy, who was probably the son of widow Percy, his Ingatestone housekeeper.*

What education Petre gave to Napper's and Berners' sons is not known, as his later accounts are lost. He did not have a uniform approach towards his wards' education, as Gostwick's case shows. Although Gostwick matriculated as a pensioner of Clare College, Cambridge, in 1554 (Venn, *Alumni Cantab.*), there is no indication that he studied there; Petre may have changed his mind and taken him to Court, where indeed he spent the last ten weeks of that year, evidently attending on his guardian. By his will, Petre made provision for Griselda Berners' marriage to be 'bestowed honestly, without disparagement and according to her condition and degree'; Lady Petre discharged this duty by marrying her in due course to Thomas, the Bakers' second son. This and other evidence points to Petre having assumed the full obligations of a guardian, and there is not the slightest suggestion of any extra profit-chasing. The number of wardships he secured over a fifteen-year period was probably well up to the average for a man holding a key position at Court, but he is excluded from 'the corrupt circle which reaped a golden harvest' during Edward's minority (J. Hurstfield, *op. cit.*, 10). He obtained the grants while Paulet Lord St. John (Winchester), Englefield and Parry successively were Masters of the Court of Wards, but, despite his friendship with Cecil who became Master in 1561, he certainly did not acquire any wardships in the early years of his mastership. (Petre's accounts end in 1562 and the unpublished calendars of the Patent Rolls to 1567 contain no such grant.) No hint occurs of any private payments to Cecil's predecessors such as the £350 'gift' to Cecil's son in 1595 when he was Master (J. Hurstfield, *op. cit.*, 82–3).

* For Fountains, see Boase, *op. cit.*; for Percy, see Foster's *Alumni Oxonienses*.

Appendix E

PROVISION ACCOUNT BOOK,
INGATESTONE HALL, 8–14 JANUARY 1548

Setterday 14 January

	Recevid	Spent	Remayne
Oxe cut owt into lyvere peces	28	27	1
Rostinge peces	10	10	—
Legges	4	4	—
Maribons	2	2	—
Chynes	2	—	2
Muttons	4	4	$\frac{1}{2}$
Capons in grese	8	8	
Mallardes	—	10	—
Tealles	—	6	—
Larkes	—	3 dosen	—
Snipps	—	8	—
Wodcokes	—	2	—
Wigions	—	5	—
Oxburdes	—	12	—
Blake byrdes	—	12	—
Pranes	—	9	—
Goodwynes	—	1	—
Nettes tonges	1	2	1
Conies	14	10	4
Partriches	5	5	—
Linges old Sturbridge	2	$1\frac{1}{2}$	$\frac{1}{2}$
Haberdens	3	3	—
Butter	3 quartes	3 quartes	—
Egges	30	146	24
Chese	2	2	—

Spent of provicion

Oxen, 1.
Shepe, 4.
Whete white, 3 bus.
Whete redde, 4 bus.
Otes, 20 bus.
Malte, 20 bus.

Empcions

Edwarde Ingref, for 6 cople of capons 7*s*., 3 dosen larkes 12*d*., 6 mallardes & 5 shelfowles 4*s*., eight snipps 12*d*., see fyshe and oysters 3*s*. 8*d*., egges 2*s*. 1*d*., rosting bef 20*d*., 6 pigges 3*s*., este to brew & bake 6*d*., a capon bought by the butler by my ladies commaundment 6*d*.
Summa, 24*s*. 5*d*.

Presentes

A peycoke, 2 capons, a bundell of apple seates, from Robert Smythe of Sowthe Hanvile [Hanningfield].
2 capons from Edget of Dunton.
2 capons from Drywod of Dunton.
1 capon from old Rawlyns wyf.
A goodwyne, a teall, 12 oxburdes, 9 praynes from Mr. Hayes father.
A woodcoke & 7 byrdes from Burton.
A capon in grese from Johan Sawier.
A basket of wardens from Mystres Tyrrell of Warley.
2 capons from Myddleton of Ingatston.
A capon & a henne from Bexwell.
A turky hen & a dishe of apples from Mr. Clavell of Hanvile.
5 partriches from Mr. Pownset.
2 hennes from Tauerner of Buttesbury.
Whete white a quarter from Harry Stretes.

Remayne of the buttry, cellor, pantry and brewhouse

White wyne nihil, redd wyne ½ hogges hedde, French wyne 1½ hoges hedde, sacke ½ butte, Raynyshe wyne ½ punchion.
March bere ½ hogges hedde, bere 10 kilderkyns.
Manchete 14 cast, ravell bredde 7 cast, temsbredde 4 cast.

Remayne of the dery, pultry, fyshe & garners

Chese 109.
Butter 6 potes & a barell.
Capons in grese 10, lean capons [blank], hennes 20, pulletes 3, chekyns nihil.
Whete white and redd together in the lyme lofte 3 quarter.
White whete in the white whet lofte 3 quarter 1 bus.
Red whete ther 2 quarter.
Malte [blank].
Otes 10 quarter 3 bus.

Olde Sturbridge linges 6 cople.
New Sturbridge ling 14½ cople.
Westurne linge 8 cople.
Linges browght from London 1 cople.
Harbberdens brought from thens 4½ cople.

Appendix F

PROVISION ACCOUNT BOOK, INGATESTONE HALL, 20 DECEMBER 1551–9 JANUARY 1552, INCLUDING CHRISTMAS DAY, NEW YEAR'S DAY AND TWELFTH DAY

SONDAY 20° DECEMBRIS

DYNER

Boylde beiffe 3 peces, a pece rosted, a nettes tonge, a legge of motton baked, 2 conneis, a partriche.
Strangeres—Luken, Richarde Samforde, Kyns sonne of Mawdelen Laver with 2 men with him, Whelare, Sawell, Pake, Nycolas Poole, 2 laboreres.

SUPPER

2 ioyntes of motton, 2 conneis.

Dies sancti Thome

MONDAY DYNER

Boyld beiffe 3 peces, a pece rosted, a conny, a partrich.

SUPPER

5 ioyntes of motton, a conny.

TEWISDAY DYNER

Boylde beiffe 3 peces, a cony.

SUPPER

4 ioyntes of motton, a capon, a conny.

My lady cam from the Cowrte with 8 servantes.

WENISDAY DYNER

Boylde beiffe 3 peces, a pece rosted, 2 conneis.
Strangeres—Smyth, George Cole, Huntman & his man, 2 laborers.

SUPPER

5 ioyntes of motton, a conny, a pastie of venson.

THURSEDAY DYNER

A lynge, an haberden, 5 whitinges, 3 playces, 5 cakes of butter, 2 warden pyes, 6 egges.

Christmas day 25° die Decembris

FRYDAY DYNER

Boylde beiffe 6 peces & a necke of motton, 3 peces rosted, a gosse, 8 pyes, a loyne & brest of porke rosted, a capon, 4 conneis.

Strangeres of Ingatston—Petchy, Howlyng the curryar, Skylman, Toping, Horne, Yonge, & their wives, Father John, William Torner, Mr. Clyffes man, Olde Pake, 3 other pore felowes.

SUPPER

5 ioyntes of motton, a necke of porke, 2 conneis, a woodecoke, a pastye of venson.

Strangeres of Ingatston—a messe in the hall & 3 pore felowes that cam from London.

SATURDAY DYNER

Halffe a lynge, $\frac{1}{2}$ haberden, 3 mudefishes, 6 playces, 12 whitinges, a dyshe & halffe of butter, 16 egges.

Strangeres—Mr. Thomas Tyrell. Ingatston—Tho. Tabor, Olde Edyng, William Umfrey, Towsen, Dekyns & their wyves, 5 pore women and 4 strange felowes, John West, Haywoode, Stamers.

SUPPER

Halffe a lynge, $\frac{1}{2}$ haberden, 2 mudefishes, 6 playces, 10 whitinges, a coode, 2 dishes of butter, 12 egges.

Strangeres—G. Lorkyn, Dowsett, Foster the smyth, John West, Pole, Pake, William Torner, 3 pore felowes.

Memorandum received from Thorndon this weike 2 dishes of butter & 40 egges.

EXPENCE OF PROVISION THIS WEIKE

A bulle cutt owt in lyvery peces 31, rosting beiffe 5 peces, a chine etc., 3 mottons.

Whett 10 bus., $\frac{1}{2}$ bus. for the partriches.

Malte 20 bus.

Ottes to the yomans stable 6 bus., ottes to the carteres 4 bus., ottes to the mylle horses and pultry 2 bus., ottes to the doves 1 bus., ottes to the pultry at Thorndon 3 bus.

Lynges 2, haberdens 2.

Mudeffishes 5.
Butter 2 dishes.
Cheses spent 2, solde to Hilles 4 that madd a leade 6s., one to Sawell the carter 16d., & one to William Marshes wive 12d.
2 capons.
16 conneis, 2 partriches, a woodecoke.
A gosse.
34 egges.
Bread baken this weike in yomans bread 100 cast, manchettes 26 caste, carteres bread 22 cast, out of this to Thorndon 15 cast.

REMAYNING IN THE LARDER, BUTTERY AND PANTRY
Lyvery peces of beiffe 18.
A chine, a nettes tonge.
A pastie of kydd.
Halffe a motton.
Bere 41 kilderkines.

EMPTION OF CATTES THIS WEIKE
Paid to Umfrey the catur for 27 whitinges, 15 playces, a codde & 1d. horsemeat, 6s.
Paid to Lorkins wive for mylke & creyme 5d.
Paid for yest to brue with 2 bruynges 4d.
　Summa—6s. 9d.

SONDAY 27 DECEMBER

DYNER
Boylde beiffe 7 peces & a chine, 4 rosting peces, a brest of veale, a legge of motton baken, 11 pasteis of beiffe, a loyne of porke & a brest rosted.
2 gesse, a capon, 6 conneis, 2 teles, 2 pasteis of venson, 3 pasteis of kydd. A woodecoke, a pygge.
Strangeres of Ingatston—Sir Thomas the curatt, Harry Strettes, Byrde of Dawes, Hilles, Petre Preston, Storgen, Foster the smyth, olde father Gilder, Hale, olde father Foster, Byrde & Pepper brickleyeres & theyr sonnes, Ramme, Rucke, Thomas Fynche, Glover, William Marshe, William Umfrey, Huntman, Mylles, Eustace Umfrey, Sammonde, Whiskare & moste part of theyre wives, Carre, Ponde, Edmonde Finche, Foster the tylare. Mownnesing—Shordes father, Denis, Baret, Offen, Benett, Nutting, Mathew, & theyr wyves, besydes 2 messe that cam unbydd & 8 pore folkes.

SUPPER

6 ioyntes of motton, a pastie of kydd.

A feasant, a duke, 2 teles, 2 conneis.

Strangeres—Dowsett, Pole, Benet, Barett, Offen, Foster the smyth, Petre Preston, Skott, with a messe besydes.

MONDAY DYNER

Boylde beiffe 9 peces, 6 rosting peces.

A gosse, 12 pasteis of beiffe, a legge of motton baken.

A capon, an hare, a feasant, 2 dukes, 3 teles, 6 conneis, 3 pasteis of kydd, 2 pasteis of venson.

Strangeres of Margetting [Margaretting]—John Tabore, Dowsett, Swetting, Almone, Silvester the elder & Silvester the yonger, Byrde, Tabor the mason, Robert Tabor, White the tanner, & most part of their wives, Tabors sone, Mr. Bexwell, John Riges, Tho. Riges, both the Lorkins. Buttesbery—Rochel bocher, Glascoke, Blakemore, Symode, Alen, Marsheall, Prentis, Clarke, Amett, Roger Woode & his brother, Hankin, Whelare, Sawell, Sir Thomas the curatt, Finche, and most parte of their wives, besydes 6 pore folkes & a messe of boyes.

SUPPER

8 ioyntes of motton, a capon, a conny, 3 teles, a shoulder of venson, 6 oxbyrdes.

Strangeres—Dowsett, Foster the smythe, Thomas Tabor, Whiting, 4 singeres & pleyeres that cam from Margetting, besydes a messe of yonge folkes that cam from the towne [Ingatestone].

TEWISDAY DYNER

Boylde beiffe 4 peces, a pece rosted, a lege of porke, a capon, a conny.

Strangeres—Hankyn, Whelare, Sawell of Wrytle, 2 strange felowes.

SUPPER

Halffe a motton, 2 conneis, 2 teles, a snype.

WENISDAY DYNER

Boylde beiffe 5 peces, a pece rosted, a conny, 2 humble pasteis.

Strangeres—Smith the carpinter & his man, George Cole, Thomas & John Rawlins, Brokweis & 2 men myllewrightes, Hankin & Roger Woode of Stocke, 2 laborers.

SUPPER

4 ioyntes of motton, a conny, 2 teles.

Strangeres—the myllewrightes, olde Pake, Foster the smythe.

THURSDAY DYNER

Boylde beiffe 6 peces, a legge of motton rosted, a conny, 2 humble pyes.
Strangeres—Maisteres Clovell & hir servant, Brokweis & his 2 men, Carre, 2 laborers.

SUPPER

5 ioyntes of motton, a shoulder of venson, 2 conneis, 2 ploveres.

New Yers Day, primus dies Januarii

FRIDAY DYNER

A lynge, an haberden, 2 mudefishes, 6 playces, 8 whitinges, a coodd, a sammonde, 3 cakes of butter, 20 egges.
Strangeres—Sir Thomas the curatt, G. Lorkine, with 6 messe of the towne & of them that brought presentes.

SUPPER

Halffe a lynge, 2 mudefishes, 4 playces, 4 whitinges, 3 cakes of butter, 5 egges.
Strangeres—4 messe in the halle.

SATURDAY DYNER

Halffe a lynge, halffe an haberden, a mudefyshe, halffe a sammonde, 4 whitinges, 4 places, a coode, 2 cakes of butter.
Strangeres—Hankin, Roger Woode, olde Pake, Skott & [number torn away] pore felowes.

SUPPER

Halffe an haberden, 2 mudefishes, 3 playces, 8 egges, 2 cakes of butter.
Memorandum received from Thorndon this weike 30 egges.

EXPENCE OF PROVISION DEWRING THIS WEIKE

An oxe cutt owt in lyvery peces 26, rosting peces 12, a chine, a nettes tounge, etc., a cowe cutt owt in lyvery peces 35, which are barelled & a quarter of it was spent at Thorndon, a porke, a doo—Crondon, 4 mottons, a gott.
Whett 11 bus., a bus. to the kytchen besydes.
Ottes to the yomans stable 6 bus., ottes to the carteres stable 6 bus., ottes to the pultry & hogges 2 bus., ottes to the pultry at Thorndon 3 bus.
Lynges 2, haberdens 2, mudefishes 7, 1½ sammondes.
Cheses spent 2, solde 35.
Swett butter 2 dishes, salt butter 11 dishes.
3 gesse, a pygge, 4 capons, 23 conneis, an hare, 11 teles, 2 feasanes, 3 duckes, a woodecoke, 2 ploveres, a snyppe.

33 egges.

Breade bakyn this weike in yomans breade 160 caste, manchettes 60 cast, carteres bred 12 cast, owt of this to Thorndon 8 cast.

REMAINING IN THE LARDER, BUTTERY & PANTRY

3 peces of lyvery beiffe, 2 pestelles of porke, 2 nettes tonges, an hinder quarter of motton, 2 pasteis of venson.

EMPTION OF CATTES THIS WEIKE

Paid to Umfrey the catur for 18 whitinges, 17 playces, 3 coodes, a pecke of oysteres & 1*d*. horsemet, 5*s*. 6*d*.

Paid to Malbroke for 12 teles 2*s*., 2 duckes 8*d*., a woodecoke 4*d*., 2 snyppes, a plover & 6 oxbyrdes 8*d*. In all 3*s*. 8*d*.

Paid for mylke, creime & a peny worth of safforne, 4*d*.

Paid to William Finche for a breste of veale 10*d*.

Paid to Rochell for a pygge 12*d*.

Summa—11*s*. 4*d*.

SONDAY 3° JANUARII

DYNER

Boylde beiffe 9 peces, 5 rosting peces, a brest, a legge & loyne of porke, a gosse, 12 beiff pies, a legge of motton baked, 2 pasties of venson, 2 pasteis of kydd, 2 mallardes, 5 conneis.

Strangeres—Sir Thomas the curatt of Buttesbery, Sir Thomas of Ingatston, Tho. Wilton, Dale, Stamer. Stocke—Haywoode, Kynge, Dawson, Hosyer, Carre, Hankin, Tyrell, Stonarde, Marsheall, Whiting, with their wives, besides 4 messe of pore folkes of Stocke and 3 messe of Ingatston.

SUPPER

9 ioyntes of motton, a brest of porke, 2 malardes, a conny.

Strangeres—4 messe in the hall.

MONDAY DYNER

Boylde beiffe 3 peces, a legge of porke, a legge of motton rost, a conny.

My master cam from the Cowrt with 4 servantes this afternone.

SUPPER

7 ioyntes of motton, a capon, 2 conneis, 2 teles.

313

TEWISDAY DYNER

Boylde beiffe 4 peces, a legge of porke, a chine of beiffe, a shoulder of venson, a conny.

Strangeres—Hale, Tho. Finche, Benett, Clerke, olde Pake.

SUPPER

9 ioyntes of motton, a capon, 4 conneis, 2 teles, a woodecoke.

Strangeres—Mr. Baker with 6 servantes, Mr. Pownsett and 2 servantes, besydes 2 messe in the hall.

WENISDAY TWELFFE DAY

DYNER

Boylde beiffe 9 peces, a pestell & legge of porke, 2 legges of veale, rosting beiffe 6 peces, 3 gesse, a loyne & brest of veale, a pygge, 10 pasteis of beiffe, 2 pasteis of motton, 6 conneis, 4 pasteis of venson, 2 capons, 2 partriches, a woodecoke, 2 teles, a dosen of larkes.

Strangeres—Mr. Richarde Baker & his brother, Mr. Tyrell of Warley, Mr. Pownsett, with 12 messe in the hall, Harris, Drywoode, Mr. Clovell, Geffreis of Cowbridge [in Mountnessing].

SUPPER

A motton & 2 ioyntes, a shoulder of venson, a brest of porke, 6 conneis, a duke, 2 capons, 2 partriches, a pastie of venson, 2 teles.

Strangeres—Mr. Richarde Baker & his brother, Mr. Tyrell of Warley, Mr. Pownsett, with 8 messe of serving men and of Ingatston, besydes a grett a number of boys.

THURSEDAY DYNER

Boylde beiffe 6 peces, a nettes tonge, a legge of porke, 3 humble pyes, 2 loynes of porke, a shoulder, breste & racke of veale, 2 pygges, 2 ioyntes of motton, 2 capons, a conny, halffe a lambe, 3 teles, 2 woodecockes.

Strangeres—Sir Harry Tyrell & his wive, Mr. Edmonde Tyrell & his wive, Mr. Richarde Baker & his brother, Mr. William Tyrell, Mr. George & Mr. Thomas Tyrell, Hale, Wilton, with 4 messe of serving men besydes others.

SUPPER

9 ioyntes of motton, 3 capons & an henne, halffe a lambe, a feasant, a pastie of venson, a conny, 2 woodecockes, a partriche.

Strangeres—Mr. Richarde Baker & his brother, Mr. Tyrell of Warley, Mr. Pownsett, with 3 messe in the halle.

FRYDAY DYNER

A lyng, an haberden, 3 mudefishes, halffe a sammonde, 8 playces, 10 whitinges, 3 flownderes, 6 cakes of butter, 12 egges.

Strangeres—Mr. Richarde Baker & his brother, Mr. Tyrell of Warley, Smithe the carpinter, Haywoode, with 3 messe besydes in the halle.

DRINKING AT NYGHT

A mudefishe, 3 cakes of butter, 2 playces, 2 whitinges, 6 egges.

Strangeres—Mr. Baker and his servantes.

SATURDAY DYNER

Halffe a lynge, halffe an haberden, 1 mudefishe, halffe a salt sammonde, 4 cakes of butter, 4 playces, 6 whitinges, 6 egges, a flownder, a coode.

Strangeres—Mr. Richarde Baker & his brother, Mr. Browne of Flamberdes [in Cold Norton], with 4 messe in the halle.

SUPPER

Halffe a lynge, an haberden, a mudefishe, 6 egges, 3 whitinges, 5 places, 9 egges, a coode.

Strangeres—Mr. Richard Baker & his brother, Mr. Browne, with 3 messe in the halle, Mr. Garett.

Memorandum received from Thorndon this weike 30 egges and $\frac{1}{2}$ dishe of butter.

EXPENCE OF PROVISION THIS WEIKE

An oxe cutt owt in lyvery peces 32, rosting peces 10, a chine etc., 5 mottons, a calve of Rochell—tythe, a porke, a doo—Crondon, a lambe—present of G. Lorkyne.

Whett 16 bus., malte 20 bus., malt to Thorndon 2 bus.

Ottes to the yomans stable 6 bus., ottes to the carteres 4 bus., ottes to Mr. Bakers horseis, Mr. Pownsettes, & to other strangers 9 bus., ottes to the pultry here 2 bus., ottes to the pultry at Thorndon 3 bus.

Lynges 2, haberdens 4, mudefishes 6.

Cheses spent 3, but one of them into the pantry.

Swett butter 2 dyshes and 7 of salte butter.

4 gesse, 3 pygges, 11 capons & an henne, 26 conneis, 5 dukes & malardes, 11 teles, 6 woodecockes, 5 partriches, 1 feasande, 33 egges.

Bread bakine this weike in yomans bredd 216 cast, manchettes 40 cast, carters bred 12 cast, owt of this to Thorndon 10 cast.

1 pece of lyvery beiffe, a loyne & necke of veale, a nettes tonge, 2 turky pyes.
Bere, 12 kilderkines.

EMPTION OF CATTES THIS WEIKE

Paid to Umfrey the cature for 2 coodes 2s. 8d., 24 playces 2s. 8d., 25 whitinges 20d., 3 peckes of oysteres 9d., 3 buttes 4d., white & redd heringes 16 penyworth, & 1d. horsemeat, 9s. 6d.
Paid to Malbroke this weike for 12 teles 2s., 4 woodecockes 16d., a duke, malarde & wigeon 12d., in all, 4s. 4d.
Paid to G. Lorkins wive for halff a dishe of butter 5d.
Paid to hir for mylke and creyme this weike 6d.
Paid for egges bought this weike by Mary 6d.
Paid for yest to bake with 4d., for yest & safforne for the kitchen 2d.
  Summa—15s. 9d.

Appendix G

WILDFOWL AND FISH

The Ingatestone accounts, like other household and kitchen books mentioned or calendared in several of the *H.M.C. Reports* (esp. those given on p. 133n.), provide useful or earlier references supplementing those in the *O.E.D.*, the first quotations in which are in parentheses below. The following notes are taken mostly from the two kitchen accounts ('week books') of 1548 and 1552 (D/DP A12, 13). The best material, as is natural, relates to the wildfowl taken on the coastal marshlands of Essex.

Marle (*ante* 1700), the knot, a variety of snipe: the Ingatestone books have both snipe and snite, the latter perhaps the smaller species (cf. *O.E.D.*).

Shelfowl (?1593), the sheldrake.

Goodwin (godwit 1544, but godwyn only 19th cent.), probably the black-tailed (marshland) godwit, which resembled the curlew.

Prane, or praine (preen 1864, provincial name for the bar-tailed godwit, prine in Essex), recognized by Mr. Wentworth Day, the authority on wildfowl, as the Essex marshman's preen, or curlew.

Oxbird (*ante* 1547) still survives as the local (Essex and Kent creeks) name for the dunlin or sanderling.

Shovelard (*c.* 1440, long since obsolete), first called by Ray the spoonbill: not to be confused with the shoveller, or spoonbill duck.

Bret, or berte (*c.* 1460), probably the turbot: 'what they call bret . . . in all the east part of England is the turbot of the west country' (Ray, 1671).

Butt (*ante* 1300), not defined more closely than being akin to the turbot, sole, or flounder.

Rochet (*ante* 1377), almost identical with the red gurnard: not to be confused with the freshwater roach.

Choyt, or cheyt (of which an average of a dozen, costing 4*d.* the dozen, were bought almost every week in June and in autumn), not definitely identified, but may be the shad, or chad, a large bony flat-fish.

Appendix H

WYATT'S REBELLION, FEBRUARY 1554
ACCOUNT OF JOHN KYME, PETRE'S STEWARD

Here followeth the charges issued as well for the entertainment of such soldiers as my master provided for the service of the Queen, as for their coats, weapon and conduct money, besides armour and artillery.

To Hans the armourer in reward when my master had on his harness, 6*s.* 8*d.*
3 yards 'myllen' fustian to line my master's shirt of mail, 4*s.*
To the saddler for making a saddle with a seat of down, 27*s.*
Silk ribbon for my master's coat of plate, 9*d.*
A lace for his dagger and a sheath locket for the same, 22*d.*
A mail pillion and girths for my master's casket, 18*d.*

For the hire of a horse being sent for my master's horses and for his retainers, 3*s.* 4*d.* To Lorkin, Whitlocke, Drywood, Haywood, Pamplyn and Preston, my master's retainers, for their charges being here and so sent home again at 20*d.* the piece, 10*s.*

To Clerke, Aueston, Rive and Waggestaff being appointed to go with Sir Thomas Wharton and forth, one night each of them 10*s.*, 40*s.*

To Tabor my master's man for his charges at London, with 12*d.* which was bestowed in wine upon Margaretting men at their coming to London, 3*s.* Spent at Romford at the coming up of the soldiers where I received them, 4*s.* 8*d.*

To Fernefolde, being a demi-lance, 6*s.* 8*d.*; to Edward Walker, a light horseman, 6*s.* 8*d.*; to Charles Waggestaff, a light horseman, 5*s.*; to Oxenham, a light horseman, 5*s.*

3 lb. gunpowder, 3s. 8d.; 2 lb. matches for the gunners.

2 doz. shooting gloves, 12s.

15 leather girdles for the sheaf arrows, 2s. 6d.

5 doz. bracers, 5s. 6d.

3 gross of arming points, 6s.

Mending an 'Almen' rivet which one of the soldiers laid out, 8d.

24 arming swords at 2s. 8d. the piece, £3 4s.

To Eland the cutler for 44 arming swords, £7 3s. 4d.

2 doz. bowstrings, besides 2 doz. had at the Tower [see below], 12d.

Carriage of two cartloads of harness, bills, pikes, bows and arrows from the Tower to my master's house [in Aldersgate Street], 16d.

4 leather harness for horses with two musrols, 5s. 8d.

6 javelins, 9s.

A mail pillion was a letter-bag. An Almain rivet was a kind of light armour, or half suit, made in Germany (illustrated in *The London of Elizabeth* (London Museum, 1958)). A bracer was an archer's armguard giving protection from a hit by the released bowstring. A musrol was the noseband of a bridle. There is also the armourer's bill for miscellaneous work amounting to £5 13s. 3d.; of which is 'a man-at-arms harness trimmed with yellow leather' cost the surprisingly high sum of £4, a horseman's mace 2s. 4d., and 2,000 arming nails 5s. 4d.

4 ells sarcenet for the 'ensen', 22s.

Making the 'ensen', 2s.

Fustian for the staff that the 'ensen' hangeth on, 8d.

Sewing silk for the 'ensen', 8d.

This may be the only surviving account of how a sixteenth century ensign was made. The steward did not write the corrupt form 'ancient' for ensign, which first came into use at this time, Wyatt's 'ancients' being referred to in the Greyfriars' Chronicle; but it was not until Shakespeare's time that ancient began to signify also the ensign-bearer.

A drum with sticks of 'brasell', 14s.

A 'snarre' for the drum, 6d.

2 dozen halfpenny laces, 10d.; a lace for the drum, 18d.

Brazil was a specially hard wood. A drum-snare was the gut stretched over a side-drum to check the reverberation, and Petre's steward has supplied a reference to this word 144 years earlier than that quoted in the O.E.D.

Awesten's cloak being sergeant of the band, 16s.

Parchment lace and making his cloak, 4s. 5d.

Making his frieze jerkin, 12d.

35½ yards of white frieze for jerkins for my master's servants, 34s.
Raising the same frieze, 6d.
4 yards red cloth to make Waggestaff and Clerke cloaks, 32s.; making of the two cloaks with parchment lace to them, 8s. 10d.

Kyme bought:

43½ yards of red cloth which made 17 coats, £3 11s. 8d.
8 yards broad red [cloth] which made 6 coats, 20s.
26 yards red cloth which made 12 coats, 52s.
6 yards broad red [cloth] which made 5 coats, 18s.
16 yards red cloth broad which made 14 coats, £3 6s. 8d.
Making the 54 coats at 5d. the piece, 22s. 6d.
A coat for Raple, Mr. Archdeacon's man, for a coat for him being a man-at-arms, 5s. 8d.
A quarter of red cloth for the coat sleeves of him that played on the drum, 16d., for yellow and blue sarcenet for him, 14d.

Wagstaff bought the rest of the material:

29¼ yards of broad red cloth at 4s. 6d., £6 11s. 7d.
29¾ yards of like cloth at 4s. the yard, £5 19s.
22 yards at 4s. 6d., £4 19s.
Making 48 coats at 6d. and 18 coats at 5d., 31s. 6d.

6 links for the soldiers, being sent for in the night before they went to the field, 2s.
3 lb. candle for the stable, 6d.
Candle spent in the house at London in the time of this late trouble, 14d.

This account was written when the 'trouble' was over:

Paid to 142 soldiers 2nd Feb. at 8d. a piece by the day being Friday and for Saturday and Sunday 3 days, £14 4s. 8d.
To the same soldiers Monday to Thursday, £18 18s. 8d. (Paid by Waggestaff, as he asserts.)
More to 123 of the same soldiers for 2 days, Friday and Saturday, being then discharged, Mr. Pascall's men not here accompted, £8 4s.
To Fuller for a Scottish cap, 12d.
To sundry of the soldiers for mending their harness, 14d., the bowmen for piking their bows, 8d., Sawell for a dagger, 12d., and to sundry of them, some 4d., some 6d. in reward, 2s. 6d.
Given to such as were 'prest' to serve, and after returned home being of the poorest sort, besides the prest money received of some of them being able to bear their own charges, 16s.
To him that played on the drum, for his prest money, 2s.
To one Thomas Wattes in prest money, being appointed in one Robert Dyke's stead who fell sick, 2s.

The number of men under Petre's standard is confirmed in the receipts section of Kyme's account-book: 'Received of my master towards the payment of his soldiers being 142, and buying their coats.' 'Prest' does not imply compulsory service; it is a Tudor word having no etymological link with the later 'impress' and 'press-gang', and refers to earnest-money or advance pay (cf. 'To my lady in prest towards the charges of my master's household £15' and the modern 'imprest account'). The 'band' Petre raised was enlisted solely from men having a territorial connection with him; of these, 'Mr. Pascall' is John Pascall, lessee of Crondon Old Hall, described as a 'gentleman' in his lease, a cousin of Lady Petre. To 'pike' meant to trim or shave gently around the protuberances (left by the small lateral branches) of the yew bowstave.

> Summa of the charges of my master in this rebellion time, besides the prest money delivered at the soldiers coming forth which amounteth to £8 10s. or thereabouts, and besides the loss of armour and artillery—£108 8s. 10d.

The following arms were issued from the Tower armouries to Sir William Petre: A 'partizan' gilt, a poleaxe trimmed with velvet, 20 bows, 20 sheaves of arrows, 2 dozen bowstrings, 40 bills, 21 Morris pikes. The bowstrings were accounted for by Kyme, as seen above. Morris pikes, said to be of Moorish origin, were in common use, but the 'partizan' was a foot-soldier's long-handled spear with a fairly large symmetrical head, generally carried by a guard or an officer.

It may be recalled that Petre had spent £40 in military preparations in 1548 (pp. 70, 74). M. R. Holmes, *Arms and Armour in Tudor and Stuart London* (The London Museum, 1957) has useful illustrations.

Appendix I

PHARMACEUTICAL TERMS IN PETRE'S ACCOUNTS (CH. XIII)

Many of the terms used in Petre's accounts occur in the contemporary pharmacopœias and in Henry VIII's apothecary's accounts (*The Chemist and the Druggist*, special issue, 27 June 1931, 792–96). See also F. N. L. Poynter and W. J. Bishop, *A Seventeenth Century Doctor and his Patients: John Symcotts* (Pub. Beds. Hist. Rec. Soc. xxxi (1951)).

'Maidenhair' and 'scolopender' (p. 252), like hartstongue, are ferns. Of these, the first was a restorative. The second, another name for the last, originated from the resemblance of its leaf to the centipede, then called

scolopendra; the bill gives the fern half a century earlier than its oldest
quotation in *O.E.D.* 'Diacitonium' was conserve of quinces (*Dispensa-
torium* of Valerius Cordus, 1546). 'Ceny alexandrie' represents Alex-
andrian senna (*O.E.D.*, not before 1693), and coriander seeds are aromatic.
Eryngo was the candied root of the sea-holly. The earliest recorded uses
in *O.E.D.* are from Gerard's *Herball* (1597) and Shakespeare's *Merry
Wives of Windsor* (1598); a few years later the sweetmeat was well known
at Colchester, the deep roots being dug up along the north-east Essex
coast (*V.C.H.*, Essex, ii, 371–2). 'Galingale' was the aromatic root of an
East Indian plant, used in medicine from ancient times. Succory is
chicory. 'Paspere' is derived from 'parsley piert', a corruption of the well-
known French remedy 'perce pierre', a dwarf annual herb allied to 'lady's
mantle'.

'Unguentum album rasi' (p. 253) is the white ointment prepared
according to the recipe of Rhases, the Arabian physician. 'Feni cheni'
probably represents wild fennel (Latin *feniculus*). 'Cheni' is perhaps Greek
for 'common' (cf. Gunter's edn. of the *Greek Herbal of Dioscorides* (Oxford,
1934), 315, 'wild fennel being drunk cureth stranguries and breaks the
stones'); Chinese fennel was not introduced into England until about
1588, and was used merely for flavouring.

The plaster (p. 254) of 1562 had a basic lead content, litharge being
lead oxide. Another contemporary name for this plaster was dischylon,
originally an ointment prepared from vegetable juices, rose leaves and
wax; in later times it stood for the common adhesive lead-plaster made
by boiling together litharge, olive oil and water. Here is the precise
recipe favoured in 1562, including also oil of vitriol, white lead, and the
sends of fenugreek, a leguminous herb.

Appendix J

SALARIES AND FEES, ETC., FROM OFFICES

This table has been compiled from Petre's personal accounts in the E.R.O. (D/DP A3-7, 14, 83, 86). His accounting year ran from 1 December to 30 November.

	1548 £	1549 £	1550* £	1554 £	1555 £	1556 £	1564 £	1571 £
Monastic annuities	72	82	56	[56]	[56]	57	48	42
Secretary: salary	100	100	50 (½)	100	100	100	—	—
Do: signet fees	44	24	43†(½)	172	97	65	—	—
Do: hanaper & petty bag fees	73	270	99 (½)	101	41	37	—	—
Ecclesiastical seal	9	4	14	30	6	6	—	—
High steward of lands of Bp. of Winchester	100	100	[50] (½)‡	[100]	[100]	[100]	100	100
Treasurer of Court of First Fruits	—	—	120	[120]	[267]	200§	200	200
Chancellor of Garter	—	—	—	100	100	100	100	100
High steward of Savoy lands	—	—	—	[4]	4	[4]	[4]	4
King Philip's pension	—	—	—	146	[250]	250	—	—
Steward of Bishop of Rochester's lands	—	—	—	—	7	7	3	3
	406	580	674	929	1,028	871	455	449

* Petre's income given this year only for first half-year; total represents a full year.

† Under 10 June 1550: 'To Sir Thomas Smith in full payment of £114 1s. paid unto him by my master's commandment for the signet £44 1s.'; the meaning is not clear but seems to imply reimbursement of arrears due to Smith (p. 82).

‡ £50 due.

§ Compensation for loss of office plus Queen's pension reduced from £266 13s. 4d. to £200 (see p. 173).

References to Sources

CHAPTER I

EARLY LIFE

1. W. G. Hoskins, *Trans. Roy. Hist. Soc.*, 5th ser., vi (1956), 8–9. Thomas Westcote's *View of Devonshire in 1630* remained in MS. until published by G. Oliver in 1845. It was used by Tristram Risdon, whose *Survey of Devon*, begun in 1605 and completed in 1630, was published in part in 1714 (best edn., 1811). Both historians were quoted by J. Prince, *Worthies of Devon* (1701). See *Trans. Dev. Assoc.*, xiv (1882), 46.
2. Inf. given to me by Dr. W. G. Hoskins, joint author of *Devonshire Studies* (1952), etc., to whom this paragraph owes much.
3. A. Wood, *Fasti Oxonienses* (1691–2), 93.
4. J. Prince, *op. cit.*, 496.
5. West Suffolk R.O., E3/15 (manor court rolls in the Kytson archives); ref. kindly supplied by Mr. M. P. Statham, County Archivist of West Suffolk.
6. D. and S. Lysons, *Magna Britannia*, vi (1822), 523.
7. In Lord Petre's possession and on view in the long gallery at Ingatestone Hall (reproduced in *Introduction to Ingatestone Hall* (2nd edn., 1957)).
8. *Genealogical Collections illustrating the History of Roman Catholic Families*, ed. J. J. Howard and H. F. Burke—part ii, Petre (priv. printed, 1887), 38; the pedigree therein is 'based on the Lawson MS.', now in possession of Sir Ralph Lawson Bt.
9. J. Prince, *op. cit.*
10. 'He supplicated for the degree of Bachelor of Civil Law 14 Dec. 1524 and was admitted Bachelor of Civil and Canon Law 2 July 1526.' (C. W. Boase, *Register of . . . Exeter College* (1st edn., 1894), lxxxi.)
11. D. Lloyd, *State Worthies*, orig. pub. as *The Statesmen and Favourites of England* (1665), 248; *Dict. Nat. Biog.*, s.v. Petre.

CHAPTER II

VISITOR OF MONASTERIES

1. *Letters and Papers, Foreign and Domestic, Henry VIII* (1862–1910), ix, no. 741 (in accordance with the usual practice, *L. & P.* are cited by the nos. of the calendared documents, not by pages).

2. S.P. 1/101, pp. 82–5 (*L. & P.*, x, 88): to be Cromwell's deputy in all matters concerning wills (13 Jan.). Petre must also have received a separate commission, not extant, with wider powers than probate matters. Cf. his being termed (1536) Cromwell's 'auditor', or judge in the Vicar-general's court of appeal (*L. & P.*, xii, pt. i, no.1155), and 'master of the faculties to the Vice-gerent' (J. Strype, *Life of Cranmer*, i, 79); also cf. E.R.O., D/DABW 39/32 (1537).

3. D. Wilkins, *Concilia* (1737), iii, 803; J. Strype, *Ecclesiastical Memorials of the Church of England* i, pt. i, 378.

4. *Munimenta Civitatis Oxonia*, ed. H. E. Salter (Oxf. Rec. Soc., lxxi, 1917), 250.

5. Edward Lord Herbert, *Life and Reign of Henry VIII* (1672), 426; repeated by Strype, *Cranmer*, 50.

6. P.R.O., S.C., Hen. VIII, 929/2; for this ref. I am indebted to Mother Winifred Sturman, O.S.U., who has nearly completed a study of the Barking Abbey estates. For Legh's itinerary see D. Knowles, *The Religious Orders in England*, iii (1959), app. vi; Professor Knowles thinks that the visit to Barking probably formed part of the visitation of London houses in that autumn.

7. B.M., Add. MS. 20,021, cited in *L. & P.*, viii, 865, and wrongly assigned to 1535 instead of to 1536 (Dunmow); P.R.O., S.C. Hen. VIII, 940 (St. Osyth).

8. Chronicle of St. Augustine, Canterbury, in *Nichols' Narratives*, cited by R. W. Dixon, *History of the Church of England* (1878–1902), i, 498.

9. Except where otherwise noted below, all questions about the Dissolution are either from the printed calendars (*L. & P.* for 1536–41, vols. xi–xvi (1888–98), and *Addenda*, vol. i, part ii (1932)), or from the originals of the calendared documents in P.R.O. or B.M.

10. The printed calendar gives 'D. Peter's (?St. Peter's) circuit', but examination of the original shows the queried alternative reading incorrect.

11. Entered in Wye parish book; for this ref. I am indebted to Mr. A. H. Corley.

12. B.M., Cott., Cleop. E. iv, 255 (*L. & P.*, xiii, pt. i, 530; printed in full by T. Wright, *Letters relating to the Suppression of the Monasteries* (Camden Soc., xxvi, 1843), 177 (misdated as 1537 by D. Knowles, *op. cit.*, iii, 340).

13. W. B. Turnbull, *Account of Monastic Treasures* (Abbotsford Club, 1836), 12.

14. *Ibid.*

15. Rose Graham, *St. Gilbert of Sempringham and the Gilbertines*, 191.

16. The best account is by R. W. Dixon, *op. cit.*, ii, 113–17.

17. W. B. Turnbull, *op. cit.*, 23–25; E.R.O., D/DP O43.

18. Petre was not a commissioner for Hants., Wilts. and Glos. (G. Burnet, *History of the Reformation of the Church of England* (1679–1715, ed. N. Pocock, 1865, iv, 263, where his name is a misreading for Gwent, cf. iv, 255 n.).

19. *L. & P.*, xvi, 745, f. 38. A partial duplicate of this (*L. & P.*, xviii, pt. ii, 231, p. 123) is miscalendared at the entry referring to Petre, which should end with 'servants of Rochester'; the rest of the entry concerns a repayment to North, the Treasurer.

20. G. Baskerville, *English Monks and the Suppression of the Monasteries* (1937). The Roman Catholic view has been restated by P. Hughes, *The Reformation in England*, i (1954), esp. ch. v. Baskerville's opinions have been subjected to criticism by D. Knowles, *op. cit.*, 270 n., 295 n.

21. R. W. Dixon, *op. cit.*, ii, 24–5.

22. S.P. 7 (Wriothesley papers, no. 73) (*L. & P.*, xiii, pt. i, 444).

23. S.P. 7, no. 76 (*L. & P.*, xiii, pt. i, 748).

24. *L. & P.*, xvii, 299.

25. *L. & P.*, xiii, pt. i, 973.

26. *L. & P.*, xiii, pt. ii, 1182 (15); Crown grant in family archives, E.R.O., D/DP T406.

CHAPTER III

INGATESTONE HALL

1. G. A. Moriarty, 'The Early Tyrrels of Heron in East Horndon' (*New England Hist. and Gen. Reg.* (1955), cix); see pedigrees in J. J. Howard and H. F. Burke, *op. cit.*

2. *L. & P.*, xii, pt. i, no. 1155.

3. J. J. Howard and H. F. Burke, *op. cit.*, 38.

4. *Ibid.*, 49, citing the book of hours.

5. P.R.O., E315/92, f. 127; I am indebted to Dr. J. E. Oxley for this ref.

6. E.R.O., D/DP E29, f. 126v.

7. E.R.O., D/DP T2/1.

8. *L. & P.*, xiv, pt. ii, 780 (26); Crown grant in family archives, E.R.O., D/DP T2/2.

9. 27 Hen. VIII, c. 27. Cf. Joyce Youings, 'The Terms of the Disposal of the Devon Monastic Lands, 1536–58' (*Eng. Hist. Rev.*, lxix (1954), 18–38); J. Youings ed., *Devon Monastic Lands: Calendar of Particulars for Grants, 1536–1558* (Dev. & Corn. Rec. Soc., N.S., i (1955)); H. J. Habakkuk, 'The Market for Monastic Property, 1539–1603' (*Econ. Hist. Rev.*, N.S., x (1958), 362–80). The manor of Ingatestone (Yng at stone, Ging Abbess) does not seem to be represented in the 'Particulars for Grants' (P.R.O., E318).

10. E.R.O., D/DP A51.

11. Receipt for West Country religious houses treasure, E.R.O., D/DP O43.

12. P.R.O., E315/212 (rent not given in *L. & P.*, xv, 1032 (p. 559)).

13. *L. & P.*, xv, 831, g. 35; 305, g. 32.

14. E.R.O., D/DP E4, A1.

15. I owe this comment to Mr. P. Bowden of Sheffield University.

16. E.R.O., D/DP E29, f. 33.

17. J. J. Howard and H. F. Burke, *op. cit.*, 49, citing the book of hours; this agrees with the age given on her portrait at Ingatestone Hall.

18. E.R.O., D/DP F143.

19. E.R.O., D/DP M186.

20. *Calendar of Patent Rolls*, Edw. VI, iv, 110.

21. E.R.O., D/DP M186 (P1), F215, P8A. For a condensed copy of the inventory, see F. G. Emmison, *Inventory of Ingatestone Hall in 1600* (E.R.O. Pub. 22, 1954).

22. E.R.O., D/DP T1/1588.

23. P. F. Tytler, *England under Edw. VI and Mary* (1839), i, 242.

24. A. Boorde, A Compendyous Regyment or Dyetary of Helth (? 1542).

25. E.R.O., D/DP P8A.

CHAPTER IV

SECRETARY TO HENRY VIII

1. *L. & P.*, xi, 255, 1217 (22).

2. *L. & P.*, xii, pt. i, 481, 491, 901–14, 1014–19; cf. also xv, 438.

3. *L. & P.*, xi, 222. The depositions are in Petre's handwriting (B.M., Cott. MS., Otho C.x, f. 260 (old f. 254)). The three signatures are originals, but Petre signs 'per Gulielmum Petre' in an italic hand. He seems never to have used the latin form and italic signature in later years, but his italic hand is occasionally found.

4. *L. & P.*, xiv, esp. pt. ii, 779; xii, pt. i, 297, 1244.
5. R. W. Dixon, *op. cit.*, ii, 122; G. Burnet, *op. cit.*, i, 414; both quoting the *Lords' Journals*.
6. *Lords' Journals*, i, e.g. 28 April (one of the receivers of petitions) and 17 June ('A Bill was handed to the Clerks of Parliament and Dr. Petre to send to the Commons'); *L. & P.*, xiv, pt. i, 829.
7. *L. & P.*, xiv, pt. ii, 146; i, 783; ii, 318.
8. *L. & P.*, xiv, pt. i, 1193; cf. pt. ii, 781 (p. 313).
9. *L. & P.*, xiv, pt. ii, 400 (p. 141).
10. *L. & P.*, xv, 14.
11. *L. & P.*, xv, 758.
12. J. A. Froude, *op. cit.*, iii, 307 (cf. *L. & P.*, xv, 766).
13. *L. & P.*, xv, 821.
14. H. A. L. Fisher, *Hist. of England . . . Henry VIII* (1906), 434.
15. *L. & P.*, xv, 821.
16. *L. & P.*, xv, 860–1.
17. *L. & P.*, xvi, 124 (cf. xv, 138), quoting *Proceedings of the Privy Council*, ed. Nicholas (1837), vii, 51.
18. G. R. Elton, *The Tudor Revolution in Government* (1953), 320, superseding A. F. Pollard, 'Council, Star Chamber, and Privy Council under the Tudors' (*Eng. Hist. Rev.*, xxxviii, 42–44, 60).
19. *L. & P.*, xvi, 146, 211, 241.
20. The cases cited for 1541–3 are found in *L. & P.*, xvi, 596, 947 (25), 1358, 1480, and xvii, 82 (from Nicholas, *op. cit.*); and in *Acts of Privy Council* ed. J. R. Dasent (1890–1922), i, 76, 126, 128, 140.
21. *L. & P.*, xvi, 1395, 1408, 1433.
22. B. Willis, *Notitia Parliamentaria* (1750), 5.
23. *L. & P.*, xvii, 243, 509, 563.
24. E.R.O., D/DP A1.
25. 'Alterum ex duobus primariis et principalibus Secretariis nostris' (P.R.O., E.315/236, f. 38; calendared in *L. & P.*, xix, pt. i, 1036).
26. K. Pickthorn, *Early Tudor Government: Henry VIII* (1934), 492, citing G. Burnet, *op. cit.*, i, 522.
27. G. R. Elton, *op. cit.*, 314. The warrant for the appointment of Wriothesley and Sadler in 1540 clarifies some of their duties in consequence of there being two officers; it is printed in full in F. M. G. Evans, *The Principal Secretary of State* (1923), 360–1.
28. G. R. Elton, *op. cit.*, 300.
29. F. M. G. Evans, *op. cit.*, 34, correcting *L. & P.*, xv, 437.
30. I am indebted to Sir John Neale for this sentence.

31. *Collection of Ordinances and Regulations for the Royal Household* (1795) (Soc. of Antiquaries, London), 192, 210; F. M. G. Evans, *op. cit.*, 29–34, 217–19; G. R. Elton, *op. cit.*, 126; *L. & P.*, iv, 1939.
32. Patent in family archives (E.R.O., D/DP O46); cf. *L. & P.*, xix, pt. i, 278(4).
33. Detailed abstracts are in the *Calendar of Letters and Papers, Foreign and Domestic, Henry VIII*, vols. xix–xxi (1903–10) (see index *s.v.* 'Petre' at end of each volume); full transcripts of certain letters are in *State Papers, Henry VIII* (1836–49), which contain some notes about Petre's drafts not in *L. & P.* (see index in vol. xi of *State Papers*).
34. E.R.O., D/DP A2.
35. *L. & P.*, xix, pt. i, 273 (pp. 149–50), 275 (p. 161).
36. *L. & P.*, xix, pt. i, 812 (87); ii, 353–4 (no. 586).
37. *L. & P.*, pt. i, 864; for some of their duties see 812(87), 891.
38. *L. & P.*, xix, pt. ii, 167–283, 688 (the last is the Queen's expenses account).
39. Except where otherwise noted, all the relevant letters in this chapter are calendared in *Letters and Papers, Henry VIII*, vols. xix and xx.
40. His name does not appear in the list of repayments (*L. & P.*, xxi, pt. ii, 775 (f. 111)) nor do his own accounts record it.
41. *State Papers, Henry VIII*, x (1849), 161.
42. *A Treatise of th'Office of a Councellor and Principall Secretarie to her Majestie* in C. Read, *Mr. Secretary Walsingham and the Policy of Queen Elizabeth* (Cambridge, U.S.A., 1925), i, 439, cited by S. R. Gammon, 'Master of Practises: A Life of William, Lord Paget' (unpublished Princeton Ph.D. thesis, 1953, p. 79).
43. *A.P.C.*, i, 246.
44. A. F. Pollard, *The Evolution of Parliament* (1920), 336; cf. *Eng. Hist. Rev.*, xxiii, 360.
45. Cited in *L. & P.*, xx, pt. ii, 1031.
46. *L. & P.*, xx, pt. ii, 1025.
47. *L. & P.*, xx, pt. ii, 1030, 1045; cf. D.N.B. (*s.v.* Mason) and J. A. Froude, *op. cit.*, iv, 196, n.i.
48. S. T. Bindoff, *Tudor England* (1950), 148–9.
49. *L. & P.*, xx, pt. ii, 1045.
50. K. Pickthorn, *op. cit.*, 500.
51. *Eng. Hist. Rev.*, xxvi, 265.
52. Petre's patent (with Henry's signature) in family archives (E.R.O. D/DP O47).
53. Correspondence about this embassy in *L. & P.*, xxi, pt. i.
54. *L. & P.*, xxi, pt. i, 790, 810, 823.

55. *L. & P.*, xxi, pt. i, 1395; correspondence in pt. ii.
56. *L. & P.*, xx, pt. ii, 36, 94, 222, 302.
57. *A.P.C.*, i, 227.
58. *L. & P.*, xix, pt. i, 278 (4); xx, pt. i, 125 (12), 970 (19).
59. *L. & P.*, xxii, pt. ii, 513, also 509.
60. H. A. L. Fisher, *Political Hist. Eng., 1485–1547* (1906), 480.
61. *L. & P.*, xxii, pt. ii, 487, 493, 647 (10); J. A. Muller, *Letters of Stephen Gardiner* (1933), 243, is uncertain which Secretary drafted it, but Paget was not with the King.
62. *L. & P.*, xxii, pt. ii, 555 (6).

CHAPTER V

SECRETARY UNDER SOMERSET

1. *A.P.C.*, ii, 33.
2. *A.P.C.*, ii, 137 (the compiler of the index, as if incredulous, omits this reference to Petre under 'Legacies').
3. *A.P.C.*, ii, 19; P.R.O., S.P. 10/1/11. A comparable reward was that of Paulet Lord St. John who got lands worth £100 a year.
4. *A.P.C.*, ii, 33, 114–15.
5. B.M., Cott. MSS., Titus B ii, f. 76, printed in Burnet, v, 148. (Strype, *Cranmer*, i, 208, says that Petre 'went along with' this visitation, but this is not otherwise confirmed.)
6. *A.P.C.*, ii, 148.
7. *Correspondance de Odet de Selve*, 186 (Gardiner's name included in error); cf. *Span. Cal.*, x, 141.
8. Paget letter-book in Fitzwilliam (Milton) MSS., Northants. Record Office, Delapré Abbey; I have to thank Mr. P. I. King, County Archivist, for this reference.
9. C. Read, *Mr. Secretary Cecil and Queen Elizabeth* (1955), 45.
10. *Span. Cal.*, x, 199, 239; ix, 342.
11. For biographical details, see Mrs. Mary Dewar's London Ph.D. thesis (1956), 'The Career and Writings of Sir Thomas Smith'; I am indebted to her for several helpful suggestions.
12. P.R.O., S.P. 10/6/2.
13. Printed in full in S. Haynes' *State Papers* (1740), 75–77, 85 (cf. *Cal. Hatfield MSS.*, i, 65–71). The lengthy articles against Seymour entered in the Council Register (P.R.O., P.C. 2/2) are in a different hand (*A.P.C.*, ii, p. xvi), but not Petre's.
14. Tytler, *op. cit.*, i, 142.

15. P.R.O., S.P. 10/7/18, 19.

16. S.P. 10/6/25.

17. *Cal. Pat. Rolls. Edw. VI*, i, 193.

18. S.P. 10/7/40.

19. S.P. 10/7/42.

20. *A.P.C.*, ii, 313; also Edward's Journal (Burnet, *op. cit.*, v, 8).

21. *A.P.C.*, ii, 312.

22. A. F. Pollard, *England under Protector Somerset* (1900), 244.

23. N. Pocock, *Troubles connected with the Prayer Book of 1549* (Camden Soc., 1884), 34.

24. Froude, *op. cit.*, iv, 471, n. 2.

25. Froude, *op. cit.*, iv, 471.

26. S.P. 10/9/16 (printed in Tytler, *op. cit.*, i, 214–16).

27. B.M., Cott. Calig. B. vii, f. 404 (printed in Ellis, *Original Letters*, i, pt. ii, 166, and Burnet, *op. cit.*, v, 273–4); *A.P.C.*, i, 333–4.

28. P.R.O., S.P. 10/9/17.

29. The draft is in S.P. 10/9/22; the Council letter is in B.M., Cott. Titus B ii, f. 55 (printed in Ellis); a copy is in the Council Register (*A.P.C.*, ii, 335–6).

30. S.P. 10/9/28; the signatures include Petre's. (Noted in R. Steele, *Tudor and Stuart Proclamations* (1910), i, 38, and printed in full by Pocock, *op. cit.*, 95–100.)

31. S.P. 10/9/27 (printed by Tytler, *op. cit.*, i, 228–30).

32. Mrs. Dewar's Ph.D. thesis on Smith (cf. ref. 11 *supra*), p. 97.

33. S.P. 10/9/39 (printed only by Pocock, *op. cit.*, 106–7).

34. B.M., Harl. MS. 353, f. 77 (cited by Pollard, *Somerset*, 252 n.).

35. A letter from Cranmer and Paget (B.M., Cotton MS., Calig. B. vii, f. 412) proves it to be the 10th, not the 9th, as given by Pollard, *op. cit.*, 251.

36. Tytler, *op. cit.*, i, 239–40; Pollard, *Somerset*, 252.

37. B.M., Cott. MS., Calig. B. vii, f. 421.

38. *A.P.C.*, ii, 342; cf. Pollard, *op. cit.*, 251.

39. C. Read, *op. cit.*, 57.

40. S.P. 10/9/45,41,46.

41. S.P. 10/9/40.

42. Dixon, *op. cit.*, iii, 153.

43. Dr. S. R. Gammon's thesis on Paget pp. 243–4.

44. Northants. Record Office: Fitzwilliam MSS., Paget letter-book, no. 28.

45. For further particulars of the Aldersgate Street house, see Petre's deeds register (E.R.O., D/DP E29, ff. 190–3) and his (London) accounts (D/DP A3–9).

46. E.R.O., D/DP F205.
47. D/DP E29, f. 190.
48. E. A. Webb, *The Records of St. Bartholomew's, Smithfield* (1921), i, 263. The bounds of Petre's plot can be traced by a comparison of the description in his deeds register (D/DP E29, ff. 190–3) with the reconstructed plan of St. Bartholomew's and Rich's house in Webb, ii, plate opp. p. 131 (cf. i, 268).
49. D/DP E29, f. 193.

CHAPTER VI

SECRETARY UNDER NORTHUMBERLAND

1. *Commons' Journals*, 11–14.
2. B.M., Cott., Galba B. xii, ff. 117–18 (draft instructions, undated but assigned to January (*For. Cal., Edw. VI*, 48) were corrected by Petre; cf. Burnet, *op. cit.*, v, 298–301, and *A.P.C.*, ii, 379, 395).
3. Lloyd's *State Worthies* (Petre), 453 (cited by Tytler, *op. cit.*, i, 77).
4. *Span. Cal.*, x, 87.
5. *Ibid.*, 88; inventory of 1565 (E.R.O., D/DP F206).
6. *A.P.C.*, ii, 432.
7. C. Read, *op. cit.*, 67.
8. *Cal. Hatfield MSS.* (H.M.C.), i, 89.
9. S.P. 10/13/7 (not 1550, as in C. Read, *op. cit.*, 65).
10. *Span. Cal.*, x, 169.
11. Middlesex Record Office, 446/H13. I am indebted to the Earl of Anglesey for permission to quote from the accounts.
12. C. Read, *op. cit.*, 65.
13. S.P. 10/13/16.
14. Haynes' *State Papers*, 116.
15. S. T. Bindoff, *Tudor England*, 159.
16. *Dom. Cal., 1547–80*, 33–4; *A.P.C.*, iii, 268, 352; *Wriothesley's Chronicle; Machyn's Diary*, 7, 317–18.
17. S.P. 10/13/33; F. C. Dietz, Eng. Govt. Finance (Univ. of Ill., 1921), 174.
18. *A.P.C.*, iii, 306, 328.
19. *Cal. Pat. Rolls, Edw. VI*, v, 200 (E.R.O., D/DP O53), the quotation is taken from the discharge in the family archives in preference to the printed calendar, which does not mention the Cofferer's refusal. Cf. *Cal. Pat. Rolls*, iv, 278.
20. S. T. Bindoff, *op. cit.*, 140.
21. S.P. 10/13/40.

22. Strype, *Mem.*, ii, pt. i, 409–10; also 495.
23. W. J. Loftie, *Memorials of the Savoy*, 108–9.
24. S.P. 10/13/43 (printed in Tytler, *op. cit.*, i, 427).
25. S.P. 10/13/53.
26. A. F. Pollard, *Somerset*, 284, 286.
27. A. F. Pollard, *Pol. Hist.*, 60–1.
28. Middx. R.O., 466/H13.
29. *Span. Cal.*, x, 386–90.
30. Middx. R.O., 466/H13.
31. A. F. Pollard, *Somerset*, 290–305.
32. *Ibid.*, *op. cit.*, 311.
33. *Cal. Hatfield MSS.* (H.M.C.), i, 94.
34. *Span. Cal.*, x, 444.
35. There is a list of 'acts', the first eight entries in which are in Edward's own hand, and these are followed by two in Cecil's and a final one in Petre's; it has been assigned to this session (*Dom. Cal.*, 38) but it is more likely to relate to that of 1552–53. For Glastonbury, see S.P. 10/13/75, 12/14/13–4, 10/15/55; *A.P.C.*, iii, 415; cf. E. Lipson, *Econ. Hist. of England* (11th edn., 1956), 493–4.
36. His peculations have now been proved to be of a relatively minor nature (Dr. Gammon's thesis, pp. 276–7).
37. Haynes' *State Papers*, 123.
38. *Ibid.*, 124.
39. *For. Cal.*, *Edw. VI*, 75; *Span. Cal.*, x, 465–6, 483–8, 514–15, 546, 553; Edward's Journal, 29 Sept.
40. *Span. Cal.*, x, 549.
41. C. Read, *op. cit.*, 68, 73–4, 77.
42. The journal and the additional memoranda discussed in this chapter were printed by the Roxburghe Club as *Literary Remains of King Edward the Sixth* (ed. J. G. Nichols, 1857) and by G. Burnet, *History of the Reformation* (ed. N. Pocock, 1865), vol. v. Cf. *Cal. Pat. Rolls*, *Edw. VI*, iv, 144 (undated). Petre's own patent, still extant in the family archives (E.R.O., D/DP O50), is dated 2 January 1552.
43. *Cal. Pat. Rolls. Edw. VI*, iv, 352–4.
44. G. R. Elton, *The Tudor Revolution in Government* (1953), 230. Dr. Elton (*op. cit.*, 231–8) has thrown new light on this commission's activities; see also *A.P.C.*, iv, 64, 179, 183.
45. Strype, *Mem.*, ii, pt. i, 526.
46. S.P. 10/16. It ends 'Examined by William Pownsett' (of Barking in Essex).
47. *A.P.C.*, iv, 157; v, 16, 54.

48. Cf. Hester W. Chapman, *The Last Tudor King* (1958), 175–6.
49. *Span. Cal.*, x, 592.
50. S.P. 10/18/11.
51. *Cal. Hatfield MSS.* (H.M.C.), i, 101.
52. *Commons' Journals.*
53. S. T. Bindoff, *op. cit.*, 165–6.
54. Alford's well-known statement is in B.M., Cott. MS. Titus B. ii. Cf. Strype, *Annals*, iv, 485; Tytler, *op. cit.*, ii, 171–2, 202–3; C. Read, *op. cit.*, 94.
55. C. Read, *op. cit.*, 91–2.
56. These four letters are at Hatfield and are in print (Haynes, *State Papers*, 148–50).
57. Bodleian Lib., Ashmolean MSS. 1729, f. 192.
58. The signatories to a Council letter of 3 June include Petre and Cheke (B.M., Cott., Titus B. ii, f. 267).
59. *Span. Cal.*, x, 50.
60. C. Read, *op. cit.*, 93.
61. S. T. Bindoff, 'A Kingdom at Stake' (*History Today* (1953), iii, 642–8).
62. J. G. Nichols, *Queen Jane and Queen Mary* (Camden Soc., 1850), 89–90; copied in Froude, v, 160–1. The amendment is clearly illustrated in Professor Bindoff's article.
63. Tytler, *op. cit.*, ii, 166.
64. R. A. de Vertot, *Ambassades de Messieurs de Noailles* (1763), ii, 31.
65. Inner Temple (Petyt MSS.) 538/47, f. 316; printed in full in Burnet, *op. cit.*, vi, 307–8, and *Chron. of Q. Jane*, 90–1. Burnet adds 'S^y' after Petre's name, which led one historian to remark that Petre was stressing the capacity in which he signed, but 'S^y' is a misreading of the flourish with which he often ended his signature.
66. Inner Temple (Petyt MSS.) 538/47, ff. 416–17; printed in full in *Chron. Q. Jane and Q. Mary*, 101–2.
67. J. G. Nichols, *Literary Remains of King Edward VI* (Roxburghe Club, 1857), ii, 574.
68. S.P. 10/18/27,28. These are calligraphic puzzles. No. 27 begins clearly in Petre's normal cursive hand, but the remaining entries are mostly in careful italic letters which he rarely used; the last entry, in which he was hurrying, uses letters of both 'hands'. (For further proof, cf. 'depech' (i.e. dispatch) in 10/18/27 with the same word in 10/13/79, a Council agenda unmistakably Petre's.) While it is perhaps true to say that few of the agenda papers for Edward's Councils survive, it is quite incorrect to state that 'none are in Cecil's hand' (C. Read, *op. cit.*, 65 (contradicted, 71)). *Dom. Cal.*, 47, specifically

refs to one written by Cecil (S.P. 10/15/51). In addition 10/14/66, 10/15/10, 10/15/14, 10/15/40, and 10/15/72 are his, and 10/15/27 has some entries by Cecil; 10/5/24, which belongs to 1551–52, is also Cecil's; also *Cal. Hatfield MSS.*, i, 118). The number of extant agenda drawn up by Petre (S.P. 10/13/79, 10/14/26, 10/15/4) is about the same as Cecil's. A few of the agenda are in a Council clerk's hand, and more than one is the composite work of clerk and Secretaries (S.P. 10/14/4, 10/14/36, 10/14/45; *Cal. Hatfield MSS.*, i, 120).

69. The preface to *A.P.C.*, iv, p. xix, gives New Hall, Boreham, in error; Mary had been there in the previous December (*Dom. Cal.*, 48).

70. *Span. Cal.*, xi, 78.

71. *Ibid.*, 88.

72. E.R.O., D/DU 40/38.

73. B.M., Lansdowne MS. 102, f. 2 (printed in Tytler, *op. cit.*, ii, 192–5), cf. C. Read, *op. cit.*, 94; A. F. Pollard, *Pol. Hist.*, 91, n. 1.

74. Tytler, *op. cit.*, ii, 192–5.

75. There are full accounts of the visits to the Tower in Dixon, *op. cit.*, iii, 220–6, and Froude, *op. cit.*, iv, 546–50, relying on Foxe (very detailed) and the Privy Council Register.

76. *A.P.C.*, iii, 84–7.

77. *Ibid.*, 146, quoting Ellis, *op. cit.*, i, pt. ii, 161.

78. *Span. Cal.*, ix, 393–4.

79. *Idem.*

80. Foxe, *op. cit.*, vi, 7–8; H. F. M. Prescott, *op. cit.*, 143–4.

81. S.P. 10/8/30.

82. S.P. 10/8/51,52. Petre had also drafted the Council's complaint.

83. *Span. Cal.*, x, 124–37.

84. Edward's *Journal*, 13 July; cf. *A.P.C.*, iii, 77.

85. The original letters of credence have survived (Inner Temple, Petyt MSS., 538/46, f. 7).

86. *A.P.C.*, iii, 144.

87. *Span. Cal.*, x, 260–1.

88. The letter and instructions are both set out in *A.P.C.*, iii, 341–6.

89. Strype, *Mem.*, ii, pt. i, 457, citing Edward's *Journal*.

CHAPTER VII

LIFE AT INGATESTONE HALL

1. This chapter is largely based on the two provision books ('week books'), 1548 and 1552, and the two general account-books, 1550 and 1555 (E.R.O., D/DP A12, 13; 10, 11); cf. Appendices A, E and F.
2. Cf. C. Read, *Bibliography of British History (Tudor Period)* (2nd edn., 1959), 106, 345.
3. T. Tusser, *A Hundreth Good Points of Husbandrie* (1557); W. Harrison, *An Historicall Description of . . . Britaine* (1577, pub. as intro. to Holinshed's *Chronicle*).
4. W. Camden, *Britannia* (1586).
5. J. Norden, *Description of Essex, 1594* (Camden Soc., 1840), 8.
6. J. T. Rogers, *Six Centuries of Work and Wages* (14th edn., 1919), 94–5.
7. V. Cheke, *The Story of Cheese-Making in Britain* (1959), 90.
8. G. E. Fussell, 'The Elizabethan Dairy Farmer' (*Journal of British Dairy Farmers' Assoc.*, lx, 1956).
9. Cited by Miss E. Burton, *The Elizabethans at Home* (1958), 150.
10. J. C. Drummond and A. Wilbraham, *The Englishman's Food* (1958), 110.
10A. N. J. Williams, *Tradesmen in Early Stuart Wiltshire* (Wilts. Arch. Soc., Records Branch, 1960), xiii.
10B. B.M., Lans. MS. 118.
11. E.R.O., D/DP A85.
12. A. Boorde, *A Compendyous Regyment or Dyetary of Helth* (?1542).
13. F. G. Emmison, *Inventory of Ingatestone Hall in 1600* (1954), 17.
14. P.R.O., K.B. 9/606/144 (cal. made for E.R.O.).
15. *Span. Cal.*, xiii, 31.
16. G. M. Trevelyan, *Eng. Soc. Hist.* (1942), 161.
17. C. W. & P. Cunnington, *Handbook of English Costume in the 16th Century* (1954), 199.
18. G. Scott Thomson, *Life in a Noble Household* (1937), 125.
19. E.R.O., D/DP F234.
20. F. G. Emmison, *Inventory of Ingatestone Hall in 1600* (1954), 19.
21. 7 Edw. VI, c. 7 (1553).
22. W. Beveridge, *Prices and Wages in England*, i (1939), 120.
23. *V.C.H.*, Essex, ii, 414.
24. J. Berridge, *The Tudor Rose* (1925), 277.

CHAPTER VIII

SECRETARY TO MARY

1. Strype, *Mem.*, iii, pt. i, 25.
2. *A.P.C.*, iv, 419. See ref. 9 below.
3. Strype, *Annals*, iv, 489; Tytler, *op. cit.*, ii, 204.
4. S.P. 11/1/5 (*Dom. Cal.*, *1547–80*, 54). It is hastily written, and is probably earlier in date than the briefer, more formal memorandum listed as 11/1/3; dates given in the printed calendar are merely taken from later endorsements, that on Petre's memorandum being in Cecil's hand.
5. Froude, *op. cit.*, v, 228–9.
6. *Venetian Cal.*, v, 532–3.
7. Pollard, *Pol. Hist.*, 94, 95 n., quoting *Chron. of Q. Jane and Q. Mary*, 15. The earliest specific record of Petre's membership of Mary's Council is 12 Aug. (BM., Lans. 3, f. 54); its register first refers to him on 13 Aug.
8. J. A. Muller, *Stephen Gardiner and the Tudor Reaction*.
9. *Cal. Pat. Rolls, Mary*, i, 278 (the actual date is 5 Nov.); Petre's patent is still preserved (E.R.O., D/DP O52); Evans, *op. cit.*, 349n. thus wrong.
10. *Span. Cal.*, xi, 216.
11. Froude, *op. cit.*, v, 228.
12. E.g., *For. Cal., Mary*, 25, 26, 28, 54, 55, 84, 384.
13. J. W. Burgon, *Life of Sir Thomas Gresham* (1839), i, 127.
14. *Span. Cal.*, xi, 315.
15. Froude, *op. cit.*, v, 128–9, referring to S.P. 10/19.
16. J. Hurstfield, *The Queen's Wards* (1958), 10.
17. S.P. 11/1/10, 11.
18. Haynes, *State Papers*, 192–3.
19. The letters patent bear date 28 May 1554 but provided for payment of his fee from the preceding Michaelmas (*Cal. Pat. Rolls, 1553–4*, p. 160); Petre's patent is preserved (E.R.O., D/DP O55A).
20. J. Anstis, *Register of . . . Order of the Garter* (1724), p. c.
21. G. F. Beltz, *Memorials of the Order of the Garter* (1841), p. c.
22. S.P. 11/1/15.
23. *For. Cal., Mary*, 52–3 (Tytler, *op. cit.*, ii, 283–6).
24. *Commons' Journals*, 28, 31, 32.
25. *A.P.C.*, iv, 317–18.

26. *Span. Cal.*, xi, 270, 320, 327, 343, 349.

27. *Span. Cal.*, xi, 397.

28. A. Strickland, *Lives of the Queens of England*, iii, 58.

29. *Span. Cal.*, xi, 400.

30. E.R.O., D/DP O57; the marriage articles (probably Dec. 1553) were signed by 23 privy councillors including Petre (S.P. 11/1/20).

31. *Span. Cal.*, xi, 444, also 412, 414, 428.

32. S.P. 11/2/20, printed in *The Letters of Stephen Gardiner* (ed. J. A. Muller, 1933), 459; cf. Froude, *op. cit.*, v, 330.

33. *Span. Cal.*, xii, 78.

34. *Chronicle of Q. Jane and Q. Mary* (Camden Soc., 1850), 48 n.

35. 1 Mary, sess. 2, c. 12.

36. E.R.O., D/DP M94; I owe this ref. to my colleague Mr. Newton.

37. *For. Cal.*, *Mary*, 61 (S.P. 69/3/159). Petre's name is not in the list of those active in the field (S.P. 11/3/36).

38. S.P. 12/1/53.

39. S. T. Bindoff, *op. cit.*, 172.

40. A. F. Pollard, *Pol. Hist.*, 113.

41. *A.P.C.*, iv, 392.

42. *For. Cal.*, 54.

43. S.P. 11/3/22; the letter is printed in Muller, *op. cit.*, p. 462.

44. *Holinshed's Chronicle.*

45. *Cal. Patent Rolls, Philip & Mary*, ii, 245.

46. *D.N.B.*, art. Petre.

47. Lloyd, *State Worthies* (1665), art. Petre.

48. *Span. Cal.*, xii, 175, 197.

49. J. E. Neale, *Queen Elizabeth* (1934), 45.

50. *Span. Cal.*, xii, 140.

51. *Cal. Patent Rolls, Mary*, i, 164; ii, 91, 173; E.R.O., D/DP O55.

52. *Span. Cal.*, xii, 137–8.

53. *Ibid.*, 168–9, 176, 197.

54. *A.P.C.*, iv, 398.

55. *Span. Cal.*, xii, 220.

56. *Ibid.*, 220–5.

57. *Ibid.*, 261.

58. *Ibid.*, 260.

59. This and other letters during the progress are in *Span. Cal.*, xii.

60. *A.P.C.*, v, 53–4.

61. *Span. Cal.*, xiii, 23–4.

62. *For. Cal.*, *Mary*, 113.

63. A. F. Pollard, *Pol. Hist.*, 127.

64. See *Span. Cal.*, xii, pp. xix–xxi, 14, 22, 30, 47–8, 115–16, 141, 143, 149, 158, 295, 315.

65. *Span. Cal.*, xiii, 49, 51.

66. *Ven. Cal.*, v, 559–60.

67. *Span. Cal.*, xiii, 21.

68. C. Read, *op. cit.*, 103–4; the long draft minute of the envoy's instructions (*For. Cal.*, 135; Tytler, ii, 445–7) is Petre's.

69. *Span. Cal.*, xiii, 87–91, 101.

70. *Chron. of Queen Jane & Queen Mary* (Camden Soc., 1850), 82.

71. S.P., 69/5, f. 122; C. Read, *op. cit.*, 103, has misread several words.

72. P. F. Tytler, *op. cit.*, ii, 436–7, citing a numbered B.M. pamphlet.

73. *For. Cal.*, *Mary*.

74. *Ibid.*, 139.

75. Foxe, *op. cit.* (ed. Cattley), vi, 568.

76. *Commons' Journals*, i, 38.

77. A. J. Kempe, *Loseley MSS.* (1835), 90–2.

78. *Commons' Journals*, i, 38.

79. *Span. Cal.*, xiii, 130.

80. *Span. Cal.*, xii, 241, and xiii, 64; *A.P.C.*, i; *For. Cal.*

81. *For. Cal.*, *Mary*, 180.

82. Sir W. Dugdale, *Monasticon Anglicanum* (1665–73), ed. of 1846, vi, 1645; plate in J. J. Howard and H. F. Burke, *Geneal. Coll. of R.C. Families*, Part i, Petre (1887); original in E.R.O., D/DP F147.

83. The chief primary source is of course John Foxe, *Acts and Monuments*, first printed in 1563, and popularly known as 'The Book of Martyrs'; S. R. Cattley's edn. (8 vols., 1837–41) has been used. Dixon's and Froude's accounts are mainly based on Foxe. The most recent studies are J. F. Mozley, *John Foxe and his Book* (1940), esp. pp. 175–203 (pro Foxe), and P. Hughes, *The Reformation in England*, ii (1953), 255–9 (R.C. view). For the Essex martyrs, see T. W. Davids, *Annals of Evangelical Nonconformity in Essex* (1863), 26–55.

84. *Span. Cal.*, xiii, 31.

85. *Richard Grafton's Chronicle* (ed. 1569), 350.

86. P. F. Tytler, *op. cit.*, ii, 470 (*For. Cal.*, *Mary*, 165).

87. *For. Cal.*, *Mary*, 166.

88. J. Foxe, *op. cit.*

89. *Span. Cal.*, xiii, 165.

90. *For. Cal.*, *Mary*, 167.

91. *A.P.C.*, v, 75, 101, 128.

92. *Span. Cal.*, xiii, 229.

93. B.M., Cott. MS., Titus B. ii, f. 176 (now 160).

94. J. D. Mackie, *The Earlier Tudors* (1952), 532.
95. Details of the feast printed *in extenso* by Sir W. Dugdale, *Origines Judiciales* (1666 and 1680).
96. J. Foxe, *op. cit.*, vii, 592, cited by J. M. Stone, *History of Mary Queen of England* (1901), 378.
97. *For. Cal., Mary*, 105, 112, 134.
98. *Ibid.*, p. ix.
99. See *A.P.C.*
100. *A.P.C.*, vi, 388.
101. A. F. Pollard, *Pol. Hist.*, 156–7.

CHAPTER IX

RESIGNATION—BUT NO REST

1. S. H. Cassan, *Lives of the Bishops of Winchester* (1827), i, 509, quoting Strype.
2. C. Read, *op. cit.*, 107.
3. E. H. Harbison, *Rival Ambassadors*, 274, citing R. Vertot, *Messieurs de Noailles* (Leyden, 1763), v, 167–8.
4. *Commons' Journal*, i, 43; *Ven. Cal.*, vi, 239.
5. *Commons' Journal*, i, 42.
6. *Ibid.*, 44.
7. *Ven. Cal.*, vi, pt. i, 154; Dixon, *op. cit.*, iv, 385–6.
8. C. Read, *op. cit.*, 110–12.
9. *For. Cal., Mary*, 199; J. W. Burgon, *Life of Sir Thomas Gresham* (1839), i, 181–4.
10. E.g. S.P. 11/7/10, 11/8/43, 11/8/51, 11/9/10, 11/9/15, 11/9/28, 11/9/41, 11/9/51.
11. *Dom. Cal.*, *1547–70*, 65–72; *Addenda, 1547–65*, 439.
12. *Ven. Cal.*, vi, pt. i. no. 259 (p. 233).
13. S.P. 11/9/24 (interrogatories in Petre's hand); P.R.O., French Transcripts, 3, bdle. 22 (18 and 21 Oct.); cf. E. H. Harbison, *op. cit.*, 305; *Dom. Cal.*, 86–88.
14. Froude, *op. cit.*, vi, 18–9.
15. *For. Cal., Mary*, 285–6 (cf. 282–3); E. H. Harbison, *op. cit.*, 320.
16. *For. Cal., Mary*, 294.
17. *Ibid.*, 293–4.
18. *Ibid.*, 302; cf. P.R.O., French Transcripts, 3, bdle. 23, f. 339v. (23 May 1557).

339

19. *A.P.C.*, vi, 69–70.

20. S.P. 69/9/544 (*For. Cal., Mary*, 264).

21. *Ven. Cal.*, vi, pt. i, 212.

22. *D.N.B.*, art. Petre (A. F. Pollard).

23. *D.N.B.*, art. Cecil.

24. E. H. Harbison, *op. cit.*, 316.

25. *Ibid.*, 319.

26. P.R.O., French Transcripts, 3, bdle. 22 (15 Dec. 1556).

27. *The Statutes of the Most Noble Order of the Garter* (1906), 38.

28. *Machyn's Diary*, 60.

29. T. S. Willan, *The Early History of the Russia Company* (1956); Machyn, 85, 104, 134; Strype, *Mem.*, iii, pt. ii, 3. The early records kept by the Company were destroyed by the Great Fire of 1666.

30. *Cal. Pat. Rolls, Phil. & Mary*, ii, 55–9.

31. B.M., Lans. 118, f. 27.

32. *Stow's Chronicle*; T. S. Willan, *op. cit.*, 16.

33. Strype, *Mem.*, iii, pt. i, 521.

34. *Ibid.*

35. Lloyd, *Statesmen* (1665), edited by *D.N.B.*

36. *A.P.C.*, vi, 229, 232.

37. S.P. 69/11.

38. S.P. 11/11/58, 59 (both given in J. W. Burgon, *op. cit.*, i, 225–8).

39. Burgon, *op. cit.*, 483.

40. Pollard, *Pol. Hist.*, 172.

41. *Ibid.*, 171.

42. S.P., 11/12/50.

43. *Cal. Pat. Rolls, Phil. & Mary*, iii, 317, also 314.

44. *For. Cal., Mary*, 314–63 (*passim*); these drafts and autograph minutes are correctly attributed to Petre.

45. Pollard, *Pol. Hist.*, 164.

46. *Span. Cal.*, xiii, 349, 366–7.

47. *Span. Cal.*, xiii, 403.

48. Her will is set out in full in H. M. Stone, *op. cit.*, 507–21, taken from F. Madden, *Privy Purse Expenses of Princess Mary* (1831), see esp. clxix, cciii.

CHAPTER X

LEISURE AND PLEASURE

1. Grove's *Dictionary of Music and Musicians* (5th edn., 1954).
2. Cf. W. L. Woodfill, *Musicians in Elizabethan Society* (1953), 276 'one broken "gyttrone" (?gittern), 1577'.
3. E.R.O., D/DP F205.
4. Grove, *op. cit.*
5. W. L. Woodfill, *op. cit.*, 60.
6. See F. G. Emmison, 'The Household Accounts of Sir William and Sir John Petre, 1548–90' (*Galpin Society Journal*, xiii).
7. E. H. Fellowes, *William Byrd* (1st edn., 1936), 208; M. Kenyon, *Harpsichord Music* (1949), 39–40.
8. E. H. Fellowes, *op. cit.*, 208; M. Kenyon, *op. cit.*, 49.
9. E.R.O., D/DP A20, 21.
10. E. H. Fellowes, *op. cit.*, 42; M. Kenyon, *op. cit.*, 31, 36. His name often occurs in Sir John's accounts in 1589–91; see L. G. Langwill's art. on 'Double and single' in Grove's *Dict. of Music and Musicians* (5th edn.).
11. E. H. Fellowes, *op. cit.*, 17; E.R.O., Q/SR and D/AEC.
12. W. L. Woodfill, *op. cit.*, App. B.
13. See L. G. Langwill, 'The Waits', in Hinrichsen's *Music Book*, vol. iii (1952); W. L. Woodfill, *op. cit.*, ch. iv.
14. Chaucer, *Roman de la Rose*, 764.
15. W. L. Woodfill, *op. cit.*, ch. iii.
16. *L. & P., Hen. VIII*, xiv, pt. ii, 329.
17. E.R.O., D/DP A15.
18. *Shakespeare's England* (1916), ii, 473. Primero and gleek, another card-game, occur in *Cal. Rutland MSS.* (H.M.C.), iv, 362, but specific references in private accounts are rare.
19. *Privy Purse Expenses of Princess Mary*, ed. F. Madden (1831), index *s.v.* 'Cards'.
20. F. G. Emmison, *Inventory of Ingatestone Hall in 1600* (1954).
21. *For. Cal., Mary*, 19, quoted by Tytler, *op. cit.*, ii, 247–8.
22. P.R.O., S.P. 69/4/186 (*For. Cal., Mary*, 72).
23. C. Read, *op. cit.*, 114.
24. C. W. Boase, *Register of Exeter College, Oxford* (2nd edn., 1894), clxvii.
25. *Wriothesley's Chronicle* (Camden Soc., N.S., 1877), ii, 121.

CHAPTER XI

COUNSELLOR TO ELIZABETH

1. C. Read, *op. cit.*, 118 and n. 3; Tytler (*op. cit.*, ii, 499) adds Wotton and Mason, Froude (*op. cit.*, vi, 117), only Mason.
2. S.P. 12/1/7.
3. Strype, *Annals*, i, pt. 1, 9.
4. *Cal. Pat. Rolls, Eliz.*, i, 57 (*D.N.B.* incorrectly gives 1566).
5. C. Dodd, *Church History* (1737–42).
6. Pollard, *Political History*, 185.
7. Cf. J. E. Neale, *Queen Elizabeth* (1934), 67–70; A. L. Rowse, 'The Coronation of Queen Elizabeth I' (*History Today*, iii, 301–10).
8. S.P. 12/1/57.
9. *A.P.C.*, vii, 48, 50; cf. *Cal. Pat. Rolls, Eliz.*, i, 67.
10. *A.P.C.*, vii, 38; *Dom. Cal.*, *1547–80*, 168–9; E. E. Rich, *The Ordinance Book of the Merchants of the Staple* (1937), 28; *For. Cal., Mary*, 216, 220, 386, 393–4; *For. Cal., Eliz.*, iv, 110. (For the rivalry between the three bodies, see E. Lipson, *Econ. Hist. of Eng.* (11th edn., 1956), 565–84; A. L. Rowse, *The England of Elizabeth* (1950), 149–51.)
11. *For. Cal., Eliz.*, i, 103–4, 137–9.
12. E.R.O., D/DP A8. Records of election dinners are rare (cf. J. E. Neale, *The Elizabethan House of Commons* (1949), 328–31). There is no evidence that any elections had been contested by Petre.
13. C. Read, *op. cit.*, 129.
14. The most recent and by far the fullest account is in J. E. Neale, *Elizabeth I and her Parliaments, 1559–1581* (1953), 33–84.
15. *Ibid.*, 37.
16. *Ibid.*, 80.
17. P.R.O., Ass. 35/3/2 (typescript calendar made for E.R.O.).
18. S.P. 12/3/8.
19. *A.P.C.*, vii, 69.
20. 14 Nov., 23, 24 Dec. 1559 (*Cal. For., Eliz.*, ii, 112, 219, 224).
21. S. T. Bindoff, *op. cit.*, 184.
22. *For. Cal., Eliz.*, ii, 224.
23. J. E. Neale, *Queen Elizabeth*, 99.
24. Haynes, *State Papers*, 268; cf. C. Read, *op. cit.*, 164.
25. S.P. 12/12/1; and *Cal. Salisbury MSS.* (H.M.C.), i, 212.
26. For the Cecil–Petre correspondence, see *Cal. Salisbury MSS.*, i, 226–48; *For. Cal., Eliz.*, iii, 115, 125, 132, 139; also *Scot. Cal. Papers, 1547–63*.

27. S.P. 52/4, f. 86 (*Cal. Salis. MSS.*, 198); *For. Cal.*, *Eliz.*, iii, 198, 199.
28. J. E. Neale, *op. cit.*, 103.
29. S.P. 12/13/21; not Brentford in Middlesex (*D.N.B.*, art. Robert Dudley).
30. S.P. 12/13/52 (*Dom. Cal.*, *1547–80*, 160); P.R.O., E407/52 (Star Chamber dinner accounts).
31. S.P. 12/33/68, f. 3; *Machyn's Diary*, 257, 258; Froude, *op. cit.*, vi, 487. About this time Petre was appointed senior commissioner, with Lord Chief Justice Catlin and others, to determine the scale of charges which prisoners in the Fleet should pay towards their keep (Inner Temple, Petyt MSS., 538/20 (H.M.C., 11th *Report*)).

CHAPTER XII

QUEEN ELIZABETH AT INGATESTONE HALL

1. B.M., Cott. MS., Vesp. C.xiv.481, printed by J. Nichols, *The Progresses of Queen Elizabeth* (edn. of 1823).
2. E.R.O., D/P 94/5/1.
3. S. Dale, *History of Harwich* (1730), 250.
4. M. Craze, *History of Felsted School* (1955), 25 (Rich); P.R.O., S.P. 12/19/29 (Oxford).
5. J. E. Neale, *Queen Elizabeth* (1934), 209–12 For the provisions and victuals consumed in Elizabeth's three-day visit to Lord North's mansion at Kirtling in 1578, see *D.N.B.*
6. S.P. 12/21/39; for Catherine Grey see R. Davey, *The Sisters of Lady Jane Grey* (1911) and Hester W. Chapman, *Two Tudor Portraits* (1960).
7. T. Wright, *Queen Elizabeth and her Times* (1838), i, 179–80.
8. *Ibid.*, 174.
9. J. J. Howard and H. F. Burke, *Geneal. Coll.—Petre* (1887), i, 49.
10. S.P. 12/36/65, quoted by C. Read, *op. cit.*, 324.
11. E.R.O., D/DP Q13/1/1.
12. S.P. 12/34/14.
13. S.P. 12/39/75.
14. S.P. 12/39/70.

CHAPTER XIII

ELDER STATESMAN

1. W. M. Palmer, 'Canbridge Doctors' (*Proc. Camb. Antiq. Soc.*, xv (N.S., ix)).
2. *For. Cal., Mary*, 266.
3. *Dom. Cal.*, vi (*Addenda, 1547-65*), 518; *For. Cal., Eliz.*, iv, 600.
4. *Cal. Pat. Rolls, Eliz.*, i, 118; ii, 279.
5. E.407/53 (Star Chamber diet expenses, 22 April).
6. *Machyn's Diary*, 281.
7. S.P. 12/33/68, ff. 6, 7.
8. *Span. Cal., Eliz.*, i, 232-3; cf. C. Read, *op. cit.*, 253; *For. Cal., Eliz.*, v, 83.
9. *A.P.C.*, vii, 114, 121.
10. C. Read, *op. cit.*, 242-3, quoting B.M., Add. MSS. 35631, f. 22.
11. *Span. Cal., Eliz.*, i, 260.
12. T. Wright, *Queen Elizabeth* (1838), i, 109; also his boathire entry for 20 Nov.
13. S.P. 12/25/64 (Cecil's draft can now be read only under an ultra-violet lamp). For Rich's endowment see M. Craze, *History of Felsted School* (1955).
14. J. A. Giles, *Works of Roger Ascham* (1865), ii, 381-8, 393-6, 399-402, 405-9.
15. *Ibid.*, i, pp. lxxxv-vi; ii, 388-91, 436-42. Dedicating to Petre his (Ascham's) 'Osorius de Nobilitate Christiana' is the *D.N.B.*'s misleading reference (*s.v.* Petre).
16. *Cal. Pat. Rolls, Mary*, i, 383; ii, 412; iii, 47, 259; *D.N.B.* is incorrect in giving the sum as £20, which was the amount he received from a separate grant (*ibid.*, i, 278).
17. S.P. 12/29/63.
18. C. Read, *op. cit.*, 216.
19. *Cal. Pat. Rolls, 1560-3*, 623; *Dom. Cal., 1547-80*, 254.
20. *For. Cal., 1563*, 395.
21. Star Chamber diet accounts (P.R.O., E407/53).
22. *Span. Cal., 1558-67*, 368; *A.P.C.*, vii, 147; see also *A.P.C.*, vii, 152.
23. Strype, *Annals*, i, pt. ii, 119; B.M., Lans. MS., cii, 55 (quoted by C. Read, *op. cit.*, 293); *Span. Cal., 1558-67*, 380; all name Petre first.
24. P.R.O., E407/53.
25. *A.P.C.*, vii, 218, 277, 304; see also 208.

26. *Cal. Hatfield MSS.* (H.M.C.), ii, 129 (misread as 1576); I am indebted to Mrs. Woodfill (née Iselin), formerly assistant librarian, Hatfield House, for verifying the date.

27. *A.P.C.*, vii, 265–6, 272, 293; C. Read, *op. cit.*, 344.

28. S.P. 12/39/75.

29. *Span. Cal.*, *1558–67*, 405–6, 615–16.

30. C. Read, *op. cit.*, 352.

30A. J. E. Neale, *The Elizabethan House of Commons* (1949), 310.

31. Miss N. Fuidge's London M.A. thesis, 'The Parliament of 1563', ch. i.

32. Pat. Roll (ref. given by courtesy of P.R.O. from unpublished calendar).

33. S.P. 12/46/21, 25 (*Dom. Cal.*, *1547–80*, 306).

34. Haynes, *State Papers*, 487–91; cf. C. Read, *op. cit.*, 410–13.

35. *L. & P., Henry VIII*, xx, pt. i, 623 (p. 322); also p. 325 (commissioner for collecting benevolence in Essex).

36. *Ibid.*, 622 (p. 314); for commissioners of sewers in Essex, see Hilda Grieve, *The Great Tide* (1959), 14.

37. *Cal. Pat. Rolls, Edw. VI*, i, 83.

38. W. Lambard, *Eirenarcha: or the Office of the Justices of Peace* (many edns. from 1581), bk. i, ch. 5; iv, 3.

39. S.P. 11/5/3.

40. E.R.O., D/AER9.

41. S.P. 12/60/53.

CHAPTER XIV

MAN OF FORTUNE AND CHARITY

1. Sir Henry Ellis (ed.), *Speculi Britanniæ Pars: An Historical and Chorographical Description of the County of Essex* (Camden Society, 1840).

2. F. Hull's London Ph.D. thesis, 'Agriculture and Rural Society in Essex, 1560–1640' (copy in E.R.O.), p. 359.

3. All documents quoted are in E.R.O. (D/DP) or in *L. & P.* and *Cal. Pat. Rolls.*

4. A miniature drawing of the house and gardens is in John Walker's map, 1598 (D/DP P5).

5. *Cal. Pat. Rolls, Philip & Mary*, i, 258, 311.

6. *Cal. Pat. Rolls, Edw. VI*, v, 200.

7. Dr. Hull's thesis, map 10.

8. Miss J. Youings, 'The Terms of the Disposal of the Devon Monastic Lands, 1536–58' (*Eng. Hist. Rev.*, lxix (1954), 28), and 'Devon Monastic Lands: Calendar of Particulars for Grants, 1536–58' (*Dev. & Corn. Rec. Soc.*, N.S., i (1955)).

9. W. R. Emerson's Oxford D.Phil. thesis, 'The Economic Development of the Petre Family, 1540–1640' (copy in E.R.O.), p. 97.

10. E.R.O., e.g. D/DP A86, and Petre (West Country estate archives), Devon R.O., e.g. 123M, 26/36; I have to thank Miss J. Sinar, County Archivist of Devon, for this document.

11. H. J. Habakkuk, 'The Market for Monastic Property, 1539–1603' (*Econ. Hist. Rev.*, 2nd series, x (1958), 366).

11A. E.R.O., D/DP E5.

12. E.R.O., D/DP A14.

13. J. Hurstfield, *The Queen's Wards* (1959), 278.

14. *For. Cal., Mary*, 109–10.

15. W. K. Jordan, *Philanthropy in England, 1480–1660* (1959), 18.

15A. *Ibid.*, 59.

16. *Cal. Pat. Rolls, Phil. & Mary*, iii, 542–3: full copy in E.R.O., D/DP Q11/1, which also contains a copy of Petre's grant.

17. A full copy of the statutes, in English, made by Petre 'for the good order and government of the priest and the poor of Ginge Petre' exists in his charities enrolment register (D/DP Q11/1).

18. *Ibid.*

19. C. G. Robertson, *All Souls College* (Oxford College Histories, 1899).

20. Copy of will and inventory in Petre's archives (E.R.O., D/DP F234). Both documents are of considerable interest. There is a list of books formerly belonging to Barking Abbey. One of the foundation indentures, dated 10 Sept. 1557, is in the Petre archives (D/DP Q13/2).

21. R. Newcourt, *Repertorium Ecclesiasticum Parochiale Londinense* (1710), ii, 34; also the executors' accounts (D/DP F235, f. 24). The rectory was unsuccessfully claimed for the Crown in 1581. The college still owns both the rectory and the advowson of Barking.

22. E.R.O., D/DP Q13/2.

23. C. G. Robertson, *op. cit.*, 91.

24. C. W. Boase, *Register of . . . Exeter College* (2nd edn., 1894), lxxxi.

25. Boase, *op. cit.*, lxxxix, n. 2.

26. *V.C.H., Oxon.*, iii, 244, 252; C. E. Mallet, *A History of the Univ. of Oxford* (1924–7), ii, 250.

27. For the first fellows' names, see Boase, *op. cit.*, xciv, 74–5.

28. For an abstract of the new statutes, see Boase, *op. cit.*, lxxxix–xciv, and (more briefly) *V.C.H. Oxon.*, iii, 109–10.

29. W. K. Stride, *Exeter College* (Oxford College Histories, 1900), 43.

30. The Bodleian Library possesses a faithfully drawn copy of the drawings. As they are the oldest views, the series is now of much antiquarian interest.

31. Translation in W. K. Stride, *op. cit.*, 48–9; an elaborate description of Elizabeth's memorable visit was prepared by Bereblock, who dedicated it to Lord Cobham and to Petre, but the pamphlet was not published until 1729, when Hearne printed it as an appendix (pp. 251–96) to his edn. of *Historia et Vita Ricardi II* (*D.N.B.*, *s.v.* Bearblock).

32. B.M., Lans. MS. 614.x.67 (so cited by C. W. Boase, *op. cit.*, lxxxiii).

33. E.R.O., D/DQ 13/1/1.

34. Misdated as 1578 in *H.M.C 9th Rep.*, pt. i (St. Paul's Dean and Chapter MSS.), 53.

35. E.R.O., D/DP Z23.

35A. H. P. R. Finberg, 'The Gostwicks of Willington' (*Pub. Beds. Hist. Rec. Soc.*, xxxvi (1956), 77, 88–9).

36. E.R.O., D/DP F1.

37. E.R.O., D/DP A17. Cf. A. R. Ingpen, *The Middle Temple Bench Book* (1912).

38. *Dom. Cal.*, *Addenda 1566–79* (1871), 279.

39. E.R.O., D/DP F2.

40. Testament (personal chattels), 12 April; will (real estate), 27 April (E.R.O., D/DP F3–5); proved 31 Jan. 1572 (P.C.C., 1 Petre).

41. E.R.O., D/DP F151.

42. W. K. Jordan, *op. cit.*, 147.

43. J. J. Howard and H. F. Burke, *op. cit.*, 51, 55; Ingatestone parish register.

44. C. Dodd, *Church History of England* (1737–42), ii, 56.

45. F. Chancellor, *The Ancient Sepulchral Monuments of Essex* (1890), plates cxi, cxii.

46. E.R.O., D/DP F8.

47. 'John Payne's Treason' (*Brentwood* [R.C.] *Diocesan Magazine* (1921), i, 65–71, 91–6); Canon B. C. Foley's account in *The Essex Recusant* (1960), ii, 48–75, includes new material in the Essex Assize Files (P.R.O.), recently calendared for the E.R.O.

48. J. J. Howard & H. F. Burke, *op. cit.*, 51, 55; Ingatestone parish register.

49. Cf. Miss M. E. Finch, *The Wealth of Five Northamptonshire Families, 1540–1640* (Northants. Rec. Soc., 1956), 165.

50. His shrievalty record-book (a rare type of archive) is preserved (E.R.O., D/DP O58).

Index

W.P.: Sir William Petre.   I.H.: Ingatestone Hall.

All the appendices except F, H and I are indexed. Fish, fowl, birds, crafts and occupations are indexed under their own heads.

A A   *349*

Garter, chancellor of Order of the, 98, 106, 164, 177, 203-4, 228, 236, 255, 265, 270-2, 322
Gates, Sir John, vice-chamberlain, sheriff of Essex, 99, 101, 105, 119-20, 122 n., 161, 164; Lady, 132
'George' (Garter emblem), 98, 177, 203
Germany, 63, 172, 235 n.
Geste ('jesse'), 237
Gidea hall, Romford (Essex), 74, 229
Gifts. See Presents
Ging Abbess (Ging Petre). See Ingatestone
Gittern, 210
Glass windows, 35, 302; stained, 32, 302
Glasses, 158
Glastonbury (Som.), 98, 267, 271; abbey, 16
Gloucestershire, 7, 267, 287
Glynne, Dr., bp. of Bangor, 209 n.
Goats, 137, 144, app. F
Godsalve, Sir John, clerk of signet, 69, 89
Godstow priory (Oxford), 21 n.
Gold and goldsmiths. See Jewellery; Plate
Goodrich, Tho., bp. of Ely, lord chancellor, 98, 101, 116
Goodwins, 138, 306-7, 316
Gosfield hall (Essex), 245
Goshawks. See Hawks
Gostwick, John s. of Wm., W.P.'s ward, 286-7, 289, 303, 305
Grafting, 140
Grafton (Worcs.), 287, 303
Grammar schools, 93-4, 257
Granary at I.H., 34
Gravesend (Kent), 87-8
Great Harry, 57
Greenfish (cod), 142
Greenwich palace and park, 44, 53, 61, 69, 72, 82, 99, 105-6, 115, 117, 121, 191-2, 198, 202, 219, 233-5, 256, 260-1, 288; friary, 188
Gresham, Sir Tho., royal agent in Flanders, 63, 163, 172, 176, 185, 188, 197-8, 207, 240, 248 n.
Greville, Ludovick son of Sir Edw., 247, 287, 289; Wm. s. of L., 289; Edw. and John his sons, 290
Grey, Lady Cath., 231, 246-8, 251 n., 261
Grey, Henry, 3rd marquis of Dorset, duke of Suffolk, 71, 97, 105, 161, 164, 173, 246, 268
Grey, Jane, Queen, 71, 105-11, 162, 168, 172
Grey, Lord John (s. of Tho. 2nd marquis), 207, 232, 246
Grey, Lady Mary, 248 n.
Greyhounds, 177, 222-3
Griffin, Maurice, bp. of Rochester, 209 n., 250
Guests at I.H., 123-32, 299, 308-15
Guildford, 99, 175-6, 215
Guinea-fowl, 35, 146
Guise, Mary of, Regent of Scotland, 231-3
Guisnes, 61, 63

Gulls, 241
Gunpowder, 224, 299
Gurnards, 139, 241, 317
Gye, Walter, brickmaker, 157
Gylham, ——, musical instrument maker, 211-12

Haberdin, 139-45, 241, 299, 301, 306, 308, app. F
Haddon, Mr. 259
Hadleigh (Suff.), 187, 244
Hales, Sir James, justice of common pleas, 116
Hales, John, author, 246
Hallingbury (Essex), 245
Hall's chronicle, 58-60
Ham, West (Essex), 193
Hampshire, 128
Hampton, Bernard, 259
Hampton court, 32, 53, 62, 68, 75-6, 82, 94, 100, 121, 180, 188, 190, 219, 222, 256, 275, 304
Hanaper office. See Fees
Hanningfield (Essex), 307
Hans, ——, armourer, 171, 176
Hanse merchants, 163; towns, 228
Hanworth park (Middx.), 190
Harbinger, 178-9
Harness, horse, 68, 74
Harpers, 216
Harrison, Wm., historian, 134, 150
Hartland abbey (Devon), 15
Harvest, 132, 145, 149
Harwich (Essex), 55, 244, 299
Hastings, Sir Edw., master of horse, 97, 110, 179, 182, 199, 244; Francis, 2nd earl of Huntingdon, 90, 97, 109-11, 122 n., 161; Lord, 244
Hatfield house (Herts.), 32, 42, 51, 71, 206 n., 226-7
Havering (Essex) palace and park, 223, 239-40; see also Pyrgo
Hawkhurst (Kent), 186
Hawks and hawking, 34, 69, 177, 197, 223-4
Haymaking, 131, 145, 149
Heath, Nich., bp. of Rochester, archbp. of York, lord chancellor, 45, 208, 226-7, 230, 262
Hedingham castle (Essex), 111, 224 n., 231 n., 244
Hemsworth hosp. (Yorks.), 209 n.
Henry II, King of France, 167, 229
Henry VIII, 4-6, 43-5; regency council, 53-4; W.P.'s drafts corrected by, 55; will, 65-6; music, 210
Herbert, Wm., earl of Pembroke, 73, 75, 79, 97, 100, 109-11, 115, 161-2, 168-70, 173-5, 178-9, 190-1, 208, 227, 230, 256, 262
Herbs, 140, 242-3, 252
Heresy acts and commissions, 42, 75, 174, 184, 200

INDEX

Plympton priory (Devon), 15
Pole, Reginald, legate, cardinal, archbp. of
    Canterbury, 125 n., 166, 181–94, 205, 209,
    258, 279 n.
Politiques, 195
Pollard, Sir Hugh, monastic visitor, 13
Polslow priory (Devon), 13, 15
Polypharmacy, 252
Poor relief, 271, 276–7, 299
Pope, Sir Tho., 17, 69, 177, 282
Popes, 92, 197, 202, 205
Portsmouth, 18 n., 57, 234
Portugal, King of, 236
Potters, 157
Poultry, 35, 144, app. F
Pownsett, Wm., 9, 124, 154, 273, 278, 303,
    307
Praines (pranes), 138, 146, 306–7, 316
Prayer book, first English, 70, 73, 112–18;
    second, 98, 230
Prescriptions, medical, 252–3
Presents to and from W.P., 69, 139, 146–7,
    189, 197, 222–3, 241–3, 256, 271, 274–5,
    299, 307; *see also* New year gifts
Priests' hiding holes, 292
Prince, J., Devon historian, 1
Privy Council, 44–51; clerk of, 47–9, 59, 69,
    70; agenda, 49, 108–9; register, 49; plan
    for reorganization of work, 100–4; inner
    council (Mary), 174, 182, 191; select (dur-
    ing Philip's absence), 191, 198–9; *see also*
    Council
Privy seals (loans), 207 n.
Progresses, 99–100, 175–80, 234, 237–45, 298
Protector. *See* Seymour, Edw.
Prunes, 147
Pulton priory (Wilts.), 14
Pyrgo palace, Havering (Essex), 223, 232,
    246–8

Quadra, Alvarez de, Spanish ambassador,
    232, 255–6
Quail, 144–6, 239–42
Quarter sessions (Essex), 187, 263–5
Quinces, 146

Rabbit warren, 241; *see also* Coneys
Radcliffe, Henry 2nd earl of Sussex, 110;
    Tho. 3rd earl, 230, 234, 263
Raisins, 147, 301
Ramme, Tho., 150
Ramsden (Essex), 124
Rawreth (Essex), 292
Raylton, Gregory, W.P.'s signet clerk,
    183
Reaping, 145
Rectories, W.P.'s, 186
Redshanks, 138, 146
Regent, Queen Cath. Parr, 53–5
Relief of the poor, 276–7
Religious houses. *See* Monasteries

Renard, Simon, Imperial ambassador, 166–7,
    169, 171–85, 190, 196
Rents on W.P.'s estates, 269–74, 298
Requests, court of, 41, 45
Retainers, W.P.'s, 53, 82, 154 n., 161, 170
Revolts, South-western and Norfolk, 73–5;
    Wyatt's, 169–72, 298, app. H
Rewards, 69, 275, 299
Rich, Richard 1st baron Rich, 17, 44, 54, 65–
    7, 70–1, 78–81, 84, 98, 111, 112, 117–22,
    128, 161, 183, 187, 194, 223, 235, 245, 251,
    256–7, 262–5, 267; Rob. 2nd baron, 256–7,
    264–5
Richmond (Surrey), 73, 167, 175, 179
Rickmansworth (Herts.), 45–6
Ridley, Nich., bp. of Rochester, 3, 113, 116,
    191–2
River Thames transport. *See* Barges; Tilt-
    boats; Wherries
Roach, 139
Robsart, Amy, 235
Robertsbridge abbey (Sussex), 21 n.
Roche abbey (Yorks.), 12
'Rochepot's affair', 42
Rochester, steward of lands of bp. of, 209 n.,
    322
Rochester priory, 10, 17, 18, 51
Rochester, Rob., 121–2, 161–2, 165–7, 173–4,
    185, 187–8, 207, 262
Rochets, 139, 317
Rochford, viscount. *See* Boleyn, George
Rogers, Sir Edw., 227
Rogers, John, martyr, 187
Romford (Essex). *See* Gidea hall
Roxwell (Essex), 285
Russell, John, 1st earl of Bedford, 65, 68, 71,
    73, 75, 79, 86–7, 99, 101, 110–11, 115, 161,
    170, 173, 206 n., 275; Francis 2nd earl,
    227–30, 256, 262
Russia, trade relations with, 204–5
Ryche, ——, apothecary, 252

Sackville, Sir Rich., 199, 227–8, 240, 259–60,
    262
Saddles and saddlers, 157, 176, 299
Sadler, Sir Ralph, principal secretary, 47, 78,
    112, 162, 232, 245, 262–3
Saffron, 141, 316
Saffron Walden (Essex), 69, 74, 141, 217 n.;
    school, 94; *see also* Audley End
St. Alban's abbey, 12, 21 n., 69
St. George's day and feast, 203, 236, 255
St. German's priory (Cornwall), 15
St. James's palace, 164, 191, 199, 209
St. John, baron. *See* Paulet, Wm.
St. Leger, Sir Anthony, deputy of Ireland,
    69; Mr., 127
St. Osyth's priory (Essex), 119, 132, 136 n.,
    244
St. Valentine's day, 217–18
Salads, 140